POETS

OF AMERICA

BY

EDMUND CLARENCE STEDMAN

AUTHOR OF "VICTORIAN POETS"

BOSTON AND NEW YORK
HOUGHTON MIFFLIN COMPANY
The Riverside Press Cambridge

TO

THE YOUNGER WRITERS OF AMERICA

THIS WORK,

CHIEFLY A REVIEW OF OUR FIRST DISTINCTIVE
LYRICAL PERIOD,

Is cordially Inscribed.

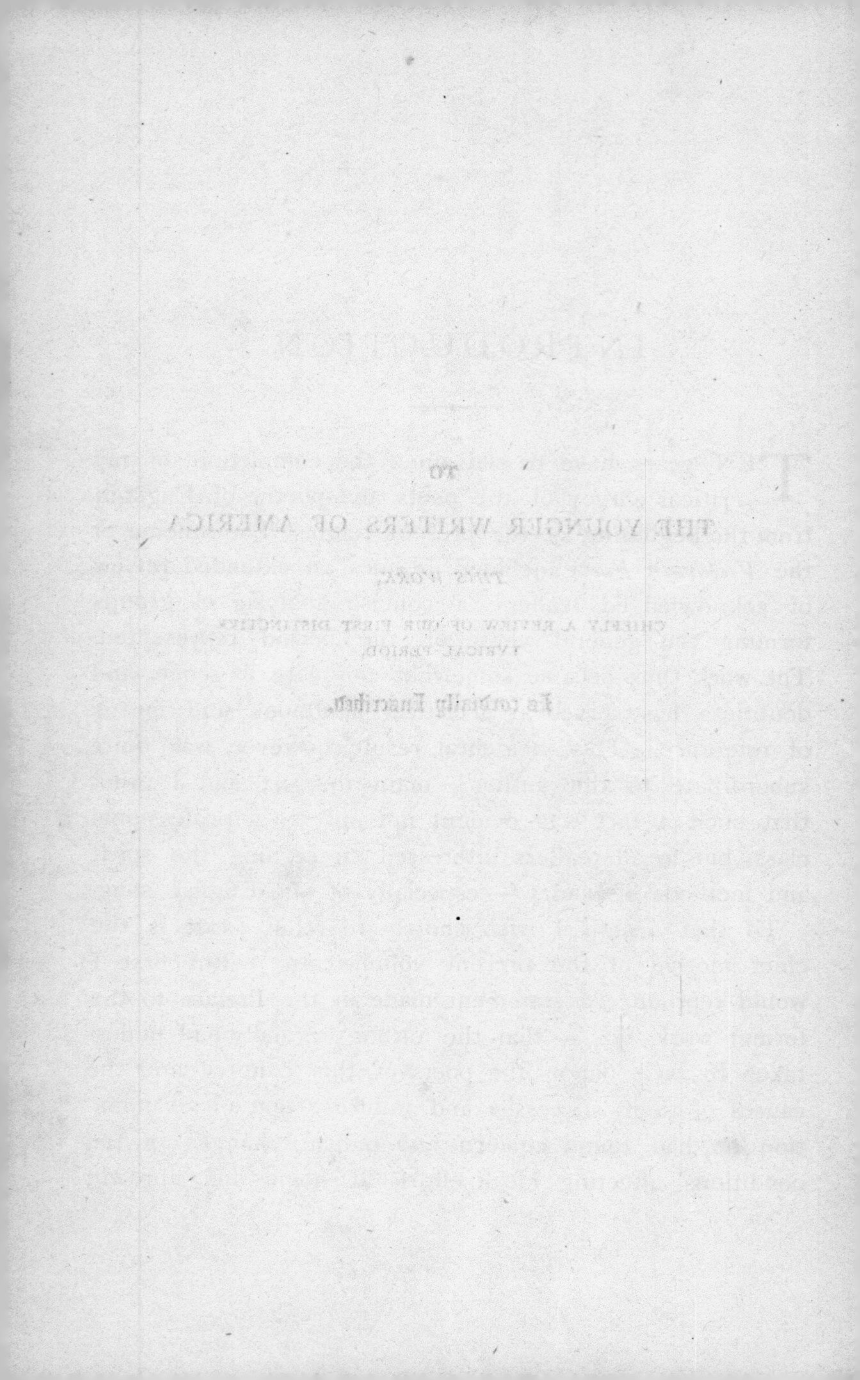

INTRODUCTION.

TEN years have passed since the completion of my critical survey of the poets and poetry of England from the beginning of the present reign. The scheme of the *Victorian Poets* included, besides an extended review of acknowledged leaders, a concise analysis of groups forming the general choir of the period represented. The work thus became somewhat complete in scope, and doubtless has served as a critical handbook and means of reference. This incidental result, however, was quite subordinate to the author's main design; and I think that such a fact was evident not only to a professional class, but to all readers interested concerning the spirit and methods of poetry,—especially of our English song.

To that design I wish shortly to refer, as it is the chief motive of the present volume also. But first I would reproduce a statement made in the Preface to the former work, viz.,—that the author originally had undertaken to write upon the poets of this country and the causes of their successes and failures; that on examination he had found modern and radical changes in the conditions affecting ideal effort, at home and abroad;

that for this and other reasons he could "more freely and graciously begin by choosing a foreign paradigm than by entering upon the home-field, and that none could be so good for the purpose as the poetry of Great Britain." It seemed to him, also, that, until after some training of this kind, "affection, reverence, national feeling, or some less worthy emotion, might be thought to prevent an American from writing without prejudice" of the poets of his own country. Certainly he could attempt this more profitably when the changes mentioned should be more complete, and the careers more rounded of the chief American writers who would pass under review.

The time came when I felt emboldened to renew my original undertaking, and the result is set forth in this volume. My belief is strengthened that the earlier treatise was essential to it, and, in fact, the most expedient preliminary task that could be chosen. The modern conditions, as far as they relate to both countries, could be observed more directly in England than in America, their stress being there of earlier origin and less diffused. My previous synopsis of them now has only to be condensed, and supplemented by discussion of those other conditions that are peculiar to this country alone. Furthermore, I regard the treatise on British poetry as of less significance, in its field of observation, than the work now following it; and I trust that reasons for this opinion — to which some at first may demur — will become apparent to those who give more than a cursory reading to these essays. Even now few Americans set a proper value on the relative bearing of our ideal and intellectual progress thus far. The instinctive deference of a young nation to its elders, and the frequent assurance of the latter that our progress has been restricted chiefly to physical achievement, have united until a recent date to make us accept that view of the matter. Aesop's lion discovered that the honors of a contest depend largely upon the sculptor that commemorates it. If there were a stake-boat, a winning-post, by which the comparative import (waiving the question of inherent value) of national activities could be measured exactly, various estimates might be disestablished. What is of most concern, in relation to the *theme* of this work, is the fact that the literature — even the poetic literature — of no country, during the last half-century, is of greater interest to the philosophical student, with respect to its bearing on the future, than that of the United States. My judgment is to this effect, after years in which I have read a good deal of native and foreign comment upon the subject. The reasons for it are generally perceptible in the ensuing chapters, but three may be stated here succinctly: 1. American poetry, more than that of England during the period considered, has idealized — often inspired — the national sentiment, the historic movements, of the land whose writers have composed it. 2. This nation already, — in the second century of a growth which began not in barbarism, but in political civilization, — is gaining in strength, population, and the liberal arts, at an accelerative speed that soon must make it a typical exemplar of ideal as well as material production. Nor can there be a time when the bent of its ideality will be more suggestive than now, for the present angle determines the arc of the future. 3. The first true course of American poetry has distinguished the principal term covered in these essays; a first heat has been run during that time, to whose leaders special chapters are devoted. It is rare that an epoch so definitely begun and ended can be selected as the object of synthetic examination. The reader is invited to study a period as distinct in literature as our Constitutional period in politics, or the Thirty Years' War in history; one, moreover, in which poetry bore closer relations to the life and enthusiasm of a people than it often has borne in other lands and times.

We see, also, that this term has been singularly concurrent with that of the Victorian hemicycle, so that an examination of the poetry of our English tongue for the last fifty years is compassed in my two books. In order to perceive the evolution of a new minstrelsy from its foreign and native germs, the opening chapters of this volume are occupied partly with the efforts of the Colonial verse-writers and their immediate successors. A final chapter contains a rapid summary of what is now doing, as a basis for speculation on the outlook and the chances of a revival in the future. The reader thus obtains a general view of American poets and poetry from their outset to the present date.

Nevertheless, the main purpose of this work, as suggested heretofore, is to continue my former effort, by obtaining further illustrations of the poetic life, and ideas with respect to the spirit and methods of the art of poetry. The marginal Analysis and topical Index are planned to accord with this intention. My views were formulated to some extent in our consideration of the transatlantic field. They can be emphasized in no way more readily than by fresh and personal examples which are a kind of object-lessons; by criticism of a new series of poets, employing the same tongue, but varying in genius and temperament, and influenced by the conditions of a distinct environment.

The tenor of the original discussion, which I have no reason to modify seriously, was in favor of simplicity, impulse, sincerity, as opposed to obscurity, didacticism, and the affectation either of refinement or a "saucy roughness," — always in behalf of imagination, and against the multiform devices proffered, consciously or unconsciously, in lieu of that supreme quality. It placed construction before decoration, the tone of a composition above its detail, and looked to the spirit rather than the structure, — not content, however, with the half-truth of a writer who declares that poetry is a spirit, not a form, — the truth being that poetry is a spirit, taking form. Finally, I welcomed every sign of healthy passion and every promising dramatic tendency, both invigorating after a prolonged reflective period. Various sins of commission were discoverable among the lesser pupils of

Wordsworth, the "spasmodic" lyrists, the Neo-Romantic artificers, etc., and frequently an absence was noted of merits that undoubtedly are found in our native verse — simplicity and honest impulse. The last-named traits do not of themselves suffice, for spontaneity must be allied with power. American singers often have been more natural than imaginative, and have risen to passion only in rare individual or public crises. Our most noted group, that of New England, distinguished for grace and scholarship, fervent in conviction and of marked intellectuality, has been pronounced too thin-blooded; what sensuousness enriches American poetry has appeared chiefly in the work of its middle and younger schools. On the other hand, our verse has been measurably free from the vice of over-decoration, prevalent in the writings of the minor British romanticists ten years or more ago. It is to be hoped that the trace of this now observed is something from which the new school soon will free itself. And I here say to our young writers, as I have said again and again with respect to their foreign standards, that in literature, as in architecture, construction must be decorated, not decoration constructed, — that invention must precede them both, — and that, if imagination be clouded and the glow of passion unfelt, it is utter and worthless jugglery to compose at all. An enumeration, in a closing chapter, of younger poets and their efforts is purposely uncritical, except in the case of Lanier; it aims to show these at their best, but the fact is not gainsaid that there is a lull in the force and efficacy of American song. My conclusion is that we are not experiencing a decadence, but rather a diversion of imaginative energy to new forms of employment, and this not without a fair compensation. It may be well that our verse thus should escape the phase of minute realism and analysis through which modern literature is passing, and which probably will give way before a dramatic and inventive impulse by the time a second epoch of poetic achievement shall be inaugurated.

My review of the exquisite productions of Tennyson and his compeers led to consideration of the methods of poetry as an art. Apt illustrations were at hand, and my remarks often and designedly were addressed to fellows of the craft. The present work is less technical; I have more to say of the poetic temperament and the conditions that affect it; more of poetry as the music of emotion, faith, aspiration, and all the chords of life. The atmosphere in which our poets have flourished is observed, as well as their special aids and hindrances and whatever has been significant in their various careers. The *personality* of the noted American minstrels has been more suggestive than that of their English contemporaries. In this respect they bear a likeness to the poets of the Georgian era. With few exceptions the Victorian brotherhood, living under advanced social and literary systems, have been neither greatly involved with the action and history of their time nor picturesquely conspicuous as individuals. Nevertheless, it is not the main thing, in writing of a poet, to consider the experiences which he shares in common with other men. He must be judged by things peculiar to himself — the creative gift and work that bring him within the franchise of literary criticism. The estimate, then, to a certain extent must be technical; and so far as my own comment has been addressed to the literary class, its endeavor is, as a Californian author pleases me by saying, to get down to the bed-rock of poetry as an art and to its pure gold as an inspiration. If passages occur where the agreement of polite thinkers, as to established processes and conclusions, is not assumed as a matter of course, it is because I hope this volume will be read by some who hitherto have paid slight attention to its topics. There is no good reason why a critical treatise, like any other work, should not appeal to both select and general readers, though possibly on very diverse grounds of interest.

During the preparation of this work, the last of its kind that I shall publish, I have had my share of the ills from which none are quite exempt. It has been delayed by the rarity of intervals at which I could devote a wholesome energy to its completion, and feel assured that it would betray no tinge of personal discouragement. If injustice has been done, in the delicate task of making even the slightest reference to one's literary associates, it has not been of malice aforethought.

Acknowledgment is due to friends, — especially to Messrs. Gilder, Johnson, Buel, and Carey, of "The Century" office, — and to Mr. G. T. Elliot, the scholarly corrector at the Riverside Press, and his assistants, for professional courtesies in aid of my labor now ended; also to my son, Arthur Stedman, for expert revision of copy and verification of names and dates. Where authorities differ, or are silent, with respect to matters of fact, I have consulted — as far as practicable — the persons directly interested, except in the cases of living female writers whose dates of birth are not given already in standard compilations.

E. C. S.

New York, September, 1885.

CONTENTS.

POETS OF AMERICA

POETS OF AMERICA.

CHAPTER I.

EARLY AND RECENT CONDITIONS.

I.

The author's purpose.

IT is my design to trace the current of poesy, deepening and widening in common with our streams of riches, knowledge, and power; to show an influence upon the national sentiment no less potent, if less obvious, than that derived from the historic records of our past; to watch the first dawning upon an eager people of "the happy, heavenly vision men call Art"; to observe closely and to set down with an honest hand our foremost illustrations of the Rise of Poetry in America. Such is my purpose, and I deem it not a mean one. We think of power and wealth as things in themselves, but they are strong and rich only in their relations to the life of man. The essential part of that life is in his spirit, of which imagination is the king, — and the sister arts, with poetry at their front, are to be accounted its highest forms of expression.

National song.

The song of a nation is accepted as an ultimate test of the popular spirit; as the earliest form of speech and the ripest, — whether the utterance of feelings common to all, or of the fine and daring speculations of the noblest minds. Examine it, and form opinions of the country's general literature, of the hold upon art and action and scientific achievement. If we have seen a true poetic movement in America, we may be sure that we have had marches in other fields of progress. The inquiry concerning the genuineness and value of such a movement affords a title to this work, and a review of the conditions that have helped or hindered it must be included. Upon the method chosen for a study of the recent period in England, my present researches are devoted chiefly to the careers and productions of leading poets whose reputations are long-established, and who, upon the whole, fairly represent the various tendencies of American song. And thus, incidentally and with fresh opportunities, we may extend our knowledge of "the aim and province of the art of Poetry," and obtain under a new atmosphere further illustrations of the poetic temperament and life.

Cp. "Victorian Poets": p. 1.

The subject cannot be lightly entered upon, and as if for entertainment merely. Properly considered, there is no more suggestive undertaking than to review the first displays of lyrical genius in a land as notable as any upon earth. These may seem crude and familiar to ourselves, and possibly are not fully estimated by older nations whose very age and glory make them self-contained. But, if the future is to have a greatness of its own, a study of New World poetry is of equal importance with that devoted to the earlier or contemporary verse of the mother-land. The reader, then, will do well to bear with the details of a prefatory analysis, though they lack that interest which adheres to the lives and works of the various poets to whom his attention will be invited. The points which I shall make will not be wholly novel, but by grouping them newly, and in a logical manner, we may get some notion of the real quality of the first genuine awakening of our home-song.

Suggestion to the reader.

For that there has been such an awakening is the

very cause and foundation of these essays, and if I did not perceive this fact I should have no excuse for their general endeavor. It is true that a nation's literature will not appear out of season. Poetry, its most spontaneous form, is a growth rather than an artifice, or it does not come to strengthen and to stay. Let me acknowledge, as heretofore, the bearing of the conditions under which it is produced, and that a poet must be viewed in the light and shadow of his environment; furthermore, that when a time is ripe there are found both idealists and men of action to represent it, — springing up as when, in the physical world, the pines and fir-trees of a virgin forest have been cleared away, and a novel flora suddenly appears, whose germs have been hidden in the undermould, awaiting their own season of room and light and air. But let me also, and at present no less than in our foreign excursions, include a factor which the new criticism often overlooks. Too little allowance is made for the surprises of genius. We forget that now and then some personage comes without a summons, like a stray leader from the skies; that works appear under adverse circumstances, so new, so strong, so revolutionary, as to seem inspired creations, — men and works that overleap the stages of development, that demand the spiritual factor, the personal equation, the allowance for exception, in the problem of national growth. In the absence of a sunlit atmosphere, they shine by inward light, and communicate heat and lustre to their surroundings. When a link in the chain of evolution is missing, such are the forces that make up for it. But there are other forces, and certain modes of intellectual effort, which assist growth and somewhat forestall the ordinary process. Even criticism may do a share, and

Law of environment;

and the factory which modify its effect.

often by penetrative study of the leaders that reflect or stimulate the various tendencies of a people's ideality. Of course a poet must represent his age and habitat; a Grecian temple beside an Alleghanian trout-brook might be lovely, but surely would be out of place and date. It is now my province to discover what special aids the poets of America have experienced, and what hindrances. In no modern country has ideality been more retarded than in our own; and I think that certain restrictions have peculiarly limited production in the field of Poetry,— the chief of imaginative arts. Yet I see that, in spite of these, the ultimate rise of an American school of poetry was swift and strong, and that its chiefs have had their aids no less than their obstacles, and have bravely confronted the latter. And thus we are brought directly to the preliminary issue.

Matters first to be considered.

II.

Question of a Home-School and its characteristics.

MUCH has been written of late upon the topic of our native literature. Is there a distinctly American school? If not, when and where shall we look for one? What are, or should be, its special characteristics? These and similar questions are frequently and somewhat vaguely discussed.

Essential quality.

Now, it is first to be observed that the radical quality of any national school, in any country or period, does not wholly depend upon the types, personages, localities, and other materials utilized by its artists and men of letters; and this is especially true with regard to the work of a poet, in distinction from that of a painter. The specific tone of the former artist is not derived from the images which his genius informs with life, and from the plots that serve his expression of the thought, passion, imagination, of his people and time. Mere reliance upon these will not suffice. Even a painter might devote his life to copying the groups he finds in his own streets, the streets themselves, and the fields and woods beyond them, yet not produce an original art, nor execute it in a fresh and native way. The mere dialect and legends of a province or section are powerless to convey their essential quality to the song of a poet who calls them to his aid. Mr. Grant White, therefore, was perfectly right when he suggested, for these and other reasons, that it is the spirit, not the letter, which giveth life; that we must pay regard to the flavor, rather than to the form and color, of the fruit, — to the distinctive character, not the speech and aspect, of the personage. Unless the feeling of our home-poet be novel, his vision a fresh and distinctive vision, — unless these are radically different from the French, or German, or even the English feeling and vision, — they are not American, and our time has not yet come.

R. G. White, in the N. Y. Times, Feb. 1, 1880.

But I am not with this distinguished writer in his further claim that we still are essentially English, and shall be so for a long series of years to come; that our literature, like the language we inherit, is wholly English, and must remain so for centuries, until "Anglo-Saxon and Hollander and German and Irishman and negro and Chinese shall have so blended their blood . . . that from the fusion a new race shall have sprung." What I first call to mind is that there are few Americans, even those of but one remove, who are not instantly recognized abroad as being very different from Englishmen, not only with respect to feature, mould, and speech, — which vary according to the sections from which they come, — but in their senti-

A reservation.

ment, modes of thought and feeling, and way of looking at things. In both outward and inward traits they are pronounced distinctively un-English and "American," however divided among themselves. Again, by so much as the style is the man, I believe that the literary product of this new people differs from the literary product of the English, or any other people of the Old World, and I hope to make that difference clear in the course of these chapters. And I will remark, in passing, that "The Scarlet Letter," a romance which Mr. White cited in illustration, to me appears thoroughly un-English in its mystical temper, and its undertone and atmosphere; if not broadly American, it is locally so, — the fruit and outgiving of the New England sentiment that brooded in its author's spirit, and of which it is a soul-wrought witness and dramatic chronicle.

"The Scarlet Letter."

In fine, recognizing the error of those who, by a forced effort, would anticipate creations that will come only of themselves, or through the natural impulse of foreordained artists, I also perceive that already, in various walks of art, and in none more than in that to which our present study is devoted, we have exhibited the new and broad results, both of acclimation and of a blending process, to which the ruling divisions of our population thus far have been subjected. Equally obvious are the minor distinctive phases, which, on the other hand, arise from the differentiation of the American people by influences that, in widely separated districts, have acted upon their inhabitants from the early settlements to the present time. The first-named phenomena are national, while those of the latter class may be termed sectional; but all are American, whether they appertain to the whole, or to the subdivisions, of our intellectual yield.

A distinctive national character.

Its incompleteness must be acknowledged.

The type first suggested, that of a broadly national character, is plainly incomplete, and has wide room for maturer development. Let us measure it only at its worth. A restless and ill-adjusted spirit still pervades the heterogeneous elements of our nationality. Here is a country as large as all Europe, embracing zones as far apart, in physical attributes, as those of Norway and Sicily. Here are the emigrants or descendants of every people in Europe, — to go no farther, — and all their languages, and customs, and traditions, and modes of feeling, at one time or another, have come with them. Hence our unconscious habitude of variety, the disinclination to cling to one way of life or thought until its perfect conclusion. There is a ferment in new blood. The American travels, and at first is delighted with the color and flavor of the region to which he has come, but soon wearies of them, and pushes on to some new place where novel characteristics can be enjoyed. This is observable of all Anglo-Saxons, capricious yet steadfast as they are, but more so among ourselves than with respect to our British kinsmen. America has absorbed the traits of many lands and people ; the currents still set this way ; our modern intercourse with the world at large is close and unintermitting, so that the raw ingredients of our national admixture are supplied quite as rapidly as the whirl and stir of the popular system can triturate and commingle them. It is too much, then, to expect that our art or song, from whatever section either may come, will exhibit a quality specifically American in the sense that the product of Italy is Italian, or that of France is French. At this distance, we who watch others as we are watched ourselves can readily see that the same causes which make our civilization assume the composite type are blend-

The national elements :

ing the politics, manners, dress, art, and letters of the several European countries, — and this, however distinct their nationalities, in proportion to the growth of travel and interculture. But the United States are homogeneous in what pertains to the language and methods of their master-race, and to this extent their homogeneity is definitely assured. Concerning the primal influences that affect the general tone of art and literature, mutual communication and understanding are so perfect that any changes or advances are almost simultaneous throughout our territory. This being the situation, foreign critics are not far wrong in requiring that our home-product shall differ from their own; that it shall be, at least, un-European, — manifestly of the New World, and not of the Old.

To what extent homogeneous?

Return to a consideration of the family likeness, physical and mental, which instantly is apparent to others as we visit the mother-land. If we ourselves are unconscious of it, or wonted to it; if the air and fashion that we display seem to us imperceptible or of small account, they are not so regarded by our kinsmen, or by the guest who lands upon these shores. The stranger quickly perceives, and holds at its value, the general, the national, type. Material and psychological changes are correlative, and almost equally sure of external recognition.

A recognizable type.

So far, therefore, from demanding absolute novelty in structure, language, or theme, of our home-poet, it is the duty of the critic to value the Americanism which great and small have displayed in quality of tone, and in faithful expression of the dominant popular moods. Thus considered, it will be found they have not fallen short. Those arbiters of foreign taste who do not acknowledge this may be suspected of some unconscious insincerity. Not every mother as fair

Foreign criticism.

and ripe as England, however affectionate, can look with perfect complacence upon a daughter growing to her own height and beauty before the world. To her eyes the maiden is still a child, and she owns with reluctance and very slowly that child's attractiveness and the claims of her suitors. One by one the points of youth and inferiority, brought against America, have worn away, and now, when so many of us grant England this last defence of her supremacy, it is with the respect due a mother, and with a courtesy perchance no less insincere than her avowal. The new Americanism is not so modest as to surrender any freehold or to be unconscious of its smallest advantages.

Minor characteristics.

The less essential novelties of structure, theme, and dialect already are discernible in the yield that represents our territorial subdivision. The local flavor of our *genre* and provincial literature has long been unquestioned, but our conceit was not overfed by an acknowledgment almost wholly due to grotesque and humorous exploits, — a welcome such as a prince in his breathing-hour might give to a new-found jester or clown. American poetry, however, has not represented the popular life of our continental slopes and corners merely in their coarser traits. These sections are not so isolated as the Scottish highlands, or as those mountain nooks in Italy, where peasant women contentedly whirl the spindle, and never visit the plains that glisten below; yet some of them are long-settled and have an abiding population, with habits more or less confirmed. Where there is the least of change and interruption, and the colonial blood is most unmixed, the national *ennui* does not prevail; the sentiment and instinct of the people, if limited, are clearly understood, and have been fairly expressed in poetry and prose romance.

In a certain sense, it is natural for the citizen of so vast and various a country to find his patriotism and his gift of expression respond most easily to the appeals of his own locality. There is still a lagging behind full nationality, just as Federal supremacy, in the hearts of a great multitude, gives precedence to "state rights." Yet there are signs of growth toward an imagination in keeping with our political enlargement. The new Americanism, with relation to literature and the arts of beauty and construction, is seen in the very search for it, in the closer inspection of our own ground, in our more realistic method, in the genuine quality of our modern poetry and creative prose, so much more indigenous than the work of the Neo-Romantic English school, and presenting so fresh a contrast to the poetry and prose of our early periods; finally, in the greater value set upon our home-workers, upon our ventures for ourselves. It is curious to note the minor symptoms of this change. As time has lessened our yearning for the mother-country, native Americans less fondly cling to the old words and traditions. The landlords who cater to foreign or provincial guests still give English and French names to their hotels, and a fresh English colony, after the manner of our ancestors, calls its village Rugby; but the reproach of this barrenness of nomenclature is fast passing away, and the time has come when the declaration of our independence may be made to include the fields of literature and art.

The new Americanism.

And indeed, if art, under the free system of a democracy, does not show in time as proud a result — whether in the product of its disciples or in the wealth of its libraries and museums — as in countries where it is fed by governmental patronage and sub-

Republicanism in these respects is on trial.

sidies, then our republicanism, upon its æsthetic side, is itself a failure. So far as poetry is concerned, I see that we have already had the first period of what may be called, for want of a better term, a true American school. I see that this school was slow to rise, until suddenly a number of its leaders appeared at once; that its first tuneful season has been completed, so that, in the temporary pause, we now, for the first time, may honestly recount its triumphs. But that our lyrical product has not been so obvious as our material grandeur, that it has put on a national type less complete than the types of various sections, that it has been but a delightful promise of what a new song will create for us when poetry comes in vogue again throughout the world, — this, too, is not to be gainsaid. Before examining what we have done, let us see what we have not been able to do until recently, and what not at all. It is time to indicate the early and later restrictions that have hemmed in the poets, and limited the poetry, of the Western world.

III.

Early and later Restrictions of the American poets.

THE poets themselves, naturally, would be slow to perceive the causes of their difficulties. The brain is not always conscious of its own *malaise*. Nevertheless, I think that to each true singer, as he arrived at a period when his intellectual faculty sought the rationale of his successes and failures, the facts have been more or less apparent. The idealism of this people was long retarded by certain interdicts, and at last forced its way to expression under very baffling and perplexing conditions, some of which are even now felt. So far as the embarrassments peculiar to the new epoch are involved, it was a perception of these that led me to observe their bearing on the poets of England, before venturing to write upon our own. To these matters I shall again refer, after some mention of the absolute barriers which shut out the Muses from these shores until so late a time.

The first two hundred years.

For two centuries, in truth, the situation here was so adverse to art, and especially to song, as to nullify even our complement to Taine's theory; to stifle, or to divert to other than ideal uses,[1] any exceptional genius that existed, and that would have made its way against restrictions not of themselves quite as exceptional. The modified results of this situation may still be observed. As a rider to all I have said of the essential superiority of art to its materials, we must not fail, also, to consider the repugnance of the general mind to disassociate things and ideas, — to separate the spirit of a work from what is used for its construction. There is a natural expectation that the art of a country will convey to us something of the national history, aspect, social law. On the whole, it has been the instinct of masters to avail themselves, so far as might be, in their plots, manners, and scenery, of the region nearest them; a wise instinct, through which they reach closely to nature, and are more sure to make their work of interest elsewhere and afterward. Shakespeare's men are apt to be Englishmen, though they may figure in Illyria

[1] I am not considering the question whether a poet of the first rank may, or may not, find his natural vocation under the most adverse conditions, and overcome them; but am trying to see why a general poetic movement, embracing many true poets, was deferred until Longfellow, Poe, Whittier, Emerson, Lowell, Whitman, and others of their generation appeared almost simultaneously.

or Rome. Nor is it entirely through unfairness and caprice that the free range allowed to English poets has been denied our own. The Old World has drawn its countries together, like elderly people in a tacit alliance against the strength of youth which cannot return to them, the fresh, rude beauty and love which they may not share. There is, also, something worth an estimate in the division of an ocean gulf, that makes us like the people of a new planet; and when those on the other side hear us sounding the changes upon familiar themes, with voices not unlike their own, they well may feel as if the highest qualities of our song were not full compensation for its lack of "something rich and strange." A response may fairly be expected to the search for novelty, to the curious yearning of those who look to us from across the seas.

Novelty of the situation.

Here begin the special restrictions of an American poet. He represents, it is true, the music and ardor of a new country, of a land his race has peopled for two hundred and fifty years, a nation that has completed its first century. A new land, a new nation, yet not forced, like those which have progressed from barbarism to a sense of art, to create a language and literature of their own; a new land with an old language, a new nation with all the literature and traditions behind it of the country from whose colonies it has sprung. While the thought and learning of this people began in America just where it had arrived in the mother-land at the dates of the Jamestown and Plymouth settlements, the physical state and environment of Americans were those of men who find themselves encountering the primitive nature of a savage world; with this difference, that they were equipped for the struggle, not as an abo-

The "Colonial" restriction:

riginal race, but with the logic, courage, experience, of the civilization behind them. All the drags, the anchorage, the limitations, involved in the word "colonial" retarded a new ideality. The colonial restriction has been well determined. It made the western lyre, until the period covered by this survey, a mechanism to echo, without fresh and true feeling, notes that came from over sea. It so occupied this people with a stern, steadfast, ingenious, finally triumphant contest with Nature that their epic passion was absorbed in the clearing of forests, the bridging of rivers, the conquest of savage and beast, the creation of a free government; and this labor is not yet ended, — it goes on with larger cohorts and immensely widening power. But the imagination never dies, and when our first leisure came for its exercise it was awakened by contact with the nature thus tamed, — by communion with the broadest panorama of woods and hills and waters, under the most radiant skies, that civilized man has ever found himself confronting. Pioneers in art and poetry here caught their inspiration, and naturally the field of painting was the first to give token of novel results. The very ease with which books containing the world's best literature were obtainable in the backwoods made our early writers copyists. The painters, meanwhile, had to lament the absence of galleries in this country, and their own inability to go abroad and study. Thrown upon themselves, and deficient in technical knowledge, they sought for models in the nature about them; and thus began our landscape-school of painting, the work of which, however rude and defective, was more original than the verse wherewith it was contemporary.

its dissimilar effects upon Poetry and Painting.

A poet of the first rank is not given to every country, nor to every age. But poets of gifts approaching those of our living favorites doubtless have been born in America, according to Nature's average, at different times of our history. Until recently, the stimulants of their genius must have been wanting. It may be that the people had no real need of them, and song and art, like invention, come not without necessity. What poetry was latent here and there does not concern us. The stone on which our colonial life was founded was frigid as an arctic boulder, — there was no molecular motion to give out life and heat. Who were the mute, inglorious Miltons? Of what kind is the verse that was produced? Does it move us? Is it poetry? However fine the cast of individuals, the effect of a perpetual contest with the elemental, often sinister, always gigantic forces of a new continent would be so adverse to art, so directly in the line of necessity and temporal gain, as to stifle their poetic fire, to develop a heroism that was stolid and unimaginative, to mark persons and communities with sternness and angularity, leading them to a homely gauge of values, not wont to esteem the ideal at its true worth. The aspiration of a refined nature would seem to the multitude foolishness and a stumbling-block. For a prolonged season the art of writing verse was almost solely a luxury of the professional classes in America, and its relics bear witness to their pedantry and dulness. It is not to the wigged and gowned that we instinctively listen for the music and freedom of creative song. And if poetry even in England, from the middle of the seventeenth century to the close of the eighteenth, stupidly fashioned itself upon the models of worn-out schools, how should it do more in England's colonies, that brought hither certain shoots of taste and

Latent genius not to be considered.

Colonial pedantry.

learning from the Old World, and found it hard to protect them at all in the sterile wild-woods of the New?

Prolonged sterility.

Such was the nature of the barriers which, in the early and later colonial periods, absolutely defied the overleaping of a single notable poet. We find little of more significance in the transition era of the Revolution, although a nation took on life. No poetry was begotten in the rage of that heroic strife; its humor, hatred, hope, suffering, prophecy, were feebly uttered, as far as verse was concerned, in the mode and language inherited years before from the coarsest English satirists. There came at last a time when the nation felt itself in vigorous youth, and began to have a song. Some few original notes were heard among our pipings. The positive barriers were broken, and in their stead came the restrictions that are felt in some degree down to the present time.

The first stages of Republicanism opposed to ideal art.

At the outset it may be said of Republicanism itself — in which our pride and faith are based, and which we trust is ultimately to promote a literature and an art not below the standard of our bravest hope — that it originally somewhat lessened the ardor of our poets, or kept this within temperate bounds. There was a craving for ideality of a certain kind, and in our liberal regions the sense of utility was not the sole controlling power. There was a wide manifestation of that which bears to pure ideality an inferior relationship. Our system diffused the intelligence which lifts our people quite above the dulness and stolidity of the middle classes elsewhere, but did not speedily bring them to the pitch of high emotion.

A leveller.

It is a leveller, and in its early stages raises a multitude to the level of the commonplace; so that there have been few tall heads of grain above the even field.

The general independence and comfort have not bred those dramatic elements which imply conditions of splendor and squalor, glory and shame, triumph and despair. In their stead we have the spirit of the American homesteads, and the loss to the artist of some darker contrast, that would make their virtue and piety more inspiring, certainly is their gain. In no other country are there so many happy little households, — although there is a curious foreign belief to the contrary, derived from travelling acquaintanceship. This must be so in the one land where every man can own a portion of the soil and be a freeholder, and where a man's toil meets no doubtful reward. The popular thrift and freedom, joined with the necessity for labor to steadily maintain them, are not at first productive of the tragic or entrancing dreams of effective art. Wisely bettering their material chances, men are too busy to feel a spiritual want. And the labor of our representative men is so extended and heroic as of itself to feed the popular imagination. In default of Homer, we at least have Hector and Achilles; and the peerless exploits of our engineers, capitalists, discoverers, speak louder than a minstrel's words. In all this amazing drama of triumphant effort and organization; in the adjustment of our political theory, dependent on statesmanship, and leading to oratory and journalism rather than to art and song; in the despotism of our social unwritten law that an American must be a good citizen first of all, and that the first duties of a citizen are to rear and maintain a family; in the implied doubt as to the sanity of enduring privations for the sake of the ideal, when, by deserting it, a practical success may be had, — amid all this the man of genius has too often betaken himself to the work of his neighbors, and those who keep

The American homestead.

Material effort.

faith with the Muse have found themselves perplexed and out of time. Nevertheless, I repeat that, up to a certain grade, our people have required their poetry, — just as they will have their votes, their seats in church, their county papers, and the piano or melodeon in every house. A throng of minor singers have answered to the demand with very natural and unaffected voices. The select few, whose efforts placed them above their comrades, often have suffered from the undue favor awarded their minor and ordinary productions.

Diffusion of the commonplace.

These adverse influences, belonging to the soil and air, perhaps have not been so directly comprehended by the American poet as the obvious and technical impediments which had force when he essayed a sustained and novel work.

Technical difficulties; which, however, do not greatly affect the lyric poet.

In considering these, let us acknowledge that they do not greatly concern the emotional and lyric poet. He is at no loss for a method or a theme; the latter is at once the cause and modulator of his song. Personal joys and griefs, special occurrences in history or related to the individual life, — these have inspired, and do inspire, the briefer poems, the lyrics which still make up the choicest portion of our verse. Their range is wide, from the simple fireside ballad to the impassioned ode, and my estimate of their remarkable freshness and variety will be given more fully hereafter. At present I would say that among them are many admirable of their kind, and that the relative number of these is not less than can be found in the popular verse of other lands. An American critic fails in discernment or independence who does not see this and avow it.

To what extent the

But, while the lyrical songster need not cast about for a subject, and does not even look into his heart to write, — for his heart has already moved him, — the ambitious poet is best equipped for a larger effort by some adequate theme awaiting his hand. The moment arrives when poets of the upper cast desire to forego their studies and brief lyrical flights, and to produce the composite and heroic works that rank as masterpieces. These leaders often have been arrested, with respect to romantic or inventive structures, by a scarcity of home-themes, no less than by the lack of sharp dramatic contrast in our equable American life. I am aware that this statement frequently is derided, and that many poets, while realizing that their product is too meagre, will not acknowledge its force. Others, and these among our foremost, who have thought to analyze their experience, confess that it is true in no small measure, and have stated this over their own hands.

more ambitious have felt their weight.

Up to a recent date, absence of theme for a national masterpiece, for a work belonging to our own atmosphere and history, has been a result of the condition under which we started. Original art is long deferred among a people cultured at the outset. A writer has well said that "the cause of the absence of the legendary and poetic in our early history may be attributed to the mental development of the colonists, who had already passed through that historic stage." They started at once with both church and school-house. The imagination was controlled by precedent, and "Art was cheated of its birthright." They made little history in a dramatic sense. What there was of the poetic or wondrous in their arduous compelling life had a local range, — such as the trials for witchcraft, finely utilized by New England's great romancer, and too inadequately, it must be owned, by her most famous poet. In Park-

Primitive absence of theme.

Otis, in "Sacred and Constructive Art."

man's elegant survey of certain picturesque epochs in colonial history, the feminine element, essential to complete dramatic quality, is usually wanting; in other annals, like those of Spanish-American adventure, it scarcely appears at all. American antiquity is a rude settler's antiquity; a homely fashion that palls, because not long out of date; a story everywhere the same, — furnishing at times the basis of some exquisite idyl, like "Evangeline," but for none too many of the class. "Evangeline" still remains the most notable of the longer American poems; and how much of that is otherwise than scenic and idyllic, and how much of it does not fit the story to the landscape, rather than the landscape to the story? No material, no stirring theme, with all your freedom, your conquest, your noble woods and waters, your westward spread of men! These are motives, accessories, atmosphere, often grander in magnitude than elsewhere to be found, but not perforce more new. The poetic instinct does not always hold the macrocosm superior to the microcosm, the prairie to the plain of Marathon, the Hudson to the Cephisus or the Tweed. As for latter-day history, this is not far enough removed. From the Revolution to the Civil War, the incidents of our life and passion are so recent and so plainly recorded as to gather no luminous halo from the too slight distance at which we observe them. The true poet will profit by them to the uttermost; the limits are to be overcome, but still are limits and in his way. He is thrown upon the necessity of inventing dramatic themes for the broader range of poetic venture. This the great poets always have avoided, for the product of such invention usually has seemed artificial and remote from human concern.

"Evangeline."

Indistinct background.

Disenchantments.

Bear in mind, also, that our wide-awake people are removed, not only from the superstitions that were a religion to our forefathers, but from the wondercraft and simple faith prevailing among the common folk of other lands than our own. The beautifying lens of fancy has dropped from our eyes. Where are our forest and river legends, our Lorelei, our Venusberg, our elves and kobolds ? We have old-time customs and traditions, and they are quaint and dear to us, but their atmosphere is not one in which we freely move. Just so with our heroism. No national changes and struggles have been of more worth than our own, but critics are not far wrong who point out that, however lofty the action and spirit of our latest crisis, heroism is not with us so much the chief business that one must be always " enthusiastic and on guard."

The forcing process.

One of our poets aims to be especially national. He sings, upon theory, as the American bard must sing when the years have died away. The result is a striking assumption of what can only come of itself, and after long time be past ; a disjointed series of kaleidoscopic pieces, not constituting a master-work, but, with all their strength and weakness, as unsatisfactory as the ill-assorted elements which he strives to represent. Yet, even in this effort, he is representative and a personage of mark, if not precisely in the direction of his own choice and assurance.

More clearly to understand how far, and in what way, our poets have felt the lack of background, of social contrasts, and of legendary and specific incident, we may observe the literature of some region where different conditions exist. In an isolated country of established growth and quality, a native genius soon discovers his tendency and proper field.

Look at Scotland. Her national melodies were

An illustration by contrast.

ready and waiting for Burns; her legends, history, traditions, for Walter Scott. The popular tongue, costumes, manners, all distinctively and picturesquely her own, affect the entire outcome of her song and art. Embraced in English literature, her literature is so un-English that it affords the paradigm we need. Enter the cathedral in Glasgow. Within the last thirty years that edifice has been refitted throughout with stained glass, contributed by the ancient families and clans. What associations are called up by the devices upon the windows in the chancel and nave, and in the impressive crypt below! Among all the shields and names, — those of Sterling, Hay, Douglas, Montrose, Campbell, Montgomerie, Lawrie, Buccleuch, Hamilton, — not one that is not utterly, purely Scottish. Even in our oldest and most characteristic sections in Virginia or New England, influences like these are discovered to no such extent. In a certain sense, they are not only influences, but aids: they move, they stimulate, they belong to the life and memory of the native poet, and he avails himself of them without effort or consciousness. Not that they are the essential, the imperative aids. But to be without them is a restriction, and one which our first genuine school of poets has had more or less to endure.

Strange, indeed, if the material wants of New World life, its utilitarian test of values, and the general conditions of a primitive democracy had not forced our early idealists into a struggle for existence which even the sturdiest found it hard to prolong.

The poet's food and fame.

Two things are essential to the poetic aspiration that results in fine achievement: the sympathetic applause which ministers to the last infirmity of noble minds, and the common wage that enables a laborer to do his work. The rewards of authorship have been sufficiently doubtful and varying in times before our own. In older lands, the poet, like his predecessor the minstrel, was at least protected and nourished by the good or great to whom he dedicated his song. Happily this kind of support was from the first impracticable in a liberal republic. But it long was impossible, on material grounds alone, — although enthusiasts might attempt to live upon love and fame — that any vigorous and prevailing flood of poesy should be sustained in toiling, practical, frugal America. We now know that in art, as in life, ideal productiveness follows, and does not precede, material security and wealth. The most creative eras of historic lands were those when their cities were the richest, when their galleons sought out distant ports, and their nobles and burgesses, sure of life's needs, craved for the luxuries of taste and emotion. Literature thrives as a means of subsistence, nor is poetry an exception to the rule. The supply answers to the demand. Not long ago in this country, few books, except school-books, were required by the people ; and how should poetry, that looked from the printed page for its welcome and sustenance, be naturally composed ? We are speaking of an ethereal art, but quietly examining the law of its activity.

Law of production.

It is, moreover, in America that the popular instinct, which resists whatever is asserted to be a tax upon knowledge, has worked with peculiar force against the development of a home-school. So long as our purveyors could avail themselves without cost or hindrance of foreign master-works, they scarcely could be expected to risk their means in behalf of native authorship. Pure idealists, men like Poe and Hawthorne, are little able to push their own fortunes.

The copyright question.

Until a state of law shall exist that will induce American publishers, driven from their distant foraging-grounds, to seek for genius at home and make it available, the support of our authors will not be so assured as to tend "in the end to the advancement of literature." International copyright at least would have made it feasible for the poet to earn his living by general literary work, and to reserve some heart and thought for his nobler calling. Now, when an organized movement at last seems under way toward copyright reform, it still is so hampered with reservations and class-interests that many ask whether it were not better to have no change at all than to have one that is partial, and that may postpone indefinitely the one thing needful, to wit: honest recognition of an author's right of property in his own creations, without any more limits of space and time than those appertaining to other kinds of estate.

International copyright.

Literature verily has been almost the sole product of human labor that has not been rated as the lasting property of the producer and his heirs or assigns. This want of permanent copyright has borne severely upon authors in all countries, but most severely upon those of America, who have had to await the formation of public taste, to create their audiences, and who, while willing to suffer in their own persons, are less ready to devote lifetimes to the production of what will be valueless to those whom they hold most dear. The want of international copyright has been a wrong to our brother-writers in Europe. Their complaints are just; their cry has gone up for years. Great as the spoliations have been which they have endured, the effect upon our native literature and authorship has been far more disastrous. Our authors themselves do not comprehend it. A few of the great

Disastrous effect upon American literature.

publishing houses, grown rich upon the system of free reprints, of late have felt this wrong, and the men of heart and culture who control them are generously atoning for it. We see them leaders in artistic and literary movements, the friends of authors and artists, receiving for their public and private humanities our warmest tributes of honor and affection. It is said that every wrong in this world is surely, if slowly, righted; and the wrongs of authors doubtless will be set right. But who shall pick up water spilled to the ground? The writers of a new generation will never realize how bitter was the bread eaten by those who went before them and made their paths straight.

Unsatisfactory tests of merit.

Critical periods are sometimes uncreative, yet there is little doubt that our poetry has suffered, also, from the lack of those high and exquisite standards of criticism which have been established in older lands. The poet, the artist, alike need the correction of a fine censorship and the tonic of that just appreciation which is the promise of fame. American verse, within recent memory, has experienced, first, a popular favor gained by its weakest and most effeminate sentiment; and, secondly, a rude exaggeration of its defects, a refusal to acknowledge its value as compared with that of the foreign product, or to consider its higher aspirations as practicable and worthy of respect. The people at large have passed from sham emotion to irreverence, and to a relish for what is flippant and ephemeral. Then, too, our most sincere and painstaking authorities often seem at a loss to estimate the nature of art, and criticise it from metaphysical or doctrinarian points of view. The poet or painter feels the wrong and the error, and, though he makes no complaint, they tell upon his buoyancy and application. Only of late have we begun to look for criti-

Criticism as it should be.

cism which applies both knowledge and self-knowledge to the test; which is penetrative and dexterous, but probes only to cure; which enters into the soul and purpose of a work, and considers every factor that makes it what it is; — the criticism which, above all, esteems it a cardinal sin to suffer a verdict to be tainted by private dislike, or by partisanship and the instinct of battle with an opposing clique or school. Such criticism is now essayed, but often is too much occupied with foreign or recondite subjects to search out and foster what is of worth among ourselves.

IV.

These local and primitive difficulties are now succeeded by the general restrictions of the new era.

These, it seems to me, have been the local and organic difficulties with which the American poet, wittingly or unwittingly, has had to contend. They are not figments of the brain; their force has been real; time and national development alone have lessened them; during the continuation of their serious pressure the rise of poetry was delayed. It is curious to note that, just as their adverse influence began to pass away, a new class of restrictions came in play throughout the enlightened world, affecting our own idealists in common with those of the mother-land. When I long since began to think of the present work, I saw that the modern intellectual change was so absolute that I was compelled to seek for the general conditions of the period, and to attempt a review of the poets of England before entering upon our home-field, in order to comprehend justly the effect of the new atmosphere upon the spirit of poetry itself. In the first chapter of the *Victorian Poets*, certain perplexing elements are considered which have made the recent time one to which a hackneyed word, "transitional," is more correctly applied than to any former period. The new learning — the passage from the childlike and phenomenal way of regarding things to the absolute, scientific penetration of their true entities and relations — has directly told upon the work of the poet, requiring new language, imagery, invention, as he adapts himself to a deeper purpose and the hope of a sublimer faith. I have pointed out, as well, the struggles, devices, defeats, and victories of the English minstrels under the stress of latter-day iconoclasm and the invincible demands of modern thought; taking into account, also, the minor and obvious forces antagonistic to a devoted pursuit of the ideal, — among the rest the world's material activity, displayed in labor, invention, construction, — the world's realistic eagerness, that makes of the newspaper, the novel, and the bulletins of science the food and outlets of the imagination, and renders mankind intent alone upon each day's labor, so to hasten on the golden year. Reluctant to confront these ceaseless and perturbing manifestations, until out of them the world shall have derived a more assured philosophy, many of the latest singers have ignored them altogether: the weaker busying themselves with mere dilettanteism and the technique of their vocation, the nobler being devoted to the worship of beauty pure and simple, and often going back to its early revelations and the antique forms.

Cp. "Victorian Poets": pp. 7–21.

V.

Dawn at last.

THESE generic burdens of the age itself have borne even more severely upon American idealists than upon their transatlantic brethren. Yet it was when they first began to have their weight, and not until then, that the true light of Poetry in America ventured to appear. Under the very shadow of the whirlwind it brightened into dawn. Possibly the new learning was most of all needed here, as an offset to puritanism, superstition, and sentimentalism in its mawkish forms. Honest fact and a search for our own resources gave an impulse to healthy inspiration. But the opportunity for the achievements of our leading poets, so famous and beloved in their hoary years, really came when the specific restrictions, to which so much space has been here devoted, at last yielded measurably to time and national progress. Coincidently with their decline, certain positive aids to our lyrical genius became apparent, and were felt, and aroused to joyous activity its instinct, courage, and imagination.

Special advantages of our home-poets.

American landscape.

First of all, as I have shown, the American with an eye for natural beauty, led by his seclusion to close and musing observation, had a subject for poetic expression in the landscape of the New World, by turns impressive, bewildering, reposeful, but always beautiful and strong. If its primeval aspect stupefied the toiling settlers, while its grandeur seemed to belittle humanity and to defer the proper study of mankind, it afterward compelled our ideal recognition, and inspired the early and reverent anthems of the father of our choir. Next, and most vital of the elements required for the promotion of a home-school, a national feeling grew up when the compactness and growth of the United States, as a nation, became assured. Half a century was needed to bring this feeling to the blossoming form of art. Meanwhile, it had been strengthening and finding expression in other ways; for example, in the patriotic eloquence which marked our oratory, and which warmed the blood and stirred the impulse of many a poetic youth, as he read

National feeling

in his school-books the speeches of the founders and preservers of liberty. Hence our strongest emotional traits, — love of freedom, hatred of oppression, respect for ancestral faith, the sense of independence which makes an American stand erect and believe himself the peer of any man, the audacity and ambition found among no other people; finally, an adventurous habit of experimenting without much regard to precedent or training. Out of some of these traits came, it is true, a commonplace and widely scattered product in literature. But if a host of writers ended in mediocrity, this, too, was in the order of evolution. The feeble books of one generation are often horn-books for the people, the promise and cause of better work in the next. The late Civil War was not of itself an incentive to good poetry and art, nor directly productive of them. Such disorders seldom are; action is a substitute for the ideal, and the thinker's or dreamer's life seems ignoble and repugnant. But we shall see that the moral and emotional conflicts preceding the war, and leading to it, were largely stimulating to poetic ardor; they broke into expression, and buoyed with earnest and fervid sentiment our heroic verse. Lastly, it must be observed that, about the time from which I date the appearance of a group of noteworthy poets, a material support was afforded to ideal work. Both artists and writers began to be paid, and found their respective gifts to some extent a means of subsistence. American publishers, as I have said, took heart, and made ventures in behalf of our own literature. Journalism also lent its aid, paying critical attention to native authors, and enabling not a few of them to gain a foothold by labor upon the great newspapers and magazines. All these aids, I repeat, came into service after the scientific

Growth of the market.

restraint of the modern period began to have weight. They assisted us to bear up against it, and alleviated the special restrictions of an earlier time. The sweet and various measures of a band of genuine singers at length were heard, and found an audience in whatsoever regions know the English tongue. American poetry took its place in literature, and entered upon a first term, now brought to an end, and constituting the main field of this review.

Advent of a true poetic school.

CHAPTER II.

GROWTH OF THE AMERICAN SCHOOL.

I.

HAVING given an outline of the situation which rendered the new country, in the earlier periods of settlement, an untoward region for the pursuit of song, and also of the specific aids which at last have enabled America to have some voice and inspiration of her own, I now wish to glance at the actual record of her lyrical exploits that culminated with the rise of the group of poets to whom this work is chiefly devoted. To do this minutely would require us to travel over dreary wastes indeed, though gaining rest at last upon the borders of a land of promise. From what has been written, I shall rightly be understood to agree with Mr. Whipple in his statement that the course of our literature has been, upon the whole, subsidiary to the general movement of the American mind; that our imagination has found exercise in the subjugation of a continent, in establishing liberty, in war, politics, and government, — above all, in the inventive and constructive energy and the financial boldness needed to develop and control the material heritage which has fallen to us. But to this let me add that the course of our poetry, for the same reasons, was long subsidiary to the course of other literature, — at once, or by turns, to our theological, political, and educational achievements in prose, and

A retrospective summary: 1607–1860.

"The First Century of the Republic": Harper's Mag., 1876.

to those in the departments of historical narrative and romance.

Authorities.

The means for a survey of the early waste, and of its few and unimportant oases, are to be found in the libraries of collectors, and in the compilations of the Duyckincks, Griswold, and others, who have made for us as cheery a showing as they could. But a reader who has not access to the rare books of a succession of by-gone authors gains with more satisfaction a correct idea of their worth and purport by the study of such a work as Professor Tyler's "History of American Literature." He well may avail himself, so far as it is completed, of a critical digest whose facts will not be gainsaid, a clear and wholesome exposition of our early literature, presenting judgments and inferences with which he usually must be in accord. It is a result of scholarly labor, closely examining the field, and failing not to detect whatever may be found of value in those new plantations. Can this mould of the Colonial period be touched with the sunlight of to-day? Can these dry bones live? Yes, under the hands of a man with the patience, enthusiasm, and kindly humor of their historian, to whom American literature is so indebted for this review of its progress that his name will be enviably connected with it henceforth.

Prof. Moses Coit Tyler's review of the Colonial periods.

And in the two large volumes, covering our first and second periods, more than a century and a half, — from 1607 to 1765, — the product of the poets appears so valueless and meagre that, if the narrative depended on them alone, there would be no great reason for its compilation. A larger proportion of educated men belonged to the early colonies than is to be found elsewhere upon the rolls of emigration. Nearly all writers then wrote verse, at first printing their works in London, and afterward by means of the few and meanly furnished presses along this coast. These folk were simply third-rate British rhymesters, who copied the pedantry of the tamest period known. The only marks of distinction between their prose and verse were that, while the former might be dull, the latter must be, and must pay a stilted regard to measure and rhyme. How hard for our amiable historian to make poetical finds that can lighten the pages of his record! How he seizes upon some promising estray, — like the anonymous ode on the death of picturesque Nat. Bacon, like Norton's "Funeral Elegy" upon Mistress Anne Bradstreet, or Urian Oakes's upon Thomas Shepard, — and makes the most of it! Surely a time that fed its imagination with the offerings of the "Tenth Muse," and expressed religious exaltation in those measures of the *Bay Psalm Book* that seem to break from a cow's horn or a Roundhead's nose, and in the lyrical damnations of Michael Wigglesworth, — such a time, from its beginning with George Sandys even to the generation that founded hopes of a native drama upon the genius of Thomas Godfrey, had derived few creative impulses from its own experience, and could give no real intimation of a national future. This was a time which now seems more venerable to us than the daylight eras of ancient civilization, — drearily old-fashioned, like its town halls and college barracks, still remaining, all the older and mouldier because they are not antique. To its very close, when the different colonies began to move toward cohesion, the most of it seems to me night, — utter night. Its poetical relics are but the curios of a museum, — the queer and ugly specimens of an unhistoric age.

Ode on the Death of Nathaniel Bacon: 1676.

John Norton: 1651–1716.

Urian Oakes: 1631–81.

Anne Bradstreet: 1612–72.

The "Bay Psalm Book": Cambridge, 1640.

Michael Wigglesworth: 1631–1705.

Sandys, the translator of Ovid: 1577–1644.

Thomas Godfrey: 1736–63.

A rayless period.

Manifestly, and as at a later time, New England

New Eng

land in the van.

claimed the lead in whatsoever there was of thought, or wit, or fancy; and Cambridge even then had her poets, who accounted themselves true children of Parnassus. Tyler plainly shows how the feudal policy of dispersion, and a contempt for book-learning as compared with active life, placed a ban upon letters in Virginia; while the New England policy of numerical and intellectual concentration brought forward the learned men of that region, and made its colonists a literary people from the first. In spite of their moroseness, pedantry, asceticism, a lurking perception of beauty, an æsthetic sensibility, was to be found among them. But the manifest, the sincere genius of the colonies is diplayed elsewhere than in their laborious verse.

The Early Chroniclers.

Noble English and a simple, heroic wonder give zest to the writings of the early chroniclers, the annals of discovery and adventure. Such traits distinguish the narratives of the gallant and poetic Captain John Smith, and of Strachey, whose picture of a storm and wreck in the Bermudas so roused the spirit that conceived "The Tempest."

Historians.

They pervade the memorials of Bradford and Winthrop, of Johnson and Gookin, of Francis Higginson and Winslow and William Wood. There are power and imagination in the discourses of the great preachers,

Divines.

— Hooker, Cotton, Roger Williams, Oakes, — who founded a dominion of the pulpit that was not shaken until after the time of Edwards and Byles. Verse-making was but the foible of the colonial New Englanders; law, religious fervor, superstition, were then the strength of life; and the time that produced Increase and Cotton Mather fostered a progeny quite as striking and characteristic as the melodists of our late Arcadian morn.

The Mid-

When the Middle Colonies began to have a literature, it was natural that the chief writers — men of the learned professions, busied in affairs, and already feeling that instinct of government which animates territorial centres — should be publicists, setting forth the principles of order, economy, and social weal. The colonial separation ended; the national movement began with stormy agitation, and progressed to union in council and war. With the Revolution came not only the great orators, but an outburst, otherwise than tuneful, of patriotic ballads, songs, and doggerel satires, — to all of which, at this distance, the sounds of the Continental fife and drum seem a fitting accompaniment. Nor did staid and learned personages disdain to pay homage to the precept of Andrew Fletcher, and to supplement the new-born national ardor by the aid of their muses. Trumbull's *M'Fingal* is a work that will not go quite out of repute. It still speaks well for the character, wit, and facility of the staunch and acute author, and shows genuine originality although written after a model. Not even "Hudibras" more aptly seizes upon the ludicrous phases of a turbulent epoch. In New York, bluff Captain Freneau, mariner, journalist, and poet, proved himself the ready laureate of the war. Read the story of his impetuous life, and look through the collection of his ditties and poems, with their pretentious defects and unwittingly clever touches. A strange and serio-comic medley they are, and no less a varied representation of the poetic standards reached in America a hundred years ago. Among the relics which I call to mind of the jingling verse produced in quantity by Treat Paine and his contemporaries, there is scarcely a lyric that breathes what we now recognize as the essential poetic spirit, excepting five or six of Freneau's, such as "The Wild Honeysuckle," "The Parting Glass,"

dle Colonies.

Revolutionary Period: 1765-87.

John Trumbull: 1750-1831.

Philip Freneau: 1752-1832.

Rhymesters of his time.

"To a Honey Bee" (which last is good enough to be Landor's), and a delicate little song, by John Shaw, of Maryland, entitled "Who has Robbed the Ocean Cave?" Practical efforts, however, were made in the composition and production of native dramas, by Tyler and Dunlap, — our earliest playwrights, — in Boston and New York respectively.

Royall Tyler: 1757–1826.

William Dunlap: 1766–1839.

1787–1815.

After the close of the Revolution, and until the War of 1812, the genius of our people was devoted to the establishment, through peaceful labor, of the security and resources which should be the first-fruits of a conflict for independence. Writers occupied themselves with analyzing the science of government, its principles and practice. No American library, however, was complete without copies of Dr. Dwight's historico-didactic masterpiece, *Greenfield Hill*, and Joel Barlow's quarto epic, *The Columbiad.* The popular ear was content with patriotic songs, among them "Hail Columbia," which owed their general adoption, like a successor, "The Star-Spangled Banner," to the music that carried them and to an early possession of the field. It was not until peace, for a second time, became a habit that the imagination of a young people, assured of nationality, slowly found expression upon the written page. In view of the conditions already described, what traits might we reasonably expect would characterize poetic effort at this stage of development?

Timothy Dwight: 1752–1817.

Joel Barlow: 1755–1812.

Patriotic ditties.

First, — and although the form and ideal of American verse still should correspond, like all our early fashions, to the modes prevailing in England, — it would seem that, gradually, poets should appear, hampered by this instinct of correspondence, and not quite knowing or daring to be original, yet possessing graces and thoughts of their own, and looking at things, after

A natural course of development.

all, in a different way from the English; that they should seek for home themes, and study their surroundings, most likely in a doubtful and groping manner; that a diversity of subject, thought, and language should be observed in the distinct sections of the republic,—the poets of the South being more courtly and romantic, and those of the Middle States more national and more upon the search for aboriginal and historical flavor; that local successes should be marked where there was the least inflow of new foreign elements, the sincerest faith, the most intelligent thought; that poetry should be the more learned, the more subtle and earnest, in the scholarly region of the East, and that poets should thrive best there, where the practice of literature had long obtained,—since all forms of art require more time for growth than other products of national organization.

Differentiation.

Somewhat after this wise, in fact, as we recur to the earliest promise of an American school, we find that it began with the second quarter of this century. Imaginative youths, born and educated in the new republic, discovered that they were poets, and strove to express the spirit of their birth and training. Among them, Pierpont, Dana, Allston, Sprague, Bryant,—the gentle stars of the East,—began to show their light, and offered their tender or patriotic lyrics, their meditative verse, their placid monographs on the phases of American scenery and tradition. Of these, Bryant was the one whose genius had the elements that give permanence to the work of poets. In the South, a few scattered minstrels, such as Wilde and Pinkney, sang their Lovelace lyrics. Their type has survived, almost to our day. Throughout the swift development of the Northern States, the South—agricultural, feudal, provincial—loyally clung to its eight-

Earliest promise of a Home-School, 1815–

John Pierpont: 1785–1866.

Richard Henry Dana: 1787–1879.

Washington Allston: 1779–1843.

Charles Sprague: 1791–1875.

Bryant.

Richard Henry Wilde: 1789–1847.

Edward Coate Pinkney: 1802–28.

The South. eenth-century taste, making no intellectual changes so long as human slavery was the basis of its physical life. I shall hereafter refer to the quality of the new-born Southern imagination. That it exists, in fresh and hopeful promise, is now beyond doubt. A few of the earlier Southern writers — one of whom was Simms, the novelist-poet — worked courageously, but with more will and fluency than native power; so that, in spite of their abundant verse, such a lyrist as Pendleton Cooke was long the typical Southern poet, — a name joined with the memory of a single song. A collection of the earlier Southern poetry worth keeping would be a brief anthology, which a little volume might contain, and in which more than one of Albert Pike's productions certainly should be found. Poe, whose pieces would occupy one third of it, sought the literary market, deserting Richmond and Baltimore for Philadelphia and New York. He lived in the Northern atmosphere, and, like Bryant, took his part in the busy movement of its civic life and work.

William Gilmore Simms: 1806–70.

Philip Pendleton Cooke: 1816–50.

Poe.

Besides the Eastern poets whom I have named, there were others who still more closely followed English models: among them, the orthodox bards of Connecticut, Hillhouse and Brainard, compared with whom Percival, the eccentric scholar and recluse, shines by virtue of a gift improved by no mean culture. His lyrics and poems of nature, though inferior to Bryant's, so resemble them that he would be called the latter's pupil, had not the two composed in the same manner from the outset.

James Abraham Hillhouse: 1789–1841.

John Gardiner Calkins Brainard: 1796–1828.

James Gates Percival: 1795–1856.

These writers and some others of their time must, in all fairness, be judged by it. They had their modest laurels and rewards, and were the bright selected few of their country and period, — no less distinguished, though within a smaller horizon, than their

Allowances to be made.

latter-day successors. Their work was the best of its kind which America could show; it had the knack of making itself read in the annuals and school-books, and influenced the sentiment of more than one generation. Were Dana and Allston flourishing now, they would accomplish feats then impracticable, and doubtless would be at no disadvantage among our present favorites, nor less receive our honor and support. Fashion is a potency in art, making it hard to judge between the temporary and the lasting. Are we sure that our popular poets are better in native faculty? If they have a finer understanding and a defter handling of their craft, these may be partly a consequence of the fact that not Montgomery and Wilson, but Keats, and Wordsworth, and Tennyson, and their greater masters, have supplied the models of a recent school.

New York.

It was natural, also, that the literary centre should shift from place to place, along a sea-board whose capital was scarcely yet defined. New York early drew together a number of bright young wits and songsters. The fame of the prose-romancers, Cooper and Irving, and their success with home themes, were gratifying to the local and national pride, and encouraged at the time, as far as literature was concerned, a broader American sentiment than prevailed in New England. That was a spirited little group of rhyming satirists whose fancy brightened the pages of Coleman's "Evening Post." Two young writers, Halleck and Drake, worked in comradeship until the one sustained a more than common misfortune in the other's untimely death. These two men were real poets; such is the impression left as one reads, after many years, the verse composed by them. Had they been born half a century later, they now would work

Cooper and Irving.

"The Croakers," 1819-25.

more elaborately, but with less certainty of reputation. Their best pieces were at once so received into popular affection that the authors' names still last. Both of these poets had humor, and a perception of its legitimate use. They, with Bryant and his school, — with Brockden Brown, Paulding, Cooper, Irving, and Miss Sedgwick, writers of prose, and the dramatist Payne, author of "Brutus" and other bygone plays, and of that abiding carol, "Home, Sweet Home," — were the first Americans whose work gave any substantial evidence of a native movement in ideal or creative literature. Drake died in his twenty-sixth year, leaving a daughter, through whom his poetic gift has been transmitted to our day. He had a quick, genuine faculty, and could be frolicsome or earnest at will. As an exercise of that delicate imagination which we term fancy, *The Culprit Fay*, although the work of a youth schooled in fairy-lore and the metres of Coleridge, Scott, and Moore, boded well for his future. "The American Flag" is a stirring bit of eloquence in rhyme. The death of this spirited and promising writer was justly deplored. His talent was healthy; had he lived, American authorship might not so readily have become, in Griswold's time, a vent for every kind of romantic and sentimental absurdity. Drake also would have stimulated the muse of Halleck, whose choicest pieces were composed before he had outlived the sense of that recent companionship. He, too, was a natural lyrist, whose pathos and eloquence were inborn, and whose sentiment, though he wrote in the prevailing English mode, was that of his own land. As we read those favorites of our schoolboy days, "Burns" and "Red Jacket" and "Marco Bozzaris," we feel that Halleck was, within his bounds, a national poet. Circumstances dulled his fire, and

Pioneers.

John Howard Payne: 1791–1852.

Joseph Rodman Drake: 1795–1820.

Fitz-Greene Halleck: 1790–1867.

he lived to write drivel in his old age. But the early lyrics remain, nor was there anything of their kind in our home-poetry to compete with them until long after their first production.

Growing literary activity.

The impulse given to poetry and belles-lettres by the example of the early poets and novelists increased with the appearance of fresh strivers after literary fame. In the East, names began to be mentioned that now are great indeed; others, then more commonly known, have passed almost out of memory. A few teachers of sound literary doctrine, like E. T. Channing, of Cambridge, were sowing good seed for future harvests. In New York, the writings of Willis and Tuckerman, of the song-makers Hoffman, Morris, and English, of Verplanck, the Duyckincks, Benjamin, Griswold, and other editors and bookwrights, and the parade of new versifiers, male and female, betokened a taste, however crude and ill-regulated, for the pursuit of letters. Occasionally a note of promise was heard, from some quaint genius like Ralph Hoyt, or some aspirant like Lord, of whom great things were predicted, and who, in spite of Poe's vindictive onslaught, was and is a poet. A good deal of eloquent and high-sounding verse was produced by such writers as Ross Wallace and Albert Pike. In the East, John Neal, William Ware, Lunt, Hillard, Mrs. Child, — and in regions farther south, Conrad, Kennedy, and Simms, — were active at this time. There were others whose claim to attention will be frequent throughout this work. But to enumerate all who, in the second quarter of this century, held themselves of much account is quite beyond my need and intention. Of the New York group, Willis perhaps had the most adroit and graceful talent, but it was not always exercised as by one possessing convictions. His kindness,

Henry Theodore Tuckerman: 1813–71.

Charles Fenno Hoffman: 1806–84.

George Pope Morris: 1802–64.

Thomas Dunn English: 1819–

Park Benjamin: 1809–64.

Ralph Hoyt: 1810–78.

William Wilberforce Lord: 1819–

William Ross Wallace: 1819–81.

Albert Pike: 1809–

John Neal: 1793–1876

George Lunt: 1803–85.

Robert Taylor Conrad: 1810–58.

Nathaniel Parker Willis: 1806-67.

tact, and experience of the world made him an arbiter in a provincial time. They also seriously exposed him to the three worldly perils of which, no less than in the days of the Apostle John, the children of the Lord must have a care. A few of his lyrics are charmingly tender and delicate, but he never did himself full justice as a poet, nor realized the purpose of his ambitious boyhood. The bustle of the Literati, as Poe chose to call them, and the concentration of thriving journals and book-houses in Philadelphia and New York, — whither most roads then seemed to lead, — made for a while the scribbling class of this middle region very conspicuous and alert. Their kith and kin, scattered throughout the States, multiplied in numbers. The first green fruit of a school-system, under which boys and girls had models set before them, and were incited to test their own skill in composition, fell in plenty from the tree. Each county had its prodigy contributing to the annuals and magazines. Lowell's "mass-meeting" of poets was in continuous session, — made up of those who wrote verse, read and praised it one to another, and printed it for their countrymen to read and praise. The dull and authoritative felt the responsibilities of the situation. Never was a more united effort made, with malice prepense, to create an indigenous school. It was thought essential that purely American themes and incidents should be utilized. Cockney poets, emulating the method of Cooper, sent fancy ranging through the aboriginal forest, and wreaked their measures upon the supposititious Indian of that day. Powhatan and Tecumseh became the heroes of hot-pressed cantos, now extinct. The Spirit of Wakondah was invoked by one bard, and made to tower above the Rocky Mountains, more awe-inspiring than Camoëns's Spirit

"The Literati."

Pseudo-Americanism.

of the Cape. Each poet, moreover, tried his hand at every form of work, and each thought it specially incumbent upon himself to write a drama, — not solely for the stage, but that America might not be deficient in the most complex order of poetical composition. Since the heyday of the Della Cruscans never were so many neophytes and amateurs suffered to bring their work before the public. Women took part in the campaign, and, truth to say, were often more spontaneous and natural than their brother-writers. One of the sex, Mrs. Sigourney, long had been supplying the prose and verse that answered to the simple wants of a primitive constituency. Another, "Maria del Occidente," gained something like fame, and even beyond the seas. She was, in fact, a woman of ardent feeling, instinctive art, and undoubted metrical talent, though scarcely meriting the praise which Lamb and Southey awarded her, or the extravagant eulogium of her modern editor. There was no lack of rivals to her success among the American pupils of Mrs. Hemans and Miss Landon. Such caterers to the literary market were found not only upon this side of the Atlantic. England was slowly escaping from her own sentimentalists; the "Annuals" and "Souvenirs" were still in vogue, and the fashions of the two countries were less divided than now. Poe, with a critical eye made somewhat keen by practice, saw the ludicrous side of all this, and poured out vials of wrath upon his contemporaries, though with no just claim to impartiality. Lowell, from a classical distance, celebrated their follies in the lines beginning,

Lydia Howard Huntley Sigourney: 1791–1865.

Maria Gowen Brooks: 1795–1845.

The Sentimentalists.

Curative applications.

"But stay, here comes Tityrus Griswold, and leads on
The flocks whom he first plucks alive, and then feeds on!"

But this reminds us that Poe, Lowell, Longfellow,

and Emerson were gaining influence at that very time; that others since eminent in our literature were gradually distinguished from the multitude; that, however absurd and depressing the condition just set forth, a superficial literary movement may be better than no movement at all. As the voyage progressed, it really was surprising how soon the dullards and pretenders went below, while the born sailors helped the vessel forward. The fit survivors of a brood of poets and authors soon obtained a grateful hearing, and a few publishers found pleasure and profit in nursing the works of these home-writers. A number of poets — men of individual traits, but allied in sentiment and taste, and belonging to the same generation — seemed to arise at once, and gained the position which they have steadfastly held to the present day.

Survival of the fittest.

II.

Experimental failures needful to ultimate success.

ALL this preliminary ferment, then, was in some way needful. The experiments of many who thought themselves called enabled the few who were chosen to find motives and occasions for work of real import. The first year of the new dispensation was worth more in its product than the score of years preceding it. The poets who now came to the front have gained distinction justly, vying with those of other countries in finish and thought, and in that reflection of the life about them which alone could make them the leaders of a national school. At the recent date when the formation of such a school became manifest, these poets spoke truthfully for our people as they were and had been. One who gives their verse the fair consideration which he would extend to that of any foreign land or language is led to this conclusion.

Genuine quality of the more recent school.

The new poetry was not autochthonous in the sense of differing from all previous outgrowth of the universal human heart, and as at variance with forms that have long seemed natural to our mother-tongue, but rather in unaffected presentation of the feeling and ideas of its constituency, and after this wise was as national, fresh, and aspiring as America herself. If this land has not yet grown to full voice, it has not lacked a characteristic expression in the verse of our favorite poets. Their careers, we have seen, began almost simultaneously at the close of the second fifth of this century, and have been prolonged until now, through a period of nearly fifty years. Let me again briefly refer to the elements which our literature hitherto might justly be called upon to idealize, and make some mention of the leading poets whose song has been the response to such a call.

III.

Traits of American verse.

1. Truthful reflection of Nature.

I HAVE said that a fellowship with the spirit of natural Landscape, and the recognition of its beauty and majesty, were the earliest, as they are the most constant, traits of American verse. The contemplation of nature has not often been the first step, or the second, in the progress of ideality. But this remark applies to primitive races. The aborigines of a country are almost a part of its mould, — or, at least, so closely related to its dumb fauna that they reflect but little on the mountains, woods, and waters which appear to surround them as a matter of course. Heroic or savage deeds of prowess are their first incitements to poetic utterance. Even an extended period of culture and growth has not always led them to consider the landscape objectively. Of this the Greeks, with their curious disregard of natural scenery, are a familiar example. They observed nature only to inform it with their own life, until there was no river or tree without its genius. First, epic action; next, patriotism and devotion; afterward, dramatic passion; last of all, analysis and reflective art. In our own settlements, a race that already had gone through these stages took possession of a new world. A struggle with its conditions involved a century of hardship and distrust. The final triumph, the adjustment of the people to their locality, brought a new understanding, out of which came the first original quality in our poetry and design. Here it is to be remembered that descriptive literature, poetry or prose, though not earlier upon the record of intellectual development, is lower as respects the essential worth of Art than that which is emotional or dramatic. In the full prime of creative work, the one must serve as a background for the other, upon which attention chiefly is concentrated. All in all, it was a foregone conclusion that our first independent artists should betake themselves to the study and utilization of American scenery. In painting, our first distinctive school — for such I do not term the early group of historical and portrait painters, from West to Allston — has been that of the landscapists. Let us own that when either poetry or painting deals with nature in no copyist's fashion, but with a sense of something "deeply interfused," it may reach the higher plane of art-expression. To this end our modern painters, upon the whole, have striven, from the time of Cole. The hands of Durand, Inness, Kensett, the two Giffords, Whittredge, McEntee, Church, Bierstadt, Brown, Martin, Wyant, have given us a landscape-school that, for sincerity and freshness, is notable on either continent, and is constantly gain-

The usual order reversed.

Our first distinctive group of painters.

ing in technique and variety from the experiments of younger men. The literary counterpart of this school began with Bryant, the Druid of our forests, the high-priest of Nature in her elemental types. These he has celebrated with the coolness and breadth that were traits of the earlier painters named, though lacking the freedom and detail of their successors. It is dangerous to measure one art by another, or to confuse their terms; yet we feel that the relationship between the pictures of Durand and Kensett, for example, and the meditative verse of Bryant — from "Thanatopsis" and "A Forest Hymn" to "The Night Journey of a River" — is near and suggestive. Bryant was at the head of our reflective poets, finding his bent at the outset, and holding it to the very close. His work rose to an imaginative height which descriptive poetry of itself rarely attains.

Their compeers in Song.

Bryant.

He was followed — at an obvious distance — by Percival, Wilcox, Street, and other mild celebrants of nature, who failed of his breadth and elevation. Their patient measures show how strongly the scenery of America has impressed her people. To the present day, the landscape, however incidental to the poetry of Emerson, Whittier, Thoreau, Lowell, and Taylor, is constantly there, and fresh as a rocky pasture-ground in New England or Pennsylvania compared with a storied park of Warwickshire. In the work of Mrs. Thaxter, Piatt, and other recent idyllists, it is natural, sympathetic, — in short, thoroughly American. And for me the value of the poetry of Whitman and Joaquin Miller does not belong to the method and democratic vistas of the one, and the melodramatic romance of the other; but to Whitman's fresh, absolute handling of outdoor nature, and to the fine surprises which Miller gives us in haunting pictures of the plains, the sierra, and the sundown seas.

Carlos Wilcox: 1794–1827.

Alfred Billings Street: 1811–81.

Fresh and original treatment of landscape.

2. Presentation of the national sentiment.

Our poetry has been equally fortunate as the language of the ideas and human emotions to which, as a people, we most readily incline. Notwithstanding the change and unrest of a new country, the *milieu* which Taine found in England here exists, and with fewer qualifications. Not that America is all middle class, as some have asserted. But her ideal is derived from sentiments which, even more than in Great Britain, preserve a Saxon quality, — those of domesticity, piety, freedom, loyalty to the institutions of the land. If unessential to various dramatic and impassioned art-creations, they have an art and passion of their own, and, in recognizing this, our singers are more national than their English contemporaries. The latter, except through the odes and idyls of Tennyson, have conveyed to us little of the home-sentiment, the English faith and feeling, which brought the motherland to greatness. Doubtless it is because these qualities were so general in the song of their predecessors that the Victorian choir has earnestly concerned itself with mediæval and legendary work, and with those technical diversions which are counted as art for art's sake.

Our poets true to their own time and kind.

The instinct of our poets has led them first to charge their lyrics with the feeling of their time and people, and in doing this they have, almost without exception, given voice to their own heart. Bryant's verse is an illustration. It everywhere breathes of liberty and patriotism. But as an apostle of all the sentiments just named, — taken singly or in combination, — Whittier, the Quaker bard of Amesbury, whose art is by turns so homely and so refined, certainly is preëminent, and in a sense has made himself that uncrowned laureate, the people's poet. His legend is *pro aris et focis.* He glows with faith, strong by

Bryant.

Whittier.

Pro aris et focis.

heredity in New England, and thence outflowing to the West, nor forgets the beauty and duty of temperance, charity, and virtue. Nothing restrains his democratic conception of the freedom of the soil, the nobility of work, the right to labor for one's self. He represents (to borrow Hugo's formula) our conflict with oppression, and was the herald and inspired seer of the enduring fiery conflict that preceded the antislavery war. His earnestness and burning effort contrast with Bryant's stern repose. In various national qualities the more polished work of Longfellow and Lowell has rivaled Whittier's, and sustained it. They, in their ways, and Gallagher, Holland, Trowbridge, and Taylor, each in his own, have paid tribute to the charm of American home-life, and have repeated the ancestral and prevalent feeling of regions which they thoroughly comprehend. In this direction they have been accompanied by many writers in verse or prose, — simple balladists like the Vermonter, Eastman, and tale-writers with the insight and fidelity that belong to Sylvester Judd, Mrs. Harriet Beecher Stowe, and Rose Terry Cooke. In times of concentrated emotion, our poets of all degrees have broken out in vivid strains. Mrs. Howe's "Battle Hymn" is memorable. There is native fire in the lyrics of McMaster, Melville, O'Hara, Finch, Palmer, Randall, Forceythe Willson, and that brave, free singer, Brownell, to whom Ticknor, sounding the war-cry of the South, bore a half-likeness in manner and spirit. There have been many single voices, heard but for a moment, of this class. Nor should we quite forget the humbler song-makers for the people, such as Foster, the negro melodist, — and Work, to whose stirring music our soldiers marched with a will, and of whose songs two or three at least should preserve the name of their

Conflict with oppression.

William Davis Gallagher: 1808–

Josiah Gilbert Holland: 1819–81.

John Townsend Trowbridge: 1827–

Charles Gamage Eastman: 1816–61.

Julia Ward Howe: 1819–

Herman Melville: 1819–

Byron Forceythe Willson: 1837–67.

Henry Howard Brownell. 1820–72.

Francis Orrery Ticknor: 1822–74.

(*See Index.*)

composer. In closing this section I will add a word in regard to a kind of verse which, of all, is the most common and indispensable, — that devoted to reverence and worship. The religious verse of America, whether the work of poets at large, or of those whose range is chiefly confined to it, — Muhlenberg, Coxe, Doane, Peabody, Croswell, Sears, S. Johnson, S. Longfellow, Abraham Coles, Ray Palmer, Harriet Kimball, Hedge, Dr. Frothingham, Randolph, Chadwick, Savage, and many other orthodox or liberal composers, — ranks in quality, if not in quantity, with the hymnology of other lands.

Religious Verse.

Arthur Cleveland Coxe: 1818–

(See Index.)

No one can enter upon the most cursory review of our literature without being struck by the share which women have had in its production. A sisterhood of song, expressing its own delicate and heroic nature, and many thoughts and affections that are sweet and high and impassioned, has won in America a just and distinctive regard. The female voices early added softness, and at times strength, to the general song. The names of Maria Lowell, Mrs. Osgood, Mrs. Whitman, the Cary sisters, Mrs. Judson, Mrs. Sewall, Elizabeth Lloyd Howell, Mrs. Oakes Smith, Mrs. E. C. Kinney, and Mrs. Botta, some of whom have passed away, are cherished by not a few. They have had successors — of whom are Mrs. Cooke, Mrs. Stoddard, Mrs. Allen, Mrs. Whitney, Mrs. Dorr, Mrs. Greenough, Lucy Larcom, Mrs. Hudson, and others to whom I shall refer in a later chapter — some of whose names are veritably household words throughout the country, and much of whose work, in verse and prose, has taken a subtler range, a better finish, a definite and influential hold upon the public attention.

American female poets.

The early and later sisterhoods of song. (See Index.)

American culture, if not so exact and diligent as that of more learned nations, is sympathetic, and ex-

University group.

plores all literatures for its delight and betterment. It is most advanced in the sections where it took its start, but there and elsewhere is well represented in our poetry. A university school has sent out rays from Cambridge, the focus being the home of a poet with whose rise the new poetic movement fairly began. He grew to be not the poet of a section, nor even of a people, but one rendered into many languages, and known throughout the world. Longfellow, on the score of his fame, and his almost exclusive devotion to the muse, became the centre of a group distinguished by culture, elegant learning, regard for the manner of saying no less than for what is said. His early legend rightly was *Outre Mer*, for he stimulated our taste by choice presentation of what is rare abroad, until it grew able to perceive what is rare and choice at home. With thoughts of this singer come thoughts of peace, of romance, of the house made beautiful by loving hands. Lowell and Holmes, no less than Longfellow, and wonted to the same atmosphere, represent our conflict with rudeness, ignorance, and asceticism. They laugh the Philistine to scorn, and with their wit and learning advance the movement toward sweetness and light. Near them are others, such as Parsons, Story, Robert Lowell, Mrs. Fields, who may be classed more readily with a composite group of whom I have yet to speak. But first let us observe that an imaginative and unique division of the recent school is that which represents the liberal philosophy of New England and its conflict with ancestral superstition. The mind and soul of Transcendentalism seemed to find their predestined service in the land of the Puritans. The poetry which sprang from it had a more subtle aroma than that whose didacticism infected the English Lake school. The latter made

Longfellow.

"Outre Mer."

Conflict with asceticism.

Robert Traill Spence Lowell 1816–

Transcendental group.

Concord and Grasmere.

Andrews Norton: 1786–1853.
Emerson.
Amos Bronson Alcott: 1799–
Henry David Thoreau: 1817–62.
Sarah Margaret Fuller Ossoli: 1810–50.
Jones Very: 1813–80.
Christopher Pearse Cranch: 1813–
William Ellery Channing: 1818–
David Atwood Wasson: 1823–
Thomas Wentworth Higginson: 1823–
Franklin Benjamin Sanborn: 1831–
Erastus Wolcott Ellsworth: 1822–
William Bull Wright: 1838–80.

prosaic the verse of famous poets; out of the former the quickest inspiration of our down-East thinkers seemed to grow. Their philosophy, beginning with the prose and verse of Andrews Norton, and the exalted spirituality of Dr. Channing, and soon going beyond the early liberties, has attained its riper expression in lyrical work, prophetic, mystical, or quaintly wise. It borrowed, in truth, the wisdom of the Orient and the speculations of Germany, but has not failed to apply the vision that so inspired it to the life and action of the New World. The white light of Emerson, the pure and elevated master of the Concord group, has been a steadfast beacon for his companions. Among these, Alcott, Thoreau, Margaret Fuller, Jones Very, Cranch, Ellery Channing, Wasson, Higginson, and Sanborn may be reckoned, with due allowance for the individuality of each. Here and there stray singers, like the shy and philosophic minstrel, Ellsworth, have seemed to belong to this peculiarly American caste. Another such was the lamented Dr. Wright, whose gift was delicately pure and thoughtful. Poe was right in claiming that the speculative tendency of these poets was at odds with the artistic effect of their work, but ought to have seen that a more exquisite feeling and insight, allied with that tendency, often made amends for it.

Meantime, as I was about to point out, we have had a number of poets, including most of those who do not live in New England, who have clung to their art from sheer love of the beautiful, under varying chances of favor and discouragement. They have paid slight regard to their respective localities, writing after their own versatile moods, and looking wherever they pleased for models and themes. Some have followed other than literary pursuits, or, if earning their bread by the pen, have accepted the vicissitudes of their craft under the conditions heretofore mentioned. Their tastes and habits have made them composite, if not cosmopolitan. Their work is not provincial, though often less original than that of some whom we have named. But in escaping the rigors of a chosen section, they have also foregone its distinctions. The East has loved its poets, and, what is more, has listened to them. The New England spirit has been that of Attica, which state, we are told, "secure in her sterility, boasted that her land had never been inundated by these tides of immigration," and that "she traced the stream of her population in a backward course through many generations." With respect to philosophy and economics, and in fields of taste and literary judgment, the trust of the modern Athens is founded on her own usage and her men of note. It is true that the reverence paid our elder poets is now general throughout the land, and as sincere and beautiful as that which the bards of Germany and Scandinavia always have received at the hands of their countrymen. It even has its jealous side, and renders it hard for new aspirants to gain their share of welcome. But New York has been to her later poets, somewhat as Oxford Street was to De Quincey, a stony-hearted mother. This is partly due to the standards of success established by monetary power and prosperity, and partly to the accident that here, more than in the East, idealists have had to live by all sorts of very practical work. Writers have been tolerated and even welcomed, but not honored and taken as counsellors until they have proved themselves worldly wise, or gained their influence elsewhere. Then New York has been proud of them, in her awkward way, and used them at need, but has assigned to the provinces

An independent class.

Eastern regard for letters and song.

Wordsworth's "Greece," p. 72.

Metropolitan indifference.

the duty of reading their works. Bryant came to be her most honored citizen, and for some years was a kind of literary Doge; his city knew that he was a poet, for the country had told her so. It would be interesting to learn how large a proportion of the wealthy classes among whom he was a peer, and who placed him at the head of feasts and civic gatherings, knew this through an appreciative knowledge of his poetry. Such, however, is apt to be the state of things in a great commercial centre, — so great that it matures slowly, and must long await that splendid prime of which smaller towns earlier furnish types in miniature; and under just such conditions many a poet has struggled, yet gone down to time and fame.

Poets of the artistic and cosmopolitan type. *(See Chap. XII., and Index.)*

The artistic bent of Parsons and Story, of Poe, Taylor, Stoddard, and Aldrich, in New York; of the Philadelphians, Boker and Read; of the Southerners, Thompson, Timrod, Hayne, Lanier, and Esten Cooke; and of various younger writers who justify future notice, has been plainly seen in the application of each man's gift, whatever its degree. They have cared for poetry alone, and have believed its country to be universal, and that England, whose poets conspicuously avail themselves of the materials and atmosphere of other lands, should be the last to lay down a law of restriction. Herein, nevertheless, they subject their work, upon its general merits, to comparison with models which they scarce could hope to surpass; for only the highest excellence could draw attention to them as poets of America. Some of our verse composed in this wise has been so charming, and withal so original, as to make reputations. Poe's lyrics are an example, and others besides Poe, less conspicuous as victims of unrest and heroes of strange careers, also have represented the conflict with materialism, and have shown as genuine a gift and a wider range. Dr. Parsons holds a place of his own. He is one of those rare poets whose infrequent work is so beautiful as to make us wish for more. In quality, at least, it is of a kind with Landor's; his touch is sure, and has at command the choicer modes of lyrical art, — those which, although fashion may overslaugh them, return again, and enable a true poet to be quite as original as when hunting devices previously unessayed. His independence, on the other hand, is exhibited in his free renderings of Dante. These, with Eliot Norton's exquisite translation of the "Vita Nuova," and Longfellow's of the entire "Commedia," with Bryant's of the "Iliad" and "Odyssey," Brooks's of various German authors, Taylor's of "Faust," and with the kindred achievements of Munford, Cranch, Leland, Macdonough, Alger, Long, Duffield, Wilstach, Coles, Howland, Miss Preston, Miss Frothingham, and Emma Lazarus (whose poetic version of Heine recently appeared), have made the American school of translation somewhat eminent. Parsons' briefer poems often are models, but occasionally show a trace of that stiffness which too little employment gives even the hand of daintier sense. "Lines on a Bust of Dante," in structure, diction, loftiness of thought, is the peer of any modern lyric in our tongue. Inversion, the vice of stilted poets, becomes with him an excellence, and old forms and accents are rehandled and charged with life anew. It is to be regretted that Dr. Parsons has not used his gift more freely. He has been a poet for poets, rather than for the people; but many types are required to fill out the hemicycle of a nation's literature. Story's various talents and acquirements as a scholar, painter, sculp-

Thomas William Parsons: 1819–

Translations.

Charles Eliot Norton: 1827–

Charles Timothy Brooks: 1813–83.

(*See Index.*)

Parsons a master of lyric verse.

William Wetmore Story: 1819–

tor, author, and what not, and his prolonged residence and studies abroad, are mirrored in his verse. This, indeed, is so un-American that I was held to blame by a prominent London journal for not reviewing him as a British-born and Victorian poet. He has extreme refinement, but is a close follower of Browning's lyrico-dramatic method, and more novel in his choice of themes than in their treatment. "Cleopatra" and "Praxiteles and Phryne" are striking pieces, and show him at his best. Among the group under notice was the ardent and generous Taylor, whose seniority in death has caused my selection of him as one of those who illustrate the rise of the American school, and upon whom alone I venture any extended criticism. Poe, the eldest of the art-group, and the subject of a future chapter, is related to the others as a toiling professional writer, whose ideality maintained itself apart from the atmosphere about him. In many respects he is an exception to the rest, but, on the whole, may be counted the first to revolt against didacticism, from the artist's point of view; while Whitman, on the other hand, is hostile to art-tradition and conventionalism, as an apostle of the democracy of the future. Another artist-poet was Buchanan Read, whose song was of a more genuine quality than the painting which he made his vocation. His idyllic verse fairly portrayed the rural life of his own State, but his successes were a few rhymed lyrics and idyls that will be preserved. "The Closing Scene" gained a reputation through its descriptive beauty and clever treatment of a standard form of verse. His townsman, Boker, is the eldest of a little group to be described in a chapter on Bayard Taylor. A close study of the English poets, especially of the Elizabethan brotherhood, led him to dramatic

Taylor.

Conflicts with didacticism and tradition.

Thomas Buchanan Read: 1822–72.

George Henry Boker: 1823–

composition. Although his plays follow old models, and are founded upon the historic themes of foreign lands, they have sterling dramatic and poetic qualities. Thirty-five years ago, in an essay upon the condition and prospect of our literature, Dr. Griswold said that "the success of the plays of Bird and Conrad, and the failure of those of Longfellow and Willis," showed that there was still "patriotism enough among us to prefer works with the American inspiration to those of any degree of artistic merit without it." But it is recorded to the credit of some of Boker's plays, which are of a poetic and literary mould, and bear the test of reading, that, like their humbler prototypes, — the acting plays of Bird, Conrad, Sargent, Mathews, and others, — they were found to have the life and substance that could gain them favor, not only in the closet, but on the stage. Some of them are antecedent to the realistic manner of our own time; others have won renewed success in the present day, and proved themselves to be of a type superior to the chance and change of fashion. They show, one and all, a manly hand, and the healthy imagination of the poet, their author. His minor pieces are of uneven quality, some of them thoroughly national and spirited. Such lyrics as "On Board the Cumberland," "A Ballad of Sir John Franklin," and the "Dirge for a Soldier," often continue a poet's name more surely than the efforts which in truth are his masterpieces.

Introduction to "The Prose Writers of America." By R. W. Griswold. 1847.

Epes Sargent: 1813–80.

Cornelius Mathews: 1817–

Boker's lyrics.

Stoddard, the life-long friend and brother in song of Taylor and Boker, is still in full voice. A New Englander born, the honors of his life and service belong to New York. The whole range of his poetry has the unrestricted or cosmopolitan tendency of which I speak. He had poor advantages in youth, but an

Richard Henry Stoddard. 1825–

absolute bent for letters, and a passion for the beautiful resembling that of Poe. His knowledge of English literature, old and new, early became so valuable that his younger associates, drawn to him by admiration of his poetry, never failed to profit by his learning and suggestions. His life has been peculiarly that of a writer, with its changes and pleasurable pains, and is marked by independence, sensitiveness, devotion to his calling, and pride in the city with whose literary growth and labor he is identified. The characteristics of Stoddard's verse are affluence, sincere feeling, strength, a manner unmistakably his own, very delicate fancy, and, above all, an imagination at times exceeded by that of no other American poet. This last quality pervades his ambitious pieces, and at times breaks out suddenly in the minor verse through which he is best known. The exigencies of his profession have too constantly drawn upon his resources; the bulk of his miscellaneous verse is large, and to this is somewhat due its unevenness. No poet is more unequal; few have more plainly failed now and then. On the other hand, few have reached a higher tone, and a selection could be made from his poems upon which to base a lasting reputation.

An imaginative poet.

"The Fisher and Charon," "The Dead Master," and the "Hymn to the Sea," are noble pieces of English blank verse, the secret of whose measure is given only to the elect; one is impressed by the art, the thought, the imagination, which sustain these poems, and the Shakespeare and Lincoln odes. Stoddard's abundant songs and lyrics are always on the wing and known at first sight, — a skylark brood whose notes are rich with feeling. The sweet and direct method of *The King's Bell* placed him high in the ranks of writers of narrative verse. Among poets

His blank-verse, lyrics, etc.

equal to him in years, he is, perhaps, the foremost of the artistic or cosmopolitan group.

American satire and Jeux-d'Esprit.

John Godfrey Saxe: 1816-87.

Charles Godfrey Leland: 1824-

James Thomas Fields: 1816-81.

William Allen Butler: 1825-

(*See Chap. XII.*)

If I cared to give, in detail, various by-road illustrations of the American spirit, I could cite many instances where the brooding humor, the quaintness and frankness, the pluck and fun and carelessness, of our new people long since cropped out in rhyme. These characteristics give life to the wise and witty purpose of Holmes's and Lowell's satires, and to the verses of Saxe, Leland, Fields, and Butler. We have their continuance and diversity in the clever, off-hand fantasies of younger men. There is no lack of dialect, bric-à-brac, and society verse. Some of our young Bohemians all at play, twenty years ago, — of whom George Arnold was American by birth, as were Halpine and O'Brien by adoption, — while not without their earnest moods, did rollicking work of this kind, and in Arnold's case it seemed to his friends but an offshoot of the better work he had it in him to do.

Holmes.

The Dean among our writers of poems for occasions is unquestionably Dr. Holmes, by virtue of his apt response to the instant call, and of the wit, wisdom, conviction, and the scholarly polish that relegate his lightest productions to the select domain of art.

Whitman.

To Whitman a chapter will be given, and is needed for the fair consideration of his traits and attitude. He represents, first of all, his own personality; secondly, the conflict with aristocracy and formalism. Against the latter he early took the position of an iconoclast, avowing that the time had come in which to create an American art by rejection of all forms, irrespective of their natural basis, which had come to us from the past. In their stead he proffered a form of his own. If I rightly understand the meaning of one or two recent papers by Mr. Whitman, his extreme views, in deprecation of what is and anticipation of what is to be, are now somewhat tempered by years and experience. He is a man of striking physical and mental qualities, and excels most writers in personal influence, tact, and adroitness as a man of the world. He is an avowed champion of democracy, and accepted as such by the refined classes at home and abroad. I shall refer to his minute knowledge and healthy treatment of the American landscape, of the phases and products of outdoor Nature, for in this respect his most fragmentary pieces show the handicraft of an artist and poet.

A genuine home-school, thus having existed, should be valued at its worth.

We need not continue farther the analysis suggested in the previous chapter. I have not tried to make a rigid classification of all who have borne a part in the rise of a home-school, but to observe the general groups of which some of our elder poets may be called the leaders, and the condition and sentiment by which their work has been affected. Enough has been said, I think, to justify the assertion that such a school already has had a career which Americans should be swift to recognize and slow to undervalue.

See "No. Am. Review": Jan. 1881.

One "of your own poets" has taken a different view, declaring that a barren void exists,— that our poetry has been marked by an absence of patriotism, and that it has shown brain and no soul. A more incorrect or wilfully pessimistic statement never was made. In every department of art, times of energy are divided by times of calm.

The first course ended.

The first course is run, and there is a temporary halt, so far as poetry is concerned. The imaginative element in our literature is active as ever, but in other directions. Meantime, we have singers in their prime, resting their voices for the moment, and others whose fresh notes will soon be more definitely heard. Both these classes will come within our review. The younger poets, upon whom the future depends, must prove themselves well endowed, if they are to succeed to the laurels of those who, blessed with years and honors, have held the affection of life-long readers scattered far and wide. It is of those elders only, the representative founders of our school, that I have undertaken to write at any length. To pass critical judgments upon those of my own, or a younger, generation is beyond my province. The time will come when some of them will in turn occupy the high places, and furnish typical illustrations of poetry and the poetic life. In that near future there will not be wanting critics to measure their works, nor hands to award the recompense that is due to them who add to the sum of human pleasure by their ministry of song.

(*See Chapter XII.*)

CHAPTER III.

WILLIAM CULLEN BRYANT.

I.

Impressive feeling excited by the poet's death.

WHEN Bryant died, in the flowery season that had inspired his sweetest lyric, the general pause and hush were singularly impressive. To the death of no other American, for a long time before and after, could be applied so aptly that Indian metaphor of the sound of the fall of a great oak in the forest. The feeling was not one of unexpectedness, although his old age was free from decrepitude, — as if some deity kinder than Aurora had given him immortality without decay; not one of sorrow, for he lived beyond the usual limit of life; not that which we have when some man of office, rank, entanglement in great affairs, suddenly passes away. Yet the station of "the father of American song" was unique, and his loss was something strange and positive. He stood alone, — in certain respects, an incomparable figure. He had become not only a representative citizen, journalist, poet, but the serene, transfigured ideal of a good and venerable man.

Born in Cummington, Mass., Nov. 3, 1794.

As a writer he had been before the public from a date near the beginning of the century, and so changeless through all its changes that his critics, in estimating the poet just dead, really were judging the poet of fifty years before, instead of guessing at the verdict of time upon his productions. Howsoever they might differ as to the measure of Bryant's gift, and of Bryant the man, one thing was sure: no minor personage could gain, and retain to the last, such a hold upon popular interest, honor, deferential esteem. Others, before reaching his years, have had their rise and decline, outlasting themselves, and finding occasion to declare with Cato Major, "It is a hard thing, Romans, to render an account before the men of a period different from that in which one has lived!" But here was one who steadily grew to be the emblem of our finest order of citizenship, possibly its most acceptable type. This, as constantly was evident, became impressed even upon coarse and ordinary persons, singly or associated in legislative bodies; hardly judges, one would think, of such a matter, but accepting without cavil the public conception and the estimate of the thoughtful and refined. There is good reason at the base of every sustained opinion of the sort. What gave Bryant just this degree of special eminence? Not alone that he was a virtuous man, and a patriot in every sense; a journalist, linked with traditions of sturdy service in the past; a clear and vigorous writer and thinker; a wise and reverend sage, most sound of body and mind. He was not a great and representative editor, according to our modern standard. Otherwise, he was all these, and in their combination held a rank excelled by none and reached only by the excepted few. Beyond and including all these, he was a poet. It may be placed to the credit of the art of song that, being a person of such attributes, the addition of the poetic gift made him a bright, particular star. It is the poet, above all, that we must observe and estimate.

"Fashioned to much honor."

The "foremost citizen."

The poet.

Yet in order to discover the quality and limitations

The man.

of his genius, he must be considered not only as an American poet who represented his country at a certain time, but as a man speaking for himself. And in this wise, first seeking a key to his literary value, we see that he had become a most satisfying type of the republican, joining the traditional gravity, purity, and patriotic wisdom of the forefathers with the modernness and freshness of our own day. His life, public and private, was in keeping with his speech and writings. We often say of a poet or artist that he should not be judged like other men by his outward irrelevant mark or habit; that to see his best, his truest self you must read his poems or study his paintings. In reading Bryant's prose and verse, and in observing the poet himself, our judgments were the same. He always held in view liberty, law, wisdom, piety, faith; his sentiment was unsentimental; he never whined nor found fault with condition or nature; he was robust, but not tyrannical; frugal, but not too severe; grave, yet full of shrewd and kindly humor. Absolute simplicity characterized him. Ethics were always in sight. He was, indeed, an "old man for counsel"; what he learned in youth from the lives and precepts of Washington, Hamilton, and their compeers, that he taught and practised to the last. His intellectual faculties, like his physical, were balanced to the discreetest level, and this without abasing his poetic fire. His genius was not shown by the advance of one faculty and the impediment of others; it was the spirit of an even combination, and a fine one.

A typical republican.

Mental and moral traits.

It is true that his practical success — the worldly substance he had gained by the thrift and prudence that "poor Richard's" maxims inculcate — gave him a prestige in the wealth-respecting metropolis which as a poet alone he could not, in his generation, have

His position strengthened by worldly success.

secured. It brought him near, as Mr. Hazeltine has pointed out, to the hosts of the Philistines, but it also impressed them with a conviction that there must be something in poetry after all. They saw him visibly haloed with a distinction beyond that which wealth and civic influence could bestow. Besides, even Philistia has its æsthetic rituals and pageantry, and it was with a gracious and picturesque sense of the fitness of things that he bore his stately part in our festivals and processions. To this extent he was conventional, but he made conventionalism suggestive and often the promoter of thought and art.

Philistia.

II.

"The Bard."

HERE, then, was a minstrel who, in appearance, more than others of a readier lyrical genius, seemed not unlike the legendary bard of Gray: —

> "The poet stood,
> (Loose his beard and hoary hair
> Streamed, like a meteor, to the troubled air),
> And with a master's hand, and prophet's fire,
> Struck the deep sorrows of his lyre."

A prolonged and equable career.

Look at the extent of the period through which he flourished. He began in the early springtime of Wordsworth, and long outlived new men like Baudelaire and Poe. The various epochs of his career scarcely bear upon our consideration of its product, which, after his escape from the manner of Pope, was of an even quality during seventy years. In this he was fortunate and unfortunate. The former, because his early pieces were so noteworthy that, in the dearth of American poetry, they at once became home classics for a homely people, and one generation after another learned them admiringly by heart. At this time, even though composed in the latest fashion and of greater merit than Bryant's, an author's pieces could not obtain for him such recognition and fame. But, owing to this otherwise good fortune, he worked under restrictions from which he never was even measurably freed. Before observing these, it again may be noted that his poetic career had neither rise, height, nor decline. He formed certain methods wholly natural to him in early youth, and was at once as admirable a poet as he ever afterward became. Throughout his prolonged term of life he sang without haste or effort, and always expressed himself rather than the varying methods of the time.

His feeling American.

From the first he was in sympathy with the aspect, atmosphere, feeling, of his own country. His tendency and manner were determined during the idyllic period of this republic, when nature and the thoughts which it suggested were themes for poets, rather than the dramatic relations of man with man. His sentiment was affected by the meditative verse of Cowper and Wordsworth, who rose above didacticism, or made it imaginative by poetic insight. Emerson said of Bryant: "This native, original, patriotic poet. I say original: I have heard him charged with being of a certain school. I heard it with surprise, and asked, What school? For he never reminded me of Goldsmith, or Wordsworth, or Byron, or Moore. I found him always original, — a true painter of the face of this country, and of the sentiment of his own people." This is, in a sense, true; yet there can be little doubt that, in most respects, Wordsworth was the master of his youth. All pupils must acknowledge masters at the beginning, but Murillo was Murillo none the less, although he ground colors for Castillo and studied with Velasquez. Bryant ground his colors

Emerson, at the Century Club, on Bryant's 70th birthday.

in the open air. His originality consisted in deriving from his studies a method natural to his own gift and condition. The elder Dana puts him on record as saying that "upon opening Wordsworth a thousand springs seemed to gush up at once in his heart, and the face of nature of a sudden to change into a strange freshness and life." Certainly he was not cradled into poetry by wrong, nor perturbed by the wild and morbid passions of a wayward youth. We can imagine him a serious and meditative lad, directed by the guidance of a scholarly father, well versed in the favorite poets of that day, — Pope, Thomson, Akenside, Cowper, — and at first accepting them as models; finally, obtaining for himself the clues to a true perception of Nature, and with his soul suddenly exalted by a sense of her

Wordsworth's pupil.

Our meditative poet of nature.

> "Authentic tidings of invisible things;
> Of ebb and flow, and ever-during power;
> And central peace, subsisting at the heart
> Of endless agitation."

This sense was fostered, throughout the changing year, by the landscape of the pastoral region of Massachusetts in which he had his growth. I have referred in a previous chapter to Hugo's works illustrating the conflicts by which man progresses to his enfranchisement, the conflicts with Nature, Superstition, Tyranny, and Society. From the third of these opponents our fathers fled to a new continent, choosing to found a nationality, and entering upon that primeval conflict with nature which to an already civilized people is not without compensations. It results, like a quarrel between generous lovers, in a betrothal of the one to the other, and of such an alliance Bryant was our celebrant. The delights of nature, and meditations upon the universality of life and death, withdrew him from the study of the individual world. Thus he became a philosophic minstrel of the woods and waters, the foremost of American landscape-poets. In the contest with primeval Nature, man signalizes his victories by educating and rendering more beautiful his captive ; she, in turn, gains a potent influence over him, for a long while driving her rivals from his heart, and compels him in his art and song to express her features and her inspiration.

Allied to our early landscape-painters. *See p. 47.*

The first enduring American school of painting was a landscape-school. We have observed the analogy between Bryant's poetry and the broad, cool canvas of the founders of that school, — the works of Durand, Cole, Kensett, Inness, various as they may be in depth, tranquillity, or power. Such a harmony exists between the soil, the climate, the fauna, and the flora of an isothermal zone. Bryant, who at once became eminent in his special walk, therein excelled and has outlasted all his compeers and followers. It is not unlikely that he will outlast many of his latest successors, notwithstanding his inferiority when persistence and minuteness of observation are taken into account. Others group together details, compose with enthusiasm, but are deficient in tone, sentiment, imaginative receptivity.

Tone, and breadth of treatment.

Tone is the one thing needful to a true interpretation of nature. Thoreau felt this when he wrote in his diary, "I have just heard the flicker among the oaks on the hillside ushering in a new dynasty. . . . Eternity could not begin with more security and momentousness than the Spring. The Summer's eternity is reëstablished by this note. All sights and sounds are seen and heard both in time and eternity; and when the eternity of any sight or sound strikes the eye or ear, they are intoxicated with delight. . . . *It is not important that the poet should say some particular thing, but that he should speak in harmony with nature. The tone and pitch of his voice is the main thing.*" Bryant is, in one respect, peculiarly unmodern. Thoreau, despite his own language, caught and observed every detail. Our poet's learning was not scientific; he lacked the minor vision which, an added gift, enables Tennyson and others to give such charm and variety to their work. The ancients may have recognized all shades and colors, but they specified fewer than we specify. Byron, among moderns, painted Nature in her simple, broad manifestations, — the sea, the mountains, the sky, — subordinating her spirit to his own passion, as Bryant allies it with his own tenderness and wisdom, but even he was not her poet in the delicate, microcosmic, recent sense. Both certainly lacked the cleverness and infinite precision of the new school. Bryant regarded nature in its phenomenal aspect, careless of scientific realities. What he gained in this wise was the absence of disillusionizing fact, and a fuller understanding of the language of nature's "visible forms"; what he lost was the wide and various range opened by the endless avenues of new-found truth.

Unscientific vision

III.

RIGHT here it is well for us to observe his limitations as a poet, — limitations so undeniable as to be a stumbling-block in the way of those who lightly consider his genius, and sometimes to throw him out of the sympathetic range of elegant and impartial minds. His longevity was not allied with intellectual quickness and fertility, but seemed almost the biologic result of inborn slowness and deliberation. He was not flexible, not facile of ear and voice. He con-

Bryant's limitations.

Stiffness.

sorted with nature in its still or majestic moods, and derived wisdom and refreshment from its tenderness and calm. His gift, as expressed by its product, was not affluent, and scarcely availed itself of his length of years. His reticence in verse was habitual. In old age, poets are apt to write the most, and often to the least advantage, but his pen through much of this period was chiefly devoted to translation. How little of his own poetry he produced in seventy years, — a few scant volumes! Think of Milton, Landor, Wordsworth, Tennyson, Hugo, Longfellow; of the impetuous work of Scott and Byron; of what Shelley, who gave himself to song, accomplished before he died, at twenty-nine. Bryant was thought to be cold, if not severe, of temperament. The most fervent social passions of his song are those of friendship, of filial and fraternal love; his intellectual passion is always under restraint, even when moved by patriotism, liberty, religious faith. There is still less of action and dramatic quality in his verse. Humor, the overflow of strength, is almost absent from it, — when present, sufficiently awkward; yet it should be noted that in conversation, or in the after-dinner talks and speeches so frequent in his later years, his humor was continuous and charming, full of kindly gossip, wisdom, and mirth. He made, as we have seen, little advance upon the early standard of his work. It would seem as if, under the lessons of a father, "who taught him the value of correctness and compression, and enabled him to distinguish between poetic enthusiasm and fustian," he there and then matured, reached a certain point, and became set and stationary. There are few notable expressions and separable lines in his poetry. In his stanzaic verse, following the established eighteenth-century patterns, he scarcely

Infertility.

Deficient in passion, humor, and individuality.

can be said to have a style of his own. Stanzas might be quoted from Collins, Goldsmith, Cowper, even Watts, any one of which would pass for Bryant's. A painter said to me, when I referred to the mannerism of a "characteristic" picture by a certain artist, "Yes, but it is well that it should not look like anybody else's; it is well to be known by one's manner, and to have one's manner known." Where Bryant was most impressive — that is to say, in his blank-verse poems — he had a positive and unmistakable style, quite distinct even from that of his master, Wordsworth. Finally, his diction, when not confined to that Saxon English at every man's use, is bald and didactic, — always sententious, but less frequently rich and full. He had a limited vocabulary at command; I should think that no modern poet, approaching him in fame, has made use of fewer words. His range is like that of Goldsmith, restricted to the simpler phrases of our tongue. Other poets, of an equally pure diction, show here and there, by rare and fine words, the extent of their unused resources, and that they voluntarily confine themselves to "the strength of the positive degree."

A scant vocabulary.

In the face of all this, Bryant's poetry has had, and will continue to have, a lasting charm for many of the noblest minds. Since this is not due to his length of years, — for he was not alone in that possession, — nor to richness of detail and imagery, nor to his having adapted himself, like Whittier, to successive changes of thought and diction, how is it that his genius triumphed over its confessed limitations? To understand this, his poetry must be judged as a whole, and not by its affluence or flexibility; and it also must be studied in connection with its author's surroundings and career.

IV.

A child of the far past.

THE fact must be kept in sight that he was the creature of our early period. Owing to an extreme precocity, his literary career began at a date prior even to that which the record of his age would suggest; he was writing and printing verse in a time when the eighteenth-century notabilities on his father's shelves were still the approved models of style. We find him in his fourteenth year publishing *The Embargo*, a political satire, of course in rhymed pentameters, and it reached a second edition. With the anticipatory instinct of youth, he shortly passed from the influence of Pope to that of Wordsworth, and quite before the founder of a natural school brought the writers of England into a saving consciousness of his worth. So that Bryant's quick allegiance, fostered by companionship with nature in his own region, really placed him then as far ahead of his time as he seemed, half a century afterward, to be behindhand. "Thanatopsis" was not printed in the "North American Review" until his twenty-first year, but some of it probably was composed when he was sixteen, and it certainly was completed two years before its appearance. Other youths have written good verse as precociously, but no one else of like years ever composed a single poem that had so continuous and elevating an effect upon the literature of a country. Its natural tone, its solemn and majestic cadences, deeply impressed writers other than himself, so that "Thanatopsis," and the lyric, "To a Waterfowl," and various pieces which followed it, became the suggestive models of American poets until the rise of Longfellow. The latter's early verse, and more than one poem in the "Voices of the Night," show very plainly the influence of Bryant, — that Long-

"The Embargo," 1808.

"Thanatopsis."

Its influence on our poets.

fellow was Bryant's pupil until he formed his own peculiar style, and, in fact, we have his word for it.

The "Inscription for the Entrance to a Wood," given to the "Review" at the same time with "Thanatopsis," is of interest as the earliest specimen in blank-verse of Bryant's nature-painting. His grave, didactic poem, in Spenserian stanzas, *The Ages*, which was delivered before the Harvard alumni, would make little impression in these days, but nothing so good of its kind then had been written in America, and it is marked by occasional fervor and touches of imagination. The author's specific dignity of handling is everywhere maintained. "The Ages" was printed at Cambridge, together with his other poems then written, in a little book of forty-four pages, now excessively rare. The product of his muse grew very slowly; he was nearing middle age before there was enough of it to make a collective edition. The London counterpart of this was edited, with a laudatory preface, by Washington Irving, and gave the poet a foreign reputation. His verse was received as the metrical supplement of Cooper's prose, and as confirming Irving's praise of its imaginative and thoroughly national delineation of American landscape "in its wild, solitary, and magnificent forms." Small volumes of new poems appeared in 1840 and 1844, and illustrated editions of Bryant's poetical works, which foreign and native artists made attractive, were brought out in Philadelphia and New York respectively. When he reached the age of threescore years and ten a collection was made of his later poems. This embraced not a few as sonorous and imaginative as "Thanatopsis" and "A Forest Hymn," and lyrics in every way equal to those of his youthful prime; yet, if I remember rightly, there was little sale for it, and the chief profit which the poet and

"The Ages"; read before the Φ. B. K. of Harvard, Aug. 30, 1821.

"Poems," 1821.

"Poems," 1832.

"The Fountain, and Other Poems," 1842.

"The White-footed Deer," etc., 1844.

Illustrated Editions, 1847, 1858.

"Thirty Poems," 1864.

his publishers received from his metrical works came through new editions, some of which were elaborately illustrated, that were issued when his conspicuousness as a personage, as a striking figure at all civic and literary gatherings of note, increased with his increasing years. The *Thirty Poems*, in fact, displayed the same inflexible restriction to an early key, now quite out of popular accord; not a particle of concession, — scarcely any consciousness of the radical changes, the advance in diction, imagery, variety of motive, and rhythm, effected by successive generations.

No change in style.

All this indicated a rigid and self-contained nature, but his long absorption in the practical affairs of life must be taken into account. As a youth, with slender means, he started out to make a living; first, as a lawyer in Berkshire County. After nine years at the bar, he threw up his profession, in view of chances offered by a growing literary reputation, and somewhat out of temper with the chicanery which even then seemed inseparable from the practice of the law, and which in any form was repugnant to his life-long and Roman sense of justice. Yet in the very traits we are observing — in diffident reserve, apparent coldness, real warmth of feeling and personal tenderness vouched for by those who knew him best, respect for abstract truth and right, wrath vehemently aroused by public and private wrongs — he was not unlike the great advocate, Charles O'Conor, who nevertheless devoted his life to enforcing the law's original claim to the perfection of reason and the majesty of power without taint. Bryant came to New York and entered upon journalism as the editor of a literary magazine, but soon found himself connected with the daily newspaper of which he ultimately became the chief proprietor and editor, and so remained until his dying day. During the

The poet's life and occupations.

Distaste for the law.

Journalism.

early portion of this town-life he took an active part, that of a leader, in what there was of literary effort and production, — associated with Dana, Halleck, Drake, Verplanck, Sands, young Willis, and other poets and wits of the time. But he became more engrossed in political and economic journalism, seldom yielding to the lyrical impulse, and when in age he again found leisure and desire for song, his voice had grown somewhat alien to modern ears, although there is no sign that he himself perceived it. I am speaking of his poetry: at intervals he wrote books of travels, made up chiefly of letters to the "Evening Post," besides many essays, addresses, orations, which were always clear and adequate, but rarely displaying anything like genius, or striking in their effect.

Absorption in this profession.

"Letters of a Traveller," and similar prose works, 1850–69.

"Orations and Addresses," 1873; and see his "Life and Works," by Godwin, 1883.

It is quite plain that he did not give himself to poetry, but added poetry to his ordinary life and occupation. The reverse of this, only, can make the greatest poet. His lack of devotion to a jealous mistress was the fault of his time, and of circumstances which decided his course in life. To him the parting of the ways came early; and what was there in our literary atmosphere and opportunities, sixty years ago, to make poetry the vocation of any thorough-trained, aspiring, and resolute man? The nation called for workers, journalists, practical teachers. If, after accomplishing their daily tasks, they found time to sing a song, it thanked them, and did little more. Poetry was the surplusage of Bryant's labors, or, more likely, their restoring complement. In all likelihood his meditations would not have been expressed in song but for the influence of those early readings, under a discerning father's care. Otherwise, though he could not have failed to become a writer, as a poet he might have been one of the mute oracles whose lot is mourned by Wordsworth: —

Poetry little more than his avocation.

Cp. "Victorian Poets": pp. 81, 82.

> — "men endowed with highest gifts,
> The vision and the faculty divine;
> Yet wanting the accomplishment of verse,
> Which, in the docile season of their youth,
> It was denied them to acquire."

But read "The Evening Wind," see him in his most spontaneous mood, and you feel that, once having learned the art of verse, the poet within him thereafter must break out from time to time. He did not hoard his reputation. But his passion and tenderness did not so readily force him to metrical expression as a feebler amount of either has forced many a weak but more facile singer trained in a less rude and inartistic age.

Absolute sincerity.

On the other hand, he never, by any chance, affected passion or set himself to artificial song. He had the triple gift of Athene, "self-reverence, self-knowledge, self-control." He was incapable of pretending to rapture that he did not feel, and this places him far above a host of those who, without knowing it, hunt for emotions and make poetry little better than a trade. As for his diction, he began when there was no Feast of Pentecost with its gift of tongues. I think that the available portion of a poet's vocabulary is that which he acquires in youth, during his formative period. It is easier for an adult to learn a foreign language than to enlarge greatly his native range of words, and have them at every-day command. Bryant's early reading was before the great revival which brought into use the romance-words of Chaucer, Spenser, and the Elizabethan age. It was derived from the poorest, if the smoothest, English period — that which began with Pope and ended with Cowper. The rich advantage of a modern equipment is visible in Tennyson, who had Keats and Shelley for his predecessors; not to

Effect of early studies on literary diction.

consider Swinburne, who, above his supernatural gifts of rhythm and language, owes much to youthful explorations in classic and Continental tongues. No doubt Bryant's models confirmed his natural restrictions of speech. But even this narrow verbal range has made his poetry strong and pure; and now, when expression has been carried to its extreme, it is an occasional relief to recur to the clearness, to the exact appreciation of words, discoverable in every portion of his verse and prose. It is like a return from a florid renaissance to the antique; and indeed there was something Doric in Bryant's nature. His diction, like his thought, often refreshes us as the shadow of a great rock in a weary land. He refused to depart from what seemed to him the natural order of English verse, — that order which comes to the lips of childhood, and is not foreign to any life or age. The thought was like the measure, that which was old with the fathers and is young in our own time, the pure philosophy of nature's lessons. Give his poems a study, and their simplicity is their charm. How easy it seems to write those natural lines! Yet it is harder than to catch a hundred fantastic touches of word-painting and dexterous sound. He never was obscure, because he dared not and would not go beyond his proper sight and knowledge, and this was the safeguard of his poetry, his prose, and his almost blameless life.

A pure and simple style.

Verse, to Bryant, was the outflow of his deepest emotions; a severe taste and discreet temperament made him avoid the study of decoration. Thus he was always direct and intelligible, and appealed to the common people as strongly as to the select few. I have compared him to our stately men of an older time. Among others Daniel Webster might be mentioned as one whose mood and rhetoric are in keeping with the

Webster and Bryant.

poetry of Bryant. Like Webster, our poet always selected the leading, impressive thought, and brushed the rest aside. This he put in with a firm and glowing touch. Many have thought the works of both the statesman and the poet conventional, but the adjective might be brought to apply to all simple and essential truth and diction. Adopting Arnold's distinction, we see that Bryant's simplicity was not *simplesse*, but *simplicité*. Everett made a good presentation of its strongest claim when he said that poetry, at its best, is "easily intelligible, touching the finest chords of taste and feeling, but never striving at effect. This is the highest merit in every department of literature, and in poetry it is well called inspiration. Surprise, conceit, strange combinations of imagery and expression, may be successfully managed, but it is merit of an inferior kind. The beautiful, pathetic, and sublime are always simple and natural, and marked by a certain serene unconsciousness of effort." "This," he added, "is the character of Mr. Bryant's poetry."

V.

Bryant's favorite measures.

LET us again, then, observe its forms and themes, and discover clues to the quality of the genius which idealized them. Bryant's chosen measures were few and simple. Two were special favorites, most frequently used for his pictures of nature and his meditations on the soul of things, and in their use he was a master.

The iambic quatrain.

One was the iambic quatrain, in octosyllabic verse, of which the familiar stanza, "Truth crushed to earth will rise again," may be recalled as a specimen. Many of his best modern pieces are composed in this measure, so evenly and firmly that the slightest change would mar their sound and flow. "A Day Dream," written in the poet's old age, is perfect of its kind, and may rank almost with Collins's nonpareil, "To fair Fidele's Grassy Tomb." Witness such stanzas as these: —

> I sat and watched the eternal flow
> Of those smooth billows toward the shore,
> While quivering lines of light below
> Ran with them on the ocean floor."
>
> . . . .
>
> "Then moved their coral lips; a strain
> Low, sweet and sorrowful, I heard,
> As if the murmurs of the main
> Were shaped to syllable and word."

His variations upon the iambic quatrain, as in the celebrated poems, "To a Waterfowl" and "The Past," are equally successful. The second of the forms referred to is that blank-verse in which his supremacy always was recognized. Among the distinct phases of our grandest English measure that have been observed in literature, Bryant's may be classed with the Reflective, of which Wordsworth, succeeding the didacticians, held unquestioned control, but from the outset it was marked by a quality plainly his own. The essence of its cadence, pauses, rhythm, should be termed American, and it is the best ever written in the New World. Blank-verse is the easiest and the most difficult of all measures; the poorest in poor hands; the finest when written by a true poet. Whoever essays it is a poet disrobed; he must rely upon his natural gifts; his defects cannot be hidden. In this measure Bryant was at his height, and he owes to it the most enduring portion of his fame. However narrow his range, we must own that he was first in the first. He reached the upper air at once in "Thanatopsis," and again and again, though none too frequently, he

His blank-verse.

renewed his flights, and, like his own waterfowl, pursued his "solitary way."

A panoramic series.

The finest and most sustained of his poems of nature are those written in blank-verse. At intervals so rare throughout his life as to resemble the seven-year harvests, or the occasional wave that overtops the rest, he composed a series of those pieces which now form a unique panorama of nature's aspects, moving to the music of lofty thoughts and melodious words. Such are "A Winter Piece," the "Inscription for the Entrance to a Wood," "A Forest Hymn," "Summer Wind," "The Prairies," "The Fountain," "A Hymn of the Sea," "A Rain-Dream"; also a few written late in life, showing that the eye of the author of "Thanatopsis" had not been dimmed, nor was his natural force abated: these are "The Constellations," "The River, by Night," and "Among the Trees." In all the treatment is large and ennobling, and distinctly marks each as Bryant's. The method, that of invocation, somewhat resembles the manner of Coleridge's Hymn in the Vale of Chamouni. When in a less enraptured strain, they exhibit repose, feeling, wise and reverent thought.

Lofty contemplative poems.

In the same eloquent verse, and with like cæsural pauses and inflections, we find his more purely meditative poems, upon an equal or still higher plane of feeling, — "Thanatopsis," the "Hymn to Death," "Earth," "An Evening Revery," "The Antiquity of Freedom," and one of his latest and longest, "The Flood of Years." Yet, in both his reflective verse and that devoted to nature, he often employed lyrical measures with equal excellence; as in the breezy, exquisite poem on "Life," "The Battle Field," "The Future Life," and "The Conqueror's Grave," — the latter one of his most elevating pieces. Especially in his lyrics he seemed like a wind-harp yielding tender music in response to every suggestion of the great Mother whom he loved. Such poems as "June," "The Death of the Flowers," and "The Evening Wind" show this, and also indicate the limits within which his song was spontaneous. Each is the genuine expression of a personal mood, and has by this merit taken its place in metrical literature.

A bard of the elements.

At last, then, we are brought to a recognition of the power in Bryant's verse which has given him a station above that which he could hope to win by its amount or range. It is the *elemental quality* of his song. Like the bards of old, his spirit delights in fire, air, earth, and water,—the apparent structures of the starry heavens, the mountain recesses, and the vasty deep. These he apostrophizes, but over them and within them he discerns and bows the knee to the omniscience of a protecting Father, a creative God. Poets, eminent in this wise, have been gifted always with *imagination.* The verse of Bryant often is full of high imaginings. Select any portion of "Thanatopsis":—

Imagination.

> "Pierce the Barcan wilderness,
> Or lose thyself in the continuous woods
> Where rolls the Oregon, and hears no sound
> Save his own dashings—yet the dead are there!"

or this, from "The Prairies":—

> "The bee
> . . . .
> Fills the savannas with his murmurings,
> And hides his sweets, as in the golden age,
> Within the hollow oak. I listen long
> To his domestic hum, and think I hear
> The sound of that advancing multitude
> Which soon shall fill these deserts. From the ground
> Comes up the laugh of children, the soft voice
> Of maidens, and the sweet and solemn hymn

6

Of Sabbath worshippers. The low of herds
Blends with the rustling of the heavy grain
Over the dark-brown furrows. All at once
A fresher wind sweeps by and breaks my dream,
And I am in the wilderness alone."

His "hand on Nature's keys."

Read the entire poem of "Earth." Take such stanzas as this, from "The Past": —

"Far in thy realm withdrawn
Old empires sit in sullenness and gloom,
And glorious ages gone
Lie deep within the shadow of thy womb";

such phrases as,

"Old Ocean's gray and melancholy waste";

or, from "A Rain-Dream," an impersonation of

"the Wind of night,
A lonely wanderer between earth and cloud,
In the black shadow and the chilly mist,
Along the streaming mountain-side, and through
The dripping woods, and o'er the plashy fields,
Roaming and sorrowing still, like one who makes
The journey of life alone, and nowhere meets
A welcome or a friend, and still goes on
In darkness."

Take passages like these, — and they are not infrequent in Bryant's poetry, — make allowance for the law by which any real poet's work is sure to grow upon us in close examination, and we still are confronted with an "elemental" imagination often higher than that of more productive poets. Modern singers excel in richness of phrase, redundant imagery, elaborate word-painting; but every period has its forerunners and masters, and our rising men must acknowledge Bryant as a laurelled master of the early American School. He seldom touched the keys, yet they gave out an organ tone.

Slight lyrical faculty.

Indeed, when he essayed piano-music, and was in a light or fanciful mood, he was unable to vie with sprightlier and defter hands. His lyrics, in swift and simple measures, had a ringing quality, noticeable in the "Song of Marion's Men," the best of them, and in "The Hunter of the Prairies." A pleasant surprise awaits us in certain later pieces, such as "The Planting of the Apple-Tree," the delicate "Snow-Shower," and "Robert of Lincoln," — so full of bird-music and fancy. Usually it was with an air of uncouthness and doubt that he ventured beyond established precedents, as if he were in strange waters and would gladly touch firm land; but then, he seldom ventured. As he grew older, beyond the asperities of life, he became less brooding, sad, and grave. His Fancy, what there was of it, came in his later years, and suggested two of his longest pieces, "Sella" and "The Little People of the Snow," tales of folk-lore, in which his lighter and more graceful handling of blank-verse may be studied without fatigue.

Fancy.

VI.

His translation of Homer: "The Iliad," 1870; "The Odyssey," 1871.

A SHREWD confidence in his own mental and bodily strength was justified by the execution, in his old age, of that monumental task, — a full translation of the epics of Homer. Such labor undoubtedly is adapted to the afternoon of life, when creative energy is spent and the discretionary faculties are trained to their extreme; still, the completed evidence of Bryant's vigor, even at life's sunset, is hardly less notable than Landor's retention of ideality to his ninetieth year.

A congenial task.

After the manner of *De Senectute*, one well might recommend this special labor to a poet of Bryant's cast, as the solace of his advancing age. There was something in the old bard himself which his admirers called Homeric; and there were these traits, at least, common to the genius of the epics and that of their translator, — a primitive way of regarding things, a stately utterance, a vision clear and suited to the theme. The best characteristics of Bryant's *The Iliad* and *The Odyssey* are: (1), general, though not invariable, fidelity to the text, as compared with former versions by poets of equal rank; (2), simplicity of phrase and style; (3), approximate transfusion of the heroic spirit; (4), a purity of language that pleases a sensible reader. It is not likely that Bryant possessed a scholar's mastery of even the familiar Ionic Greek, but the text of Homer long has been substantially agreed upon by European editors, there are special lexicons devoted to it, and it is faithfully rendered in German and English translations: so that the poet could have little trouble in adjusting it to his metrical needs. His choice of words is meagre, and so — in a modern sense — was that of Homer; there is no lack of minstrels, nowadays, who ransack their vocabularies to fill our jaded ears with "words, words, words." As a presentment of standard English the value of these translations is beyond serious cavil. When they are compared with the most faithful and poetic blank-verse rendering which preceded them, the work of Cowper, they show an advance in both accuracy and poetic quality. Lord Derby's contemporaneous version is dull and inferior. Bryant naturally handled to best advantage his descriptive passages, — the verses in the Fifth Odyssey, which narrate the visit of Hermes to Calypso, furnishing a case in point. His rendering of these is more literal than the favorite transcript by Leigh Hunt, and excels all others in ease and choice of language. The following extract from another pas-

How far Bryant's work may be commended.

The descriptive passages.

Od. V., 43–74.

sage will show how well he occasionally substitutes, for the Greek color and rising harmony, the gloom and vigor of our Saxon tongue :—

Od. II. 427–434.

"The steady wind
Swelled out the canvas in the midst; the ship
Moved on, the dark sea roaring round her keel,
As swiftly through the waves she cleft her way.
And when the rigging of that swift black ship
Was firmly in its place, they filled their cups
With wine, and to the ever-living gods
Poured out libations, most of all to one,
Jove's blue-eyed daughter. Thus through all that night
And all the ensuing morn they held their way."

Very often, in fact, where the original text is high-sounding and polysyllabic, he obtains his English effect by reliance upon the strength of monosyllabic words :—

"For his is the black doom of death, ordained
By the great gods."

"Hear me yet more:
When she shall smite thee with her wand, draw forth
Thy good sword from thy thigh and rush at her
As if to take her life, and she will crouch
In fear."

"I hate
To tell again a tale once fully told."

Style and language.

But occasionally he uses to advantage the Latinism peculiar to his reflective poems. Such lines as Shakespeare's

"The multitudinous seas incarnadine"

show by what process the twin forces of our language are fully brought in play. Verses of this sort, formed by the juxtaposition of the numerous Greek particles with ringing derivative and compound words, make up a good deal of the Homeric song. Bryant accordingly varied his translation with lines which remind us of "Thanatopsis" or "A Forest Hymn":—

"The innumerable nations of the dead."

"That strength and these unconquerable hands."

"And downward plunged the unmanageable rock."

His paraphrases of the Greek idioms are noticeable for English idiomatic purity, so much so that the idea of a translation frequently absents itself from the reader's mind. While in one respect this is the perfection of such work, in another it is the loss of that charm pertaining to the sense of all rare things which are foreign to our own mode and period. His restraint, also, is carried to the verge of sterility by the repetition of certain adjectives as the equivalents of Greek words varying among themselves. The words "glorious" and "sagacious," for example, not uncommon in this translation, do not always represent the same, or even synonymous, expressions in the original text. But some of his epithets and renderings, such as "the large-souled Ulysses," "the unfruitful sea," "passed into the Underworld," and his retention of Cowper's paraphrase of γέρων ἅλιος, "the Ancient of the Deep," give a more elevated and poetical tone to the work.

The measure chosen for this translation.

It must be acknowledged that these translations, executed without haste or rest during eight years of an old man's life, are not without dignity and value. The question is debatable whether there was any real need of a new rendering of Homer into our rhymeless iambic pentameter. If so, did Mr. Bryant's labors fill the void? It was proper and natural that he should make blank-verse the vehicle for his use, as the one above all others in which he was sure to reach a measure of success. And had Tennyson undertaken the full translation of Homer, after the manner indicated by that magnificent early production, the "Morte d'Arthur," something very fine would have been the result. Bryant's verse is noticeably different from that of Tennyson. Only in an occasional passage, like the following, the one reminds us of the other: —

> "The formidable baldric, on whose band
> Of gold were sculptured marvels, — forms of bears,
> Wild boars, grim lions, battles, skirmishings,
> And death by wounds, and slaughter."

Inefficacy of blank-verse.

Yet in every blank-verse rendering there is an inefficacy, — least felt, perhaps, in those elevated passages, the fiery glow of which for a time lifts us above contemplation of the translator's art. In the more mechanical portions blank-verse cannot of itself, by the music and flexibility of its structure, have the converse effect of holding us above the level of the theme. Here the deficiency is painful; and for this reason, amongst others, that in Greek the names of the most common objects are imposing and melodious. Those lines whose poverty of thought is greatest, upborne by the long roll of the hexameter, have a quality as aristocratic as the grace and dignity of a Spanish beggar. A translator discovers the weakness of blank-verse in those intercalary lines which are such a feature in Homer, and which constitute a kind of refrain, affording rest at intervals along the torrent of the song. In the best lyric and epic poetry of all nations a disdain of minor changes is observable; but Bryant, seeing that blank-verse does little honor to a purely mechanical office, often varied his translations of such lines, instead of following the Homeric method of recurrence to one chosen form. The very directness of his syntax, leading to the rejection, even, of such inversions as Tennyson's

Prosaic lapses.

> "To whom replied King Arthur, much in wrath"

made it almost prosaic in this respect. Such lines as

> "Telemachus, the prudent, thus rejoined"
>
> "And then discreet Telemachus replied"
>
> "Ulysses, the sagacious, answered her"

are tame substitutes for the courtly and sonorous interludes,

> Τὴν δ' αὖ Τηλέμαχος πεπνυμένος ἀντίον ηὔδα·
> Τὴν δ' ἀπαμειβόμενος προσέφη πολύμητις Ὀδυσσεύς·

We feel still more the shortcomings of blank-verse in the paraphrases of those resonant dactylic lines, which make up so large a portion of the Iliad and Odyssey, and give splendor to the movement of whole cantos. We might cite innumerable examples, like the following: —

> Ἦμος δ' ἠριγένεια φάνη ῥοδοδάκτυλος Ἠώς.
>
> "But when the Morn,
> The rosy-fingered child of Dawn, looked forth."
>
> Αὐτὰρ ἐπεὶ ποταμοῖο λίπεν ῥόον Ὠκεανοῖο
> Νηῦς, ἀπὸ δ' ἵκετο κῦμα θαλάσσης εὐρυπόροιο.
>
> "Now when our bark had left Oceanus
> And entered the great deep."

Lack of movement.

All this points to the one deficiency in a blank-verse translation, and this, unquestionably, relates to the *movement.* Can a version in our slow and stately iambics, which are perfectly adequate to represent the dialogue of the Greek dramas, approximate to the rhythmic effect of a measure which originally was chanted or intoned? The rush of epic song has been caught by Chapman, in his "Iliads," and to some extent by Pope and others, at the expense of matter and style. But only in one instance, that I now recall, has modern blank-verse attained to anything like the Homeric swiftness. I refer to the

Cp. "Victorian Poets": p. 166.

tournament scene, which closes the fifth book of "The Princess." Even the splendid movement of this passage is unrestful, and like the fierce spurt of a racer that can win by a dash, but has not the bottom needed for a three-mile heat.

Recent prose translations.

To the present date I know of no metrical version of Greek hexameter text, epic or idyllic (unless in brief experiments like one or two of Dean Hawtrey's), that can vie in beauty and fidelity with the prose rendering of Homer by Butcher and Lang, and with Mr. Lang's exquisite translation of Theocritus, Bion, and Moschus.

Available forms of verse.

There are two of our metrical forms in which, I think, the Homeric *rhythmus* may be more nearly approached than by the means of blank-verse. A good objection has been made to the rhymed heroic measure, as used by Pope (and by Dryden in his Virgil), that it disturbs the force of the original by connecting thoughts not meant to be connected; that it causes a "balancing of expression in the two lines of which it consists, which is wholly foreign to the Homeric style." Professor Hadley suggested that this might be obviated by a return to the measure as written by Chaucer, not pausing too often at the rhymes, but frequently running the sentences over, with the cæsura varied as in blank-verse. This usage, in fact, was revived by Keats and Leigh Hunt, and is notable in William Morris's flowing poetry, to which Hadley referred for illustration. Chapman translated the Odyssey upon this plan, but in a slovenly fashion, not to be compared with his other Homeric work. There is room, perhaps, for a new translation of Homer into the rhymed Chaucerian verse. The merits of the so-called "English hexameter" were long ago so clearly set forth by Mr. Arnold, the main

The rhymed iambic pentameter.

The "English hexameter."

points of whose argument seem to me irrefutable, that I shall write at no great length upon it here. Professor C. T. Lewis, in his brilliant review of Bryant's Homer, after justly stating that our hexameter verse could not be written classically, says that it is peculiar among English metres, because it is so very like prose. It is less metrical than any form of English verse. "Blank-verse," he adds, "can stoop to the simplest speech without approaching prose." True, but it does not always do so. Run together the opening lines of Bryant's Odyssey, which in Greek are made highly poetical by the structure and sound, and see if they have not a prosaic effect:—

See "No. Am. Rev." CXII. 328.

A test.

"Tell me, O Muse, of that sagacious man who, having overthrown the sacred town of Ilium, wandered far and visited the capitals of many nations, learned the customs of their dwellers, and endured great suffering on the deep."

Cp. "Victorian Poets": p. 251.

Now where, in Mr. Kingsley's "Andromeda,"— a fair specimen of English hexameter, with liquid cadences throughout,—can five lines be made to read like that? In a future chapter, when we come to Longfellow's "Evangeline," it may be worth while to consider the features that this measure is likely to assume. No master has brought it to the perfection which attracts *both* scholars and laymen; yet I am confident that we shall have an English verse of six feet, with the billowy roll of the classical hexameter, and that by its form it will be suited to the reproduction of Homer, line for line. If Bayard Taylor, who, by argument and practice, demonstrated the value of Form to the translator's work, could reach so near his mark in rendering the hundred metres of "Faust," surely there is encouragement for a future attempt to represent more closely the one de-

See Chap. VI.

fiant measure of heroic song. To the point made that English is too consonantal for such representation, we reply that it is no more consonantal in hexameter than in pentameter verse, and that, of the two kinds, the former is nearer to the verse of Homer. This objection would apply more forcibly to the still harsher German; yet we conceive Voss's Iliad to have given German readers a truer idea of the original than any English translation has conveyed to ourselves.

In a review of Bryant's Odyssey, at the date of its completion, I criticised his employment of those Roman names by which the deities of Grecian mythology have been familiarly known. It was a failure to realize the advances in taste and learning even then nearly popularized by Grote, Tennyson, the Brownings, Swinburne, and by younger poets and scholars without end. If Lord Derby in England, and Mr. Bryant in America, had adopted the true nomenclature, the transition speedily would have been complete. But the order of our poet's mind, even in its epic mood, was slow and stately, Latin rather than Grecian. Hence, as a translator from the Spanish he was successful, reproducing the calm and royal quality of Castilian song.

See "The Atlantic Monthly," May, 1872.

VII.

Poets of freedom.

AMERICAN poets have been true to their own land in expressing its innate freedom, patriotism, aspiring resolve. Throughout Bryant's life his scattered poems upon political events, at home and abroad, have been consecrated to freedom and its devotees. He breathed a spirit of independence with the wind of his native hills. The country is the open wild of liberty. All our poets of nature are poets of human rights. Should

America ever become monarchical it will be due to the influence of cities and those bred in them. Bryant's regard for law, for the inheritance of just political and social systems, was unquestionable. He might have been a constitutionalist in France ; here, though bred a Federalist, he was sure to oppose undue centralization. After all, he was of no party further than he conceived it to be right. Witness his contest with slavery and his desertion of a Democracy which finally, he thought, belied its name. That he did not, with Lowell and Whittier, summon his muse to oppose the greatest wrong of our history was owing to two causes : First, it was his lyrical habit to observe and idealize general principles, the abstract rather than the concrete. Whittier's poems are alive with incident, and burn with personal feeling. Once, only, Bryant wrote a mighty poem on Slavery : when it had received its death-blow, when the struggle ended and the right prevailed. Jehovah had conquered, His children were free, and Bryant raised a chant like that of Miriam, —

Bryant's poem on the Emancipation.

> "O thou great Wrong, that, through the slow-paced years,
> Didst hold thy millions fettered ;
>
> . . . .
>
> "Go, now, accursed of God, and take thy place
> With hateful memories of the elder time!
>
> . . . .
>
> "Lo! the foul phantoms, silent in the gloom
> Of the flown ages, part to yield thee room."

This swelling poem, "The Death of Slavery," was not needed to assure us that the cause of freedom touched his heart. For, secondly, his true counterpart to Whittier's work was to be found in the vigorous antislavery assaults he made for years in the journal of which he died the editor. There it was that he exercised his influence and mental power upon "the rebuke of fraud and oppression of whatever clime or race."

His prose labors.

His prose labors were an outlet, constantly afforded in his journalism, through which much of that energy escaped which otherwise would have varied the motives and increased the body of his song. On the whole, though he was without a philologist's equipment, there were few better writers of simple, nervous English. He made it for half a century the instrument of his every-day thought and purpose; as a leader-writer, a traveller and correspondent, an essayist and orator, a political disputant. His polemic vigor and acerbity were worked off in his middle-life editorials, and in defence of what he thought to be right. There he was, indeed, unyielding, and other pens recall the traditions of his political controversies. He never confused the distinct provinces of prose and verse. Refer to anything written by him, of the former kind, and you find plainness, well-constructed syntax, free from any cheap gloss of rhetoric or the "jingle of an effeminate rhythm."

W. C. B. died in New York, N. Y., June 12, 1878.

As in written prose and verse, so in speech and public offices. The long series of addresses on civic occasions closed with one which brought him to his death. Mastering his work to the very end, it was his lot at last to bow, as became a poet of Nature, before her own life-nurturing, life-destroying forces, and thus submit to her kindest universal law. The question of a passage in "An Evening Revery" was answered, and the prophecy fulfilled:—

> "O thou great Movement of the Universe,
> Or Change, or Flight of Time — for ye are one!
> That bearest, silently, this visible scene
> Into night's shadow and the streaming rays
> Of starlight, whither art thou bearing me?

I feel the mighty current sweep me on,
Yet know not whither. Man foretells afar
The courses of the stars; the very hour
He knows when they shall darken or grow bright;
Yet doth the eclipse of Sorrow and of Death
Come unforewarned."

CHAPTER IV.

JOHN GREENLEAF WHITTIER.

I.

His standing with typical Americans of his own time.

A PLEASANT story, that went the round shortly after the close of our Civil War, shows the character of Whittier's hold upon his countrymen. It was said that one among a group of prominent men, when conversation on politics and finance began to lag, asked the question, Who is the best American poet? Horace Greeley, who was of the party, replied with the name of Whittier, and his judgment was instantly approved by all present. These active, practical Americans, patriots or demagogues, — some of them, doubtless, of the "heated barbarian" type, — for once found their individual preferences thus expressed and in accord. At that climacteric time the Pleiad of our elder poets was complete and shining, — not a star was lost. But the instinct of these stern, hard-headed men was in favor of the Quaker bard, the celibate and prophetic recluse; he alone appealed to the poetic side of their natures. We do not hold a press item to absolute exactness in its report of words. The epithet "best" may not have been employed by the questioner on that occasion; were it not for the likelihood that those to whom he spoke would not have laid much stress upon verbal distinctions, one might guess that he said the most national, or representative, or inborn, of our poets. The value of the incident remains; it was discovered that Whittier most nearly satisfied the various poetic needs of the typical, resolute Americans, men of his own historic generation, who composed that assemblage.

English opinion: "Pall Mall Gazette," Jan. 30, 1882.

With this may be considered the fact that it is the habit of compilers and brief reviewers, whose work is that of generalization, to speak of him as a "thoroughly American" poet. An English critic, in a notice marked by comprehension of our home-spirit, and with the honest effort of a delicate mind to get at the secret of Whittier's unstudied verse, and gain the best that can be gained from it, finds him to be the "most national" of our writers, and the most characteristic through his extraordinary fluency, narrow experience, and wide sympathy, — language which implies a not unfriendly recognition of traits which have been thought to be American, — loquacity, provincialism, and generosity of heart.

How far a national poet.

In sentiments thus spoken and written there is a good deal of significance. But the words of the foreign verdict cannot be taken precisely as they stand. Has there been a time, as yet, when any writer could be thoroughly American? What is the meaning of the phrase, — the most limited meaning which a citizen, true to our notion of this country's future, will entertain for a moment? Assuredly not a quality which is collegiate, like Longfellow's, or of a section, like Whittier's, or of a special and cultured class, which alone can enjoy Whitman's sturdy attempt to create a new song for the people before the accepted and accepting time. During the period of these men America scarcely has been more homogeneous in popular characteristics than in climate and topography. I have discussed the perplexing topic of our nationalism, and am willing to believe that these States are blending

See pp. 5-10.

into a country whose distinctions of race and tendency will steadily lessen; but whether such a faith is well grounded is still an open question. And whatsoever change is to ensue, in the direction of homogeneity, will be the counterswing of a vibration whose first impulse was away from the uniformity of the early colonies to the broadest divergence consistent with a common language and government. At Whittier's time this divergence was greater than before, — greater, possibly, than it ever can be again. In fact, it is partly as a result of this superlative divergence that he is called our most national poet. If his song was not that of the people at large, it aided to do away with something which prevented us from being one people; and it was national in being true to a characteristic portion of America, — the intense expression of its specific and governing ideas.

Distinctively, the Poet of New England.

The most discriminating *précis* is that which Mr. Parkman contributed at a gathering in honor of the Quaker bard. The exact eye of the author of "Frontenac" saw the poet as he is: "The Poet of New England. His genius drew its nourishment from her soil; his pages are the mirror of her outward nature, and the strong utterance of her inward life." The gloss of this sentiment belonged to the occasion; its analysis is specifically correct, and this with full recognition of Whittier's most famous kinsmen in birth and song. The distinction has been well made, that the national poet is not always the chief poet of a nation. As a poet of New England, Whittier had little competition from the bookish Longfellow, except in the latter's sincere feeling for the eastern sea and shore, and artistic handling of the courtlier legends of the province. He certainly found a compeer in Lowell, whose dialect idyls prove that only genius is needed to enable a scholar, turned farmer, to extract the richest products of a soil; and the lyric fervor of Lowell's odes is our most imaginative expression of that New England sentiment which has extended itself, an ideal influence, with the movement of its inheritors to the farthest West. Emerson, on his part, has volatilized the essence of New England thought into wreaths of spiritual beauty. Yet Mr. Parkman, than whom no scholar is less given to looseness of expression, terms Whittier the poet of New England, as if by eminence, and I think with exceeding justice. The title is based on apt recognition of evidence that we look to the people at large for the substance of national or sectional traits. The base, not the peak, of the pyramid determines its bearings. There is, to be sure, as much human nature in the mansion as in the cottage, in the study or drawing-room as in the shop and field. But just as we call those *genre* canvases, whereon are painted idyls of the fireside, the roadside, and the farm, pictures of "real life," so we find the true gauge of popular feeling in songs that are dear to the common people and true to their unsophisticated life and motive.

A test of this statement.

Here we again confront the statement that the six Eastern States were not and are not America; not the nation, but a section, — the New Englanders seeming almost a race by themselves. But what a section! And what a people, when we take into account, superadded to their genuine importance, a self-dependence ranking with that of the Scots or Gascons! As distinct a people, in their way, as Mr. Cable's Creoles, old or new. Go by rail along the Eastern coast, and note the nervous, wiry folk that crowd the stations; — their eager talk, their curious scrutiny of ordinary persons and incidents, make it easy to believe that the

New England's influence upon the country at large.

trait chosen by Sprague for the subject of his didactic poem still is a chief motor of New England's progress, and not unjustly its attribute by tradition. This hive of individuality has sent out swarms, and scattered its ideas like pollen throughout the northern belt of our States. As far as these have taken hold, modified by change and experience, New England stands for the nation, and her singer for the national poet. In their native, unadulterated form, they pervade the verse of Whittier. It is notable that the sons of the Puritans should take their songs from a Quaker; yet how far unlike, except in the doctrine of non-resistance, were the Puritans and Quakers of Endicott's time? To me, they seem grounded in the same inflexible ethics, and alike disposed to supervise the ethics of all mankind. Time and culture have tempered the New England virtues; the Eastern frugality, independence, propagandism, have put on a more attractive aspect; a sense of beauty has been developed, — the mental recognition of it finally granted to a northern race, who still lack the perfect flexibility and grace observable wherever that sense comes by nature and directs the popular conscience. As for the rural inhabitants of New England, less changed by travel and accomplishments, we know what they were and are, — among them none more affectionate, pious, resolute, than Whittier, beyond doubt their representative poet.

A notable constituency.

He belongs, moreover, — and hence the point of the incident first related, — to the group now rapidly disappearing, of which Horace Greeley was a conspicuous member, and to an epoch that gave its workers little time for over-refinement, Persian apparatus, and the cultivation of æsthetics. That group of scarred and hardy speakers, journalists, agitators, felt that he was of them, and found his song revealing the highest purpose of their boisterous, unsentimental careers. These men — like all men who do not retrograde — had an ideal. This he expressed, in measures that moved them, and whose perfection they had no thought or faculty of questioning. Many of them came from obscure and rural homes, and to read his verse was to recall the scent of the clover and apple-bloom, to hear again the creak of the well-pole, the rattle of the bars in the lane, — the sights and freshness of youth passing for a moment, a vision of peace, over their battlefield. They needed, also, their own pibroch and battle-cry, and this his song rang out; their determination was in it, blended with the tenderness from which such men are never wholly free.

The bard of an historic time.

His ultimate reputation, then, will be inseparable from that of his section and its class. He may not hold it as one of those whose work appeals to all times and races, and whose art is so refined as to be the model of after-poets. But he was the singer of what was not an empty day, and of a section whose movement became that of a nation, and whose purpose in the end was grandly consummated. We already see, and the future will see it more clearly, that no party ever did a vaster work than his party; that he, like Hampden and Milton, is a character not produced in common times; that no struggle was more momentous than that which preceded our Civil War, no question ever affected the destinies of a great people more vitally than the antislavery issue, as urged by its promoters. Neither Greece nor Rome, not even England, the battle-ground of Anglo-Saxon liberty, has supplied a drama of more import than that in which the poets and other heroes of our Civil Reformation played their parts.

II.

John Greenleaf Whittier: born near Haverhill, Mass., Dec. 17, 1807.

WHITTIER'S origin and early life were auspicious for one who was to become a poet of the people. His muse shielded him from the relaxing influence of luxury and superfine culture. These could not reach the primitive homestead in the beautiful Merrimack Valley, five miles out from the market-town of Haverhill, where all things were elementary and of the plainest cast. The training of the Friends made his boyhood still more simple; otherwise, as I have said, it mattered little whether he derived from Puritan or Quaker sources. Still, it was much, in one respect, to be descended from Quakers and Huguenots used to suffer and be strong for conscience' sake. It placed him years in advance of the comfortable Brahmin class, with its blunted sense of right and wrong, and, to use his own words, turned him "so early away from what Roger Williams calls 'the world's great trinity, pleasure, profit, and honor,' to take side with the poor and oppressed." The Puritans conformed to the rule of the Old Testament, the Friends to the spirit of the New. One has only to read our colonial annals to know how the Jews got on under the Mosaic law, inasmuch as to the end of the Mather dynasty the pandect of Leviticus, in all its terror, was sternly enforced by church and state. The Puritans had two gods, Deus and Diabolus; the Quakers recognized the former alone, and chiefly through his incarnation as the Prince of Peace. They exercised, however, the right of interference with other people's code and practice, after a fashion the more intolerable from a surrender of the right to establish their own by rope and sword. Whittier's Quaker strain, as Frothingham has shown, yielded him wholly to the "intellectual pas-

The Puritans and the Quakers.

The poet's Quakerism.

sion" that Transcendentalism aroused, and still keeps him obedient to the Inward Light. And it made him a poet militant, a crusader whose moral weapons, since he must disown the carnal, were keen of edge and seldom in their scabbards. The fire of his deep-set eyes, whether betokening, like that of his kinsman Webster, the Batchelder blood, or inherited from some old Feuillevert, strangely contrasts with the benign expression of his mouth, — that firm serenity, which by transmitted habitude dwells upon the lips of the sons and daughters of peace.

Youth on the farm.

There was no affectation in the rusticity of his youth. It was the real thing, — the neat and saving homeliness of the Eastern farm. All the belongings of the household were not the equivalent of a week's expenses in a modern city home, yet there was no want and nothing out of tone. We see the wooden house and barn, set against the background of rugged acres; indoors, still the loom and wheel, and still the Quaker mother, dear old toiling one, the incarnation of faith and charity, beloved by a loyal, bright-eyed family group. There was little to read but the Bible, "Pilgrim's Progress," and the weekly newspaper; no schooling but in the district school-house; nothing to learn of the outer world except from the eccentric and often picturesque strollers that in those days peddled, sang, or fiddled from village to village. Yet the boy's poetic fancy and native sense of rhythm were not inert. He listened eagerly to the provincial traditions and legends, a genuine folk-lore, recounted by his elders at the fireside; and he began to put his thoughts in numbers at the earliest possible age. A great stimulus came in the shape of Burns's poems, a cheap volume of which fell into his possession by one of those happenings that seem ordained for poets.

Influence of Burns.

His first printed efforts were an imitation of the dialect and measures of the Scottish bard, and perhaps no copybook could have been more suitable until he formed his own hand — a time not long postponed. He well might have fancied that in his experience there was much in common with that of his master; that he, too, might live to affirm, though surely in words less grandiloquent, "The Genius of Poetry found me at the plough, and threw her inspiring mantle over me." Of our leading poets, he was almost the only one who learned Nature by working with her at all seasons, under the sky and in the wood and field. So much for his boyhood; his after course was affected greatly by the man then coming into notice as a fanatic and agitator, the lion-hearted champion of freedom, long since glorified with the name he gave to his first pronunciamento, the Liberator. A piece of verse sent by young Whittier to the Newburyport "Free Press" led Garrison, its editor, to look up his contributor, and to encourage him with praise and counsel. From that time we see the poet working upward in the old-fashioned way. A clever youth need not turn gauger in a land of schools and newspapers. Whittier's training was supplemented by a year or more at the academy, and by a winter's practice as a teacher himself, — fulfilling thus the customary *Lehrjahre* of our village aspirants. In another year we find him the conductor of a tariff newspaper in Boston. Before his twenty-fifth birthday he had experienced the vicissitudes of old-time journalism, changing from one desk to another, at Haverhill, Boston, and Hartford, still pursuing literature, erelong somewhat known as a poet and sketch-writer, and near the close of this period issuing his first book of Legends, in prose and verse. At Hartford also he edited, with

First acquaintance with William Lloyd Garrison.

See p. 114.

a well-composed preface, the posthumous collection of his friend Brainard's poems.

Consecration to the anti-slavery struggle.

But the mission of his life now came upon him. He received a call. In 1831 Garrison had begun "The Liberator." He was Whittier's ally and guide; the ardor of the poet required an heroic purpose, and Garrison's crusade was one to which his whole nature inclined him. It was no personal ambition that made him the psalmist of the new movement. His verses, crude as they were, had gained favor; he already had a name, and a career was predicted for him. He now doomed himself to years of retardation and disfavor, and had no reason to foresee the honors they would bring him in the end. What he tells us is the truth: "For twenty years my name would have injured the circulation of any of the literary or political journals in the country." During this term his imaginative writings were to be "simply episodical," something apart from what he says had been the main purpose of his life. He was bent upon the service which led Samuel May to declare that of all our poets he "has, from first to last, done most for the abolition of slavery. All my anti-slavery brethren, I doubt not, will unite with me to crown him as our laureate." Bryant, many years later, pointed out that in recent times the road of others to literary success had been made smooth by anti-slavery opinions, adding that in Whittier's case the reverse of this was true; that he made himself the champion of the slave "when to say aught against the national curse was to draw upon one's self the bitterest hatred, loathing, and contempt of the great majority of men throughout the land." Unquestionably Whittier's ambition, during his novitiate, had been to do something as a poet and man of letters.

Not that he had learned what few, in fact, at that time realized, that the highest art aims at creative beauty, and that devotion, repose, and calm are essential to the mastery of an ideal. But he was a natural poet, and, if he had not been filled with convictions, might have reached this knowledge as soon as others who possessed the lyrical impulse. The fact that he made his rarest gift subsidiary to his new purpose, in the flush of early reputation, when one is most sensitive to popular esteem, has led me to dwell a little upon the story of his life, and to observe how life itself may be made no less inspiring than a poem. I would not be misunderstood; we measure poetry at its worth, not at the worth of its maker. This is the law; yet in Whittier's record, if ever, there is an appeal to the higher law that takes note of exceptions. Some of his verse, as a pattern for verse hereafter, is not what it might have been if he had consecrated himself to poetry as an art; but it is memorably connected with historic times, and his rudest shafts of song were shot true and far and tipped with flame. This should make it clear to foreigners why we entertain for him a measure of the feeling with which Hungarians speak of Petöfi, and Russians of Turgénieff. His songs touched the hearts of his people. It was the generation which listened in childhood to the *Voices of Freedom* that fulfilled their prophecies.

His gift subsidiary to "the cause."

"The Voices of Freedom," 1849, *etc., etc.*

Garrison started his journal with the watchword of "unconditional emancipation," and the pledge to be "harsh as truth and uncompromising as justice; . . . not to retreat a single inch, and to be heard." Whittier reënforced him with lyre and pen, — though sometimes the two differed in policy, — and soon was writing abolition pamphlets, editing "The Freeman,"

Record and experience.

In the field.

and active in the thick of the conflict. He was the secretary of the first anti-slavery convention, a signer of the Declaration of Sentiments, and, at an age when bardlings are making sonnets to a mistress's eyebrow, he was facing mobs at Plymouth, Boston, Philadelphia. After seven or eight years of this stormy service, he settled down in quarters at Amesbury, sending out, as ever, his prose and verse to forward the cause. But now his humane and fervent motives were understood even by opponents, and the sweetness of his rural lyrics and idyls had testified for him as a poet. In 1843 the most eclectic of publishing houses welcomed him to its list; the rise of poetry had set in, and Longfellow, Emerson, Lowell, were gaining a constituency. As he grew in favor, attractive editions of his poems appeared, and his later volumes came from the press as frequently as Longfellow's, — more than one of them, like "Snow-Bound," receiving in this country as warm and wide a welcome as those of the Cambridge laureate. After the war, Garrison — at last crowned with honor, and rejoicing in the consummation of his work — was seldom heard. Whittier, in his hermitage, the resort of many pilgrims, has steadily renewed his song. While chanting in behalf of every patriotic or humane effort of his time, he has been the truest singer of our homestead and wayside life, and has rendered all the legends of his region into familiar verse. The habit of youth has clung to him, and he often misses, in his too facile rhyme and rhythm, the graces, the studied excellence of modern work. But all in all, as we have seen, and more than others, he has read the heart of New England, and expressed the convictions of New England at her height of moral supremacy, — the distinctive enjoyment of

After the campaign.

which, in view of the growth of the Union, and the spread of her broods throughout its territory, may not recur again.

III.

Unstudied quality of his verse.

It would not be fair to test Whittier by the quality of his off-hand work. His verse always was auxiliary to what he deemed the main business of his life, and has varied with the occasions that inspired it. His object was not the artist's, to make the occasion serve his poem, but directly the reverse. Perhaps his *naïveté* and carelessness more truthfully spoke for his constituents than the polish of those bred in seats of culture; many of his stanzas reflect the homeliness of a provincial region, and are the spontaneous outcome of what poetry there was in it. His feeling gained expression in simple speech and the forms which came readily. Probably it occurred somewhat late to the mind of this pure and duteous enthusiast that there is such a thing as duty to one's art, and that diffuseness, bad rhymes, and prosaic stanzas are alien to it. Nor is it strange that the artistic moral sense of a Quaker poet, reared on a New England farmstead, at first should be deficient. A careless habit, once formed, made it hard for him to master the touch that renders a new poem by this or that expert a standard, and its appearance an event. His ear and voice were naturally fine, as some of his early work plainly shows. "Cassandra Southwick," "The New Wife and the Old," and "The Virginia Slave Mother" were of an original flavor and up to the standards of that day. If he had occupied himself wholly with poetic work, he would have grown as steadily as his most successful compeers. But his

Its defects.

Hasty composition.

vocation became that of trumpeter to the impetuous reform brigade. He supplied verse on the instant, often full of vigor, but often little more than the rallying-blast of a passing campaign. We are told by May that "from 1832 to the close of our dreadful war in 1865, his harp of liberty was never hung up. Not an important occasion escaped him. Every significant incident drew from his heart some pertinent and often very impressive or rousing verses." It is safe to assume that if he had been more discriminating, or had cherished the resolve of Longfellow or Tennyson to make even conventional pieces artistic, many occasions would have escaped him. We see again that Art will forego none of its attributes. Sincerity and spontaneity are the well-springs of its clearest flow; yet, if dependent on these traits alone, it may become cheap and common, and utterly fail of permanence. In the time under notice there was nothing more likely to confuse the imagination than the life of a journalist, especially of a provincial or reform editor. The case of Hood, one of the truest of poets by nature, has shown us something of the dangers that beset a journalist-poet. This Whittier emphatically became, though in every way superior to the band of temperance, abolition, and partisan rhymesters that, like the shadows of his own failings, sprang up in his train. He wrote verses very much as he wrote editorials, and they were forcible only when he was deeply moved by stirring crises and events. Some of his best were tributes to leaders, or rebukes of great men fallen. But he was too apt to write weak eulogies of obscurer people; for every friend or ally had a claim upon his muse.

Cp. "Victorian Poets": pp. 81, 82.

His imperfections were those of his time and class, and he was too engrossed with a mission to overcome them. He never learned compression, and still is troubled more with fatal fluency than our other poets of equal rank, —by an inability to reject poor stanzas and to stop at the right place. Mrs. Browning was a prominent sufferer in this respect. The two poets were so much alike, with their indifference to method and taste, as to suggest the question (especially in view of the subaltern reform-verse-makers) whether advocates of causes, and other people of great moral zeal, are not relatively deficient in artistic conscientiousness and in what may be called æsthetic rectitude.

The Poets of Reform.

An occasional looseness in matters of fact may be forgiven one who writes from impulse. We owe "Barbara Frietchie" to the glow excited by a newspaper report; and the story of "Skipper Ireson's Ride," now challenged, if not true, is too well told to be lost. Whittier became, like a mother's careless, warm-hearted child, dearer for his very shortcomings. But they sometimes mar his bravest outbursts. Slight changes would have made that eloquent lyric, "Randolph of Roanoke," a perfect one. Feeling himself a poet, he sang by ear alone, in a somewhat primitive time; but the finest genius, in music or painting for example, with the aid of a commonplace teacher can get over more ground in a month than he would cover unaided in a year; since the teacher represents what is already discovered and established. There came a period when Whittier's verse was composed solely with poetic intent, and after a less careless fashion. It is chiefly that portion of it, written from 1860 onward, that has secured him a more than local reputation. His ruder rhymes of a day bear witness to an experience which none could better illustrate than by citing the words of the poet himself:

Culture an aid to genius.

"Hater of din and riot,
He lived in days unquiet;
And, lover of all beauty,
Trod the hard ways of duty."

Prose writings.

In prose he soon became skilled. His letters often are models of epistolary style; the best articles and essays from his pen are written with a true and direct hand, though rather barren of the epigram and original thought which enrich the prose of Lowell, Holmes, and Emerson. *Margaret Smith's Journal* is a charming *nuova antica;* a trifle thin in plot, but such a quaint reproduction of the early colonial period — its people, manners, and discourse — as scarcely any other author save Hawthorne, at the date of its production, could have given us.

"Margaret Smith's Journal," 1849.

IV.

Whittier's poetical style, genius, and works.

HIS metrical style, except in certain lyrics of marked individuality, is that of our elders who wrote in diffuse measures, and whose readers favored sentiment more than beauty or wit. It is a degree more old-fashioned than styles which are so much older as to become new by revival; that is to say, its fashion was current within our own recollection and is now passing away. Some forms put on a new type with each successive period, such as blank-verse and the irregular ode-measures in which Lowell, Taylor, and Stoddard have been successful. Whittier uses these rarely, and to less advantage than his ballad-verse. He has conformed less than any one but Holmes to the changes of the day. Imagine him with an etching-needle, tracing the deft lines of a triolet or villanelle! If he could, and would, it would be seen that when one leaves a natural vein, the yield, lacking what is characteristic, is superfluous. Even his recent sonnets, "Requirement," "Help," etc., are little more than fourteen-line homilies. Those who know their author find something of him in them, but such efforts do not reveal him to a new acquaintance. A poet's voice must have a distinct quality to be heard above the general choir.

A wholesome intent.

We turn to his early verse, as still acknowledged, to see in what direction his first independent step was made, and we note an effort to become a true American poet — to concern himself with the story and motive of his own land. For a time it was rather ineffective. The author of *Mogg Megone* and *The Bridal of Pennacook* was on the same trail with the New York squadron that sought the red man's path. It is queer, at this distance, to see the methods of Scott and Coleridge applied to the Indian legendary of Maine. Among works of this sort, however, these were the best preceding "Hiawatha." Longfellow had the tact to perceive that if the savage is not poetical his folk-lore may be made so. The prelude to Whittier's "Bridal" is quite modern and natural. It contains a suggestive plea that this experiment in a home field may not seem amiss even to those who are best pleased

"Mogg Megone," 1836.

"The Bridal of Pennacook," 1848.

> "while wandering in thought,
> Pilgrims of Romance o'er the olden world."

And, after all, "Mogg" was a planned and sustained effort, and full of promise. Its writer's later management of local themes was more to the point. The *Songs of Labor* are American chiefly in topic, — in manner they are much like what Mackay or Massey might have written, — yet they became popular, and their rhetorical flow adapted them to recitation in the

"Songs of Labor," 1850.

Indications of his true bent.

country schools. The poet's distinctive touch first appears in the legendary ballads which now precede the "Voices of Freedom" in his late editions. "The New Wife and the Old" is almost our best specimen of a style that Mrs. Hemans affected, and which Miss Ingelow, Mrs. Browning, and others have employed more picturesquely. It is a weird legend, musically told, and clearly the lyric of a poet. The early Quaker pieces are as good, and have all the traits of his verse written forty years afterward. His first ballads give the clew to his genius, and now make it apparent that most of his verse may be considered without much regard to dates of production. "Cassandra Southwick," alone, showed where his strength lay: of all our poets he is the most natural balladist, and Holmes comes next to him. The manner of that poem doubtless was suggested by Macaulay's "Battle of Ivry," and nothing could better serve the purpose. The colonial tone is well maintained. Here is a touching picture of the inspired maid's temptation to recant, of her endurance, trial, and victory. A group, also, of the populace — cloaked citizens, grave and cold, hardy sea-captains, and others — gathered where

Our foremost balladist.

> "on his horse, with Rawson, his cruel clerk, at hand,
> Sat dark and haughty Endicott, the ruler of the land."

The bigoted priest, a "smiter of the meek," is a type that was to reappear in our poet's scornful indictments of the divines who, within public remembrance, upheld the slavery system under the sanction of Noah's curse of Canaan. This ballad is well-proportioned, and thus escapes the defect of "The Exiles," which is otherwise a good piece of idiomatic verse.

Ballads on Quaker themes.

On the whole, it is as a balladist that Whittier displays a sure metrical instinct. The record of the Quakers has always served his muse, from the date of "Cassandra Southwick" to the recent production of "The Old South," "The King's Missive," and "How the Women went from Dover." Neither Bernard Barton nor Bayard Taylor is so well entitled to the epithet of the Quaker Poet. His Quaker strains, chanted while the sect is slowly blending with the world's people, seem like its swan-song. It is worth noting that of the nine American poets discussed in these essays, one is still a Friend, and two others, Whitman and Taylor, came of Quaker parentage on both sides. The strong ballad, "Barclay of Ury," would be almost perfect but for the four moralizing stanzas at the close. It is annoying to see a fine thing lowered, and even in moral effect, by an offence against the ethics of art. Whittier's successes probably have been scored most often through ballads of our eastward tradition and supernaturalism, such as those pertaining to witchcraft, — a province which, from "Calef in Boston" to "The Witch of Wenham," he never has long neglected. Some of his miscellaneous ballads are idyllic; others, in strong relief, were inspired by incidents of the War, during which our non-combatant sounded more than one blast, like that of Roderick, worth a thousand men. His ballads vary as much in excellence as in kind; among the most noteworthy are "Mary Garvin," "Parson Avery," "John Underhill," and that pure bit of melody and feeling, the lay of "Marguerite." Yet some of the poems which he classes in this department properly are eclogues, or slow-moving narratives. He handles well a familiar measure; when aiming at something new, as in "The Ranger," he usually is

Ballads of witch-craft, colonial romance, etc.

8

less at ease, despite the fact that the nonpareil of his briefer pieces is thoroughly novel in form and refrain, and doubtless chanced to come to him in such wise. "Skipper Ireson's Ride" certainly is unique. Dialect-poems are too often unfaithful or unpoetic. Imagination, humor, and dramatic force are found in the ballad of the Marblehead skipper's dole, and its movement is admirable. The culmination is more effective than is usual in a piece by Whittier. We have the widow of the skipper's victim saying "God has touched him! why should we?" — an old dame, whose only son has perished, bidding them "Cut the rogue's tether and let him run"; and

"Skipper Ireson's Ride."

"So, with soft relentings and rude excuse,
Half scorn, half pity, they cut him loose,
And gave him a cloak to hide him in,
And left him alone with his shame and sin.
Poor Floyd Ireson, for his hard heart,
Tarred and feathered and carried in a cart
By the women of Marblehead!"

The change of feeling is indicated by the single word "poor." This is only a minor piece, but quantity is the plane, and quality the height, of lyrical verse. Were it not for two of Collins's briefest poems, where would his name be?

A balladist should be a good reciter of tales. Our poet's prose work on *The Supernaturalism of New England* was devoted to the ghost and witch stories of his own neighborhood. In general design his chief story-book in verse, *The Tent on the Beach*, like Longfellow's "Tales of a Wayside Inn," — the first series of which it post-dated and did not equal, — follows the oft-borrowed method of Boccaccio and Chaucer. The home tales of this group are the best, among them "The Wreck of Rivermouth" and "Abraham Daven-

(1847.)

"The Tent on the Beach," 1867.

port." Throw out a ballad or two, and, but for a want of even finish, "The Tent on the Beach" might be taken for a portion of Longfellow's extended work. As a bucolic poet of his own section, rendering its pastoral life and aspect, Whittier surpasses all rivals. This is established chiefly by work that increased, after he reached middle age, with a consciousness of his lost youth. In some breathing-spell from the stress of his reform labors, he longed for the renewal of

Our chief bucolic poet.

> "boyhood's painless play,
> Sleep that wakes in laughing day,
> Health that mocks the doctor's rules,
> Knowledge never learned of schools."

His eye fell upon the Barefoot Boy, and memory brought back a time when he too was

> "rich in flowers and trees,
> Humming-birds and honey-bees."

Rural verse, and its begetters.

To rate the country life at its worth, one must have parted from it long enough to become a little tired of that for which it was exchanged. The best eclogues are those which, however simple, have a feeling added by the cast of thought. Poets hold Nature dear when refined above her. Goldsmith, after years of wandering; Burns, when too well acquainted with the fickle world. The maker of rural verse, moreover, should be country-bred, or he will fall short. Unless Nature has been his nurse in childhood, he never will read with ease the text of her story-book. The distinction between artifice and sincerity is involved. Watteau's pictures are exquisite in their way, but Millet gave us the real thing. Longfellow's rural pieces were done by a skilled workman, who could regard his themes objectively and put them to good use. Lowell delights in outdoor life, and his Yankee studies are perfect;

still, we feel that he is, intellectually and socially, miles above the people of the vale. Whittier is of their blood, and always the boy-poet of the Essex farm, however advanced in years and fame. They are won by the sincerity and ingenuousness of his verse, rooted in the soil and native as the fern and wild rose of the wayside. His brother-poets are more exact: which of them would hit upon "Maud" as a typical farm-girl's name? But incongruities are the signs manual of a rural bard, as one can discover from Burns's high-sounding letters and manifestoes. Whittier himself despises a sham pastoral. There is good criticism, a clear sense of what was needed, in his paper on Robert Dinsmore, the old Scotch bard of his childhood. He says of rural poetry that "the mere dilettante and the amateur ruralist may as well keep their hands off. The prize is not for them. He who would successfully strive for it must be himself what he sings,— part and parcel of the rural life, . . . one who has added to his book-lore the large experience of an active participation in the rugged toil, the hearty amusements, the trials and pleasures he describes." I need not dwell upon our poet's fidelity to the landscape and legends of the Eastern shore and the vales of the Piscataqua and Merrimack. Those who criticise his pastoral spirit as lacking Bryant's breadth of tone, Emerson's penetration, and Thoreau's detail, confess that it is honest and that it comes by nature. His most vivid pictures are of scenes which lie near his heart, and relate to common life — to the love and longing, the simple joys and griefs, of his neighbors at work and rest and worship. Lyrics such as "Telling the Bees," "Maud Muller," and "My Playmate" are miniature classics; of this kind are those which confirmed his reputation and still make his volumes real household books of song.

Whittier's pastoral spirit.

These rustic verses, as we have seen, came like the sound of falling waters to jaded men and women. Years ago, when *Snow-Bound* was published, I was surprised at the warmth of its reception. I must have underrated it in every way. It did not interest one not long escaped from bounds, to whom the poetry of action then was all in all. And in truth such poetry, conceived and executed in the spirit of art, is of the higher grade. But I now can see my mistake, a purely subjective one, and do justice to "Snow-Bound" as a model of its class. Burroughs well avows it to be the "most faithful picture of our northern winter that has yet been put into poetry." If his discussion had not been restricted to "Nature and the Poets," he perhaps would have added that this pastoral gives, and once for all, an ideal reproduction of the inner life of an old-fashioned American rustic home; not a peasant-home, —far above that in refinement and potentialities,— but equally simple, frugal, and devout; a home of which no other land has furnished the coadequate type.

"Snow-Bound. A Winter Idyl," 1866.

This poem is not rich in couplets to be quoted for their points of phrase and thought. Point, decoration, and other features of modern verse are scarcely characteristic of Whittier. In "Snow-Bound" he chose the best subject within his own experience, and he made the most of it. Taken as a whole, it is his most complete production, and a worthy successor to "The Deserted Village" and "The Cotter's Saturday Night." Here is that air which writers of quality so often fail to capture. "Hermann and Dorothea," "Enoch Arden," even "Evangeline," memorable for beauty of another kind, leave the impression that each of their authors said, as Virgil must have said, "And now I will compose an idyl." Whittier found his idyl already pictured for him by the camera of his own heart. It is a

Among the famous poems of its class.

work that can be praised, when measured by others of the sort, as heartily as we praise the "Biglow Papers" or "Evangeline," and one that ranks next to them as an American poem. This "Winter Idyl" is honestly named. Under the title, however, is a passage from Cornelius Agrippa on the "Fire of Wood," followed by Emerson's matchless heralding of the snow-storm. Devices of this kind add to the effect of such a poem, only, as "The Ancient Mariner." The texts are needless at the outset of a work whose lovely and unliterary cast is sufficient in itself. From the key struck at the opening to the tender fall at the close, there is a sense of proportion, an adequacy and yet a restraint, not always observed in Whittier. This is a sustained performance that conforms to the maxim *ne quid nimis*. Its genuineness is proved by a severe test, the concord with which imaginative passages glide into homely, realistic verse:

Realism.

"The wind blew east: we heard the roar
Of Ocean on his wintry shore,
And felt the strong pulse throbbing there
Beat with low rhythm our inland air.

"Meanwhile we did our nightly chores, —
Brought in the wood from out of doors,
Littered the stalls, and from the mows
Raked down the herd's-grass for the cows;
Heard the horse whinnying for his corn;
And, sharply clashing horn on horn,
Impatient down the stanchion rows
The cattle shake their walnut bows."

The gray day darkens to

"A night made hoary with the swarm
And whirl-dance of the blinding storm;

. . . . .

The white drift piled the window-frame,
And through the glass the clothes-line posts
Looked in like tall and sheeted ghosts."

The poet's child-vision makes this fancy natural and not grotesque. The whole transfiguration is recalled:

Fancy.

> "The old familiar sights of ours
> Took marvellous shapes; strange domes and towers
> Rose up where sty or corn-crib stood,
> Or garden-wall, or belt of wood;
> . . . . .
> The bridle-post an old man sat
> With loose-flung coat and high cocked hat;
> The well-curb had a Chinese roof;
> And even the long sweep, high aloof,
> In its slant splendor, seemed to tell
> Of Pisa's leaning miracle."

Imaginative touches follow:

Imagination.

> "The shrieking of the mindless wind,
> The moaning tree-boughs swaying blind,
> And on the glass the unmeaning beat
> Of ghostly finger-tips of sleet.
> . . . . .
> From the crest
> Of wooded knolls that ridged the west,
> The sun, a snow-blown traveller, sank
> From sight beneath the smothering bank."

The building and lighting of the wood-fire, the hovering family group that

A graphic interior.

> "watched the first red blaze appear,
> Heard the sharp crackle, caught the gleam
> On whitewashed wall and sagging beam,"

the rude-furnished room thus glorified and transformed, while even

> "The cat's dark silhouette on the wall
> A couchant tiger's seemed to fall,"—

all this is an interior painted by our Merrimack Teniers. His hand grows free in artless delineations of each sharer of the charmed blockade: the father, with his stories of woodcraft and adventure; the Quaker mother rehearsing tales from Sewell and Chalkley "of faith fire-winged by martyrdom"; then a foil to these, the unlettered uncle "rich in lore of fields and brooks,"

> "A simple, guileless, childlike man,
> Content to live where life began";

the maiden aunt; the elder sister, full of self-sacrifice, a true New England girl; lastly, the "youngest and dearest," seated on the braided mat,

> "Lifting her large, sweet, asking eyes."

The guests are no less vividly portrayed. The schoolmaster, distinct as Goldsmith's, is of an original type. The group is completed, with an instinct for color and contrast, by the introduction of a dramatic figure, the half-tropical, prophetic woman, who was born to startle,

> "on her desert throne,
> The crazy Queen of Lebanon
> With claims fantastic as her own."

The poem returns to its theme, and records the days of farm-house life during the chill embargo of the snow, until

> "a week had passed
> Since the great world was heard from last."

But the treading oxen break out the highways, the rustic carnival of sledding and sleighing is at hand,

> "Wide swung again our ice-locked door,
> And all the world was ours once more."

The poet's masterpiece.

From the subject thus chosen and pursued, an unadventured theme before, our poet has made his masterpiece. Its readers afterward loved to hear his voice, whether at its best or otherwise; and the more so for his pleased and assured reflection,

> "And thanks untraced to lips unknown
> Shall greet me like the odors blown
> From unseen meadows newly mown."

A claim that he has found and preserved in fit and winning verse the poetic aspect of his own section can be grounded safely on this idyl. We return from the work in which his taste is most effectual to that inspired by his life-long convictions. It is in this that the faults heretofore noted are most common, but here also his natural force is at its height, and results from what is lacking in some of his group — the element of passion. The verse of his period, especially the New England verse, is barren enough of this. For what there was, and is, of love-poetry we must look south of the region where poets are either too fortunate or too self-controlled to die because a woman 's fair. The song of the Quaker bard is almost virginal, in so far as what we term the master-passion is concerned. Its passion comes from the purpose that heated his soul and both strengthened and impeded lyrical expression. Active service in any strife, even the most humane, is unrest, and therefore hostile to the perfection of art. But the conflict often engenders in its cloud the flash of eloquence and song. Three-fourths of Whittier's anti-slavery lyrics are clearly effusions of the hour; their force was temporal rather than poetic. There are music and pathos in "The Virginia Slave Mother," and "The Slave-Ships" is lurid and grotesque enough to have furnished Turner with his theme. The poet's deep-voiced scorn and invective rendered his anti-slavery verse a very different thing from Longfellow's, and made the hearer sure of his "effectual calling." Even rhetoric becomes the outburst of true passion in such lines as these upon "Elliott": —

The passion of a fiery heart.

> "Hands off! thou tithe-fat plunderer! play
> No trick of priestcraft here!
> Back, puny lordling! darest thou lay
> A hand on Elliott's bier?"

Personal lyrics.

A little of this, however, goes quite far enough in poetry. As a writer of personal tributes, whether pæans or monodies, the reform bard, with his peculiar faculty of characterization, has been happily gifted. Scarcely one of these that might not be retouched to advantage, but they are many and various and striking. John Randolph lives for us in the just balancing, the masterly and sympathetic portraiture, of Whittier's fine elegy. Channing, Elliott, Pius IX., Foster, Rantoul, Kossuth, Sumner, Garibaldi, — all these historic personages are idealized by this poet, and haloed with their spiritual worth; his tributes are a lyrical commentary, from the minstrel's point of view, upon an epoch now gone by. The wreath his aged hands have laid upon the tomb of Garrison is a beautiful and consecrated offering. One of his memorable improvisations was "Ichabod," the lament for Webster's defection and fall, — a tragical subject handled with lyric power. In after years, his passion tempered by the flood of time, he breathes a tenderer regret in "The Lost Occasion": —

"Ichabod."

> "Thou shouldst have lived to feel below
> Thy feet Disunion's fierce upthrow, —
> The late-sprung mine that underlaid
> Thy sad concessions vainly made.
> . . . . .
> Ah, cruel fate, that closed to thee,
> O sleeper by the Northern sea,
> The gates of opportunity!"

But the conception of "Ichabod" is most impressive; those darkening lines were graven too deeply for obliteration. In thought we still picture the deserted leader, the shadow gathering about his "august head," while he reads such words as these: —

> "All else is gone; from those great eyes
> The soul has fled:

When faith is lost, when honor dies,
The man is dead.

"Then, pay the reverence of old days
To his dead fame;
Walk backward, with averted gaze,
And hide the shame!"

Among our briefer poems on topics of dramatic general interest, I recall but one which equals this in effect, — and that, coming from a hand less familiar than Whittier's, is now almost unknown. I refer to the "Lines on a Great Man Fallen," written by William W. Lord, after the final defeat of Clay, and in scorn of the popular judgment that to be defeated is to fall. The merit of this eloquent piece has been strangely overlooked by the makers of our literary compilations.

Deep religious feeling.

It is matter of history that our strictest clerical monitors, during the early struggle for abolition, opposed agitation of the slavery question, and often with a rancor that Holy Willie might envy. Not even this one-sided *odium theologicum* could long debar Whittier from the respect of the church-going classes, for he is the most religious of secular poets, and there is no gainsaying to a believer the virtues of one who guides his course by the life and teachings of Jesus Christ. A worshipful spirit, a savor "whose fragrance smells to heaven," breathes from these pages of the Preacher-Poet's song. The devotional bent of our ancestors was the inheritance of his generation. Domesticity, patriotism, and religion were, and probably still are, American characteristics often determining an author's success or failure. A reverent feeling, emancipated from dogma and imbued with grace, underlies the wholesome morality of our national poets. No country has possessed a group, equal in talent, that has pre-

Morality of American verse.

sented more willingly whatsoever things are pure, lovely, and of good report. There is scientific value in an influence, during a race's formative period, so clarifying to the general conscience. We have no proof that the unmorality of a people like the French, with exquisite resources at command, can evolve an art or literature greater than in the end may result from the virile chastity of the Saxon mind. Whittier is the Galahad of modern poets, not emasculate, but vigorous and pure; he has borne Christian's shield of faith and sword of the Spirit. His steadfast insistence upon the primitive conception of Christ as the ransomer of the oppressed had an effect, stronger than argument or partisanship, upon the religiously inclined; and of his lyrics, more than of those by his fellow-poets, it could be averred that the songs of a people go before the laws. Undoubtedly a flavor smacking of the caucus, the jubilee, and other adjuvants of "the cause" is found in some of his polemic strains; but again they are like the trumpeting of passing squadrons, or the muffled drum-beat for chieftains fallen in the fray.

A poet militant and ministrant.

The courage that endures the imputation of cowardice, as in "Barclay of Ury," the suffering of man for man, the cry of the human, never fail to move him. He celebrates all brave deeds and acts of renunciation. The heroism of martyrs and resistants, of the Huguenots, the Vaudois, the Quakers, the English reformers, serves him for many a song and ballad. At every pause after some new devotion, after some supreme offering by one of his comrades, it was the voice of Whittier that sang the pæan and the requiem. His cry, —

> "Thou hast fallen in thine armor,
> Thou martyr of the Lord!"

compares with Turgénieff's thought of the Russian

maiden crossing the threshold of dishonor and martyrdom, the crowd crying "Fool!" without, while from within and above a rapturous voice utters the words, "Thou saint!" His sympathy flows to prisoners, emancipationists, throughout the world; and in "The May-Flower" he has a lurking kindness even for the Puritans, — but of the sort that Burns extends to Auld Hornie. This compassion reaches a climax in the lyric of the two angels who are commissioned to ransom hell itself. The injunction to beware of the man of one book applies to the poet whose Bible was interpreted for him by a Quaker mother. Its letter rarely is absent from his verse, and its spirit never. His hymns, than which he composes nothing more spontaneously, are so many acts of faith. The emancipationists certainly fought with the sword in one hand and the Bible in the other, — and Whittier's hymns were on their lips. The time came when these were no longer of hope, but of thanksgiving. Often his sacred numbers, such as the "Invocation," have a sonorous effect and positive strength of feeling. It was by the common choice of our poets that he wrote the "Centennial Hymn"; no one else would venture where the priest of song alone should go. The composition begins imposingly: —

Hymns of prayer and praise.

> "Our fathers' God! from out whose hand
> The centuries fall like grains of sand";

and it is difficult to see how a poem for sacred music, or for such an occasion, could be more adequately wrought.

His occasional and personal pieces reveal his transcendental habit of thought. We find him imagining the after-life of the good, the gifted, the maligned. The actuality of his conceptions is impressive: —

Transcendental spirit.

"I have friends in spirit-land;
Not shadows in a shadowy band,
Not others, but themselves, are they."

The change is only one from twilight into dawn: —

"*Thou livest, Follen!* — not in vain
Hath thy fine spirit meekly borne
The burthen of Life's cross of pain."

And in "Snow-Bound" he thus invokes a sister of his youth: —

"And yet, dear heart, remembering thee,
Am I not richer than of old?
Safe in thy immortality,
What change can reach the wealth I hold?"

An abiding mood.

Whittier's religious mood is far from being superficial and temporary. It is the life of his genius, out of which flow his ideas of earthly and heavenly content. In outward observance he is loyal to the simple ways of his own sect, and still a frequenter of the Meeting, where —

"from the silence multiplied
By these still forms on either side,
The world that time and sense have known
Falls off and leaves us God alone."

God should be most, he says, —

"where man is least;
So, where is neither church nor priest,
And never rag of form or creed
To clothe the nakedness of need, —
Where farmer-folk in silence meet, —
I turn my bell-unsummoned feet."

He clings in this wise to the formal formlessness of the Quakers, as he would cling, doubtless, to the usages of any church in which he had been bred, provided that its creed rested upon the cardinal doctrines of the Master. Channing seemed to him a hero and saint, with whom he could enter into full communion: —

> "No bars of sect or clime were felt, —
> The Babel strife of tongues had ceased, —
> And at one common altar knelt
> The Quaker and the priest."

Scorn of bigotry.

With this liberal inclusion of all true worshippers, he is so much the more impatient of clerical bigotry. "Woe unto you, scribes and Pharisees, hypocrites!" has been often on his lips, — sometimes the outbreak of downright wrath, —

> "Woe to the priesthood! woe
> To those whose hire is with the price of blood, —
> Perverting, darkening, changing, as they go,
> The searching truths of God!"

at other times varied with grim and humorous contempt, as in "The Pastoral Letter" and "The Haschish"; and never more effectively than in the vivid and stinging ballad of the fugitive slave-girl, captured in the house of God, in spite of tearful and defying women's eyes, and of the stout hands that rise between "the hunter and the flying." Down comes the parson, bowing low: —

> "Of course I know your right divine
> To own and work and whip her;
> Quick, deacon, throw that Polyglot
> Before the wench, and trip her!"

The "inward light."

The basic justification of Whittier's religious trust appears to be the "inward light" vouchsafed to a nature in which the prophet and the poet are one. This solvent of doubt removes him alike from the sadness of Clough and Arnold and the paganism of certain other poets. In the striking "Questions of Life," a piece which indicates his highest intellectual mark and is in affinity with some of Emerson's discourse, he fairly confronts his own share of our modern doubts; questioning earth, air, and heaven; perplexed with the mystery of our alliance to the upper and lower worlds; asking what is this

> "centred self, which feels and is;
> A cry between the silences."

He finds no resource but to turn from

> "book and speech of men apart
> To the still witness in my heart."

Faith, essential to the highest art.

His repose must come from the direction in which the Concord transcendentalists also have sought for it, the soul's temple irradiated by the presence of the inward light. I have seen a fervent expression of this belief, in a voluntary letter of Whittier's, to a poet who had written an ode concerning intuition as the refuge of the baffled investigator. In fine, the element of faith gives a tone to the whole range of his verse, both religious and secular, and more distinctively than to the work of any other living poet of equal reputation. What he has achieved, then, is greatly due to a force which is the one thing needful in modern life and art. Faith, of some kind, in things as they are or will be, has elevated all great works of human creation. The want of it is felt in that insincere treatment which weakens the builder's, the painter's, and the poet's appeal; since faith leads to rapture and that to exaltation, — the *passio vera*, without which art gains no hold upon the senses and the souls of men.

V.

American poets, as personages.

THE leaders of our recent poetic movement, with the exception of Longfellow, — who, like Tennyson and Browning, devoted himself wholly to ideal work, — seem to have figured more distinctively as personages, in both their lives and writings, than their English contemporaries. This remark certainly applies to Poe, Emerson, Whitman, Holmes, and Lowell, and to none more clearly than to the subject of this review. His traits, moreover, have begotten a sentiment of public affection, which, from its constant manifestation, is not to be overlooked in any judgment of his career. In recognition of a beautiful character, critics have not found it needful to measure this native bard with tape and calipers. His service and the spirit of it offset the blemishes which it is their wont to condemn in poets whose exploits are merely technical. A life is on his written page ; these are the chants of a soldier, and anon the hymnal of a saint. Contemporary honor is not the final test, but it has its proper bearing, — as in the case of Mrs. Browning, whom I have called the most beloved of English poets. Whittier's audience has been won by unaffected pictures of the scenes to which he was bred, by the purity of his nature, and even more by the *earnestness* audible in his songs, injurious as it sometimes is to their artistic purpose. Like the English sibyl, he has obeyed the heavenly vision, and the verse of poets who still trust their inspiration has its material, as well as spiritual, ebb and flow.

Whittier's endearing traits.

Purity and zeal.

It must be owned that Goethe's calm distinction between the poetry of humanity and that of a high ideal is fully illustrated in Whittier's reform-verse. Yet even his failings have "leaned to virtue's side." Those who gained strength from his music to endure defeat and obloquy cherish him with a devotion beyond measure. For his righteous and tender heart they would draw him with their own hands, over paths

Philanthropy.

strewed with lilies, to a shrine of peace and remembrance. They comprehend his purpose — that he has "tried to make the world a little better, . . . to awaken a love of freedom, justice, and good will," and to have his name, like Ben Adhem's, enrolled as of "one that loved his fellow-men." In their opinion a grace is added to his poetry by the avowal, "I set a higher value on my name as appended to the Anti-Slavery Declaration of 1833, than on the title-page of any book."

Pro aris et focis.

Our eldest living poet, then, is canonized already by his people as one who left to silence his personal experience, yet entered thoroughly into their joy and sorrow; who has been, like a celibate priest, the consoler of the hearts of others and the keeper of his own; who has best known the work and feeling of the humble household, and whose legend manifestly is *pro aris et focis*. He has stood for New England, also, in his maintenance of her ancient protest against tyranny. He is the veteran of an epoch that can never recur; that scarcely can be equalled, however significant future periods may seem from the artist's point of view. The primitive life, the old struggle for liberty, are idealized in his strains. Much of both his strength and incompleteness is due to his Hebraic nature; for he is the incarnation of Biblical heroism, of the moral energy that breathed alike, through a cycle of change from dogma to reason, in Hooker, Edwards, Parker, Garrison, and Emerson. In his outbursts against oppression and his cries unto the Lord, we recognize the prophetic fervor, still nearer its height in some of his personal poems, which popular instinct long ago attributed to him. Not only of Ezekiel, but also of himself, he chanted in that early time of anointment and consecration: —

Hebraic fervor.

"The burden of a prophet's power
Fell on me in that fearful hour;
From off unutterable woes
The curtain of the future rose;
I saw far down the coming time
The fiery chastisement of crime;
With noise of mingling hosts, and jar
Of falling towers and shouts of war,
I saw the nations rise and fall,
Like fire-gleams on my tent's white wall."

The Prophet Bard.

Oliver Johnson's tribute, a complement to Parkman's, paid honor to "The Prophet Bard of America, poet of freedom, humanity, and religion; whose words of holy fire aroused the conscience of a guilty nation, and melted the fetters of the slaves." This eulogy from a comrade is the sentiment of a multitude in whose eyes their bard seems almost transfigured by the very words that might be soonest forgotten if precious for their poetry alone. I confess to my own share of this feeling. It may be that he has thought too little of the canons which it is our aim to discover and illustrate; yet it was to him above all that the present writer felt moved to dedicate a volume with the inscription "Ad Vatem," and to invoke for Whittier

"Ad Vatem."

"the Land that loves thee, her whose child
Thou art, — and whose uplifted hands thou long
Hast stayed with song availing like a prayer."

For surely no aged servant, his eyes having seen in good time the Lord's salvation, ever was more endowed with the love and reverence of a chosen people. They see him resting in the country of Beulah, and there solacing himself for a season. From this comfortable land, where the air is sweet and pleasant (and he is of those who here have "met abundance of what they had sought for in all their pilgrimage"), they are not yet willing to have him seek the Golden City of his visions, but would fain adjure him, —

> "And stay thou with us long! vouchsafe us long
> This brave autumnal presence, ere the hues
> Slow-fading, ere the quaver of thy voice,
> The twilight of thine eye, move men to ask
> Where hides the chariot, — in what sunset vale,
> Beyond thy chosen river, champ the steeds
> That wait to bear thee skyward."

CHAPTER V.

RALPH WALDO EMERSON.

I.

A clew to his work as a poet.

THE grasses had scarcely taken root on Emerson's grave among the pines when a discussion of his genius began, to which so many have contributed, that we already are asking Lowell's question concerning Shakespeare, — Can anything new be said of him? One thing, it seems to me, may be said, at least in a new way and as a clew to his work as a poet. While, of all his brotherhood, he is the radiant exemplar of his own statement, that in spirit "the true poet and the true philosopher are one," nevertheless, of all verse his own shows most clearly that the Method of the poet not only is not one with that of the philosopher, but is in fact directly opposed to it. The poet, as an artist, does not move in the direction which was Emerson's by instinct and selection. The Ideal philosophy scrutinizes every phase of Nature to find the originating sense, the universal soul, the pure identity; it follows Nature's trails to their common beginning, inverting her process of evolution, working back from infinite variety to the primal unity. This, too, is the spirit of the poet, — to find the soul of things. But in method he is an artist: his poetry is an art that imitates Nature's own habit. He works from unity to countless results and formations, from the pure thought to visible symbols,

Difference between artistic and philosophic processes.

from the ideal to the concrete. As a poet, Emerson found himself in a state, not of distraction, but often of indecision, *between the methods of philosophy and art.* To bear this in mind is to account more readily for the peculiar beauties and deficiencies of his verse, — and thus to accept it as it is, and not without some understanding of its value.

A combination.

Hermann Grimm recurs to the dispute whether our sage was a poet, a philosopher, or a prophet. The fact is that he was born with certain notes of song; he had the poet's eye and ear, and was a poet just so far as, being a philosopher, he accepted poetry as the expression of thought in its rare and prophetic moods, and just so far as, in exquisite moments, he had the mastery of this form of expression.

Ideal prose and verse.

Emerson's prose is full of poetry, and his poems are light and air. But this statement, like so many of his own, gives only one side of a truth. His prose is just as full of every-day sense and wisdom; and something different from prose, however sublunary and imaginative, is needed to constitute a poem. His verse, often diamond-like in contrast with the feldspar of others, at times is ill-cut and beclouded. His prose, then, is that of a wise man, plus a poet; and his verse, by turns, light and twilight, air and vapor. Yet we never feel, as in reading Wordsworth, that certain of his measures are wholly prosaic. He was so careless of ordinary standards, that few of his own craft have held his verse at its worth. It is said that his influence was chiefly, like that of Socrates, upon the sensitive and young, and such is the case with all fresh influences; but I take it that those who have fairly assimilated Emerson's poetry in their youth have been not so much born poets as born thinkers of a poetic cast. It is inevitable, and partakes of

His natural disciples.

growth by exercise, that poets in youth should value a master's sound and color and form, rather than his priceless thought. They are drawn to the latter by the former, or not at all. Yet when poets, even in this day of refinement, have served their technical apprenticeship, the depth and frequent splendor of Emerson's verse grow upon them. They half suspect that he had the finest touch of all when he chose to apply it. It becomes a question whether his discords are those of an undeveloped artist, or the sudden craft of one who knows all art and can afford to be on easy terms with it. I think there is evidence on both sides;— that he had seasons when feeling and expression were in circuit, and others when the wires were down, and that he was as apt to attempt to send a message at one time as at the other. But he suggested the subtilty and swiftness of the soul's reach, even when he failed to sustain it.

At times the finest touch of all.

I have said that of two poets, otherwise equal, the one who acquires the broadest knowledge will draw ahead of him who only studies his art, and the poet who thinks most broadly and deeply will draw ahead of all. There can be little doubt of Emerson as a thinker, or as a poet for thinkers satisfied with a deep but abstract and not too varied range. Yet he did not use his breadth of culture and thought to diversify the purpose, form, symbolism, of his poems. They are mostly in one key. They teach but one lesson; that, to be sure, is the first and greatest of all, but they fail to present it, after Nature's method, in many forms of living and beautiful interest, — to exemplify it in action, and thus bring it within universal sympathy. That this should be so was, I say, inevitable from the field of Emerson's research, — that of pure rather than of applied philosophy. Thus

A single thought conveyed, but that the greatest.

far, however, he represents Thought in any adjustment of our poetic group, and furthermore, — his thought being independent and emancipatory, — the American conflict with superstition, with servility to inherited usage and opinion.

Essentially a poet.

We shall see that he had himself a noble and comprehensive ideal of what a typical poet should be, and was aware that his own song fell short of it. Still, he called himself a poet, and the consent of the best minds has sustained him in his judgment. His prose alone, as Lowell said, showed that he was essentially a poet; another with reason declared of his spoken essays that they were "not so much lectures as grave didactic poems, theogonies," adorned with "odes" and "eclogues." Thirty years later a cool and subtile writer looks back to find them the "most poetical, the most beautiful, productions of the American mind." For once the arbiters agree, except in a question akin to the dispute whether all things consist solely of spirit or solely of matter. Common opinion justified Mr. Sanborn's fine paradox that, instead of its being settled that Emerson could not write poetry, it was settled that he could write nothing else. We know his distaste for convention, his mistrust of "tinkle" and "efficacious rhymes." But his gift lifted him above his will; even while throwing out his grapnel, clinging to prose as the firm ground of his work, he rose involuntarily and with music. And it well may be that at times he wrote verse as an avowal of his nativity, and like a noble privileged to use the language of the court. Certainly he did not restrict himself to the poet's calling with the loyalty of Tennyson and Longfellow. In verse, however careful of his phrase, he was something of a rhapsodist, not apt to gloss his revelations

An apt paradox.

and exhortings with the nice perfection of those others. He must be reviewed as one whose verse and parable and prophecy alike were means to an end, — that end not art, but the enfranchisement and stimulation of his people and his time. When Longfellow, the poet of graceful art and of sympathy as tender as his voice, took his departure, there went up a cry as from a sense of fireside loss. People everywhere dwelt upon the story of his life and recalled his folk-songs. Emerson glided away almost unperceived under the shadow of the popular bereavement. But soon, and still multiplying from the highest sources, tributes to his genius began to appear, — searching, studying, expounding him, — as when a grand nature, an originating force, has ceased to labor for us. This is the best of fame: to impress the selected minds, which redistribute the effect in steadfast circles of extension. More than his associates, Emerson achieved this fame. He had the great man's intellect, which, according to Landor, "puts in motion the intellect of others." He was, besides, so rare a personage, that one who seeks to examine his writings apart from the facts and conduct of his life needs must wander off in contemplation of the man himself. Yet anything that others can write of him is poor indeed beside a collect of his own golden sayings. He felt his work to be its own and best interpreter, and of recent authors who have justly held this feeling he doubtless was the chief.

His office.

Order of intellect.

II.

HIS writings, then, are the key to his biography — the scroll of a life which, as for essential matter, and as he said of Plato's, was chiefly "interior." To quote his own language further, "Great geniuses have

R. W. E.: born in Boston, Mass., May 25, 1803.

the shortest biographies." Among the external points of significance in Emerson's story are those derived from his ancestral strain, for he was of pure and even gentle English blood, "through eight generations of cultured, conscientious, and practical ministers." He himself, as we know, assumed the profession of his father and forefathers, and for a time was a Unitarian preacher in Boston; this, after the stated courses at Harvard, where he read and wrote philosophy, nor failed to cultivate the Muse — for whose art he had shown a rare aptness even in childhood. The office and honors of the Class Poet fell to him, as to Lowell in after years. In letters he had Everett, Ticknor, and Edward Channing for instructors. In theology he was deeply influenced by Channing, the divine, — the true founder, through the work of Emerson and lesser pupils, of our liberal religious structure. Emerson projected the lines of the master so far beyond their first draft that he was unable long to remain within the Unitarian limits of that day. Some one has cleverly said that his verse, "Good-bye, proud world!" came from one whose future gave no cause for epigrams like that of Madame de Sévigné on Cardinal de Retz — of whom she wrote that he pretended to retire from a world which he saw was retiring from him. The separation from the church, and the retreat to Concord, were the beginning of Emerson's long career as poet, lecturer, essayist, thinker and inspirer. The details of his social, domestic, and civic relations are all upon record. Nothing could be more seemly than his lifelong abode in the New England village of Concord, the home of his line, the birth-place of our liberties; and it became, largely through his presence, the

Ancestry.

Training.

Influence of Channing.

Retirement from the pulpit.

source of our most resultful thought. Here he blended, in his speech and action, the culture of the university, nigh at hand, with the shrewd prudence of the local neighborhood, as became a poet and sage imbued with patriotism, morals, and the wisdom of practical life. Here, though crossing the ocean more than once, and inspecting other lands with the regard that sees for once and all, he otherwise exemplified during half a century his own conception of the clear spirit — that needs not to go afar upon its quests, because it vibrates boundlessly, and includes all things within reach and ken. For the rest, the life of Emerson appertained to the household, the library, the walk, the talk with all sorts and conditions of men, communion with rare natures, the proper part in local and national movement. As a lecturer, his range was the country at large, but the group that drew about him made Concord a modern Academe. Unconsciously he idealized them all with the halo of his own attributes. To him they all were of the breed so exquisitely characterized in his reference to Margaret Fuller's "Friends." "I remember," he says, "these persons as a fair, commanding troop, every one of them adorned by some splendor of beauty, of grace, of talent, or of character, and comprising in their band persons who have since disclosed sterling worth and elevated aims in the conduct of life." Thus year after year a tide, that ceases not with the death of him who mainly attracted it, has set toward Concord, — a movement of pilgrims craving spiritual exaltation and the interplay of mind with mind. The poet's moral and intellectual experiences are revealed in discourses, always beginning with the memorable sermon on the Lord's Supper, which pre-

After-life and career.

Pupils and associates.

Concord.

Sermon on the Communion, 1832.

Essay on "Nature," 1836.

figured his emancipation from dogma,[1] and the essay on Nature, wherein he applied a new vision to the world about us. These were the Alpha of his conviction and insight; his after-speech followed consistently and surely, "as the night the day." He created his own audience, whose demand for his thought grew by what it fed on, beginning in a section, and spreading not only through a country but over many lands. If it is true that "he was not the prince of transcendentalists but the prince of idealists," the history of New England transcendentalism is no less a corollary to the problem of Emerson's life.

The transcendental movement.

Our starry memories of the places and people that once knew Emerson radiate always from one centre — the presence of the sage himself. Many pupils, catching something of his own sure and precise art of delineation, have drawn his image for us, dwelling upon the sinewy bending figure, the shining and expectant face, the union of masculinity and sweetness in his bearing. His "full body tone" is recalled, "full and sweet rather than sonorous, yet flexible, and haunted by many modulations." Persuasion sat upon his lips. The epithet "sun-accustomed" is applied to Emerson's piercing eyes by one, a woman and a poet, who marked the aquiline effect of his noble profile. I, too, remember him in this wise, and as the most serene of men: one whose repose, whose tranquillity, was not the contentment of an idler housed in worldly comforts, but the token of spiritual adjustment to all the correspondences of life; as the bravest and most deferential, the proud-

His personal traits and bearing.

[1] Definitely set forth in his Address before the Senior Class in Divinity College, Cambridge, July 15, 1838.

est in self-respect, yet recognizing in deep humility the supremacy of universal law. No man so receptive, and none with so plain and absolute a reservation of his own ground. Even in the shadow and silence of his closing years, he bore the mien of one assured that

Died at Concord, Mass., April 27, 1882.

> "the gods reclaim not from the seer
> Their gift, although he ceases here to sing,
> And, like the antique sage, a covering
> Draws round his head, knowing what change is near."

III.

Emerson's philosophy.

It is not my province to take part in the discussion of Emerson's philosophy, his system or lack of system. Some notion of this, however, must affect our thoughts of him as a poet, since of all moderns he most nearly fulfilled Wordsworth's inspired prediction, uttered sixty years ago, of the approaching union of the poet and the philosopher. He deemed the higher office that of the poet, — of him who quaffs the brook that flows fast by the oracles, — yet doubtless thought himself not so well endowed with melody and passion that his teaching should be subordinate to his song. But the latter was always the flowering of his philosophic thought, and it is essential to keep in view the basis of that pure reflection. He looked upon Nature as pregnant with Soul; for him the Spirit always moved upon the face of the waters. The incomprehensible plan was perfect: whatever is, is right. Thus far he knew, and was an optimist with reverent intent. It was in vain to ask him to assert what he did not know, to avow a creed founded upon his hopes. If a theist, with his intuition of an all-pervading life, he no less felt himself a portion of

Optimism.

that life, and the sense of omnipresence was so clearly the dominant sense of its attributes, that to call him a theist rather than a pantheist is simply a dispute about terms; to pronounce him a Christian theist is to go beyond his own testimony. Such a writer must be judged by the concurrence of his books; they are his record, and the parole evidence of no associate can weigh against his written manifest for an instant.

Reverence without dogma.

His writings assure us that he accepted all bibles and creeds for what good there was in them. One thing for him was "certain": "Religions are obsolete when lives do not proceed from them." He saw that "unlovely, nay frightful, is the solitude of the soul which is without God in the world"; but the creeds and dogmas of anthropomorphic theology were merely germinal. "Man," thus far, has "made all religions, and will yet make new and even higher faiths."

An idealist and eclectic.

Emerson, a man of our time, while a transcendentalist, looking inward rather than to books for his wisdom, studied well the past, and earlier sages were the faculty of his school. A latter-day eclectic, he took from all literatures their best and essential. A Platonic idealist, he was not averse to the inductive method of Aristotle; he had the Alexandrian faith and ecstasy, the Epicurean zest and faculty of selection;

Morals.

like the Stoics, he observed morals, heroism, self-denial, and frugality. There is much in his teachings that recalls the beautiful ethics of Marcus Aurelius, and the words of Epictetus, as reported by Arrian. His spiritual leanings never stinted his regard of men and manners.

Life taken at its full worth.

He kept a sure eye on the world; he was not only a philosopher, but the paragon of gentlemen, with something more than the Oriental, the Grecian, or the Gallic, tact. He relished to the full the brave distinctions, the portraitures and tests of Plutarch, and found the best of all good company in the worldly wise, the cheery and comfortable Montaigne. One may almost say that he refined and digested what was good in all philosophies, and nothing more. He would get hold of Swedenborg, the mystic, yet not be Swedenborg exclusively, nor imitate the rhetoric of the Sophists, the pride of the Cynics. From all he learned what each confesses in the end, — the limitations of inquiry, — that the Finite cannot measure, though it may feel, the Infinite. No more would he formulate a philosophy, but within it he could recognize nature, art, taste, morals, laws, religion, and the chance of immortality. When it was said that he had no new system, he thought that he needed none, and was sceptical of classification.

His wisdom unformulated.

It appears that he found the key to his own nature in Plato, being an idealist first of all. His intuitive faculty was so determined that ideality and mysticism gave him the surest promise of realities; his own intellect satisfied him of the power of intellect. Plainly hearing an interior voice, he had no doubt that other men were similarly monished. Plato, the guide of his youth, remained his type of philosopher and man. To Plato's works alone should Omar's saying of the Koran be applied: "Burn the libraries, for their value is in this book." Nowhere else was there such a range of speculation. "Out of Plato come all things." And thus he held to the last. "Of Plato," he said, years afterward, "I hesitate to speak, lest there should be no end. . . . Why should not young men be educated on this book? It would suffice for the tuition of the race." Yet Emerson's philosophy was a greater advance from Neo-Platonism than the Alexandrians were able to make upon the

Plato his early guide and type.

Special likeness of Emerson to Plotinus.

lines indicated by their elemental master. In personal life and bearing, Plotinus, with whom our poet seems to have been most in sympathy, was very closely his prototype. There is first to be noted the curious resemblance between the eclectic, investigating Alexandrian age and our present time; and secondly, it is Plotinus of whom we are told that "He lived at the same time with himself and with others, and the inward activity of his spirit ceased only during his hours of sleep. . . . His written style was close, pregnant, and richer in thought than in words, yet enthusiastic, and always pointing to the main object. He was more eloquent in his oral communications, and was said to be very clever in finding the appropriate word, even if he failed in accuracy on the whole. Besides this, the beauty of his person was increased when discoursing; his countenance was lighted up with genius." Taylor's translations of selections from the Works of Plotinus, published in 1817 and 1834, must have fallen into Emerson's hands, and I am satisfied of their impression upon his mind. As one examines the lives and writings of the two men, the likeness is still more notable, especially with respect to their views of fate, will, ethics, the "higher law," the analysis of the beautiful, and in the ardor with which young students, and many of the elderly and wise, listened to their respective teachings. Emerson was a Plotinus reanimate after the lapse of sixteen centuries of Christianity. He has now, like the Neo-Platonist, "led back the Divine principle within" him "to the God who is all in all."

Standards of greatness.

To the great thinkers of the past, the New England teacher, without fear or boasting, well might feel himself allied. The accepted great, free of the ordinary bounds of place and time, recognize one another across the vague, like stars of the prime magnitude in the open night. Emerson knew the haps and signs of genius: "Whenever we find a man higher by a whole head than any of his contemporaries, it is sure to come in doubt what are his real works." We cannot say "What is master, and what school." "As for their borrowings and adaptings, they know how to borrow. . . . A great man is one of the affinities, who takes of everything." But they are not above the law of perfect life; virtue, simplicity, absolute sincerity, these are their photosphere. "Live as on a mountain. Let men see, let them know, a real man, who lives as he was meant to live." To this Roman standard the New Englander subjoined the shrewd, kindly wisdom of his stock and region. He was eminent among those whose common sense is the most telling point to be made against Locke's negation of innate ideas, — whose judgment is so apt that, granting Locke's theory, it can be accounted for only by the modern theory of ideas prenatal and inherited. His written wisdom is more effective than Montaigne's, being less dependent on citations. He knew by instinct what our novelists learn from observation and experience; or is it that they study chiefly their own time and neighborhood, while he sat aloof and with the ages? Thus strong in equipment, sound in heart, and lofty of intellect, we find him revered by his pupils, and without a living peer in the faculty of elevating the purpose of those who listened to his buoyant words. We must confess that a differentiation between master and school, and between members of the school, after awhile became manifest. That such a process was inevitable is plain, when Emerson's transcendental and self-reliant laws of conduct are kept in mind.

Innate wisdom.

Transcendental and inductive methods contrasted.

One may say, in illustration, that his philosophical method bears to the inductive or empirical a relation similar to that between the poetry of self-expression and the poetry of æsthetic creation, — a relation of the subjective to the objective. The former kind of verse often is the more spontaneous, since it has its birth in the human need for utterance. It is the cry of adolescence and femininity, the resource of sensitive natures in which emotion outvies the sense of external beauty or power. It was the voice of Shakespeare's youth, nor was it ever quieted throughout the restless careers of Byron, Heine, and De Musset. But we accept as the great works of the poets their intellectual and objective creations, wherein the artist has gone beyond his own joy and pain, his narrow intro-vision, to observe, combine, transfigure, the outer world of nature and life. Such the epics, idyls, dramas, of the masters. When subjective poetry is the yield of a lofty nature, or of an ideal and rapturous womanhood like Mrs. Browning's, it is a boon and revelation to us all; but when, as too often, it is the spring-rise of a purling, commonplace streamlet, its egotism grows pitiful and repulsive. This lesson has been learned, and now our minor poets, in their fear of it, strive to give pleasure to our sense of the beautiful, and work as artists, — though somewhat too delicately, — rather than to pose as exceptional beings, "among men, but not of them."

The master and his pupils.

As with the subjective poets, so with many of the transcendental acolytes. The force of Emerson lay in the depth and clearness of his intentions. He gave us the revelation and prophecy of a man among millions. Such a teacher aids the self-development of noble minds; his chief peril is that of nurturing a weaker class that cannot follow where he leads.

Diverse results of his influence.

Some of its enthusiasts will scarcely fail to set too high a value upon their personal impulses. They "still revere," but forget to "still suspect" themselves "in lowliness of heart." For the rest, the down-East instinct is advisory and homiletic; New Englanders are prone to teach, and slower to be taught. Emerson, however, grew to be their superior man, the one to whom all agreed to listen, and from whom all quote. His example, also, has somewhat advanced the art of listening, in which he was so perfect, with forward head and bright, expectant visage. His inculcations were of freedom, of the self-guidance that learns to unlearn and bears away from tradition; yet this, too, will breed false liberty of conceit in minor votaries, whose inward light may do well enough for themselves, yet not suffice for the light of the world. Hence the public, accepting Emerson, has been less tolerant of more than one Emersonian, with his *ego, et rex meus*. After all is said, we must see that our transcendentalists were a zealous, aspiring band of seekers after the true, the beautiful, and the good; what they have lacked in deference they have made up in earnestness and spirituality. There have been receptive natures among them, upon whom, as indeed upon the genius of his people far and wide, the tonic effect of Emerson's life and precept has been immeasurable. Goethe's declaration of himself that he had been "to the Germans in general, and to the young German poets in particular, their liberator," may, with perfect truth, be applied to Emerson, and to a generation that has thriven on his word. He has taught his countrymen the worth of virtue, wisdom, courage, — above all, to fashion life upon a self-reliant pattern, obeying the dictates of their own souls.

A liberator.

IV.

Emerson, the Poet.

RECOGNIZING Emerson's high mood as that of a most original poet, I wish chiefly to consider his relations to poetry and the poetic art. His imaginative essays are not poems. Speech is not song; the rarest mosaic lacks the soul of the canvas swept by the brush. The credentials that he presented from time to time, and mostly in that dawn when poets sing if ever, are few and fragmentary, but they will suffice. They are the trophies, the wreaths and golden vessels, the *spolia opima*, which he set before the shrine of the goddess. They are the avowal of a rare spirit that there are things which cannot be rendered in prose; that Poetry claims a finer art, a supremer utterance, for her service, and that she alone can stamp the coins and bronzes which carry to the future the likeness of her viceroy.

"Poems," 1847.

"May-Day, and Other Pieces," 1867.

"Poems," 1876.

Philosophy transfigured.

In his verse, Emerson's spiritual philosophy and laws of conduct appear again, but transfigured. Always the idea of Soul, central and pervading, of which Nature's forms are but the created symbols. As in his early discourse he recognized two entities, Nature and the Soul, so to the last he believed Art to be simply the union of Nature with man's will — Thought symbolizing itself through Nature's aid. Thought, sheer ideality, was his sovereign; he was utterly trustful of its guidance. The law of poetic beauty depends on the beauty of the thought, which, perforce, assumes the fittest, and therefore most charming, mode of expression. The key to art is the eternal fitness of things; this is the sure test and solvent. Over and again he asserted his conviction: "Great thoughts insure musical expression. Every word should be the right word. . . . The Imagina-

His view of Art.

Fitness of things.

tion wakened brings its own language, and that is always musical. . . . Whatever language the poet uses, the secret of tone is at the heart of the poem." He cites Möller, who taught that the building which was fitted accurately to answer its end would turn out to be beautiful, though beauty had not been intended. (The enforced beauty of even the rudest sailing craft always has seemed to me the most striking illustration of this truth.) In fine, Emerson sees all forms of art symbolizing but one Reason, not one mind, but The Mind that made the world. He refers "all production at last to an aboriginal Power." It is easy to discern that from the first he recognized "the motion and the spirit," which to Wordsworth were revealed only by the discipline of years; but his song went beyond the range of landscape and peasant, touching upon the verities of life and thought. "Brahma" is the presentation of the truth manifest to the oldest and most eastern East, and beyond which the West can never go. How strange that these quatrains could have seemed strange! They reveal the light of Asia, but no less the thought of Plato — who said that in all nations certain minds dwell on the "fundamental Unity," and "lose all being in one Being." Everywhere one stuff, under all forms, this the woven symbolism of the universal Soul, the only reality, the single and subdivided Identity that alone can "keep and pass and turn again," that is at once the doubter and the doubt, the slayer and the slain, light and shadow, the hither and the yon. Love is but the affinity of its portions, the desire for reunion, the knowledge of soul by soul, to which the eyes of lovers are but windows. Art is the handiwork of the soul, with materials created by itself, building better than it knows, the bloom of attraction and necessity.

All art a reflex of the universal soul.

"Brahma."

Our lyric poet.

Thus far the theory of Emerson's song. It does not follow that he composed upon a theory. At times I think him the first of our lyric poets, his turns are so wild and unexpected; and he was never commonplace, even when writing for occasions. His verse changes unawares from a certain tension and angularity that were congenital, to an ethereal, unhampered freedom, the poetic soul in full glow, the inner music loosed and set at large. Margaret Fuller wrote that his poems were "mostly philosophical, which is not the truest kind of poetry." But this depends upon the measure of its didacticism. Emerson made philosophical poetry imaginative, elevating, and thus gave new evidence that the poet's realm is unbounded. If he sought first principles, he looked within himself for them, and thus portrays himself, not only the penetrative thinker, but the living man, the citizen, the New England villager, whose symbols are drawn from the actual woods and hills of a neighborhood. Certainly he went to rural nature for his vigor, his imagery and adornments. An impassioned sense of its beauty made him the reverse of the traditional descriptive poet. Most poetry of nature justly is termed didactic; most philosophical verse the same. Miss Fuller failed to make distinctions. All feel what didacticism signifies, but let us try to formulate it.

Margaret Fuller's comment.

Why Didacticism repels us.

Didacticism is the gospel of half-truths. Its senses are torpid; it fails to catch and convey the soul of truth, which is beauty. Truth shorn of its beauty is tedious and not poetical. We weary of didactic verse, therefore, not because of its truth, but because of its self-delusive falsehood. It flourishes with a dull and prosaic generation. The true poet, as Mrs. Browning saw, is your only truth-teller, because he gives the truth complete in beauty or not at all.

Elusive nature.

Emerson doubts his power to capture the very truth of nature. Its essence — its beauty — is so elusive; it flees and leaves but a corpse behind; it is the pearly glint of the shells among the bubbles of the latest wave: —

> "I fetched my sea-born treasures home;
> But the poor, unsightly, noisome things
> Had left their beauty on the shore,
> With the sun, and the sand, and the wild uproar."

Emerson close upon her trail.

But such poems as the "Forerunners" show how closely he moved, after all, upon the trail of the evading sprite. He seemed, by the first intention, and with an exact precision of grace and aptness, to put in phrases what he saw and felt, — and he saw and felt so much more than others! He had the aboriginal eye, and the civilized sensibility; he caught both the external and the scientific truth of natural things, and their poetic charm withal. As he triumphed over the untruthfulness of the mere verse-maker, and the dulness of the moralist, his instant, sure, yet airy transcripts gave his poems of nature a quality without a counterpart. Some of his measures had at least the flutter of the twig whence the bird has just flown. He did not quite fail of that music music-born,

> —— "a melody born of melody,
> Which melts the world into a sea.
> Toil could never compass it;
> Art its height could never hit."

"Woodnotes."

He infused his meditations with the sheen of Day itself, — of

> —— "one of the charmèd days
> When the genius of God doth flow;
> The wind may alter twenty ways,
> A tempest cannot blow;
> It may blow north, it still is warm;
> Or south, it still is clear;

> Or east, it smells like a clover-farm ;
> Or west, no thunder fear."

He returns with delight to Nature's blending of her laws of beauty and use, perceiving that she

> ——"beats in perfect tune,
> And rounds with rhyme her every rune,
> Whether she work in land or sea,
> Or hide underground her alchemy.
> Thou canst not wave thy staff in air,
> Or dip thy paddle in the lake,
> But it carves the bow of beauty there,
> And the ripples in rhymes the oar forsake."

"The Problem."

"May-Day."

Always the one apt word.

Artlessness.

"Woodnotes" is full of lyrical ecstasy and lightsome turns and graces. To assimilate such a poem of nature, or "The Problem," that masterpiece of religion and art, is to feed on holy dew, and to comprehend how the neophytes who were bred upon it find the manna of noontide somewhat rank and innutritious. "May-Day" is less lyrical, more plainly descriptive of the growth and meaning of the Spring, but not in any part didactic. It is the record of the poet's training, a match to Wordsworth's portrayal of his subjective communing with Nature in youth ; its spirit is the same with Lowell's woodland joyousness, one of child-like and unquestioning zest. Finally, this poet's scenic joinery is so true, so mortised with the one apt word, as where he says that the wings of Time are "*pied* with morning and with night," and the one best word or phrase is so unlooked for, that, as I say, we scarcely know whether all this comes by grace of instinct, or with search and artistic forethought. It seems "the first fine careless rapture"; the labor, which results in the truth of Tennyson's landscape and the pathos of Longfellow's, may be there, but is not to be detected, and in these touches, if not otherwise, he excelled his compeers. His generalizations pertain to the unseen world; viewing the actual, he puts its strength and fineness alike into a line or epithet. He was born with an unrivalled faculty of selection. Monadnock is the "constant giver," the Titan that "heeds his sky-affairs"; the tiny humming-bee a "voyager of light and noon," a "yellow-breeched philosopher," and again an "animated torrid zone"; the defiant titmouse, an "atom in full breath." For a snow-storm, or the ocean, he uses his broader brush, but once only and well. His minute truth and sense of values are held in honor by his pupils Whitman and Burroughs, our poetic familiars of the field, and by all to whom the seasonable marvels of the pastoral year are not unwelcome or unknown.

His epithets.

Thus keenly Emerson's instinct responded to the beauty of Nature. I have hinted that her secure laws were the chief promoters of his imagination. It coursed along her hidden ways. In this he antedated Tennyson, and was less didactic than Goethe and kindred predecessors. His foresight gave spurs to the intellect of Tyndall and other investigators, — to their ideal faculty, without which no explorer moves from post to outpost of discovery. Correlatively, each wonder-breeding point attained by the experimentalists was also occupied by our eager and learned thinker from the moment of its certainty. Each certainty gave him joy; reasoning *a priori* from his sense of a spiritual Force, the seer anticipated the truths demonstrated by the inductive workers, and expected the demonstration. Even in "The Sphinx," the first poem of his first collection, the conservation of force, the evolution from the primordial atom, are made to subserve his mystical faith in a broad Identity. Here, thirty years before Tennyson made his most compact expression of the central truth, —

Scientific prescience.

Darwin anticipated.

"The Sphinx."

"Flower in the crannied wall . . .
Little flower — but if I could understand
What you are, root and all, and all in all,
I should know what God and man is,"

Emerson had put it in this wise: —

"Thorough a thousand voices
Spoke the universal dame:
'Who telleth one of my meanings,
Is master of all I am.'"

The seer of evolution.

The reference, in "Bacchus," to the ascent of life from form to form, still remains incomparable for terseness and poetic illumination: —

—— "I, drinking this,
Shall hear far Chaos talk with me;
Kings unborn shall walk with me;
And the poor grass shall plot and plan
What it will do when it is man."

And in "Woodnotes" he discoursed of

—— "the genesis of things,
Of tendency through endless ages,
Of star-dust and star-pilgrimages,
Of rounded worlds, of space and time,
Of the old flood's subsiding slime";

but always thinks of the universal Soul as the only reality, — of creation's process as simply the metamorphosis which

"Melts things that be to things that seem,
And solid nature to a dream."

Even in the pathetic "Threnody" he stays his anguish with faith in the beneficence of Law. With more passion and less method than afterward gave form to "In Memoriam," he declared that the "mysteries of Nature's heart" were "past the blasphemies of grief." He saw

—— "the genius of the whole,
Ascendant in the primal soul,
Beckon it when to go and come."

Such a poet was not like to go backward. The "Song of Nature" is his pæan to her verities, still more clearly manifest in his riper years. This superb series of quatrains, cumulative as thunder-heads and fired with lyric glory, will lend its light to whatsoever the poetry of the future has in reserve for us.

"Song of Nature."

It should be noted that Emerson's vision of the sublime in scientific discovery increased his distaste for mere style, and moved him to contentment with the readiest mode of expression. It tempered his eulogy of "Art," and made him draw this contrast: "Nature transcends all moods of thought, and its secret we do not yet find. But a gallery stands at the mercy of our moods, and there is a moment when it becomes frivolous. I do not wonder that Newton, with an attention habitually engaged on the paths of planets and suns, should have wondered what the Earl of Pembroke found to admire in 'stone dolls.'"

Science and Art. Cp. "Victorian Poets": pp. 12-16.

Right here we observe (deferring matters of construction) that our seer's limitations as a poet are indicated by his dependence on out-door nature, and by his failure to utilize those higher symbols of the prime Intelligence which comprise the living, acting, suffering world of man. With a certain pride of reserve, that did not lessen his beautiful deference to individuals, he proclaimed "the advantage which the country life possesses for a powerful mind over the artificial and curtailed life of cities." He justified solitude by saying that great men, from Plato to Wordsworth, did not live in a crowd, but descended into it from time to time as benefactors. Above all he declared — "I am by nature a poet, and therefore must live in the country." But here a Goethe, or De Musset, or Browning might rejoin: "And I am a poet, and need the focal life of the town." If man be the paragon of life on

Emerson's limitations.

Narrowing the poet's franchise.

this globe, his works and passions the rarest symbols of the life unseen, then the profoundest study is mankind. Emerson's theorem was a restriction of the poet's liberties. One can name great poets who would have been greater but for the trammels of their seclusion. I believe that Emerson's came from self-knowledge. He kept his range with incomparable tact and philosophy. Poets of a wider franchise — with Shakespeare at their front — have found that genius gains most from Nature during that formative period when one reads her heart, if ever, and that afterward he may safely leave her, as a child his mother, to return from time to time, but still to do his part among the ranks of men.

Life, action, and passion, wanting in his song.

Emerson makes light of travel for pleasure and observation, but ever more closely would observe the ways of the inanimate world. Yet what are man's works but the works of Nature by one remove? To one poet is given the ear to comprehend the murmur of the forest, to another the sense that times the heart-beats of humanity. Few have had Emerson's inward eye, but it is well that some have not been restricted to it. He clung by attraction, no less than by circumstance, to "a society in which introspection," as Mr. James has shrewdly written, "thanks to the want of other entertainment, played almost the part of a social resource." His verse, in fact, is almost wholly void of the epic and dramatic elements which inform the world's great works of art. Action, characterization, specific sympathy, and passion are wanting in his song. His voice comes "like a falling star" from a skyey dome of pure abstraction. Once or twice, some little picture from life, — a gypsy girl, a scarcely outlined friend or loved one, — but otherwise no personage in his works except, it may be, the poet himself, the Saadi of his introspective song: even that wise and joyous bard restored in fragments, suggested rather than portrayed. Emerson would be the "best bard, because the wisest," if the wisdom of his song illustrated itself in living types. He knew the human world, none better, and generalized the sum of its attainments, — was gracious, shrewd, and calm, — but could not hold up the mirror and show us to ourselves. He was that unique songster, a poet of fire and vision, quite above the moralist, yet neither to be classed as objective or subjective; he perceived the source of all passion and wisdom, yet rendered neither the hearts of others nor his own. His love poetry is eulogized, but it wants the vital grip wherewith his "Concord Fight" and "Boston Hymn" fasten on our sense of manhood and patriotism. It chants of Love, not of the beloved; its flame is pure and general as moonlight and as high-removed. "All mankind love a lover," and it is not enough to discourse upon the philosophy of "Love," "Experience," "Power," "Friendship." Emerson's "Bacchus" must press for him

Characteristics.

—— "wine, but wine which never grew
In the belly of the grape."

His deepest yearnings are expressed in that passionate outburst, — the momentary human wail over his dead child, — and in the human sense of lost companionship when he tells us, —

"In the long sunny afternoon,
The plain was full of ghosts."

Oftener he moves apart; his blood is ichor, not our own; his thoughts are with the firmament. We reverence his vocation, and know ourselves unfitted for it. He touches life more nearly in passages that have the acuteness, the practical wisdom of his prose works and days; but these are not his testimonials as a poet.

A layer on of hands.

His laying on of hands was more potent; a transmitted heat has gone abroad through the ministry of his disciples, who practise as he preached, and sometimes transcend both his preaching and his practice. All the same, the originator of a force is greater than others who add four-fold to its momentum. They are never so manifestly his pupils as when they are "scarifying" and "sounding and exploring" him, "reporting where they touch bottom and where not," on ground of their own, but with a pleasant mockery of the master's word and wont. There was a semblance between the poets Emerson and Rossetti, first, in the small amount of their lyrical work, and again in the positive influence which each exerted upon his pupils. In quality the Concord seer, and the English poet who was at once the most spiritual and sensuous of his own school, were wholly unlike. Rossetti was touched with white fire, but dreamed of souls that meet and glow when disembodied. The spirits of his beatified thrill with human passion. Our seer brought something of heaven to earth, while Rossetti yearned to carry life through death to heaven.

Rossetti.

Metrical style.

The technical features of Emerson's verse correspond to our idea of its meaning. In fact, his view of personal culture also applied to his metrical style. "Manners are not to be directly cultivated. That is frivolous; leave it to children. . . . We must look at the mark, not at the arrow, and perhaps the best rule is Lord Bacon's,— that to attain good forms one only needs not to despise them." Delicate and adroit artisans, in whose eyes poetry is solely a piece of design, may find the awkwardness of Emerson's verse a bar to right comprehension of its frequent beauty and universal purpose. I am not sure but one must be of the poet's own country and breeding to look quite down his vistas and by-paths: for every American has something of Emerson in him, and the secret of the land was in the poet, — the same Americanism that Whitman sees in the farmer, the deck-hand, the snag-toothed hostler, atoning with its humanities for their sins past and present, as for the sins of Harte's gamblers and diggers of the gulch. It may be, too, that other conditions are needed to open the ear to the melody, and to shut out the discords, of Emerson's song. The melody is there, and though the range be narrow, is various within itself. The charm is that of new-world and native wood-notes wild. Not seldom a lyrical phrase is the more taking for its halt, — helped out, like the poet's own speech, by the half-stammer and pause that were wont to precede the rarest or weightiest word of all.

Native wood-notes wild.

Among the followers of any art there are those whose compositions are effective in the mass, their treatment broad, the beauty pervasive; again, those who with small constructive feeling are rich in detail, and whose work is interspersed with fine and original touches; lastly, the complete artists, in whom, however vivid their originality and great their special beauties, the general design is always kept in hand. Emerson never felt the strength of proportion that compels the races to whom art is a religion and a law. He has given many a pang to lovers of the beautiful, who have endured his irreverence by allowing for his supposed disabilities. He satisfied his conscience in the same easy way, declaring that he was from his "very incapacity of mechanical writing" a "chartered libertine." But his speech bewrayeth him. Who sounds one perfect chord can sound again. His greater efforts in verse, as in prose, show that he chose to deprecate the constructive faculty lest it might limit

Deficient sense of proportion.

A nonconformist.

his ease and freedom. And his instinct of personality, not without a pride of its own, made him a nonconformist. We are told of his mode of preparing an essay, — of the slow-growing medley of thoughts on a topic, at last brought out and strung at random, like a child's variegated beads. But I do not find that his best essays read backward as well as forward; I suspect an art beneath their loose arrangement, and I see at times the proof of continuous heat. His early critic declared that he had not "written one good work, if such a work be one where the whole commands more attention than the parts." But again we see that she too rarely qualified her oracles. At that time he had written poems of which the whole and the parts were at least justly related masterpieces, — lyrical masterpieces, of course, not epic or dramatic; of such were the "Threnody" and "Woodnotes," to which was afterward added the "May-Day." Breadth and proportion, in a less degree, mark "The Problem," "Monadnock," "Merlin," and a few other pieces. But working similarly he falls short in the labored dithyrambic, "Initial, Dæmonic, and Celestial Love." He was formal enough in youth, before he struck out for himself, and at the age of eleven, judging from his practice-work, was as precocious as Bryant or Poe. But he soon gave up construction, putting a trademark upon his verse, and trusting that freedom would lead to something new. So many precious sayings enrich his more sustained poems as to make us include him at times with the complete artists. Certainly, both in these and in the unique bits so characteristic that they are the poet himself, — "Terminus," "Character," "Manners," "Nature," etc., — he ranks with the foremost of the second class, poets eminent for special graces, values, sudden meteors of thought. In that

Miss Fuller on his synthesis.

Unique lyrics and notable sayings.

gift for "saying things," so notable in Pope and Tennyson, he is the chief of American poets. From what other bard have so many original lines and phrases passed into literature, — inscriptions that do not wear out, graven in bright and standard gold? It is worth while, for the mere effect, to group some of them together, and especially those which, appearing in his first book forty years ago, long since became a constituent part of our literary thought and expression: —

"Jewels . . . on the stretched forefinger of all Time."

" 'T is the law of bush and stone,
Each can only take his own."

"The thoughts that he shall think
Shall not be forms of stars, but stars,
Nor pictures pale, but Jove and Mars."

"Hast thou named all the birds without a gun?
Loved the wood-rose and left it on its stalk?"

"Heartily know,
When half-gods go
The gods arrive."

"What is excellent,
As God lives, is permanent;
Hearts are dust, hearts' loves remain."

"Born for the future, to the future lost."

"Not for all his faith can see
Would I that cowled churchman be."

"Not from a vain or shallow thought
His awful Jove young Phidias brought;
. . . .
Out from the heart of nature rolled
The burdens of the Bible old."

"The hand that rounded Peter's dome
. . . .

Wrought in a sad sincerity;
Himself from God he could not free;
He builded better than he knew; —
The conscious stone to beauty grew."

"Earth proudly wears the Parthenon
As the best gem upon her zone;
And Morning opes with haste her lids,
To gaze upon the Pyramids."

"One accent of the Holy Ghost
The heedless world hath never lost."

"Or ever the wild Time coined itself
Into calendar months and days."

"Set not thy foot on graves."

"Good-bye, proud world! I'm going home."

"What are they all, in their high conceit,
When man in the bush with God may meet?"

"— If eyes were made for seeing,
Then Beauty is its own excuse for being."

"Leave all thy pedant lore apart,
God hid the whole world in thy heart."

"And conscious Law is King of kings."

"— Mount to paradise
By the stairway of surprise."

"Here once the embattled farmers stood,
And fired the shot heard round the world."

"Great is the art,
Great be the manners, of the bard."

"The silent organ loudest chants
The master's requiem."

New felicities.

Verses from Emerson's later poems, — which came at rare intervals, after the public had learned to seek for the sweet kernel in every nut that fell from his tree, — are scarcely less familiarized and put to use : —

"Deep in the man sits fast his fate
To mould his fortunes mean or great:
Unknown to Cromwell as to me
Was Cromwell's measure or degree."

"O tenderly the haughty day
Fills his blue urn with fire !"

"I hung my verses in the wind,
Time and tide their faults may find;
All were winnowed through and through,
Five lines lasted sound and true."

"Winters know
Easily to shed the snow,
And the untaught Spring is wise
In cowslips and anemones."

"It is time to be old,
To take in sail, —
. . . .
Obey the voice at eve obeyed at prime:
'Lowly faithful, banish fear,
Right onward drive unharmed;
The port, well worth the cruise, is near,
And every wave is charmed.'"

"He spoke, and words more soft than rain
Brought the Age of Gold again;
His action won such reverence sweet
As hid all measure of the feat."

Rhythmical compression.

The poet's rhythm and gift of compression made verse like the foregoing a kind of ambrosial pemmican, easily carried for spiritual sustenance. Phrases in his prose, which have become more current, move in foot-beats, such as, — "Hitch your wagon to a star," "Nature is loved by what is best in us," and "The hues of sunset make life great." He thought rhythm indispensable, and rhyme most efficacious, as the curators of poetic thought. "Every good poem I know I recall by its rhythm also."

Unsurpassed in lyrical "quality."

Popular instinct, recognized by those who compile our anthologies, forbids an author to be great in more than one way. These editors go to Emerson for point and wisdom, and too seldom for his truth to nature and his strictly poetic charm. Yet who excels him in quality? That Margaret Fuller had a fine ear, and an independent one, is proved by her admission that "in melody, in subtilty of thought and expression," he took the highest rank. He often captures us with absolute beauty, the poetry that poets love, — the lilt and melody of Shelley (whose vagueness irked him) joined to precision of thought and outline. Poe might have envied "Uriel" his lutings of the spangled heaven; he could not have read "Woodnotes," or he would have found something kindred in the bard who said, —

> "Quit thy friends as the dead in doom,
> And build to them a final tomb;
> Let the starred shade that nightly falls
> Still celebrate their funerals,
> And the bell of beetle and of bee
> Knell their melodious memory."

Emerson "listened to the undersong," but rejoiced no less in the "divine ideas below" of the Olympian bards,

> "Which always find us young
> And always keep us so."

His modes of expression, like his epithets, are imaginative. The snow is "the north-wind's masonry";

feeling and thought are scarcely deeper than his speech; he puts in words the "tumultuous privacy of storm," or the "sweet varieties of chance." With what high ecstasy of pain he calls upon the deep-eyed boy, the hyacinthine boy, of his marvellous "Threnody!" Time confirms the first impression that this is the most spontaneous, the most elevating, of lyrical elegies,—that it transcends even the divine verse of Bishop King's invocation to his entombed wife. How abrupt, how exquisitely ideal, the opening phrase! Afterward, and throughout, the pure spirit of poetry rarefied by the passion of its theme: the departed child is the superangelic symbol of the beauty, the excellence, that shall be when time ripens and the harmonies of nature are revealed,—when life is no longer a dream within a dream. Read the "Threnody" anew. What grace! What Æolian music, what yearning! What prophecy and exaltation! See how emotion becomes the soul of art. Or is it that true passion cannot but express itself in verse at once simple and sensuous, thus meeting all the cardinal points of Milton's law?

The "Threnody."

One readily perceives that "Merlin" conveys Emerson's spirited conception of the art and manners of the bard. His should be no trivial harp:—

"Merlin."

"No jingling serenader's art,
Nor tinkle of piano strings;
. . . .
The kingly bard
Must smite the cords rudely and hard,
As with hammer or with mace;
. . . .
He shall not his brain encumber
With the coil of rhythm and number;
But leaving rule and pale forethought,
He shall aye climb
For his rhyme."

Thus fearlessly should a poet compel the Muse; and even to a broader liberty of song one, at least, of Emerson's listeners pushed with deliberate zeal. Walt Whitman was stimulated by this teaching, and by the rugged example of Carlyle, to follow resolutely the method which suited his bent and project; and Emerson's "Mithridates," we may say, is at once the key-note and best defence of Whitman's untrammelled, all-heralding philosophy. The descriptive truth, the lusty Americanism, of the democratic chanter took hold upon the master's expectant heart. A later modification of the first welcome, and the omission of the new songs from "Parnassus," had no bearing upon the question of their morals or method; Emerson was moved solely by his taste, — and New England taste has a supreme dislike of the unsavory. The world, even the Concord world, is not wholly given over to prudery. It has little dread, nowadays, of the voluptuous in art, ancient or modern. But to those of Puritan stock cleanliness is even more than godliness. There is no "fair perdition" tempting us in the "Song of Myself" and the "Children of Adam." But here are things which, whether vessels of honor or dishonor, one does not care to have before him too often or too publicly, and which were unattractive to the pure and temperate seer, whose race had so long inhabited the clean-swept keeping-rooms of the land of mountain breezes and transparent streams. The matter was one of artistic taste and of the inclinations of Emerson's nature, rather than of prudery or censorship.

Emerson and Whitman.

As for his own style, Emerson was impressed in youth by the free-hand manner of the early dramatists, whom he read with avidity. He soon formed his characteristic measure, varying with "sixes," "sevens,"

Favorite poets and measures.

and "eights," resembling Ben Jonson's lyrical style, but even more like that of Milton, Marvell, and other worthies of the Protectorate. In spirit and imagery, in blithe dithyrambic wisdom, he gained much from his favorite Orientals — Saadi and Hafiz. One stately and various measure he rarely essayed, but showed that it was well suited to his genius. In "Musketaquid" and "Sea-Shore" we see the aptness of his ear and hand for blank verse. The little poem of "Days," imitated from the antique, is unmatched, outside of Landor, for compression and self-poise: —

"Days."

"Daughters of Time, the hypocritic Days,
Muffled and dumb like barefoot dervishes,
And marching single in an endless file,
Bring diadems and fagots in their hands.
To each they offer gifts after his will,
Bread, kingdoms, stars, and sky that holds them all.
I, in my pleachéd garden, watched the pomp,
Forgot my morning wishes, hastily
Took a few herbs and apples, and the Day
Turned and departed silent. I, too late,
Under her solemn fillet saw the scorn."

We could wish that Emerson had written more blank verse, — a measure suited to express his highest thought and imagination. Probably, however, he said all that he had to say in verse of any kind. He was not one to add a single line for the sake of a more liberal product.

Changes in style.

He is thought to have begun so near the top that there was little left to climb. None of his verse is more pregnant than that which came in the first glow, but the later poems are free from those grotesque sayings which illustrate the fact that humor and a lively sense of the absurd often are of slow development in the brain of an earnest thinker. There was, it must be owned, a tinge of provincial arrogance, and there were expressions little less than ludicrous, in his early defiance of usage. He was too sincere a personage to resort to the grotesque as a means of drawing attention. Of him, the leader, this at least could not be suspected. Years afterward he revised his poems, as if to avoid even the appearance of affectation. On the whole, it is as well that he left "The Sphinx" unchanged; that remarkable poem is a fair gauge of its author's traits. The opening is strongly lyrical and impressive. The close is the flower of poesy and thought. The general tone is quaint and mystical. Certain passages, however, like that beginning "The fiend that man harries," are curiously awkward, and mar the effect of an original, almost an epochal, poem. This would not be admitted by the old-fashioned Emersonian, — never, by any chance, a poet pure and simple, — who makes it a point of faith to defend the very passages where the master nods. Just so the thick-and-thin Browningite, who testifies his adoration by counting the *m's* and *n's* of the great dramatist's volumes, and who, also, never is a poet pure and simple, celebrates Mr. Browning's least poetic experiments as his masterpieces. I think that the weakness of "transcendental" art is as fairly manifest in Emerson's first and chief collection of verse as were its felicities, — the former belonging to the school, the latter to the seer's own genius. Poe, to whom poetry was solely an expression of beauty, was irritated to a degree not to be explained by contempt for all things East. He extolled quaintness, and justly detested obscurity. He was prejudiced against the merits of such poets as Channing and Cranch by their prophetic bearing, which he berated soundly as an effort to set up as poets "of *unusual* depth and *very* remarkable powers

"The Sphinx" again.

Strength and weakness of transcendental verse.

of mind." Admitting the grace of one, he said that it was "laughable to see that the transcendental poets, if beguiled for a minute or two into respectable English and common-sense, are always sure to remember their cue just as they get to the end of their song, and round off with a bit of doggerel." Their thought was the "cant of thought," in adopting which "the cant of phraseology is adopted at the same time." This was serviceable criticism, *et ab hoste*, though Poe's lack of moral, and keenness of artistic, sense made him too sure of the insincerity of those who place conviction above expression. And Mr. James sees that Emerson's philosophy was "drunk in by a great many fine moral appetites with a sense of intoxication." The seer himself was intoxicated at times, and spoke, like the hasheesh-eaters, with what then seemed to him music and sanity. In a more reflecting season he excluded from his select edition certain pieces from which too many had taken their cues, — for example, the "Ode" to W. H. Channing, "The World-Soul," and "Tact." The Ode begins finely with a manner caught from Ben Jonson's ode "To Himself," and we can ill spare one passage ("The God who made New Hampshire"); but was it the future compiler of "Parnassus" who preceded this with laughter-stirring rhymes, and shortly avowed that "Things are of the snake," and again that "Things are in the saddle, And ride mankind"? Well, he lived to feel that to poets, "of all men, the severest criticism is due," and that "Poetry requires that splendor of expression which carries with it the proof of great thoughts."

Poe on this school.

Philosophic "intoxication."

But the forte of bardlings is the foible of a bard. Emerson became his own censor, and did wisely and well. We have seen that his art, even now, upon its

Emerson his own best critic.

constructive side, must often seem defective, — unsatisfactory to those whose love of proportion is a moral instinct. Many poets and critics will feel it so. The student of Emerson learns that he, too, moved upon their plane, but would not be confined to it. More than other men, he found himself a vassal of the unwritten law, whether his impulse lifted him above, or sent him below, the plane of artistic expression. If he could not sustain the concert-pitch of his voice at his best, he certainly knew what is perfection, and said of art much that should be said. He was not, he did not wish to be, primarily an artist: he borrowed Art's aid for his lofty uses, and held her at her worth. His essay on Art would be pronounced sound by a Goethe or a Lessing, though such men probe less deep for the secret principle of things, and deal more featly with the exterior. Elsewhere he insists that we must "disabuse us of our superstitious associations with place and time, with number and size. . . . Where the heart is, there the muses, there the gods sojourn. . . . A great man makes his climate genial in the imagination of man, and its air the beloved element of all delicate spirits." And again (like Arnold) he speaks of the modernness of all good books: "What is well done, I feel as if I did; what is ill done, I reck not of." He revised his prose less carefully, for republication, than his verse, and doubtless felt surer of it. He himself would have been the first to declare, as to the discordant and grotesque portions of his verse or prose, that the thought was proportionately defective, — not strong and pure enough to insure the beauty of the art which was its expression. Above all he knew, he confessed, that it is the first duty of a poet to express his thoughts naturally, counting among "the traits common to all works of the highest art, — that

Essay on Art.

Its chief canon.

they are universally intelligible, that they restore to us the simplest states of mind." This was his own canon. Where he failed of it, he might not surely know; where he knew, there he rebuked himself. He struck out, in his self-distrust, many things of value to those who loved his verse. We dwell with profit on the fact that he retained so little that should be stricken out.

V.

His prose writings.

"Nature," 1836.

"Essays," First Series, 1841.

"Essays," Second Series, 1844.

"Miscellanies," 1849.

"Representative Men," 1850.

"English Traits," 1856.

"Conduct of Life," 1860.

It is but a foolish surmise whether Emerson's prose or verse will endure the longer, for they are of the same stuff, warp and woof, and his ideality crosses and recrosses each, so that either is cloth-of-gold. Of whichever a reader may first lay hold, he will be led to examine the whole fabric of the author's work. Few writers, any one of whose essays, met with for the first time, seems more like a revelation! It will not be, I think, until that time when all his prose has passed into a large book, such as the volume we call Montaigne, that its full strength and importance can be felt. In certain respects it dwarfs other modern writing, and places him among the great essayists. These are not the efforts of a reviewer of books or affairs, but chapters on the simplest, the greatest, the immemorial topics, those that lie at the base of life and wisdom: such as Love, Experience, Character, Manners, Fate, Power, Worship — lastly, Nature herself, and Art her ideal counterpart. If to treat great themes worthily is a mark of greatness, the chooser of such themes begins with the instinct of great design. Bacon's elementary essays excepted, there are none in English of which it can be more truly averred that there is nothing superfluous in them. Compare them with the rest in theme and method. Carlyle, outside of "Sartor Resartus" and "Hero-Worship," usually reviews books, histories, individuals, at extreme length, and with dramatic comment and analysis. Emerson treats of the principles behind all history, and his laconic phrases are the very honey-cells of thought. There are let-downs and surplusage even in Landor. Throughout Emerson's writings each word is of value; they are the discourse of one who has digested all the worthy books, and who gives us their results, with latter-day discoveries of his own. He is the citizen of a new world, observing other realms and eras from an unrestricted point of view.

"Society and Solitude," 1870.

"Letters and Social Aims," 1876.

The intent of our essayist is the highest, and by no means that of writing for the exercise or glory of authorship. "Fatal," he declares, "to the man of letters is the lust of display. . . . A mistake of the main end to which they labor is incidental to literary men, who, dealing with the organ of language . . . learn to enjoy the pride of playing with this splendid engine, but rob it of its almightiness by failing to work with it." He estimates books at their worth. They "are for nothing but to inspire. I had better never see a book than to be warped by its attraction clean out of my own orbit, and made a satellite instead of a system."

His style.

Thus the thought of Style, it may be, should enter into the mind of neither writer nor reader. Style makes itself, and Emerson's is the apothegmatic style of one bent upon uttering his immediate thoughts, — hence strong in sentences, and only by chance suited to the formation of an essay. Each sentence is an idea, an epigram, or an image, or a flash of spiritual light. His letters to Carlyle show that he was at one time caught by the manner of the author whose character, at least, seemed of the most import to him. This was but a passing trace. When he was fresh from the schools,

Apothegms.

his essays were structural and orderly, but more abstract than in latter years. During his mature and haply less spiritual period, had he cared to write a history, the English would have been pure English, the narrative racy and vigorous. Portions of the "English Traits" make this plain. Since De Foe, where have we found anything more idiomatic than his account of Wordsworth delivering a sonnet?

Native English.

"This recitation was so unlooked for and surprising, — he, the old Wordsworth, standing apart, and reciting to me in a garden-walk, like a schoolboy declaiming, — that I at first was near to laugh; but recollecting myself, that I had come thus far to see a poet, and he was chanting poems to me, I saw that he was right and I was wrong, and gladly gave myself up to hear."

Note also Emerson's account of an ocean voyage. For charm of landscape-painting, take such a passage as that, in the second essay on Nature, beginning: "There are days which occur in this climate." But terseness is the distinctive feature of his style. "Men," he says, "descend to meet." "We are all discerners of spirits." "He [a traveller] carries ruins to ruins." No one has compressed more sternly the pith of his discourse.

Compression.

No poet, let us at once add, has written prose and shown more incontestably his special attribute. Emerson's whole argument is poetic, if that work is poetic which reaches its aim through the analogies of things, and whose quick similitudes have the heat, the light, the actinism, of the day-beam, and of which the language is rhythmic without degeneracy, — clearly the language of prose, always kept from weakness by the thought which it conveys. No man's writing was more truly his speech, and no man's speech so rhythmic: "There are Muses in the woods to-day, and whispers

The prose of a poet.

Rhythmic, and full of noble imagery.

to be heard in the breezes"; and again, "Hawthorne rides well his horse of the night." As he spoke, so he wrote: "Give me health and a day, and I will make the pomp of emperors ridiculous"; "The conscious ship hears all the praise"; of young idealists, "The tough world had its revenge the moment they put the horses of the sun to plough in its furrow"; of Experience, "was it Boscovich who found out that bodies never come in contact? Well, souls never touch their objects. An innavigable sea washes with silent waves between us and the things we aim at and converse with." In the same essay, — "Dream delivers us to dream, and there is no end to illusion. Life is a train of moods like a string of beads, and as we pass through them, they prove to be many-colored lenses which paint the world their own hue."[1] And of Love's world, with the cadences of Ecclesiastes, — "When the day was not long enough, but the night, too, must be consumed. . . . When the moonlight was a pleasing fever, and the stars were letters, and the flowers ciphers, and the air was coined into song; when all business seemed impertinence, all the men and women running to and fro in the streets mere pictures." But to show the poetry of Emerson's prose is to give the whole of it; these essays are of the few which make us tolerate the conceit of "prose poems." Their persistent recourse to imagery and metaphor, their suggestions of the secret relations of things, at times have subjected them to the charge of being obscure. The fault was not in the wine: —

"Hast thou a drunken soul?
Thy bane is in thy shallow skull, not in my silver bowl!"

[1] "Life, like a dome of many-colored glass,
Stains the white radiance of eternity."
Shelley's "Adonais."

In mature years the essayist pays more regard to life about him, to the world as it is; he is more equatorial, less polar and remote. His insight betrays itself in every-day wisdom. He is the shrewd, the benignant, the sagacious, Emerson, writing with pleasant aptitude, like Hesiod or Virgil, of domestic routine, and again of the Conduct of Life, of Manners, Behavior, Prudence, Grace. This is in the philosophic order of progress, from the first principles to the application of them. Some of his followers, however, take him to task, unwilling that the master should venture beyond the glory of his cloud. As for his unique treatises upon Behavior, it was natural that he should be led to think upon that topic, since in gentle bearing, in his sweetness, persuasiveness, and charm of smile and voice, he was not excelled by any personage of our time, and what he said of it is of more value than the sayings of those who think such a matter beneath his regard. His views of civic duty and concerning the welfare of the Republic are the best rejoinder to his early strictures upon Homer and Shakespeare for the temporal and local features of their master-works. As a critic he was ever expectant, on the lookout for something good and new, and sometimes found the one good thing in a man or work and valued it unduly. When he made a complete examination, as in his chapter on Margaret Fuller, he excelled as a critic and delineator. *Parnassus* is not judicial, but oddly made up of his own likings, yet the best rules of criticism are to be found in its preface. With the exception of "English Traits," he published no long treatise upon a single theme. His general essays and lectures, however, constitute a treatise upon Man and Nature, and of themselves would serve as America's adequate con-

See the "Complete Works," 1885.

"*Parnassus*," 1874.

tribution to the English literature of his period. We are told of an unprinted series of his essays that may be grouped as a book on the Natural History of the Intellect. Should these see the light, it would be curious to compare them with the work of some professional logician — with the standard treatise of President Porter, for instance — upon a similar theme. Something in quantity may yet be added to Emerson's literary remains. But it will not differ in quality; we have had the gist of it: for he was a writer who, though his essays were the fruit of a prolonged life, never wrote himself out. Often an author has gained repute by one or two original works, while his ordinary efforts, if not devoted to learned or scientific research, have been commonplace. The flame of Emerson's intellect never fades or flickers, and never irks us. It burns with elemental light, neither of artifice nor of occasion, serene as that of a star, and with an added power to heat the distance which receives it.

VI.

Our most typical and inspiring poet.

In summing up the traits of Emerson one almost ceases to be critical, lest the highest praise may not be quite undue. More than when Bion died, the glades and towns lament him, for he left no heir to the Muse which he taught his pupils. In certain respects he was our most typical poet, having the finest intuition and a living faith in it, — and because there was a sure intellect behind his verse, and because his influence affected not simply the tastes and emotions, but at last the very spirit, of his countrymen. He began where many poets end, seeking at once the upper air, the region of pure thought and ideality. His speech was wisdom, and his poesy its exhalation.

When he failed in either, it seemed to be through excess of divining. His triumphs were full of promise for those who dare to do their best. He was as far above Carlyle as the affairs of the soul and universe are above those of the contemporary, or even the historic, world. His problem, like that of Archimedes, was more than the taking of cities and clash of arms. The poet is unperturbed by temporal distractions; yet poets and dreamers, concerned with the ideal, share in the world's battle equally with men of action and practical life. Only, while the latter fight on the ground, the idealists, like the dauntless ghosts of the Huns and Romans, lift the contest to the air. Emerson was the freest and most ideal of them all, and what came to him by inheritance or prophetic forecast he gave like a victor. He strove not to define the creeds, but to stimulate the intellect and purpose of those who are to make the future. If poetry be that which shapes and elevates, his own was poetry indeed. To know the heart of New England you must hear the songs of his compeers; but listening to those of Emerson, the east and west have yielded to the current of its soul.

Emerson and Longfellow.

The supreme poet will be not alone a seer, but also a persistent artist of the beautiful. Of those who come before the time for such a poet is ripe, Longfellow on the whole has done the most to foster the culture of poetry among us as a liberal art. Emerson has given us thought, the habit of thinking, the will to think for ourselves. He drained the vats of politics and philosophy, for our use, of all that was sweet and fructifying, and taught his people self-judgment, self-reliance, and to set their courses by the stars. He placed chief value upon those primitive laws which are the only sure basis of national law and letters. And as a poet, his verse was the sublimation of his rarest mood, that changed as water into cloud, catching the first beams of sunrise on its broken edges, yet not without dark and vaguely blending spots between. Emerson and Longfellow came at the parting of the ways. They are of the very few whom we now recognize as the true founders of an American literature. No successors with more original art and higher imagination can labor to more purpose. If the arrow hits its mark, the aim was at the bowstring; the river strengthens and broadens, but the sands of gold wash down from near its source.

"A poet hidden in the light of thought."

Not a few are content with that poetry which returns again and again to its primal conceptions, yet suggests infinite pathways and always inspires, — the poetry of a hermitage whose Lar is Nature, and whose well-spring flows with clear and shining Thought. To such, — who care less for sustained flights of objective song, who can withdraw themselves from passion and dramatic life, who gladly accept isolated cadences and scattered, though exquisite, strains of melody in lieu of symphonic music "wandering on as loth to die," — Emerson will seem the most precious of our native poets. He will not satisfy those who look for the soul incarnate in sensuous and passionate being.

"Unbodied joy"

Such readers, with Professor Dowden, find him the type of the New World transcendentalist, the creature of the drying American climate, one "whose nervous energy has been exalted," so "that he loves light better than warmth." He is not the minstrel for those who would study men in action and suffering, rather than as heirs to knowledge and the raptured mind. He is not a warrior, lover, raconteur, dramatist, but an evangelist and seer. The greatest poet must be all in one, and I have said that Emerson was among the foremost to avow it. Modern bards poorly satisfy him, being meagre of design, and failing to guide and console. Wordsworth was an exception, yet he had "written longer than he was inspired." Tennyson, with all his tune and color, "climbs no mount of vision." Even Shakespeare was too traditional, though one learns from him that "tradition supplies a better fable than any invention can." In face of the greatest he felt that "the world still wants its poet-priest, a reconciler, who shall not trifle with Shakespeare the player, nor shall grope in graves with Swedenborg the mourner; but who shall see, speak, and act with equal inspiration." Thus clearly he conceived of the poet's office, and equally was he assured that he himself was not, and could not be, the perfect musician. He chose the part of the forerunner and inspirer, and when the true poet shall come to America, it will be because such an one as Emerson has gone before him and prepared the way for his song, his vision, and his recognition.

Emerson's conception of the future bard.

CHAPTER VI.

HENRY WADSWORTH LONGFELLOW.

I.

Fortunate in life and death.

OUR poet of grace and sentiment left us in the after-glow of an almost ideal career. He had lived at the right time, and with the gift of years; and he died before the years came for him to say, I have no pleasure in them. Not all the daughters of music were brought low. He scarcely could have realized that people were calling his work elementary, that men whose originality had isolated them, like Emerson and Browning, — and even metrical experts, the inventors of new modes, — were gaining favor with a public which had somewhat outgrown him; that he was to be slighted for the very qualities which had made him beloved and famous, or that other qualities, too long needed, were to be overvalued as if partly for the need's sake.

But they are wrong who make light of Longfellow's service as an American poet. His admirers may form no longer a critical majority, yet he surely helped to quicken the New World sense of beauty, and to lead a movement which precedes the rise of a national school. I think that the poet himself, reading his own sweet songs, felt the apostolic nature of his mission, — that it was religious, in the etymological sense of the word, the binding back of America to the Old World taste and imagination. Our true rise of Poe-

His mission apostolic.

try may be dated from Longfellow's method of exciting an interest in it, as an expression of beauty and feeling, at a time when his countrymen were ready for something more various and human than the current meditations on nature. It was inevitable that he should first set his face toward a light beyond the sea, and I have said that his youthful legend aptly was *Outre Mer*. An escape was in order from the asceticism which two centuries had both modified and confirmed. How could this be effected? Not at once by the absolute presentation of beauty. A Keats, pledged to this alone, could not have propitiated the ancestral spirit. Puritanism was opposed to beauty as a strange god, and to sentiment as an idle thing. Longfellow so adapted the beauty and sentiment of other lands to the convictions of his people, as to beguile their reason through the finer senses, and speedily to satisfy them that loveliness and righteousness may go together. His poems, like pictures seen on household walls, were a protest against barrenness and the symptoms of a new taste.

Effect of his early works.

They made their way more readily, also, by their response to the inherited Anglo-Saxon instincts of his own region. His early predilections, strengthened during a stay in Germany, were chiefly for the poetry and romance of that land. He read his heart in its songs, which he so loved to translate for us. A new generation may be at a loss to conceive the effect of Longfellow's work when it first began to appear. I may convey something of this by what is at once a memory and an illustration. Take the case of a child whose Sunday outlook was restricted, in a decaying Puritan village, to a wooden meeting-house of the old Congregational type. The interior — plain, colorless, rigid with dull white pews and dismal galleries

A charm recalled and illustrated.

— increased the spiritual starvation of a young nature unconsciously longing for color and variety. Many a child like this one, on a first holiday visit to the town, seeing the vine-grown walls, the roofs and arches, of a graceful Gothic church, has felt a sense of something rich and strange; and many, now no longer children, can remember that the impression upon entrance was such as the stateliest cathedral now could not renew. The columns and tinted walls, the ceiling of oak and blue, the windows of gules and azure and gold, — the service, moreover, with its chant and organ-roll, — all this enraptured and possessed them. To the one relief hitherto afforded them, that of nature's picturesqueness, — which even Calvinism endured without compunction, — was added a new joy, a glimpse of the beauty and sanctity of human art. A similar delight awaited the first readers of Longfellow's prose and verse. Here was a painter and romancer indeed, who had journeyed far and returned with gifts for all at home, and who promised often and again to

> —— "sing a more wonderful song
> Or tell a more marvellous tale."

His genius not creative, but the fosterer of taste and ideality.

And thus it chanced that, well as he afterward sang of his own sea and shore, he now is said to have been the least national of our poets. His verse, it is true, was like a pulsatory cord, sustaining our newborn ideality with nourishment from the mother-land, until it grew to vigor of its own. Yet he was more widely read than his associates, and seemed to foreigners the incumbent American laureate. His native themes, like some of Tennyson's, were chosen with deliberation and as if for their availability. But from the first he was a poet of sentiment, and equally a craftsman of unerring taste. He always gave of his best; neither toil nor trouble could dismay him until art had done its perfect work. It was a kind of genius, — his sure perception of the fit and attractive. Love flows to one whose work is lovely. Besides, he was a devotee to one calling, — not a critic, journalist, lecturer, or man of affairs, — and even his prose romances were akin to poems. A long and spotless life was pledged to song, and verily he had his reward. Successors may find a weakness in his work, but who can rival him in bearing and reputation? His worldly wisdom was of the gospel kind, so gently tempered as to breed no evil. His life and works together were an edifice fairly built, — the House Beautiful, whose air is peace, where repose and calm are ministrant, and where the raven's croak, symbol of the unrest of a more perturbed genius, is never heard. Thus the clerkly singer fulfilled his office, — which was not in the least creative, — and had the tributes he most desired: love and honor during his life-time, and the assurance that no song of his took flight but to rest again and again "in the heart of a friend."

II.

An auspicious time.

POETS, like the cicalas, have occasion to envy those who compass their song and sustenance together. Few can pledge with Longfellow their lives, or even frequent hours, to the labor they delight in. There was, in fact, an "opening," — a need for just the service he could render. The circumstances of his birth and training were propitious and worked to one end. Neither he nor Hawthorne was the mere offspring of an environment. There was nothing special in the little down-east school of Bowdoin, sixty years ago, to breed the leaders of our imaginative prose and verse.

But the time was ripe; there was an unspoken demand for richer life and thought, to which such natures, and the intellects of Channing and Emerson, were sure to respond. And the concurrence certainly was special: that Longfellow, descended from Pilgrim and Puritan stock, the child of a cultured household, should be born not only with a poet's voice and ear, but with an aptitude for letters amounting to a sixth sense, — a bookishness assimilative as that of Hunt or Lamb; that he should be reared in a typical Eastern town, open alike to polite influences and to the freshness and beauty of the northern sea; that such a youth, buoyant and manly, but averse to the coarser sports, gentle, pure, — one who in France would have become at first an abbé, — should in New England be made a college professor at nineteen, and commissioned to visit Europe and complete his studies; that ten years later, having ended the pleasant drudgery of his apprenticeship, he should find himself settled for life at Harvard, the centre of learning, and under few obligations that did not assist, rather than impede, his chosen ministry of song. Here he was to have health, friendship, ease, the opportunity for travel, abundant and equal work and fame, with scarcely an abrupt turn, or flurry, or drought or storm, to the very end. Even his duties served in the direction of a literary bent, confirming his mastery of languages whose poetry and romance were his treasure-house. He wrote his text-books at an age when most poets go a-gypsying. When twenty-six, he made his translation of the "Coplas de Manrique," — a rendering so grave and sonorous that, if now first printed, it would be caught up like FitzGerald's "Rubáiyát of Omar," instead of going to the paper mill. It indicated, more than his original work of this period, that

Henry Wadsworth Longfellow: born in Portland, Me., Feb. 27, 1807.

"Coplas de Manrique," 1833.

a true poetic method was forming in a country where Berkeley's muse thus far had made no course of empire. A few essays, always on literature or the languages, complete the round of his miscellanies, the last being contributed to a review in 1840. After that time he gave up all critical writing whatsoever.

Works in prose: "Outre-Mer," 1835.

Outre-Mer, a young poet's sketch-book, reports his first transition from cloister life to travel and experience. It is a journey of sentiment, if not a sentimental journey, and made in the blithesome spirit of a troubadour. All the world was Arcady, — a land of beauty and romance; and these he found, caring for nothing else, in sunny nooks of France, Italy, and Spain, as deftly as the botanist picks out his ferns and forest flowers. Our poet's herbarium had a gift to keep its blossoms unfaded. His road-glasses illuminate the wayside: our modern travellers use stronger lenses, and see things through and through, but with the old illusions we have lost the best of all things — zest. *Hyperion* showed what changes four years can bring about while still the man is young: it is the thoughtful, and somewhat too fond, fantasy of the same pilgrim after more knowledge of the verities of life. The atmosphere of this book is that of Switzerland and Germany; but its shadows came from the maker's heart. He had been bereaved. The opening phrase is grief, a poet's grief, that consoles itself with imagery: "The setting of a great hope is like the setting of the sun. . . . We look forward into the coming lonely night. The soul withdraws into itself. Then stars arise, and the night is holy." This precise, epicurean touch, the application of art to feeling, was new in our authorship. Void of real anguish or passion, it still suggested an ideal, — a purpose beyond mere book-craft. The sketches, diversified with

"Hyperion," 1839.

not too frequent musing, the wedding of sound to sense, the daintiness of words, the feeble plot, all bear witness that "Hyperion" is the work of an idyllist. The vague manner, with its impression of rest sought in restlessness, and even the broken story, were borrowed, doubtless, from "Titan." The book naturally became the companion of all romantic pilgrims of the Rhine, for the true German spirit is here; its sentiment and fancy alike are seized by a master of the picturesque. He "knew the beauteous river all by heart, — every rock and ruin, every echo, every legend. The ancient castles, . . . they were all his; for his thoughts dwelt in them, and the wind told him tales." With Jean Paul we have Heine, also, who might have conceived the grotesque episode of Frau Kranich's "tea" in Ems. The romance and spooning of "Hyperion," and its moral conclusions, are food for adolescents; but it is easier to laugh at youth than to possess it. And this is Longfellow's youth throughout, — the frankest of confessions. Paul Flemming "buried himself in books; in old dusty books." Read the list of them, from the Nibelungenlied down, and see the diet that he garnished with grapes and Liebfrauenmilch and love-making and moonlight dreams. "How beautiful it is to love!" Ah! how happy to be young, and in love; to have known sorrow, and to use it as a foil; to visit and read the great world, yet not to be corrupted by it, still to keep a pure heart that has no taste for recklessness and vice; through all to recall one lesson: "Look not mournfully into the Past. It comes not back again. Wisely improve the Present. It is thine. Go forth to meet the shadowy Future, without fear, and with a manly heart."

Influence of Richter and Heine.

"The Scroll of Youth."

The chief import of the poet's romances was their

bearing upon his own purpose. He fixed his rules of life by writing them down. His second maxim is found in *Kavanagh*, a tale with less freshness than "Hyperion," but fashioned with the hand of greater mastery, that of a writer in his prime. Its personages are more distinctly drawn, and it was his brief and nearest approach to a novel. We have a transcript of New England village life, an atmosphere of breeding and refinement, and some pertinent criticism on literary and social topics. As before, the gist of the tale is in a text, placed, with due regard to convention, at the beginning: —

The poet's rules of life.

"Kavanagh," 1849.

> "The flighty purpose never is o'ertook
> Unless the deed go with it."

This bit of wisdom had been deeply considered by the author. By way of strengthening himself against a dreamer's temptation to be derelict, he worked it, one might say, into this "sampler" of a tale. Those who are fond of citing the formula, that genius is only a talent for persistent work, have reason to place our poet well in the van of their examples. Yet I fancy that only men of talent will heartily subscribe to this definition. Be this as it may, Longfellow's prose tales show us his equipment, and give the clew to his well-adjusted life. It was plain, also, that he was a born romanticist, in full sympathy with the German school. We shall see that, as a poet, he followed a romantic method, to the disapproval of those who feel that nothing in the New World should be done as it has been done elsewhere. It is difficult, however, to explain why even things at home should not be treated according to the genius of the designer. After strange experiments, we just now are discovering that the colonial architecture, so much like that of Cromwell's

Romantic tendency.

England, is of all our styles the best adapted to the Atlantic States; and it still becomes us to be modest in defining the types that American art and poetry finally will assume. The critical question, I take it, is not what fashion should be outlawed, but whether the thing done is good of its kind.

Nothing afterward tempted Longfellow from poetic composition, except the illustrations of the *Poetry of Europe*, many of which were his own translations, and, late in life, the diversion of editing *Poems of Places*, and the heroic labor of his complete version of "The Divine Comedy," a work to which I shall refer again.

III.

Poetical works.

LONGFELLOW'S juvenile poems have been collected recently. Those printed, before his graduation, in "The Literary Gazette," resemble the verse of Bryant and Percival, the former of whom he looked upon as his master. Tracings of browsing in the usual pasture grounds are strangely absent: I sometimes wonder if he had an early taste for the Elizabethan poets, or, indeed, for any English worthy, since no modern author has shown fewer signs of this in youth. The *Voices of the Night*, his own first collection, was postponed until after a long experience of translation and prose work. It appeared in his thirty-third year, and met with instant favor. Only nine new pieces were in the book; these, with the translations following, have characteristics that his verse continued to display. The Prelude recalls that of Heine's third edition of the "Reisebilder" (*Das ist der alte Märchenwald*), then just published. Later pieces show that Longfellow caught the manner of this poet, whose principles he severely condemned. The German's

"Voices of the Night," 1839.

Foreign influences.

rhythm and reverie were repeated in "The Day is Done," "The Bridge," "Twilight," etc., but not his passion and scorn. The influence of Uhland is equally manifest elsewhere. Prototypes of Longfellow's maturer work are found in "The Reaper," "The Psalm of Life," and "The Beleaguered City." "The Midnight Mass for the Dying Year," against which Poe brought a mincing charge of plagiarism, is as strong and conjuring as anything its author lived to write. The Translations deserved high praise. The stately "Coplas" re-appears. Various renderings from German lyric poets, such as "The Happiest Land," "Beware," and "Into the Silent Land," were new originals, examples of a talent peculiarly his own. Given a task which he liked, — with a pattern supplied by another, — and few could equal him. He made his copies in various measures and from many tongues. An essay in hexameter, the version of Tegnér's "Children of the Lord's Supper," preceded his original poems in that form. Even after completing his "Dante," he loved to toy with such work. I have heard him say that he longed to make an English translation of Homer, upon the method which Voss had used to such advantage.

"Ballads and Other Poems," 1841.

Cp. "Victorian Poets": pp. 158–160.

His volume of 1841, *Ballads and Other Poems*, may be likened to Tennyson's volume of the ensuing year, in that it confirmed its author's standing and indicated the full extent of his genius as a poet. It was choice in its way, suggesting taste rather than fertility; choicely presented, also, for with it came the fashion, new to this country, of printing verse attractively and in a shape that seeks the hand. The poet's matter, if often gleaned from foreign literatures, was novel to his readers, and his style distinct from that of any English contemporary. The book

The poet's quality now apparent.

contains examples of all the classes into which his poems seem to divide themselves, and may be examined with its successors. One sees, forthwith, that Longfellow's impulse was to make a poem, above all, *interesting*. He was no word-monger, no winder of coil upon coil about a subtle theme. He changed his topics, for some topic he must have, and one that suited him. A cheerful acceptance of the lessons of life was the moral, suggested in many lyrics, which commended him to all virtuous, home-keeping folk, but in the end poorly served him with the critics.

Lyrical homilies.

He gained a foothold by his least poetic work, — verse whose easy lessons are adjusted to common needs; by the "Psalm of Life," "Excelsior," "Prometheus," and "The Ladder of St. Augustine," — little sermons in rhyme that are sure to catch the ear and to become hackneyed as a sidewalk song. He often taught, by choice, the primary class, and the upper form is slow to forget it.

Sentiment.

Next above these pretty homilies are his poems of sentiment and twilight brooding. "The Reaper and the Flowers," "Footsteps of Angels," "Maidenhood," "Resignation," and "Haunted Houses" came home to pensive and gentle natures. Lowell has written a few kindred pieces, such as "The Changeling" and "The First Snow-fall."

Picturesqueness.

A still higher class, testing Longfellow's eye for the suggestive side of a theme and his art to make the most of it, includes "The Fire of Drift-Wood," "The Lighthouse," "Sand of the Desert," "The Jewish Cemetery," and "The Arsenal." In poems of this sort he was a skilled designer, yet they were something more than art for art's sake. Owing to the tenderness seldom absent from his work, he often has been called a poet of the Affections. It must be owned that he was a poet of the Tastes as well. He combined beauty with feeling in lyrical trifles which rival those of Tennyson and other masters of technique, and was almost our earliest maker of verse that might be termed exquisite. "The Bells of Lynn" and "The Tide Rises, the Tide Falls," show that the hand which polished "Curfew" and "The Arrow and the Song" was sensitive to the last.

Taste.

Among obvious tests of a poet are his voice, facility, and general aim. Longfellow's verse was refined and pleasing; his purpose, evidently not that of a doctrinaire. The anti-slavery poems did not come, like Whittier's, from a fiery heart, or rival Lowell's in humor and disdain. They simply manifest his recognition and artistic treatment of an existing evil. The ballad of "The Quadroon Girl" is a poem, not a prophecy, with a pathos beautified by certain "values," as a painter might term them, — the tropic shore, the lagoon, the island planter's daughter and slave. Of the higher tests of poetic genius, — spontaneity, sweep, intellect, imaginative power, — what examples has he left us? At times the highest of all, imagination, in passages where he foregoes the conceits and fancies that so possessed him. We have it in the "Midnight Mass"; in "Sir Humphrey Gilbert"; in "The Spanish Jew's Tale," when

Not a polemic reformer.

Tests of genius.

> —— "straight into the city of the Lord
> The Rabbi leaped with the Death-Angel's sword,
> And through the streets there swept a sudden breath
> Of something there unknown, which men call death."

At times also we have what is of almost equal worth, imaginative treatment. This is felt in the effect of his very best lyrics, a series of ballads, with "The Skeleton in Armor" at their front both in date and in merit. This vigorous poem opens with a rare abrupt-

Imaginative Ballads. "The Skeleton in Armor," etc.

ness. The author, full of the Norseland, was inspirited by his novel theme, and threw off a ringing carol of the sea-rover's training, love, adventure. The cadences and imagery belong together, and the measure, that of Drayton's "Agincourt," is better than any new one for its purpose. Even the poet's conceits are braver than their wont: —

> " Then from those cavernous eyes
> Pale flashes seemed to rise,
> As when the northern skies
> Gleam in December;
> And, like the water's flow
> Under December's snow,
> Came a dull voice of woe
> From the heart's chamber."

Elsewhere he is as resonant as the bard of England's "King Harry": —

> " And as to catch the gale
> Round veered the flapping sail,
> Death! was the helmsman's hail,
> Death without quarter!
> Midships with iron keel
> Struck we her ribs of steel;
> Down her black hulk did reel
> Through the black water!"

To old-fashioned people this heroic ballad, written over forty years ago, is worth a year's product of what I may term Kensington-stitch verse. A few others, mostly of the sea, count high in any estimate of Longfellow. "The Wreck of the Hesperus," though not without blemishes, "Sir Humphrey Gilbert," "Victor Galbraith," and "The Cumberland" are treated, I think, imaginatively. Boker's noble stanzas on the sinking of the Cumberland follow more closely the old ballad style, but Longfellow plainly found a style of his own. His "occasional" poems were equally fe-

Occasional Poems.

licitous: witness the touching, sympathetic imagery of "The Two Angels," the joyous grace of the chanson for Agassiz's birthday. "Hawthorne," "Bayard Taylor," and "Killed at the Ford" are examples of the fitness with which his emotion and poetic quality corresponded, each to each. But neither war nor grief ever too much disturbed the artist soul. Tragedy went no deeper with him than its pathos; it was another element of the beautiful. Death was a luminous transition. "The Warden of the Cinque Ports" is all melody and association. He made a scenic threnody, knowing the laureate would supply an intellectual characterization of the Iron Duke. His fancy dwells upon the ancient and high-sounding title, the mist and sunrise of the Channel, and the rolling salute from all those rampart guns, that yet could not arouse the old Field-Marshal from his slumber. Tennyson fills his grander strophes with the sturdy valor and wisdom of the last great Englishman, but within our own poet's bounds the result is just as undeniably a poem.

A metrical expert.

Longfellow, employing regular forms of verse, was flexible where many are awkward, — at ease in his fine clothes. "Rain in Summer," "To a Child," and a few longer poems yet to be examined, such as "The Building of the Ship," are written with a free hand. In his latter period he often used an anapestic movement, first discoverable in "The Saga of King Olaf" and "Enceladus," afterward in "Belisarius," "The Chamber over the Gate," and "Helen of Tyre." The impression conveyed is that we listen to one whose day for elaborate song is past, but whose voice still warbles in the fresh break of spring or the melting twilight of thankfulness and rest. With age, his natural tenderness grew upon him, as men's traits will for good and bad. "The Children's Hour" is one of the

"My Lost Youth."

inimitable fireside songs that made this "old moustache" the children's poet. Another delightful lyric, "My Lost Youth," was the utterance of a man who in middle age looked in his own heart to write, and found it warm and true. To comprehend its charm and sincerity, one, perchance, must also have loitered in youth along the piers, sending his hopes far across the whispering ocean to the untried world; must himself remember

> —— "the black wharves and the slips,
> And the sea-tides tossing free;
> And Spanish sailors with bearded lips,
> And the beauty and mystery of the ships,
> And the magic of the sea."

Some breezy dome of trees, with sounds and shadows like those of Deering's woods, must still haunt his memory, if he would recall

> "The song and the silence in the heart,
> That in part are prophecies, and in part
> Are longings wild and vain;
> And the voice of that fitful song
> Sings on, and is never still:
> 'A boy's will is the wind's will,
> And the thoughts of youth are long, long thoughts.'"

Of all these poems, the swallow-flights of many seasons, not one falls short of a certain standard of grace and correctness; and the same may be said of the author's more pretentious works, to which we now come. Meanwhile it is to be noted that he was the first American to compose sustained narrative-poems that gained and kept a place in literature. In fact, since the Georgian period, there has been no other poet of our tongue, save Tennyson, whose longer productions have been greeted by the public with the interest bestowed upon the successive works of novelists in the front rank.

IV.

"EVANGELINE," the first of these tales in verse, was written — as I have said of "In Memoriam," that very different production — when its author had reached the age of forty, with his powers in full maturity, and it remains his typical poem. Like "Hermann and Dorothea," it is composed in hexameter, as befits a bucolic love story. Longfellow's choice of this measure, in defiance of a noble army of censors, proves that he had, much as he shrank from discussion, the full courage of his convictions upon a point in literary art. He lived for poetry; his tastes were definite, and he felt himself justified in respecting them.

Sustained narrative poems.

"Evangeline," 1847.

Within a recent period several noteworthy extensions have been made to the technical range of English verse. Among these are: the use by Tennyson of the stanzaic form of "In Memoriam"; the example of a long poem in unrhymed trochaics, by Longfellow; Swinburne's forcible handling of anapestic measures; more recently, the revival of elegant romance forms, by the new English school. Preceding these in date we have Longfellow's success in familiarizing the "English hexameter," the measure of "Evangeline" and "Miles Standish." The popularity of those idyls assuredly proved that the common folk, in spite of critics, do not find the verse a stumbling-block. They read it, when gracefully written, without suspecting that it is not a musical and natural English form. The question of hexameter has been argued to little purpose, in consequence of a mist which has hid the true issue from the perception of both parties to the dispute. The verse usually is examined, by its friends and opponents, from the scholar's point of view. To Mr. Swinburne, hexameters are "ugly bastards of

The question of "English Hexameter" verse. Cp. "Victorian Poets": p. 251.

Wrongly argued, from the scholar's point of view.

verse"; even those of Mr. Arnold have "no metrical feet at all," but sound like "anapests broken up and driven wrong"; Clough's are admirable "studies in graduated prose"; Hawtrey's "faultless, English, hexametrical," but only "a well-played stroke," not continuable; Kingsley's "Andromeda," the "one good poem extant in that pernicious metre," and even Kingsley's feet are but "loose, rhymeless anapests." Now "Andromeda," a delicious poem for poets, never will commend its measure to the multitude, since it never will reach them. But if such lines as these, —

Kingsley's "Andromeda."

"Far through the wine-dark depths of the crystal, the gardens of Nereus,
Coral and sea-fan and tangle, the blooms and the palms of the ocean,"

are essentially anapestic, it is because one chooses to read them so; and any dactylic verse of Homer may be transposed in the same way by reading it accentually and ignoring the first and last syllables. When Mr. Swinburne adds, "Such as pass elsewhere for English hexameter, I do hope, are impossible to Eton," he strikes the key-note of the misunderstanding. The same premise is always implied, to wit: that classical analogies should govern our opinion of this measure. Unfortunately, I say, even the arguments of its defenders are based on the notion that the modern verse may approximate to the antique, in which effort, of course, it always must fail. Poe, in his turn, opposed Longfellow's hexameters because they were not classical; yet he unconsciously paid tribute to them as an English form of verse, when he said that their admirers were "deceived by the facility with which some of these verses may be read!" Lord Derby anticipated Mr. Swinburne's "pernicious metre," in denounc-

A wrong premise.

ing "that pestilent heresy of the so-called English hexameter," which "can only be pressed into the service by a violation of every rule of prosody." Whether or not the noble translator, deprived of rules of prosody, would have found it hard to write verse at all, it is plain that here again crops out the fallacy of the discussion. Fixed rules of quantitative or classical verse must be put out of mind. The question ought to be, simply: Is the verse, in six feet, of "Evangeline" or "Andromeda" a good and readable measure for an English poem?

The real point at issue.

Bryant, a good writer of blank verse, disliked a measure which he found unsuited to his slow and dignified movement. Professor Lewis took the ground of Mr. Bryant, whose Homer he so much praised. Mr. Lang is on the same side, and has said that not even Professor Arnold can alter his opinion. Yet the late Professor Hadley, an almost matchless scholar, advocated this verse for Homeric translation. Messrs. Lowell, Higginson, and Stoddard are among its friends. Matthew Arnold, in the delightful papers "On Translating Homer," has made his strongest plea for the English hexameter by unconsciously granting that its close approximation to the antique type must be the result of adroit labor, not of unstudied expression. Such a result justly might be deemed an artifice, distinct from natural English verse. And Mr. Arnold, in view of the reception awarded "Evangeline," also sees that the dislike of our present English hexameter is "rather among the professional critics than the general public." A liking for it, on the part of many poets, is evident from their successive experiments. Longfellow's foreign studies influenced his own decision in its favor; since then we have had Kingsley's "Andromeda," Clough's "Bothie," Howells's "Clem-

Views of other friends and opponents.

Arnold "On Translating Homer."

Recent poems in hexameter.

ent," Taylor's rhythmic "Pastorals," and, more recently, Mr. Munby's idyl of "Dorothy" in the elegaic measure, and its Hellenic counter-type, the "Delphic Days" of Mr. Snider. But while there are both faith and practice in favor of the hexametric verse, it is still in a stage of growth. Mr. Arnold a second time reaches the mark when he implies that its capabilities are not yet evident; that, "even now, if a version of the Iliad in English hexameter were made by a poet who, like Mr. Longfellow, has that indefinable quality which renders him popular, — something *attractive* in his talent which communicates itself to his verses, — it would have a great success among the general public." He expected yet to see an improved type of this verse, which should excel Voss's by as much as Shakespeare's blank verse excels that of Schiller. This may or may not be; but the capabilities of the measure will not be understood until some fine poet — combining the simplicity of Longfellow and the vigor of Clough, and free from the sing-song of the one and the roughness of the other — shall make it the vehicle of passion, incident, imagination. To bring out its full rhythm, while depending chiefly on accent, — the natural basis of English verse, — the ear will pay regard to such effects of quantity as the language proffers. Purely quantitative English verse, at any length, is out of the equation. To the samples of it often printed by amateurs in "Blackwood" and elsewhere, Canning's outburst, "Dactylics call'st thou them? God help thee, silly one!" may be justly applied, but not to the hexameter of Kingsley and Bayard Taylor. Call the new measure what you will — something else, if possible, than the term applied to the verse of Homer and Lucretius, for it assuredly is not composed of quantitative dactyls and spondees. But it will have six feet,

Accent and quantity.

Ultimate characteristics. Cp. "Victorian Poets": p. 251.

and natural breaks and cæsuras, and will be more or less dactylic; it may also have anapestic variations, and trochees quite as often as spondees. To sum up all, its music, sweep, and inspiriting effect will depend entirely upon the genius of the poet who writes it.

The use of this measure for translation from the Greek and Latin poets I have discussed in the chapter on Bryant. Longfellow could not be the supreme translator of Homer; but if there was nothing of the Grecian in him, there was much of the Latinist, and with Virgil's polished muse he might have been quite at ease. Meanwhile, the popularity of our new hexameter with simple readers who know little of the Homeric roll, the Sicilian *psithurisma*, or Virgil's liquid flow, has been demonstrated against all theorists by the record of "Evangeline." The poet's friends told him he must take a familiar metre, that hexameters "would never do." He found, as reported by David Macrae, that his "thoughts would run in hexameter," and declared that the measure would "take root in English soil." "It is a measure," he said, "that suits all themes. It can fly low like a swallow, and at any moment dart skyward. . . . What fine hexameters we have in the Bible: *Husbands, love your wives, and be not bitter against them*; and this line, *God is gone up with a shout, the Lord with the sound of a trumpet.* Nothing could be grander than that!" Over-dactylic, and therefore monotonous, as Longfellow's hexameters often are, they have the merit of being smooth to read, without analysis, like any other English verse. This primary, easy lilt was needed for an introduction, until, stage by stage, the popular ear should be wonted to more varied forms, and the scholar brought to realize that here is a true and idiomatic English verse, however distinct from that which he learned in the classes.

See pp. 89–91.

Popular success of Longfellow's experiment.

Notwithstanding its primitive and loose construction, the verse of "Evangeline" is at times vigorously wrought and sonorous: —

> "Wild through the dark colonnades and corridors leafy the blast rang,
> Breaking the seal of silence, and giving tongues to the forest.
> Soundless above them the banners of moss just stirred to the music.
> Multitudinous echoes awoke and died in the distance,
> Over the watery floor, and beneath the reverberant branches."

"Evangeline" the flower of American idyls.

And with the measure that came to him, the poet had chanced upon an idyllic story, seemingly made for its use, and wholly after his liking. A beautiful, pathetic tradition of American history, remote enough to gather a poetic halo, and yet fresh with sweet humanities; tinged with provincial color which he knew and loved, and in its course taking on the changing atmospheres of his own land; pastoral at first, then broken into action, and afterward the record of shifting scenes that made life a pilgrimage and dream. There are few dramatic episodes; there is but one figure whom we follow, — that one the most touching of all, the betrothed Evangeline searching for her lover, through weary years and over half an unknown world. There are chance pictures of Acadian fields, New World rivers, prairies, bayous, forests, by moonlight and starlight and midday; glimpses, too, of picturesque figures, artisans and farmers, soldiery, trappers, boatmen, emigrants and priests. But the poem already is a little classic, and will remain one, just as surely as "The Vicar of Wakefield," "The Deserted Village," or any other sweet and pious idyl of our English tongue; yet we find its counterpart more nearly, I think, in some faultless miniature of the purest French school. Evangeline, as she

"Sat by some lonely grave, and thought that perchance in its bosom
He was already at rest, and she longed to slumber beside him,"

though the subject of artists, needs no other painter than her poet, through whose verse the music of her name and the legend of her wanderings will be long perpetuated. There are flaws and petty fancies and homely passages in "Evangeline"; but this one poem, thus far the flower of American idyls, known in all lands, I will not approach in a critical spirit. There are rooms in every house where one treads with softened footfall. Accept it as the poet left it, the mark of our advance at that time in the art of song,—his own favorite, of which he justly might be fond, since his people loved it with him, and him always for its sake.

"The Song of Hiawatha," 1855.

Its measure.

The advantage of a new field, to which later authors, like Harte and Cable, are somewhat indebted, was of full service to our poet, not only on his provincial excursions, but also in the one successful attempt that has been made to treat in numbers the customs and legends of our Indian tribes. This gain was strengthened by the novelty of the rhymeless trochaic dimeter used for *Hiawatha*, a measure then practically unknown to English verse. He probably would not have ventured to compose his Algic Edda in this monotonous time-beat, had he not made sure of its effect in older literatures, and mainly, as was noted at the time, in the Finnish epic of "Kalevala." The result, on the whole, justified his course. "Hiawatha" is a forest-poem; it is fragrant with the woods, fresh with the sky and waters of the breezy north. The Indian traditions, like those of Finland, are the myths of an untutored race; they would seem puerile and affected in any but the most primitive of chanting measures. As it is, one feels that the nicest skill was required to protect the verse from gathering an effect of burlesque or commonplace; yet this it never does. The fable is not of a stimulating kind. Grown-up readers, I suspect, seldom go through it consecutively. To read here and there and at odd times, it is in every way pleasurable. It was, in a sense, the poet's most genuine addition to our native literature. Previous endeavors to make imaginative verse from aboriginal material had signally failed: witness the ludicrous heroics of the Knickerbocker poets, whose conventional ideals were utterly discarded by Longfellow. He alone had the gift to blend the kindred myths of Indian fancy in mellow and artistic simplicity; to cull from Schoolcraft what was really essential, and make it more charming for us than a sheer invention possibly could be. He made the field his own, with little room for after-comers. "Hiawatha" is the one poem that beguiles the reader to see the birch and ash, the heron and eagle and deer, as they seem to the red man himself, and to join for the moment in his simple creed and wonderment. Such is the half-dramatic merit of the work, and it was only by a true exercise of the imagination that a poet, himself no familiar of the wild-wood life, could sit in his study and utilize the books relating to it: an equally true exercise, I think, though upon a less majestic basis, with that of the poet who mastered the Arthurian legends of his own historic race and island, and wrote the "Idylls of the King." Longfellow's use of the Indian dialect and names is delightful. These cantos remind us that poetry is the natural speech of primitive races; the "song" of Hiawatha has the epic quality that pertains to early ballads, the highest enjoyment of which belongs to later ages

First successful treatment of the Indian legends.

and to the creature that Whitman terms the civilizee. He alone can relish to the full the illusions which the poet has recaptured for his episode of "The Building of the Canoe," the death of Minnehaha, and Hiawatha's mystical farewell.

"*The Courtship of Miles Standish*," 1858.

When a companion-piece to "Evangeline" appeared, every one made haste to acquaint himself with the love experience of the demure Priscilla, loyal John Alden, and bluff Captain Miles. Even now, if we had some young Tennysons and Longfellows, poetic ideals might not wholly give way to the novelist's photographs of every-day life. The author's tact guided him to the prettiest tradition of Pilgrim times. We have a romantic picture of the Plymouth settlement, with its far-away round of human life and action, through which the tide of love went flowing then as now. The bucolic wedding-scene at the close is a fine subject for the pastoral canvas. *The Courtship of Miles Standish* was an advance upon "Evangeline," so far as concerns structure and the distinct characterization of personages. A merit of the tale is the frolicsome humor here and there, lighting up the gloom that blends with our conception of the Pilgrim inclosure, and we see that comic and poetic elements are not at odds in the scheme of a bright imagination. The verse, though stronger, is more labored than that of "Evangeline"; some of the lines are prosaic, almost inadmissible. There are worse, however, in the poet's last example of hexameter, the Quaker story of "Elizabeth,"—which was written rather to fill out the "Tales of a Wayside Inn" than from any special inspiration. Nor does the Plymouth idyl show much sympathy on the part of the author with the ancestral environment, but chiefly a cavalier perception of what romance and grace there might have been in the good old colony time.

Longfellow's dramatic poems.

His works in dramatic form plainly represent the craving of a versatile poet to win laurels in every province of his art. But to compose a living drama requires just that special faculty, if not the highest, which is denied to nine out of ten. Longfellow, perchance, might have made himself either a dramatist or a novelist, if he had gone into training as doggedly as others, born essayists or poets, who have gained the secret of novel-writing through practice, aided by popular encouragement. He made a fair beginning as a romancer with "Hyperion," and even as a dramatist by the clever play of *The Spanish Student*, — equipped with the properties of a country and literature so well understood by him. As a drama, that remains his best achievement. When the desire to better it possessed him, the outcome was a motley series of writings in the form under review: one, a frigid contribution to the pseudo-antique verse at which all college-bred poets feel competent to try their hands. Nothing with the true Grecian flavor could come out of his Italian and Gothic tendencies. *Pandora*, besides reminding us of Taylor's version of the Second Part of Faust, is in every way a forced effort, and, like "Judas Maccabæus," would go a-begging if the work of a new man. The Trilogy of *Christus*, as a whole, is a disjointed failure. Parts First and Third, "The Divine Tragedy," and "The New England Tragedies," exhibit the skill to choose imposing subjects and build a framework, but little of the power required for their treatment. We have the form, the personages, and situations, rarely the action and noble fire. The author's shortcomings are even more conspicuous than Tennyson's, and by as much as his intellectual power was the less absolute. His theory that the Scriptural language should be reproduced

"The Spanish Student," 1843.

Various weak and faulty dramas.

Cp. "Victorian Poets": pp. 189, 190, 413;

grew out of the fact that he could invent no other, and resulted in a barren paraphrase of what is fine in its own place. What sublime themes! — the life and passion of Christ, the Golden Legend of Christendom, the tragedy of Puritan superstition, — and how tamely the first and last of these are handled! Their consolidation was manifestly an after-thought, to give a semblance of strength to the whole. Where we have the poet's own style, as in the soliloquies of Mary, Simon, Helen, it is a subjective utterance of the Cambridge scholar at his desk. The Interludes are put in to brace the effect, like the sham buttresses of a faulty building. He should not have preempted the sable field of the Quaker and witch persecutions, unless he felt in his utmost fibre the nerve to occupy it. The temptation was strong; the result, contrasted with Hawthorne's prose treatment of kindred subjects, is deplorable.

and see "Becket" in index to this volume.

The Golden Legend, however, should be judged by itself, and is an enchanting romance of the Middle Age cast in the dramatic mould. Brought out years before the "Tragedies," it finally was merged in the "Christus" by way of toning up the whole, the poet well knowing that this was his choicest distillation of Gothic mysticism and its legendary. It is composite rather than inventive; the correspondences between this work and Goethe's masterpiece, not to speak of productions earlier than either, are interesting. There is decided originality in its general effect, and in the taste wherewith the author, like a modern maker of stained glass, arranged the prismatic materials which he knew precisely where to collect. The Prologue, not wholly a new conception, is none the less imaginative: a scene of night and storm, with Lucifer and the Powers of the Air vainly assaulting the Strasburg Cross,

"The Golden Legend," 1851.

Delightful re-use of Gothic material.

baffled by the voices of the Bells, which repeat the sacred words graven on their sides. The Legend is a striking instance of an effort by which mediæval rituals, chants, and wonder-tales are boldly seized and molten to an alloy, whose color and tensile qualities are due to the solvent of the alchemist. Here and there are unmistakable lustres of the poet's own vein. This would be recognized at sight: —

> "His gracious presence upon earth
> Was as a fire upon a hearth;
> As pleasant songs, at morning sung,
> The words that dropped from his sweet tongue
> Strengthened our hearts."

And this, also, is after his best fashion: —

> "I have my trials. Time has laid his hand
> Upon my heart, gently, not smiting it,
> But as a harper lays his open palm
> Upon his harp, to deaden its vibrations."

The poet's freest and most affluent work.

The humor of Lucifer's soliloquies, in the Church and elsewhere, is characteristic of both Goethe and Longfellow, and therefore German with a difference. But all phases of our poet's verse and fancy are to be observed in this brilliant conglomerate. And what rare materials are brought together! Here are revived the oft-told gest of Brother Felix, Walter the Minnesinger, Lucifer and the Black Paternoster, the monkish chants and anthems, the Miracle Play, the disputes at the School of Palermo. The richest passages are those contrasting the Cellar and Refectory scenes with the prayer-like labor of Brother Pacificus illuminating the Gospel in the Scriptorium above. These, with many beautiful counterparts, lighting page after page, move one to accord with those who regard "The Golden Legend" as a piece in which the poet's versatile genius is seen at its best. Though not the work of a natural dramatist, it is vastly superior to the prosaic fabrics which are attached to it, and which fail to grow upon the reader in spite of this forced association.

"*Michael Angelo*," 1882.

A posthumous drama, *Michael Angelo*, while having the dignity that becomes its theme, does not change our view of the author's limitations. It contains elevated passages, mostly the soliloquies of the great artist, of whom in his old age it may be termed a sympathetic study, and is worth pursuing, even for something more than the perfect sonnet which forms the Dedication.

A representative volume: "The Seaside and the Fireside," 1849.

Were I to select one from the poet's long succession of books to fitly illustrate his traits, I might name the little volume of 1849, with its two divisions, "By the Seaside" and "By the Fireside." *The Building of the Ship* is the best example of his free-hand metrical style, — musical, wholesome, and suggestive of an imagination that takes heat from its own action. This celebration of a manly and poetic form of handicraft is simply cast, yet full of energy and spirit. At the close, a sunburst of patriotism, the superb apostrophe to the Union, outvies that ode of Horace on which it was modelled. In conception and structure the poem, while thoroughly national, is akin to Schiller's "Lay of the Bell." I think that the minor lyrics in this volume, from "Chrysaor" to "Gaspar Becerra," warrant my liking for it, and are peculiarly representative. The author long afterward supplied companion-pieces, *The Hanging of the Crane* and *Keramos*, to his idyl of the ship-yard. His reputation now made the production of each of these a literary event; just as any late and brief work of a favorite composer sends a murmur of interest through the musical world. Such afterpieces earn for artists, in the ripeness of their fame, a more

Free-hand idyls.

sudden reward than greater efforts which preceded them. All things come around at last, and often come too late. But Longfellow again and again received his crown of praise; and this the more frequently in return for service in which he was easily first, — the art which gained for an old-time minstrel a willing largess, that of the raconteur, the teller of bewitching tales. His station as a poet was not advanced by the different instalments of the *Tales of a Wayside Inn*, but it was much to have the delight of giving delight, as often as each appeared, to a host of unseen readers. And so in the end they formed his most extended work: a series of short stories, mostly gathered from older literatures, translated into his varying and crystalline verse, and linked together, like the tales of Boccaccio and Chaucer, by a running commentary of the poet's own. The selections are good of themselves, and the conceit of the gathering of the poet's friends at the Sudbury Inn brought them near to the interest of his audience. Nothing could be better than the prelude. A transfiguring portraiture from life is that of the musician, Ole Bull. The tales here told in song for the first time, all of them colonial, are but four in number, — few indeed, among so many gleaned from the Decameron, the Gesta Romanorum, "the chronicles of Charlemagne," and "the stories that recorded are by Pierre Alphonse." Here is the semblance of a master effort, but in fact a succession of minor ones; we perceive that no great outlay of imaginative force was required for this kind of work. With Longfellow's lyrical facility of putting a story into rippling verse, almost as lightly as another would tell it in prose, we find ourselves assured of as many poems as he had themes. Less subtle and refined than Morris, he was a better raconteur. This was due to a modern

"Tales of a Wayside Inn," 1863–1874.

Longfellow and Morris. Cp. "Victorian Poets": pp. 372–378.

and natural style, the sweet variety of his measures, and to his ease in dialogue. He intersperses many realistic passages, and by other ways avoids the monotony of the "idle singer of an empty day." As for poetic atmosphere and all the essentials of a select work of beauty, the "Tales" cannot enter into comparison with "The Earthly Paradise." Longfellow's frequent gayety and constant sense of the humanities make him a true story-teller for the multitude; not, like Morris, an exquisite, dreamy singer for companions of his own guild.

Translation: "Dante's Divine Comedy," 1865–1867.

His version of *The Divine Comedy* is one of the most signal results of American labor in the department of translation. There was nothing in the work of his predecessors to prevent the task from being not only a matter of attraction, but a duty; no one, on the score of talent or acquirements, was better fitted to renew an attempt which from its conditions never can be perfectly successful. His life-long study of Dante's text had brought to this natural translator that knowledge of it which was more than half the achievement. The theory of his version was the modern one (which it helped to confirm), — that of recent and noted English translations, and of Taylor's "Faust," — to wit, a literal and lineal rendering. Unlike Taylor, Longfellow had but one measure to reproduce, and he discarded the rhymes altogether, while striving to convey the rhythm and deeper music of the sublime original. It was fitting that the neighborhood of Cambridge, whose poets and scholars were for the most part sympathetic lovers of Dante, should furnish a new translation of the Commedia, and that Longfellow — less brilliant than Lowell, whether as a poet or a student, but his superior in patient industry and evenness of taste — should be the one to make

Theory of the work.

it. We are told that his work received, from time to time, the criticism of a pleiad of his friends. Certainly it was brought to birth with heralding by Norton, — the classical translator of "Vita Nuova," — Howells, Greene, and others of the group. As for the discussions which ensued upon its merits, my impression is that points were well taken on both sides.

Competitors in the field.

Various other translations of Dante were appearing about this time — the six-hundredth anniversary of the Tuscan's birth: in Great Britain, those of Dayman, Ford, and Rossetti; in America, Dr. Parsons's "Inferno" was before the public, — seventeen cantos in the rhymed pentameter quatrain, not so literal as Longfellow's, but the noble performance that one might expect from the author of the "Lines on a Bust of Dante." The best of the English triad was that of Rossetti. It bears the stamp of a master-hand, yet has so many blemishes, and is here and there so awkward, as to be on the whole less satisfactory than Longfellow's, to which it is kindred in principle and method.

Merits of Longfellow's version.

The reader of Longfellow's pages is secure of a faithful reproduction of the original order and meaning and of Dante's manner — so far as the latter depends on linear arrangement. All these are of the highest value, if the vital and pervading style of the lofty Florentine can likewise be transferred. The ideal translator will reproduce all these — the sense, the metrical arrangement, the grandeur of tone. Until his arrival, if one of these must be sacrificed, it cannot be the first, and it should be, I think, the second rather than the third. One would prefer a prose rendering of the same rank with Mr. Lang's "Homer" and "Theocritus" to a feebly correct transcription in English verse. Longfellow certainly aimed to meet all the foregoing requirements, and in his case a complete failure was scarcely possible, even with respect to the third. But his gifts as a translator never were more conspicuous than when, in youth, he paraphrased and almost recreated so many lyrics from the German and other tongues. Applying a literal method to the Commedia, his genius is less evident than his talent and conscientious self-restraint. What he did was to translate the whole work, line for line, almost as literally as a class recitation, and this, barring a few archaisms, with much simplicity and smoothness. Except in the more abstruse cantos, the appearance of ease is so marked that one gives credit to the story that the poet, with his facility and mastery of the text, accomplished his task in a few years by writing a stated number of verses each morning, while waiting for his coffee to boil. If this were the fact, it would not do to estimate the feat by it. Where a man's genius lies, there he works with ease, and often undervalues the result; elsewhere, he "labors." There is nothing labored in Longfellow's translation; the fault is of another kind: we lose, amid all its simplicity, the "grand manner," as Mr. Arnold would call it, of the divine master. A neophyte misses what he expected to realize of the unflinching strength and terror of the Inferno, the palpitating splendor of the Paradiso. The three divisions seem levelled, so to speak, to the grade of the Purgatorio, midway between the zenith and nadir of Dante's song. This shortcoming is to be felt, rather than proved, and tells in favor of Parsons's translation, and of others greatly inferior to this as a whole. Even Cary's old-fashioned paraphrase, full of Miltonic inversions and epithets, and thoroughly open to Bentley's stricture on Pope's "Homer," has exalted passages that jus-

Special characteristics and defects.

tify its survival to our day. Longfellow's genuine scholarship led him to pursue his method, once determined on, without the slightest protrusion of skill and learning. Grace is added by the frequent use of feminine endings, — a habit natural to Longfellow, and increasing the likeness of his own to the original verse. But his rendition of many Italian words by English derivatives, which often have quite lost the etymological meaning, is an error made in the interest of extreme fidelity and really telling against it. A kindred one is the use of derivatives in which the primitive meaning is not lost, but which do not translate the text to English ears so effectively as their Saxon synonyms. For instance, most of the translators — Wright, Cayley, Ford, Rossetti, etc. — have made havoc with the inscription over the gate of hell: —

Faulty use of derivatives.

> "Per me si va nella città dolente;
> Per me si va nell' eterno dolore;
> Per me si va tra la perduta gente."

Longfellow's rendering is superior to all the rest: —

> "Through me the way is to the city dolent;
> Through me the way is to eternal dole;
> Through me the way among the people lost."

Yet here is a forced translation of the word "dolente" by a derivative which, to English readers, is not an *equivalent*. Besides, a more effective expression of anguish can be gained by the use of a Saxon word. One step further would have made Mr. Longfellow's rendering perfect: he might have escaped an inversion, and have matched the verbal repetition in the first two lines, after this wise: —

> "Through me the way is to the woful city;
> Through me the way is to eternal woe."

Reading the whole work, and accepting the late Mr. Greene's opinion that the characteristics of Dante are Variety and Power, I think that the evenness of Longfellow's method robs us of the former; and as for the latter, it is the one thing which the lay reader of this translation, unrivalled as it is in many respects, does not adequately feel.

Later work.

The reflex influence of this effort was apparent in the elevated nature of his later poems. It is true that he occasionally used his new diction in a prosaic or weary manner. Of this, such a line as "The spiritual world preponderates," from the sonnet to Whittier, is an extreme instance. Otherwise, a firmer poetic quality was observable after this date. The sonnets which he now wrote, few as they are, entitle him to a place in the most select circle of modern poets. They rank with the best written in our century. Where, in fact, throughout the whole galaxy of English sonnets, is there a group surpassing the six which accompanied the Dante volumes? Rhythmic, perfect in structure, and full of beauty, they have captured the spirit of the Divine Song. A series written in the poet's old age, his tributes to the memory of comrades gone before, has a pathetic charm. Still later was composed the sonnet "Nature," which must be accounted one of the choicest in any language upon the theme to which its title is but a pass-word:—

Sonnets of rare beauty.

"As a fond mother, when the day is o'er,
Leads by the hand her little child to bed,
Half willing, half reluctant to be led
And leave his broken playthings on the floor,
Still gazing at them through the open door,
Nor wholly reassured and comforted
By promises of others in their stead,
Which, though more splendid, may not please him more;
So Nature deals with us, and takes away

> Our playthings one by one, and by the hand
> Leads us to rest so gently, that we go
> Scarce knowing if we wish to go or stay,
> Being too full of sleep to understand
> How far the unknown transcends the what we know."

This is, however, singularly like the translation, by Leigh Hunt, of Filicaja's sonnet on Providence, quoted by Longfellow himself in the notes to the Paradiso. With lessening use, the poet's touch lost little of its delicacy and poise. The few pieces brought together in *Ultima Thule* indicate that his ruling sense of art was clear as ever; nor was it finally dulled, like Emerson's bright intelligence, by a veil of darkness slowly drawn. He ceased from service almost without forewarning, and because his work was done.

"Ultima Thule," 1880.

V.

Longfellow's habits and mannerism.

Few poets have been more restricted to fixed habits of composition. His mode was perfectly obvious and unchanged, save by greater refinement, during fifty years. Everything suggested an image, except when his imagery suggested the thought of which he made it seem a reflection. He tells us that

> "Bent like a laboring oar that toils in the surf of the ocean,
> Bent, but not broken, by age was the form of the notary public";

and we feel that the image really grew out of a poet's conception of his personage. But again, looking upon "drifting currents of the river," or finding the day "cold and dark and dreary," or listening to the belfry-chimes, he hunts about for some emotion or phase of life which these things aptly illustrate. This process not seldom becomes a vice of style. He constantly applied his imagery in a formal way, — the very *ut . . . ita* of the Latins, the *as . . . so* of the eigh-

Formal imagery.

teenth century. But whether his metaphors came of themselves, or with prayer and fasting, they always came, and often were novel and poetic. A more trying habit was that inbred, as it seems, with the New England poets, most of whom have preached too much in verse. He tacked a didactic moral, like a corollary of Euclid, on many a lovely poem. No one better knew that "nothing is poetry which could as well have been expressed in prose," but the habit formed in youth seemed beyond his control. Still, it was through this habit that he became the most popular of University poets, and as a moralist no one could make commonplace more attractive. Lastly, the bookish flavor of his work is at once its strength and weakness: the former, because the very life of his genius depended on it; the latter, because poetry that is over-literary is so much the less creative, and is otherwise open to the objections brought against literary art. Browning's fondness for black-letter is redeemed by dramatic vigor. In reading Longfellow, we see that the world of books was to him the real world. From first to last, if he had been banished from his library, his imagination would have been blind and deaf and silent. It is true that he fed upon the choicest yield of literature; his gathered honey was of the thyme and clover, not the rude buckwheat. Take, for instance, the "Morituri Salutamus," read before his surviving classmates on the fiftieth anniversary of their graduation. Was there ever anything more beautiful, in view of the occasion? Is not the title itself a stroke of genius? But the title also defines the method of the poem: there are more than twenty learned references in this piece of less than three hundred lines, including one entire tale from the "Gesta Romanorum." He had, we see, this way of working, and for once it resulted in a poem that is the model of its kind.

Moralizing.

Excessive literary flavor.

"Morituri Salutamus," 1875.

A poet of the study and alcove.

As for Nature, he usually saw it as polarized by reflection from the mirror Art. Whether in or out of his study, he had not Emerson's interpretative eye, and his report of landscape and the country life was less genuine than Lowell's or Whittier's, not to mention the younger poets. He rarely ventured beyond the simple outlook from his mansion door. The effect of the rain, the mist, the night-fall, upon his own spirit, is what he gives us, in the manner of some landscape of the French subjective school. A starry event, the occultation of Orion, at once becomes a glorious image of the triumph of Love over Force. In "Evangeline" there are refined pictures of scenery that was familiar to him, with just as pleasing descriptions of that which he knew only through his books. He painted the landscape of half Europe in the same way, always a cosmopolitan, never the genius of the place. The flower-de-luce, with its heraldic associations, is the emblem after which he names a volume. But with respect to still life and common life, the true *genre* touch of "The Old Clock" and "The Village Blacksmith" grows firmer in "Miles Standish," where he draws so well the Plymouth interiors, the Puritan maiden at her wheel, the elders, and men-at-arms. And look! how he describes what of all is nearest his heart, an olden volume:—

> "Open wide on her lap lay the well-worn psalm-book of Ainsworth,
> Printed in Amsterdam, the words and the music together,
> Rough-hewn, angular notes, like stones in the walls of a churchyard,
> Darkened and overhung by the running vine of the verses.
> Such was the book from whose pages she sang the old Puritan anthem."

I more than half recant the statement that Longfellow was not a poet of Nature, bethinking myself how justly others have maintained that he was by eminence our poet of the Sea. He clung to the coast: looking inland, he cared most for the tide-meadows of his neighborhood; looking oceanward, his fancy throve upon the omens, the mysteries, the perpetual fascinations of "sea from shore." He loved his mighty rock-girt bay, the lights and beacons, the mist and fog-bells, the sleet and surge of winter, the coastwise vessels; and its memories were the drift-wood with which he kindled "thoughts that burned and glowed within." His imagination goes out to "the ocean old," the "gray old sea" of storms and calms; to its winged frequenters, the ancient galleons, the fleets of conquest and embassy and traffic. The names of sunny isles and far-off lands were music to him. If by chance our fireside magician drowned his books deeper than did ever plummet sound, and sang from a poet's heart alone, it was when he returned again and again to capture and repeat for us the haunting "secret of the sea."

Yet one who caught the secret of the Sea.

Reviewing our survey of his work, I observe that each of his best known efforts has led to the mention of prose or verse by some other hand which it resembles. In view of the possible inference, we now may ask, Was Longfellow, then, with his great reputation and indisputable hold upon our affections, not an original poet? It must be acknowledged, at the outset, that few poets of his standing have profited more openly by examples that suited their taste and purpose. The evidence of this is seen not in merely three or four, but in a great number of his productions,—in his briefest lyrics, in his elaborate narrative poems. Like greater bards before him, he was a good borrower. Dependence on his equipment led to unconscious as-

Question of his originality.

A persistent borrower, but

similation of its treasures. But originality is of more than one kind. As we say of some people that they have a genius for friendship, so his sympathy with the beautiful, wherever he found it, was unique and tantamount to a special inspiration. The proof of his originality, however, even where he was least inventive, hardly requires this paradox: it did not consist in word or motive, but in the distinctive tone of the singer, the sentiment of voice which made his performances in a sense new songs; in an air, a suffused quality, which rendered every phrase unmistakable. If he borrowed freely, he was freely drawn upon by others in their turn. Scores of followers have caught a manner that shows to poor advantage when transferred; but his position for years, at the head of even a sentimental school, indicated that Longfellow was not without a genius of his own.

With a distinctive air.

His cosmopolitanism,

Apart from certain exceptions already noted, his bent was cosmopolitan. He had the Anglo-Saxon longing of the pine for the palm, a love for the softer winds and skies, the pliant languages, of Italy and Spain. Besides the example of his works, we have his written theory of what our literature should be. His Mr. Churchill, in "Kavanagh," declares that in literature "Nationality is a good thing to a certain extent, but universality is better. All that is best in the great poets of all countries is not what is national in them, but what is universal. Their roots are in their native soil; but their branches wave in the unpatriotic air that speaks the same language unto all men. . . . I prefer what is natural. Mere nationality is often ridiculous." And again, "Our literature is not an imitation, but a continuation of the English." He insists upon originality, but "without spasms and convulsions." . . . "A national literature is not the growth of a day.

And ideal of a national literature. *See pp. 5-10, 96, 97.*

Centuries must contribute their dew and sunshine to it. . . . As for having it so savage and wild as you want it, . . . all literature, as well as all art, is the result of culture and intellectual refinement. . . . As the blood of all nations is mingling with our own, so will their thoughts and feelings finally mingle in our literature. We shall draw from the Germans tenderness, from the Spanish passion, from the French vivacity, to mingle more and more with our English solid sense. And this will give us universality, so much to be desired." With regard to all this, it may be said that Longfellow's service, important as it was in his time, is not that required of his successors. The greatest poets have been those who conveyed the spirit of their respective nationalities. That poetry is truest which is universal in its passion and thought, but national in motive and in all properties of the craft. The final outcome of American ideality will depend on conditions which our best thinkers are investigating, and which give rise to conflicting theories. Herbert Spencer's recent utterance is somewhat in accordance with Longfellow's views: "Because of its size, and the heterogeneity of its components, the American nation will be a long time in evolving its ultimate form, but its ultimate form will be high." And again: "From biological truths it is to be inferred that the eventual mixture of the allied varieties of the Aryan race forming the population will produce a finer type of man than has hitherto existed." This agreeable prediction may seem too optimistic; but the future type of poetry certainly will represent the future type of man. Without debating the question whether we now are forming loam for a distinct growth, or whether our literature is to be a "continuation" merely, we may be sure that both here and in foreign lands new

"Herbert Spencer on the Americans." New York, 1882.

types of genius will appear, we know not how or why, and add new species to the world's *flora symbolica* of art and song. Longfellow, if not a prophet, was a pioneer, — by choice an apostle of the best traditional culture. His verse is not of a kind to make its admirers indifferent to any other, — an effect, whether for good or ill, sometimes produced by Browning's, Emerson's, and Whitman's, — but that which, however elementary, promotes a taste for higher ideals. It is due to such as he that we have passed the age of nursing, and are now less satisfied with what is not primarily our own. That the best equipped section of the country should produce him was in the order of events: other things being equal, that region is most American which has been so the longest, and the frontier steadily grows to resemble it.

Longfellow a pioneer of taste.

In England, Longfellow has been styled the poet of the middle classes. Those classes include, however, the majority of intelligent readers, and Tennyson had an equal share of their favor. The English middle classes furnish an analogue to the one great class of American readers, among whom our poet's success was so evident. This was because he used his culture not to veil the word, but to make it clear. He drew upon it for the people in a manner which they could relish and comprehend. Would not any poet whose work might lack the subtlety that commends itself to professional readers be relegated by University critics to the middle-class wards? Caste and literary priesthood have something to do with this. Were it not for "Lucretius" and "In Memoriam," the author of "The May Queen" and "Locksley Hall" and "Enoch Arden" would be in the same category; as it is, he scarcely escapes it in the judgment of both the psychologic and neo-Romantic schools. Yet the

In what sense a "poet of the middle classes."

Tennyson.

poetry of analytics has not outlasted, in the past, that which came without gloss or obscurity, and whose melody and meaning appealed to one and all. That a poet's verse should require a commentary in its own day is not, all things considered, the best omen for its hold upon the future. But the point taken with respect to Longfellow is not unjust. So far as comfort, virtue, domestic tenderness, and freedom from extremes of passion and incident are characteristics of the middle classes, he has been their minstrel. And it is true that a cold, or even temperate quality is deadening to the higher forms of art. The creative soul abhors ennui; it glows in dramatic self-abandonment. Poets "of passion and of pain" concentrate their lives in some burning focus whose dazzling heat devours them; they suffer, but mount on their own flame. Without passion and its expiations, without the mad waste of life, and even crime and terror, where are our noble tragedies, our high dramatic themes? The compensation of man's anguish is that it lifts him beyond the ordinary. Superlative joy and woe alike were foreign to the verse of Longfellow. It came neither from the heights nor out of the depths, but along the even tenor of a fortunate life. I do not mean that he was exempt from mortal ills; he had his dark experiences, but at the mature age that has learned "what life and death is," and of them he gave little sign. If sorrow and rapture are from within, rather than from without, it may be that our benignant poet, alike through circumstance and temperament, was spared the full extremity of discipline signified in the translation from Goethe: —

Poets and their scholiasts.

Longfellow's ethics and domesticity.

Wanting in ecstasy and dramatic insight.

> "Who ne'er his bread in sorrow ate,
> Who ne'er the mournful midnight hours
> Weeping upon his bed has sate,
> He knows you not, ye Heavenly Powers."

Not his the agony and bloody sweat. We may conjecture that, aside from one or two fierce episodes, he was less tried in the furnace than poets are wont to be. From the first he had what he desired, — congenial work and associations, advancement, the love of women and friends, appreciative criticism, the pure wheat and sweet waters of life in plenitude. He had lovely things about him, and gratified his artist nature to the full, while so many makers of the beautiful are condemned to Vulcan's cavern of toil and smoke. He had the best, as by right; and in truth the world, if it but knew it, can afford to keep a poet or an artist in some luxury, like a flower for its perfume, a hound for beauty, a bird for song. If Longfellow's regard fell upon ugliness and misery, it certainly did not linger there. "The cry of the human" did not haunt his ear. When he avails himself of a piteous situation, he does so as tranquilly as the nuns who broider on tapestry the torments of the doomed in hell. He wrote few love poems, none full of longing, or "wild with all regret"; but this might come from the absolute content of his soul, — he had gained the woman whom he idolized, and songs of passion are the cry of unfulfilled desire. His song flows on an equal course, from sunny fountain-head to darkling sea; and even upon that sea he finds repose, for its billows rock to sleep, and no cradle is more peaceful than the grave. Thus fair, gentle, fortunate, — could such a poet answer to the deepest needs of men? Allowing for the factor of imagination, we still see that Longfellow shrank from efforts that would react too keenly upon his sensibilities. He touched the average heart by the sympathetic quality of a voice adjusted to the natural scale. People above or apart from the average — sufferers, aspirants, questioners —

Fortune's favorite.

A sympathetic voice, unperturbed by human passion and conflict.

are irked by his acceptance of life as it is and his enjoyable relations to it. There is something exasperating to serious minds in his placid waiver of things grievous or distasteful. They ask what cause he has advanced, how has he enlarged the province of thought, what conflict has he sung? Where are his rapture, his longing, his infinitudes? They see his fellow-poet, less prosperous and accomplished, who defied obloquy, and rose to passion in denouncing wrong, — a man of peace, yet valiant as Great-Heart in behalf of freedom and the rights of man. They recall another, who sought out the inmost laws of spiritual life. But why expect a poet to be other than he is? Recognize the instinct that defined his range, and value the range at its worth. Longfellow spoke according to his voice and vision. The attempt to do otherwise ends all. A critic must accept what is best in a poet, and thus become his best encourager.

The poet's sweet and wholesome disposition.

So far as good fortune may be supplemented by human wisdom, Longfellow was a man after the preacher's own heart. His was one of those happy natures which, as Thackeray says, are softened by prosperity and kindness. He was saved the torment that the envious feel: —

> "He did not find his sleep less sweet
> For music in some neighboring street;
> Nor rustling hear in every breeze
> The laurels of Miltiades."

Artistic tact.

We have seen his tact in the choice and use of things pertaining to his work, his carefully restrained decoration, his knowledge of limitations, which prevented him, except in the dramatic experiments, from groping for impracticable means and results. The forms which he introduced or revived were as successful as Tennyson's; in fact, his product represents

Judgment supplementing inspiration.

the full advance of American taste and feeling, during the period covered by it, though not our most significant thought. He was a lyrical artist, whose taste outranked his inspiration; and assuredly, if he had been a Minister of the Fine Arts, he never would have abolished an École at the dictation of the "impressionists," nor have adopted as a motto the phrase "Beware of the Beautiful." We have noted his industry and the self-control with which he devoted his life to poetry alone. Yet the report of his library talk shows that his brain was alert upon many topics; that in private, at least, he did not reserve his talents for his publisher, — an economy which a French critic declares to be "a bad sign, and the proof that one makes a trade of literature, and that one does not really have the impressions he assumes to have in his books." His verse is peculiarly open to the test of Milton's requirement, that poetry should be simple, sensuous, passionate. Simple, even elementary, it manifestly is, despite the learning which he put to use. It is sensuous in much that charms the ear and eye, and in little else; for the extreme of sensuousness is deeply felt, and feeling results in passion, and passionate the verse of Longfellow was not, nor ever could be. His song was a household service, the ritual of our feastings and mournings; and often it rehearsed for us the tales of many lands, or, best oi all, the legends of our own. I see him, a silver-haired minstrel, touching melodious keys, playing and singing in the twilight, within sound of the rote of the sea. There he lingers late; the curfew bell has tolled and the darkness closes round, till at last that tender voice is silent, and he softly moves unto his rest.

Final estimate.

H. W. L. died at Cambridge, Mass., Mar. 24, 1882.

CHAPTER VII.

EDGAR ALLAN POE.

I.

UPON the roll of American authors a few names are written apart from the many. With each of these is associated some accident of condition, some memory of original or eccentric genius, through which it arrests attention and claims our special wonder. The light of none among these few has been more fervid and recurrent than that of Edgar Allan Poe. But, as I in turn pronounce his name, and in my turn would estimate the man and his writings, I am at once confronted by the question, Is this poet, as now remembered, as now portrayed to us, the real Poe who lived and sang and suffered, and who died but little more than a quarter-century ago?

Distinctive reputations.

The great heart of the world throbs warmly over the struggles of our kind; the imagination of the world dwells upon and enlarges the glory and the shame of human action in the past. Year after year, the heart-beats are more warm, the conception grows more distinct with light and shade. The person that was is made the framework of an image to which the tender, the romantic, the thoughtful, the simple, and the wise add each his own folly or wisdom, his own joy and sorrow and uttermost yearning. Thus, not only true heroes and poets, but many who have been conspicuous through force of circumstances, become

The witchery of Time.

idealized as time goes by. The critic's first labor often is the task of distinguishing between men, as history and their works display them, and the ideals which one and another have conspired to urge upon his acceptance.

A twofold ideal.

The difficulty is increased when, as in the case of Poe, a twofold ideal exists, of whose opposite sides many that have written upon him seem to observe but one. In the opinion of some people, even now, his life was not only pitiful, but odious, and his writings are false and insincere. They speak of his morbid genius, his unjust criticisms, his weakness and ingratitude, and scarcely can endure the mention of his name. Others recount his history as that of a sensitive, gifted being, most sorely beset and environed, who was tried beyond his strength and prematurely yielded, but still uttered not a few undying strains. As a new generation has arisen, and those of his own who knew him are passing away, the latter class of his reviewers seems to outnumber the former. A chorus of indiscriminate praise has grown so loud as really to be an ill omen for his fame; yet, on the whole, the wisest modern estimate of his character and writings has not lessened the interest long ago felt in them at home and abroad.

Postulates.

It seems to me that two things at least are certain. First, and although his life has been the subject of the research which is awarded only to strange and suggestive careers, he was, after all, a man of like passions with ourselves, — one who, if weaker in his weaknesses than many, and stronger in his strength, may not have been so bad, nor yet so good, as one and another have painted him. Thousands have gone as far toward both extremes, and the world never has heard of them. Only the gift of genius has made the temperament of Poe a common theme. And thus, I also think, we are sure, in once more calling up his shade, that we invoke the manes of a poet. Of his right to this much-abused title there can be little dispute, nor of the claim that, whatever he lacked in compass, he was unique among his fellows, — so different from any other writer that America has produced as really to stand alone. He must have had genius to furnish even the basis for an ideal which excites this persistent interest. Yes, we are on firm ground with relation to his genuineness as a poet. But his narrowness of range, and the slender body of his poetic remains, of themselves should make writers hesitate to pronounce him our greatest one. His verse is as conspicuous for what it shows he could not do as for that which he did. He is another of those poets, outside the New England school, of whom each has made his mark in a separate way, — among them all, none more decisively than Poe. So far as the judgment of a few rare spirits in foreign lands may be counted the verdict of "posterity," an estimate of him is not to be lightly and flippantly made. Nor is it long since a group of his contemporaries and successors, in his own country, spoke of him as a poet whose works are a lasting monument, and of his "imperishable" fame.

Unique quality of Poe's genius.

After every allowance, it seems difficult for one not utterly jaded to read his poetry and tales without yielding to their original and haunting spell. Even as we drive out of mind the popular conceptions of his nature, and look only at the portraits of him in the flesh, we needs must pause and contemplate, thoughtfully and with renewed feeling, one of the marked ideal faces that seem — like those of Byron, De Musset, Heine — to fulfil all the traditions of

Personal aspect.

genius, of picturesqueness, of literary and romantic effect.

Halpin's likeness of Poe, in the complete American edition.

Halpin's engraving of Poe, in which the draughtsman was no servile copyist, but strove to express the sitter at his best, makes it possible to recall the poet delineated by those who knew and admired him in his nobler seasons. We see one they describe as slight but erect of figure, athletic and well moulded, of middle height, but so proportioned as to seem every inch a man; his head finely modelled, with a forehead and temples large and not unlike those of Bonaparte; his hands fair as a woman's, — in all, a graceful, well-dressed gentleman, — one, even in the garb of poverty, "with gentleman written all over him." We see the handsome, intellectual face, the dark and clustering hair, the clear and sad gray-violet eyes, — large, lustrous, glowing with expression, — the mouth, whose smile at least was sweet and winning. We imagine the soft, musical voice (a delicate thing in man or woman), the easy, quiet movement, the bearing that no failure could humble. And this man had not only the gift of beauty, but the passionate love of beauty, — either of which may be as great a blessing or peril as can befall a human being stretched upon the rack of this tough world.

Later portraits.

But look at some daguerreotype taken shortly before his death, and it is like an inauspicious mirror, that shows all too clearly the ravage made by a vexed spirit within, and loses the qualities which only a living artist could feel and capture. Here is the dramatic, defiant bearing, but with it the bitterness of scorn. The disdain of an habitual sneer has found an abode on the mouth, yet scarcely can hide the tremor of irresolution. In Bendann's likeness, indubitably faithful, we find those hardened lines of the

Repro- duced in the

chin and neck that are often visible in men who have gambled heavily, which Poe did not in his mature years, or who have lived loosely and slept ill. The face tells of battling, of conquering external enemies, of many a defeat when the man was at war with his meaner self.

"*Memorial Volume*," *Balt.*, 1877.

Among the pen-portraits of Poe, at his best and his worst, none seem more striking in their juxtaposition, none less affected by friendship or hatred, than those left to us by C. F. Briggs, the poet's early associate. These were made but a short time before the writer's death, — after the lapse of years had softened the prejudices of a man prejudiced indeed, yet of a kindly heart, and had rendered the critical habit of the journalist almost a rule of action.

Reprinted in the New York "Independent," June 24, 1880.

If these external aspects were the signs of character within, we can understand why those who saw them should have believed of Poe — and in a different sense than of Hawthorne — that

> "Two natures in him strove
> Like day with night, his sunshine and his gloom."

The recorded facts of his life serve to enhance this feeling. My object here is not biography, yet let us note the brief annals of a wayward, time-tossed critic, romancer, poet. Their purport and outline, seen through a cloud of obscurities, and the veil thrown over them by his own love of mystery and retreat, — made out from the various narratives of those who have contended in zeal to discover the minute affairs of this uncommon man, — the substance of them all, I say, may readily enough be told.

II.

THE law of chance, that has so much to do with the composition of a man, that makes no two alike, yet adjusts the most of us to a common average, brings about exceptional unions like the one from which the poet sprang. A well-born, dissolute Maryland boy, with a passion for the stage, marries an actress and adopts her profession, — taking up a life that was strolling, precarious, half-despised in the pioneer times. Three children were the fruit of this love-match. The second, Edgar, was born in Boston, January 19, 1809. From his father he inherited Italian, French, and Irish blood; the Celtic pride of disposition and certain weaknesses that were his bane. His mother, Elizabeth Arnold, an actress of some talent, was as purely English as her name. Two years after his birth, the hapless parents, wearied and destitute, died at Richmond, both in the same week. The orphans "found kind friends," and were adopted — the oldest, William, by his grandfather Poe, of Baltimore; Edgar and Rosalie by citizens of Richmond.

Edgar Allan Poe: born in Boston, January 19, 1809.

His childhood.

Edgar gained a protector in Mr. Allan, an English-born and wealthy merchant, who was married, but without a child. The boy's beauty and precocity won the heart of this gentleman, who gave him his name, and lavished upon him, in true Southern style, all that perilous endearment which befits the son and heir of a generous house. Servants, horses, dogs, the finest clothes, a purse well filled, all these were at his disposal from the outset. Great pains were taken with his education, the one element of moral discipline seemingly excepted. When eight years old he went with Mr. Allan to England, and was at the school in Stoke-Newington, to which it is thought his memory went back in after years, when he wrote the tale of "William Wilson." At ten we find him at school in Richmond, proficient in classical studies but shirking his mathematics, already writing verse,—instinctively

Training.

> "Seeking with hand and heart
> The teacher whom he learned to love
> Before he knew 't was Art."

His grace and strength, his free, romantic, and ardent bearing, made him friends among old and young, and at this time he certainly was capable of the most passionate loyalty to those he loved. Traditions of all this — of his dreamy, fitful temperament, of his early sorrows and his midnight mournings over the grave of an affectionate woman who had been his paragon — are carefully preserved. He was a schoolboy, here and there, until 1826, when he passed a winter at the University of Virginia. He ended his brief course in the school of ancient and modern languages with a successful examination, but after much dissipation and gambling which deeply involved him in debt. His thoughtlessness and practical ingratitude justly incensed an unwise but hitherto devoted guardian. A rupture followed between the two, Mr. Allan finally refusing to countenance Edgar's extravagances; and the young man betook himself to Boston, where, after a few months, he succeeded in finding a printer for his first little book, a revised collection of juvenile poems. But he was soon reduced to straits, and driven to enlistment, under a partly fictitious name, as a soldier; in which capacity, first a private and then by promotion a sergeant-major, he served his country for almost two years. In 1829 he was touched by news of the death of Mrs. Allan, who had always given him a sympathetic mother's

College life.

"Tamerlane and Other Poems," Boston, 1827. Reprinted, with changes and omissions, Baltimore, 1829.

Enlistment in the army.

love. He obtained a furlough, and effected a reconciliation with the widower in his hour of loneliness and sorrow. Poe's later and trustworthy biographer has spared no pains to give the true details of the youth's enlistment, service, and final discharge through the influence of his early protector.

"Edgar Allan Poe." By G. E. Woodberry: Boston, 1885.

About this time he visited his aunt, Mrs. Maria Clemm, of Baltimore. Her daughter Virginia was then six years old, and Poe interested himself in the sweet and gentle child, who loved him from the first, and made his will her law through girlhood and their subsequent wedded life.

West Point.

Poe now was asked to choose a profession; he selected that of arms, and his benefactor secured his admission to West Point. Here we find him in 1830, and find little good of him. Though now a man grown, he was unable to endure discipline. After a first success, he tired of the place and brought about his own expulsion and disgrace, to his patron's deep, and this time lasting, resentment. But here he also arranged for the issue, by subscription, of another edition of his poems, which was delivered to his classmates after his departure from the academy.

Subscription edition of his poems: New York, 1831.

A new personage now comes upon the scene. Mr. Allan, naturally desiring affection from some quarter, married again, and after a time heirs were born to the estate which Poe, had he been less reckless, might have inherited. The poet, returning in disgrace to Richmond, found no intercessor in the home of his youth. This change, and his manner of life thus far, render it needless to look for other causes of the final rupture between himself and his guardian. It was the just avenge of fate for his persistent folly, and a defeat was inevitable in his contest (if there was a contest) with a lady who, by every law of right, was stronger than he. Poe went out into the world with full permission to have the one treasure he had seemed to value — his own way. Like a multitude of American youths, often the sons or grandsons of successful men, he found himself of age, without the means proportionate to the education, habits, and needs of a gentleman, and literally, in the place of an unfailing income, without a cent. Better off than many who have erred less, he had one strong ally — his pen. With this he was henceforth to earn his own bed and board, and lead the arduous life of a working man of letters.

Adrift.

His one ally.

For the struggle now begun his resources of tact, good sense, self-poise, were as deficient as his intellectual equipment was great. Soon after the loss of a home-right, which he forfeited more recklessly than Esau, his professional career may be said to have begun. It extended, with brief but frequent intermissions, from 1832 to 1849, the year of his untimely death. Its first noteworthy event was the celebrated introduction to Kennedy, Latrobe, and Miller, through his success in winning a literary prize with "A MS. Found in a Bottle." This brought him friends, work, and local reputation, — in all, a fair and well-earned start.

A good start.

Seventeen years, thenceforward, of working life, in which no other American writer was more active and prominent. I have considered elsewhere the influence of journalism upon authorship. It enabled Poe to live. On the other hand, while he rarely made his lighter work commonplace, it limited the importance of his highest efforts, gave a paragraphic air to his criticisms, and left some of his most suggestive writings mere fragments of what they should be. He discovered the pretentious mediocrity of a host of

Summary of his career.

See Chap. XI., and cp. "Victorian Poets": pp. 81, 82.

scribblers, and when unbiased by personal feeling, and especially when doing imaginative work, was one of the few clear-headed writers of his day. He knew what he desired to produce, and how to produce it. We say of a man that his head may be wrong, but his heart is all right. There were times enough when the reverse of this was true of Poe. I do not say there were not other times when his heart was as sound as his perceptions. What, after all, is the record of his years of work, and what is the significance of that record? We must consider the man in his environment, and the transient, uncertain character of the markets to which he brought his wares. His labors, then, were continually impeded, broken, changed; first, by the most trying and uncontrollable nature that ever poet possessed, that ever possessed a poet; by an unquiet, capricious temper, a childish enslavement to his own "Imp of the Perverse," a scornful pettiness that made him "hard to help," that drove him to quarrel with his patient, generous friends, and to wage ignoble conflict with enemies of his own making; by physical and moral lapses, partly the result of inherited taint, in which he resorted, more or less frequently, and usually at critical moments, — seasons when he needed all his resources, all his courage and manhood, — to stimulants which he knew would madden and besot him more than other men. None the less his genius was apparent, his power felt, his labor in demand wherever the means existed to pay for it. But here, again, his life was made precarious and shifting by the speculative, ill-requited nature of literary enterprises at that time. From various causes, therefore, his record — no matter how it is attacked or defended — is one of irregularity, of broken and renewed engagements. From 1832 to 1835 Poe had

Head and heart.

"The Imp of the Perverse."

Precarious life of American authors at that time.

but himself to support, and a careless young fellow always gets on so long as he *is* young, with one success and the chance of a future. The next year his private marriage to his sweet cousin Virginia, still almost a child, was reaffirmed in public, and the two set up their home together. The time had come when Poe, with his sense of the fitness of things, could see that Bohemianism, the charm of youth, is a frame that poorly suits the portrait of a mature and able-handed man. So we are not surprised to find him engaged, for honest wages, upon "The Southern Literary Messenger." That his skilful touch and fantastic genius, whether devoted to realistic or psychological invention, were now at full command, is shown by his "Hans Pfaall," and by his first striking contribution to the "Messenger," the spectral and characteristic tale of "Berenice." In short, he did uncommon work, for that time, upon the famous Southern magazine, both as tale-writer and as critic, and increased its reputation and income. Yet he felt, with all the morbid sensitiveness of one spoilt by luxury and arrogance in youth, the difference between his present work-a-day life and the independence, the social standing, which if again at his command would enable him to indulge his finer tastes and finish at ease the work best suited to his powers. From this time he was subject to moods of brooding and despair, of crying out upon fate, that were his pest and his ultimate destruction. And so we again are not surprised to find this good beginning no true omen of the fifteen years to come; and that these years are counted by flittings here and there between points that offered employment; by new engagements taken up before he was off with the old; by legends of his bearing and entanglements in the social world he entered; by

Marriage with Virginia Clemm, 1835.

Journalism.

Mental suffering.

Wanderings.

alternate successes and disgraces, in Richmond, Philadelphia, Boston, New York; by friendships and fallings out with many of the editors who employed him, — the product, after all, with which we are chiefly concerned being his always distinctive writings for the "Quarterly," "The Gentleman's Magazine," "Graham's," "Godey's," "The Mirror," "The American Review," and various other fosterers and distributers of such literature as the current taste might demand. We begin to understand his spasmodic, versatile industry, his balks and breaks, his frequent poverty, despondency, self-abandonment and almost to wonder that the sensitive feminine spirit — worshipping beauty and abhorrent of ugliness and pain, combating with pride, with inherited disease of appetite — did not sooner yield, was not utterly overcome almost at the outset of these experiences. So have I wondered at seeing a delicate forest-bird, leagues from the shore, keep itself on the wing above relentless waters into which it was sure to fall at last.[1] Poe had his good genius and his bad. Near the close of the struggle he made a brave effort, and never was so earnest and resolved, so much his own master, as just before the end. But a man is no stronger than his weakest part, and with the snapping of that his chance is over. At the moment when the poet, rallying from the desolation caused by the loss of his wife, found new hope

Work.

Misfortunes.

Death, in Baltimore, October 7, 1849.

[1] Finely paraphrased, since the original appearance of this chapter, by my friend, Mr. Winter: —

> "Far from the blooming field and fragrant wood
> The shining songster of the summer sky,
> O'er ocean's black and frightful solitude,
> Driven on broken wing, must sink and die";
> . . . . .

Poem read at the Dedication of the Actors' Monument to Poe, May 4, 1885.

and purpose, and was on his way to marry a woman who possibly might have saved him, the tragedy of his life began again. Its final scene was as swift, irreparable, black with terror, as that of any drama ever written. His death was gloom. Men saw him no more; but the shadow of a veiled old woman, mourning for him, hovered here and there. After many years a laurelled tomb was placed above his ashes, and there remain to American literature the relics, so unequal in value, of the most isolated and exceptional of all its poets and pioneers.

Mrs. Maria Clemm.

Poe's misfortunes were less than those of some who have conquered misfortune. Others have been castaways in infancy and friendless in manhood, and have found no protectors such as came at his need. Still others have struggled and suffered, and have declined to wear their hearts upon their sleeves. They have sought consolation in their work, and from their bitter experiences have gathered strength and glory. The essential part of an artist's life is that of his inspired moments. There were occasions when Poe was the master, when his criticism was true, when he composed such tales as "Ligeia," "The Fall of the House of Usher," poems like "The Raven," "The Bells," "The City in the Sea." It must be acknowledged, moreover — and professional writers know what this implies — that Poe, in his wanderings, after all, *followed his market.* It gradually drifted to the North, until New York afforded the surest recompense to authors not snugly housed in the leafy coverts of New England. Nor did he ever resort to any mercantile employment for a livelihood. As we look around and see how authors accept this or that method of support, there seems to be something chivalrous in the attitude of one who never earned a dollar except by his pen.

The literary market.

See pp. 22 25, 38.

A genuine man of letters.

From first to last he was simply a poet and man of letters, who rightly might claim to be judged by the literary product of his life. The life itself differed from that of any modern poet of equal genius, and partly because none other has found himself, in a new country, among such elements. Too much has been written about the man, too little of his times.

Interest excited by Poe's life and works.

His story has had a fascination for those who consider the infirmity of genius its natural outward sign. The peculiarity of his actions was their leaning toward what is called the melodramatic; of his work, that it aimed above the level of its time. What has been written of the former — of little value as compared with the analysis derivable from his literary remains — was for a long time the output of those who, if unable to produce a stanza which he would have acknowledged, at least felt within themselves the possibilities of his errant career. Yet, as I observe the marvels of his handicraft, I seem unjust to these enthusiasts. It was the kind which most impresses the imagination of youth, and youth is a period at which the critical development of many biographers seems to be arrested. And who would not recall the zest with which he read, in school-boy days, and by the stolen candle, a legend so fearful in its beauty and so beautiful in its fear as "The Masque of the Red Death," for example, found in some stray number of a magazine, and making the printed trash that convoyed it seem so vapid and drear? Not long after, we had the collected series, *Tales of the Grotesque and Arabesque.* With what eagerness we caught them from hand to hand until many of us knew them almost by heart. In the East, at that time, Hawthorne was shyly putting out his "Mosses" and "Twice Told Tales," and it was not an unfruitful period that fostered, among its brood of chattering and

"Tales of the Grotesque and Arabesque," 1840.

aimless sentimentalists, two such spirits at once, each original in his kind. To-day we have a more consummate, realistic art. But where, now, the creative ardor, the power to touch the stops, if need be, of tragedy and superstition and remorse! Our taste is more refined, our faculties are under control; to produce the greatest art they must, at times, compel the artist. "Poetry," said Poe, "has been with me a passion, not a purpose," — a remarkable sentence to be found in a boyish preface, and I believe that he wrote the truth. But here, again, he displays an opposite failing. If poetry had been with him no less a passion, and equally a purpose, we now should have had something more to represent his rhythmical genius than the few brief, occasional lyrics which are all that his thirty years of life as a poet — the life of his early choice — have left to us.

Poetry a passion with him.

III.

In estimating him as a poet, the dates of these lyrics are of minor consequence. They make but a thin volume, smaller than one which might hold the verse of Collins or Gray. Their range is narrower still. It is a curious fact that Poe struck, in youth, the keynotes of a few themes, and that some of his best pieces, as we now have them, are but variations upon their earlier treatment.

Lyrical remains.

His first collection was made in his eighteenth year, revised in his twentieth, and again reprinted, with changes and omissions, just after he left West Point. The form of the longer poems is copied from Byron and Moore, while the spirit of the whole series vaguely reminds us of Shelley in his obscurer lyrical mood. Poe's originality can be found in them, but they would

Early books of verse: printed, respectively, in 1827, 1829, and 1831.

be valueless except for his after career. They have unusual significance as the shapeless germs of much that was to grow into form and beauty. Crude and wandering pieces, entitled "Fairy Land" and "Irene," "To ——," "A Pæan," etc., were the originals of "The Sleeper," "A Dream within a Dream," and "Lenore"; while "The Doomed City" and "The Valley Nis" reappear as "The City in the Sea" and "The Valley of Unrest." Others were less thoroughly rewritten. Possibly he thus remodelled his juvenile verse to show that, however inchoate, it contained something worth a master's handling. Mr. Stoddard thinks, and not without reason, that he found it an easy way of making salable "copy." The poet himself intimates that circumstances beyond his control restricted his lyrical product. I scarcely remember another instance where a writer has so hoarded his early songs, and am in doubt whether to commend or deprecate their reproduction. It does not betoken affluence, but it was honest in Poe that he would not write in cold blood for the mere sake of composing. This he undoubtedly had the skill to do, and would have done, if his sole object had been creation of the beautiful, or art for art's sake. He used his lyrical gift mostly to express veritable feelings and moods — I might almost say a single feeling or mood — to which he could not otherwise give utterance, resorting to melody when prose was insufficient. Herein he was true to the cardinal, antique conception of poesy, and in keeping it distinct from his main literary work he confirmed his own avowal that it was to him a passion, and neither a purpose nor a pursuit.

Germs of his later poems.

His use of poesy.

A few poems, just as they stood in his early volumes, are admirable in thought or finish. One is the sonnet, "To Science," which is striking, not as a son-

Precocity.

net, but for its premonition of attitudes which poetry and science have now more clearly assumed. Another is the exquisite lyric, "To Helen," which every critic longs to cite. Its confusion of imagery is wholly forgotten in the delight afforded by melody, lyrical perfection, sweet and classic grace. I do not understand why he omitted this charming trifle from the juvenile poems which he added to the collection of 1845. Although it first appeared in his edition of 1831, he claimed to have written it when fourteen, and nothing more fresh and delicate came from his pen in maturer years.

"The Raven and Other Poems," 1845.

The instant success of "The Raven" — and this was within a few years of his death — first made him popular as a poet, and resulted in a new collection of his verses. The lyrics which it contained, and a few written afterward, — "Ulalume," "The Bells," "For Annie," etc., — now comprise the whole of his poetry as retained in the standard editions. The most glaring faults of "Al Aaraaf" and "Tamerlane" have been selected by eulogists for special praise. Turning from this practice-work to the poems which made his reputation, we come at once to the most widely known of all.

"The Raven."

Poe could not have written "The Raven" in youth. It exhibits a method so positive as almost to compel us to accept, against the denial of his associates, his own account of its building. The maker *does* keep a firm hand on it throughout, and for once seems to set his purpose above his passion. This appears in the gravely quaint diction, and in the contrast between the reality of every-day manners and the profounder reality of a spiritual shadow upon the human heart. The grimness of fate is suggested by phrases which it requires a masterly hand to subdue to the meaning of the poem. "'Sir,' said I, 'or madam,'" "this ungainly fowl," and the like, sustain the air of grotesqueness, and become a foil to the pathos, an approach to the tragical climax, of this unique production. Only genius can deal so closely with the grotesque, and make it add to the solemn beauty of structure an effect like that of the gargoyles seen by moonlight on the façade of Notre Dame.

Not his subtlest poem.

In no other lyric is Poe so self-possessed. No other is so determinate in its repetends and alliterations. Hence I am far from deeming it his most poetical poem. Its artificial qualities are those which catch the fancy of the general reader; and it is of all his ballads, if not the most imaginative, the most peculiar. His more ethereal productions seem to me those in which there is the appearance, at least, of spontaneity, — in which he yields to his feelings, while dying falls and cadences most musical, most melancholy, come from him unawares. Literal criticisms of "The Raven" are of small account. If the shadow of the bird could not fall upon the mourner, the shadows of its evil presence could brood upon his soul; the seraphim whose footfalls tinkle upon the tufted floor may be regarded as seraphim of the Orient, their anklets hung with celestial bells. At all events, Poe's raven is the very genius of the Night's Plutonian shore, different from other ravens, entirely his own, and none other can take its place. It is an emblem of the Irreparable, the guardian of pitiless memories, whose burden ever recalls to us the days that are no more.

"The City in the Sea."

As a new creation, then, "The Raven" is entitled to a place in literature, and keeps it. But how much more imaginative is such a poem as "The City in the Sea"! As a picture, this reminds us of Turner, and, again, of that sublime madman, John Martin. Here is a strange city where Death has raised a throne. Its

> "shrines and palaces and towers
> (Time-eaten towers that tremble not!)
> Resemble nothing that is ours.
> Around, by lifting winds forgot,
> Resignedly beneath the sky
> The melancholy waters lie."

This mystical town is aglow with light, not from heaven, but from out the lurid sea, — light which streams up the turrets and pinnacles and domes, —

> "Up many and many a marvellous shrine,
> Whose wreathed friezes intertwine
> The viol, the violet, and the vine.
> . . . .
> While, from a proud tower in the town,
> Death looks gigantically down."

The sea about is hideously serene, but at last there is a movement; the towers seem slightly to sink; the dull tide has a redder glow, —

> "And when, amid no earthly moans,
> Down, down that town shall settle hence,
> Hell, rising from a thousand thrones,
> Shall do it reverence."

This poem, notwithstanding its sombreness and terror, depends upon effects which made Poe the forerunner of our chief experts in form and sound, and both the language and the conception are suggestive in a high degree.

"The Sleeper."

"The Sleeper" is even more poetic. It distills, like drops from the opiate vapor of the swooning moonlit night, all the melody, the fantasy, the exaltation, that befit the vision of a beautiful woman lying in her shroud, silent in her length of tress, waiting to exchange her death chamber

"for one more holy,
This bed, for one more melancholy."

Poe's ideality cannot be gainsaid, but it aided him with few, very few, images, and those seemed to haunt his brain perpetually. Such an image is that of the beings who lend their menace to the tone of the funeral bells: —

"And the people, — ah, the people, —
They that dwell up in the steeple
All alone,
And who, tolling, tolling, tolling,
In that muffled monotone,
Feel a glory in so rolling
On the human heart a stone, —
They are neither man nor woman,
They are neither brute nor human,
They are Ghouls."

"The Bells."

In the same remarkable fantasia the bells themselves become human, and it is a master-stroke that makes us hear them shriek out of tune,

"In a clamorous appealing to the mercy of the fire,"

and forces us to the very madness with which they are

"Leaping higher, higher, higher,
With a desperate desire,
And a resolute endeavor
Now — now to sit, or never,
By the side of the pale-faced moon."

Clearly this extravagance was suggested by the picture and the rhyme. But it so carries us with it that we think not of its meaning; we share in the delirium of the bells, and nothing can be too extreme for the abandon to which we yield ourselves, led by the faith and frenzy of the poet.

The hinting, intermittent qualities of a few lyrics

remind us of Shelley and Coleridge, with whom Poe always was in sympathy. The conception of "The Raven" was new, but in method it bears a likeness to "Lady Geraldine's Courtship," so closely, in fact, that the rhythm of the one probably was suggested by that of the other. In motive they are so different that neither Poe nor Mrs. Browning could feel aggrieved. After an examination of dates, and of other matters relating to the genesis of each poem, I have satisfied myself, against much reasoning to the contrary, that Poe derived his use of the refrain and repetend, here and elsewhere, from the English sibyl, by whom they were employed to the verge of mannerism in her earliest lyrics.

Use of the refrain and repetend, by Mrs. Browning and by Poe. Cp. "Victorian Poets": p. 145.

"The Conqueror Worm" expresses in a single moan the hopelessness of the poet's vigils among the tombs, where he demanded of silence and the night some tidings of the dead. All he knew was that

"The Conqueror Worm."

> "No voice from that sublimer world hath ever
> To sage or poet these responses given."

The most he dared to ask for "The Sleeper" was oblivion; that her sleep might be as deep as it was lasting. We lay the dead "in the cold ground" or in the warm, flower-springing bosom of dear Earth, as best may fit the hearts of those who mourn them. But the tomb, the end of mortality, is voiceless still. If you would find the beginning of immortality, seek some other oracle. "The Conqueror Worm" is the most despairing of lyrics, yet quite essential to the mystical purpose of the tale "Ligeia." But to brood upon men as mimes, ironically cast "in the form of God on high," — mere puppets, where

> "the play is the tragedy, 'Man,'
> And its hero the Conqueror Worm,"

— that way madness lies, indeed. In the lyric, "For Annie," death is a trance; the soul lingers, calm and at rest, for the fever, called living, is conquered. Human love remains, and its last kiss is still a balm. Something may be hereafter, — but what, who knows? For repose, and for delicate and unstudied melody, it is one of Poe's truest poems, and his tenderest. During the brief period in which he survived his wife, he seemed to have a vision of rest in death, and not of horror. Two lyrics, widely different, and one of them of a most singular nature, are thought to be requiems for his lost companion. It is from no baseness, but from a divine instinct, that genuine artists are compelled to go on with their work and to make their own misery, no less than their joy, promote its uses. Their most sacred experiences become, not of their volition, its themes and illustrations. Every man as an individual is secondary to what he is as a worker for the progress of his kind and the glory of the gift allotted to him.

Requiems.

Art's strong compulsion.

Therefore, whether Poe adored his wife or not, her image became the ideal of these poems. I shall add little here to all that has been written of "Ulalume." It is so strange, so unlike anything that preceded it, so vague and yet so full of meaning, that of itself it might establish a new method. To me it seems an improvisation, such as a violinist might play upon the instrument which had become his one thing of worth after the death of a companion had left him alone with his own soul. Poe remodelled and made the most of his first broken draft, and had the grace not to analyze the process. I have accepted his analysis of "The Raven" as more than half true. Poets know that an entire poem often is suggested by one of its lines, even by a refrain or a bit of rhythm. From this

"Ulalume."

it builds itself. The last or any other stanza may be written first; and what at first is without form is not void, — for ultimately it will be perfected into shape and meaning. If "Ulalume" may be termed a requiem, "Annabel Lee" is a tuneful dirge, — the simplest of Poe's melodies, and the most likely to please the common ear. It is said to have been his last lyric, and was written, I think, with more spontaneity than others. The theme is carried along skilfully, the movement hastened and heightened to the end and there dwelt upon, as often in a piece of music. Before considering the poet's method of song, I will mention the two poems which seem to me to represent his highest range, and sufficient in themselves to preserve the memory of a lyrist.

"Annabel Lee."

Poe's highest lyrical range.

We overlook the allegory of "The Haunted Palace," until it has been read more than once; we think of the sound, the phantasmagoric picture, the beauty, the lurid close. The magic muse of Coleridge, in "Kubla Khan," or elsewhere, hardly went beyond such lines as these: —

"The Haunted Palace."

> "Banners yellow, glorious, golden,
> On its roof did float and flow,
> (This — all this — was in the olden
> Time long ago;)
> And every gentle air that dallied,
> In that sweet day,
> Along the ramparts, plumed and pallid,
> A wingèd odor went away."

The conception of a "Lost Mind" never has been so imaginatively treated, whether by poet or by painter. Questioning Poe's own mental state, look at this poem and see how sane, as an artist, he was that made it. "Do you act best when you forget yourself in the part?" "No, for then I forget to perfect the part."

"*Israfel.*" Even more striking is the song of "Israfel," whose heart-strings are a lute. Of all these lyrics is not this the most lyrical, — not only charged with music, but with light? For once, and in his freest hour of youth, Poe got above the sepulchres and mists, even beyond the pale-faced moon, and visited the empyrean. There is joy in this carol, and the radiance of the skies, and ecstatic possession of the gift of song: —

> "If I could dwell
> Where Israfel
> Hath dwelt, and he where I,
> He might not sing so wildly well
> A mortal melody,
> While a bolder note than this might swell
> From my lyre within the sky!"

All this, with the rapturous harmony of the first and third stanzas, is awakened in the poet's soul by a line from a discourse on the Koran, and the result is even finer than the theme. If I had any claim to make up a "Parnassus," not perhaps of the most famous English lyrics, but of those which appeal strongly to my own poetic sense, and could select but one of Poe's, I confess that I should choose "Israfel," for pure music, for exaltation, and for its original, satisfying quality of rhythmic art.

IV.

An exquisite but limited faculty.

Few and brief are these *reliquiæ* which determine his fame as a poet. What do they tell us of his lyrical genius and method? Clearly enough, that he possessed an exquisite faculty, which he exercised within definite bounds. It may be that within those bounds he would have done more if events had not hindered him, as he declared, "from making any serious effort" in the field of his choice. In boyhood he had decided views as to the province of song, and he never afterward changed them. The preface to his West Point edition, rambling and conceited as it is, — affording such a contrast to the proud humility of Keats's preface to "Endymion," — gives us the gist of his creed, and shows that the instinct of the young poet was scarcely less delicate than that of his nobler kinsman. Poe thought the object of poetry was pleasure, not truth; the pleasure must not be definite, but subtile, and therefore poetry is opposed to romance; music is an *essential*, "since the comprehension of sweet sound is our most indefinite conception." Metaphysics in verse he hated, pronouncing the Lake theory a new form of didacticism that had injured even the tuneful Coleridge. For a neophyte this was not bad, and after certain reservations few will disagree with him. Eighteen years later, in his charming lecture, "The Poetic Principle," he offered simply an extension of these ideas, with reasons why a long poem "cannot exist." One is tempted to rejoin that the standard of length in a poem, as in a piece of music, is relative, depending upon the power of the maker and the recipient to prolong their exalted moods. We might, also, quote Landor's "Pentameron," concerning the greatness of a poet, or even Beecher's saying that "pint measures are soon filled." The lecture justly denounces the "heresy of the didactic," and then declares poetry to be the child of Taste, — devoted solely to the Rhythmical Creation of Beauty, as it is in music that the soul most nearly attains the supernal end for which it struggles. In fine, Poe, with "the mad pride of intellectuality," refused to look beyond the scope of his own gift, and would restrict the poet to one method and even to a

Poe's theory of poetry.

Cp. "Victorian Poets": p. 127.

"The Poetic Principle," 1845.

The Rhythmical Creation of Beauty.

single theme. In his *ex post facto* analysis of "The Raven" he conceives the highest tone of beauty to be sadness, caused by the pathos of existence and our inability to grasp the unknown. Of all beauty that of a beautiful woman is the supremest, her death is the saddest loss — and therefore "the most poetical topic in the world." He would treat this musically by application of the refrain, increasing the sorrowful loveliness of his poem by contrast of something homely, fantastic, or quaint.

Poe's own range was quite within his theory. His juvenile versions of what afterward became poems were so very "indefinite" as to express almost nothing; they resembled those marvellous stanzas of Dr. Chivers, that sound magnificently, — I have heard Bayard Taylor and Swinburne rehearse them with shouts of delight — and that have no meaning at all. Poe could not remain a Chivers, but sound always was his forte. We rarely find his highest imagination in his verse, or the creation of poetic phrases such as came to the lips of Keats without a summons. He lacked the dramatic power of combination, and produced no symphony in rhythm, — was strictly a melodist, who achieved wonders in a single strain. Neither Mrs. Browning nor any other poet had "applied" the refrain in Poe's fashion, nor so effectively. In "The Bells" its use is limited almost to one word, the only English word, perhaps, that could be repeated incessantly as the burden of such a poem. In "The Raven," "Lenore," and elsewhere, he employed the repetend also, and with still more novel results: —

A melodist.

The refrain and repetend.

"An anthem for the queenliest dead that ever died so young,
A dirge for her, the doubly dead, in that she died so young."

"Our talk had been serious and sober,

> But our thoughts they were palsied and sere,
> Our memories were treacherous and sere."

One thing profitably may be noted by latter-day poets. Poe used none but elementary English measures, relying upon his music and atmosphere for their effect. This is true of those which seem most intricate, as in "The Bells" and "Ulalume." "Lenore" and "For Annie" are the simplest of ballad forms. I have a fancy that our Southern poet's ear caught the music of "Annabel Lee" and "Eulalie," if not their special quality, from the plaintive, melodious negro songs utilized by those early writers of "minstrelsy" who have been denominated the only composers of a genuine American school. This suggestion may be scouted, but an expert might suspect the one to be a patrician refinement upon the melody, feeling, and humble charm of the other.

Use of simple ballad forms.

Poe was not a single-poem poet, but the poet of a single mood. His materials were seemingly a small stock in trade, chiefly of Angels and Demons, with an attendance of Dreams, Echoes, Ghouls, Gnomes and Mimes, ready at hand. He selected or coined, for use and re-use, a number of what have been called "beautiful words," — "albatross," "halcyon," "scintillant," "Ligeia," "Weir," "Yaanek," "Auber," "D'Elormie," and the like. Everything was subordinate to sound. But his poetry, as it places us under the spell of the senses, enables us to enter, through their reaction upon the spirit, his indefinable mood; nor should we forget that Coleridge owes his specific rank as a poet, not to his philosophic verse, but to melodious fragments, and greatly to the rhythm of "The Ancient Mariner" and of "Christabel." Poe's melodies lure us to the point where we seem to hear angelic lutes and citherns, or elfin instruments that make music in "the

Effects of sound.

land east of the sun and west of the moon." The enchantment may not be that of Israfel, nor of the harper who exorcised the evil genius of Saul, but it is at least that of some plumed being of the middle air, of a charmer charming so sweetly that his numbers are the burden of mystic dreams.

V.

Poe most eminent as a romancer.

If Poe's standing depended chiefly upon these few poems, notable as they are, his name would be recalled less frequently. His intellectual strength and rarest imagination are to be found in his *Tales.* To them, and to literary criticism, his main labors were devoted.

The limits of this chapter constrain me to say less than I have in mind concerning his prose writings. As with his poems, so with the "Tales," — their dates are of little importance. His irregular life forced him to alternate good work with bad, and some of his best stories were written early. He was an apostle of the art that refuses to take its color from a given time or country, and of the revolt against commonplace, and his inventions partook of the romantic and the wonderful. He added to a Greek perception of form the Oriental passion for decoration. All the materials of the wizard's craft were at his command. He was not a pupil of Beckford, Godwin, Maturin, Hoffman, or Fouqué; and yet if these writers were to be grouped we should think also of Poe, and give him no second place among them. "The young fellow is highly imaginative, and a little given to the terrific," said Kennedy, in his honest way. Poe could not have written a novel, as we term it, as well as the feeblest of Harper's or Roberts's yearlings. He vibrated between two

Revolt against the commonplace.

poïnts, the realistic and the mystic, and made no attempt to combine people or situations in ordinary life, though he knew how to lead up to a dramatic tableau or crisis. His studies of character were not made from observation, but from acquaintance with himself; and this subjectivity, or egoism, crippled his invention and made his "Tales" little better than prose poems. He could imagine a series of adventures — the experience of a single narrator — like "Arthur Gordon Pym," and might have been, not Le Sage nor De Foe, but an eminent raconteur in his own field. His strength is unquestionable in those clever pieces of ratiocination, "The Murders in the Rue Morgue," "The Mystery of Marie Rogêt," "The Purloined Letter"; in some of a more fantastic type, "The Gold Bug" and "Hans Pfaall"; and especially in those with elements of terror and morbid psychology added, such as "The Descent into the Maelstrom," "The Black Cat," "The Tell-tale Heart," and the mesmeric sketches. When composing these he delighted in the exercise of his dexterous intellect, like a workman testing his skill. No poet is of a low grade who possesses, besides an ear for rhythm, the resources of a brain so fine and active. Technical gifts being equal, the more intellectual of two poets is the greater. "Best bard, because the wisest."

Realism and mysticism.

Psychologic analysis.

His artistic contempt for metaphysics is seen even in those tales which appear most transcendental. They are charged with a feeling that in the realms of psychology we are dealing with something ethereal, which is none the less substance if we might but capture it. They are his resolute attempts to find a clew to the invisible world. Were he living now, how much he would make of our discoveries in light and sound, of the correlation of forces! He strove by a kind of

Contempt for metaphysics.

divination to put his hand upon the links of mind and matter, and reach the hiding-places of the soul. It galled him that anything should lie outside the domain of human intelligence. His imperious intellect rebelled against the bounds that shut us in, and found passionate expression in works of which "Ligeia," "The Fall of the House of Usher," and "William Wilson" are the best types. The tales in which lyrics are introduced are full of complex beauty, the choicest products of his genius. They are the offspring of yearnings that lifted him so far above himself as to make us forget his failings and think of him only as a creative artist, a man of noble gifts.

Master-pieces.

In these short, purely ideal efforts — finished as an artist finishes a portrait, or a poet his poem — Poe had few equals in recent times. That he lacked sustained power of invention is proved, not by his failure to complete an extended work, but by his under-estimation of its value. Such a man measures everything by his personal ability, and finds plausible grounds for the resulting standard. Hawthorne had the growing power and the staying power that gave us "The Scarlet Letter" and "The House of the Seven Gables." Poe and Hawthorne were the last of the romancers. Each was a master in his way, and that of Poe was the more obvious and material. He was expert in much that concerns the structure of works, and the modelling touches of the poet left beauty-marks upon his prose. Yet in spiritual meaning his tales were less poetic than those of Hawthorne. He relied upon his externals, making the utmost of their gorgeousness of color, their splendor and gloom of light and shade. Hawthorne found the secret meaning of common things, and knew how to capture, from the plainest aspects of life, an essence of evasive beauty which the senses of

Poe and Hawthorne.

Poe often were unable to perceive. It was Hawthorne who heard the melodies too fine for mortal ear. Hawthorne was wholly masculine, with the great tenderness and gentleness which belong to virile souls. Poe had, with the delicacy, the sophistry and weakness of a nature more or less effeminate. He opposed to Hawthorne the fire, the richness, the instability of the tropics, as against the abiding strength and passion of the North. His own conceptions astonished him, and he often presents himself "with hair on end, at his own wonders." Of these two artists and seers, the New Englander had the profounder insight; the Southerner's magic was that of the necromancer who resorts to spells and devices, and, when some apparition by chance responds to his incantations, is bewildered by the phantom himself has raised.

Poe failed to see that the Puritanism by which Hawthorne's strength was tempered was also the source from which it sprang; and in his general criticism did not pay full tribute to a genius he must have felt. In some of his sketches, such as "The Man of the Crowd," he used Hawthorne's method, and with inferior results. His reviews of other authors and his occasional literary notes have been so carefully preserved as to show his nature by a mental and moral photograph. His *Marginalia*, scrappy and written for effect, are the notes of a thinking man of letters. The criticisms raised a hubbub in their day, and made Poe the bogy of his generation — the unruly censor whom weaklings not only had cause to fear, but often regarded with a sense of cruel injustice. I acknowledge their frequent dishonesty, vulgarity, prejudice, but do not, therefore, hold them to be worthless. Even a scourge, a pestilence, has its uses; before it the puny and frail go down, the fittest survive. And so it was in

"*Marginalia.*"

Poe's foray. Better that a time of unproductiveness should follow such a thinning out than that false and feeble things should continue. I suspect that *The Literati* made room for a new movement, sure though long delayed, in American authorship. Mr. Higginson, however, is entirely right when he intimates that Margaret Fuller, by her independent reviews in "The Tribune," sustained her full and early part in the chase against "such small deer." The shafts of Dian were more surely sped, and much less vindictively, than the spear of her brother-huntsman. Poe's sketches are a prose Dunciad, waspish and unfair, yet not without touches of magnanimity. He had small respect for the feeling that it is well for a critic to discover beauties, since any one can point out faults. When, as in the cases of Tennyson, Mrs. Browning, Taylor, and others, he pronounced favorably upon the talents of a claimant, and was uninfluenced by personal motives, his judgments not seldom have been justified by the after-career. Besides, what a cartoon he drew of the writers of his time, — the corrective of Griswold's optimistic delineations! In the description of a man's personal appearance he had the art of placing the subject before us with a single touch. His tender mercies were cruel; he never forgot to prod the one sore spot of the author he most approved, — was especially intolerant of his own faults in others, and naturally detected these at once. When meting out punishment to a pretentious writer, he revelled in his task, and often made short work, as if the pleasure was too great to be endurable. The keenness of his satire, just or unjust, is mitigated by its obvious ferocity: one instinctively takes part with the victim. Nothing in journalistic criticism, even at that time, was more scathing and ludicrous than his conceit of a popular bookwright in the act of confabu-

"The Literati," 1846.

Cp. pp. 42–44.

Satire.

lation with the Universe. But he marred the work by coarseness, telling one man that he was by no means a fool, although he did write "De Vere," and heading a paper on the gentlest and most forbearing of poets — "Mr. Longfellow and other Plagiarists." In short, he constantly dulled the edge and temper of his rapier, and resorted to the broad-axe, using the latter even in his deprecation of its use by Kit North. Perhaps it was needed in those salad days by offenders who could be put down in no other wise; but I hold it a sign of progress that criticism by force of arms would now be less effective.

Broad-axe criticism.

VI.

SOME analysis of Poe's general equipment will not be out of place. Only in the most perfect tales can his English style be called excellent, however significant his thought. His mannerisms — constant employment of the *dash* for suggestiveness, and a habit of italicizing to make a point or strengthen an illusion — are wearisome, and betray a lack of confidence in his skill to use plain methods. While asserting the power of words to convey absolutely any idea of the human mind, he relied on sound, quaintness, surprise, and other artificial aids. His prose is inferior to Hawthorne's; but sometimes he excels Hawthorne in qualities of form and proportion which are specially at the service of authors who are also poets. The abrupt beginnings of his stories often are artistic: —

Poe's equipment and genius.

"We had now reached the summit of the loftiest crag. For some minutes the old man seemed too much exhausted to speak." ("Descent into the Maelstrom.")

"The thousand injuries of Fortunato I had borne as best I could; but when he ventured upon insult, I vowed revenge." ("The Cask of Amontillado.")

His endings were equally good, when he had a clear knowledge of his own purpose, and some of his conceptions terminate at a dramatic crisis. The tone, also, of his masterpieces is well sustained throughout. In "The Fall of the House of Usher," the approach to the fated spot, the air, the landscape, the tarn, the mansion itself, are a perfect study, equal to the ride of Childe Roland, — and here Poe excels Browning: we not only come with him to the dark tower, but we enter and partake its mystery, and alone know the secret of its accursed fate. The poet's analytic faculty has been compared to that of Balzac, but a parallel goes no farther than the material side. In condensation he surpassed either Balzac or Hawthorne.

"The Fall of the House of Usher."

Balzac.

Poe's imagination.

His imagination was not of the highest order, for he never dared to trust to it implicitly; certainly not in his poetry, since he could do nothing with a measure like blank verse, which is barren in the hands of a mere songster, but the glory of English metrical forms when employed by one commanding the strength of diction, the beauty and grandeur of thought, and all the resources of a strongly imaginative poet. Neither in verse nor in prose did he cut loose from his minor devices, and for results of sublimity and awe he always depends upon that which is grotesque or out of nature. Beauty of the fantastic or grotesque is not the highest beauty. Art, like nature, must be fantastic, not in her frequent, but in her exceptional moods. The rarest ideal dwells in a realm beyond that which fascinates us by its strangeness or terror, and the votaries of the latter have masters above them as high as Raphael is above Doré.

The fantastic.

Deficient in humor.

In genuine humor Poe seemed utterly wanting. He also had little of the mother-wit that comes in flashes and at once; but his powers of irony and satire were so great as to make his frequent lapses into invective the more humiliating. The command of humor has distinguished men whose genius was both high and broad. If inessential to exalted poetic work, its absence is hurtful to the critical and polemic essay. Poe knew this as well as any one, but a measureless self-esteem would not acknowledge the flaw in his armor. Hence efforts which involved the delusion that humor may come by works and not by inborn gift. Humor is congenital and rare, the fruit of natural mellowness, of sensitiveness to the light and humane phases of life. It is, moreover, set in action by an unselfish heart. Such is the mirth of Thackeray, of Cervantes and Molière, and of the one master of English song. Poe's consciousness of his defect, and his refusal to believe it incurable, are manifest in trashy sketches for which he had a market, and which are humorous only to one who sees the ludicrous side of their failure. He analyzed mirth as the product of incongruity, and went to work upon a theory to produce it. The result is seen not only in the extravaganzas to which I refer, — and it is a pity that these should have been hunted up so laboriously, — but in the use of what he thought was humor to barb his criticisms, and as a contrast to the exciting passages of his analytical tales. One of his sketches, "The Duc de l'Omelette," after the lighter French manner, has grace and jaunty persiflage, but most of his whimsical "pot-boilers" are deplorably absurd. There is something akin to humor in the sub-handling of his favorite themes, — such as the awe and mystery of death, the terrors of pestilence, insanity, or remorse. The grotesque and nether side of these matters presents itself to him, and then his irony, with its repulsive fancies, is as near humor as he ever

Quality of the great humorists. *Cp. "Victorian Poets": pp. 73, 77.*

The grotesque.

approaches. That is to say, it is grave-yard humor, the kind which sends a chill down our backs, and implies a contempt for our bodies and souls, for the perils, helplessness, and meanness of the stricken human race.

Character of his scholarship.

Poe is sometimes called a man of extraordinary learning. Upon a first acquaintance, one might receive the impression that his scholarship was not only varied, but thorough. A study of his works has satisfied me that he possessed literary resources and knew how to make the most of them. In this he resembled Bulwer, and, with far less abundant materials than the latter required, employed them as speciously. He easily threw a glamour of erudition about his work, by the use of phrases from old authors he had read, or among whose treatises he had foraged with special design. It was his knack to cull sentences which, taken by themselves, produce a weird or impressive effect, and to reframe them skilfully. This plan was clever, and resulted in something that could best be muttered "darkly, at dead of night"; but it partook of trickery, even in its art. He had little exact scholarship, nor needed it, dealing, as he did, not with the processes of learning, but with results that could subserve the play of his imagination. Shakespeare's anachronisms and illusions were made as he required them, and with a fine disdain. Poe resorted to them of malice aforethought, and under pretence of correctness. Still, the work of a romancer and poet is not that of a book-worm. What he needs is a good reference-knowledge, and this Poe had. His irregular school-boy training was not likely to give him the scholastic habit, nor would his impatient manhood otherwise have confirmed it. I am sure that we may consider that portion of his youth to have been of

Affectation of learning.

A good reference-knowledge.

most worth which was devoted, as in the case of many a born writer, to the unconscious education obtained from the reading, for the mere love of it, of *all* books to which he had access. This training served him well. It enabled him to give his romance an alchemic air, by citation from writers like Chapman, Thomas More, Bishop King, etc., and from Latin and French authors in profusion. His French tendencies were natural, and he learned enough of the language to read much of its current literature and get hold of modes unknown to many of his fellow-writers. I have said that his stock in trade was narrow, but for the adroit display of it examine any of his tales and sketches, — for example, "Berenice," or "The Assignation."

His materials.

In knowledge of what may be called the properties of his romance, he was more honestly grounded. He had the good fortune to utilize the Southern life and scenery which he knew in youth. It chanced, also, that during some years of his boyhood — that formative period whose impressions are indelible — he lived in a characteristic part of England. He had seen with his own eyes castles, abbeys, the hangings and tapestries and other by-gone trappings of ancient rooms, and remembered effects of decoration and color which always came to his aid. These he used as if he were born to them; never, certainly, with the surprise at their richness which vulgarizes Disraeli's "Lothair." In some way, known to genius, he also caught the romance of France, of Italy, of the Orient, and one tale or another is transfused with their atmosphere; while the central figure, however disguised, is always the image of the romancer himself. His equipment, on the whole, was not a pedant's, much less that of a searcher after truth; it was that of a poet and

"Eureka: a Prose Poem," 1848.

a literary workman. Yet he had the hunger which animates the imaginative student, and, had he been led to devote himself to science, would have contributed to the sum of knowledge. In writing *Eureka* he was unquestionably sincere, and forgot himself more nearly than in any other act of his professional life. But here his inexact learning betrayed him. What was begun in conviction — a swift generalization from scientific theories of the universe — grew to be so far beyond the data at his command, or so inconsistent with them, that he finally saw he had written little else than a prose poem, and desired that it should be so regarded. Of all sciences, astronomy appeals most to the imagination. What is rational in "Eureka" mostly is a re-statement of accepted theories: otherwise the treatise is vague and nebulous, — a light dimmed by its own vapor. The work is curiously saturated with our modern Pantheism; and although in many portions it shows the author's weariness, yet it was a notable production for a layman venturing within the precincts of the savant. The poetic instinct hits upon truths which the science of the future confirms; but as often, perhaps, it glorifies some error sprung from a too ardent generalization. Poe's inexactness was shown in frequent slips, — sometimes made unconsciously, sometimes in reliance upon the dulness of his rivals to save him from detection. He was on the alert for other people's errors; for his own facts, were he now alive, he could not call so lightly upon his imagination. Even our younger authors, here and abroad, now are so well equipped that their learning seems to handicap their winged steeds. Poe had, above all, the gift of poetic induction. He would have divined the nature of an unknown world from a specimen of its flora, a fragment of its art. He felt himself

A layman's imaginative venture. Cp. "Victorian Poets": pp. 19, 20.

Poetic induction.

something more than a bookman. He was a creator of the beautiful, and hence the conscious struggle of his spirit for the sustenance it craved. Even when he was most in error, he labored as an artist, and it is idle criticism that judges him upon any other ground.

Accept him, then, whether as poet or romancer, as a pioneer of the art feeling in American literature. So far as he was devoted to art for art's sake, it was for her sake as the exponent of beauty. No man ever lived in whom the passion for loveliness more plainly governed the emotions and convictions. His service of the beautiful was idolatry, and he would have kneeled with Heine at the feet of Our Lady of Milo, and believed that she yearned to help him. This consecration to absolute beauty made him abhor the mixture of sentimentalism, metaphysics, and morals, in its presentation. It was a foregone conclusion that neither Longfellow, Emerson, Lowell, nor Hawthorne should wholly satisfy him. The question of "moral" tendency concerned him not in the least. He did not feel with Keats that "Beauty is truth, truth beauty," and that a divine perfection may be reached by either road. This deficiency narrowed his range both as a poet and as a critic. His sense of justice was a sense of the fitness of things, and — strange to say — when he put it aside he forgot that he was doing an unseemly thing. Otherwise, he represents, or was one of the first to lead, a rebellion against formalism, commonplace, the spirit of the bourgeois. In this movement Whitman is his countertype at the pole opposite from that of art; and hence they justly are picked out from the rest of us and associated in foreign minds. Taste was Poe's supreme faculty. Beauty, to him, was a definite and logical reality, and he would have scouted Véron's

Poe's absolute love of beauty.

His protest against didacticism.

Taste.

claim that it has no fixed objective laws, and exists only in the nature of the observer. Although the brakes of art were on his imagination, his taste was not wholly pure; he vacillated between the classic forms and those allied with color, splendor, Oriental decoration; between his love for the antique and his impressions of the mystical and grotesque. But he was almost without confraternity. An artist in an unartistic period, he had to grope his way, to contend with stupidity and coarseness. Again, his imagination, gloating upon the possibilities of taste, violated its simplicity. Poe longed for the lamp of Aladdin, for the riches of the Gnomes. Had unbounded wealth been his, he would have outvied Beckford, Landor, Dumas, in barbaric extravagance of architecture. His efforts to apply the laws of the beautiful to imaginary decoration, architecture, landscape, are very fascinating as seen in "The Philosophy of Furniture," "Landscape Gardening," and "Landor's Cottage." "The Domain of Arnheim" is a marvellous dream of an earthly paradise, and the close is a piece of word-painting as effective as the language contains. Regarding this sensitive artist, this original poet, it seems indeed a tragedy that a man so ideal in either realm, so unfit for contact with ugliness, dulness, brutality, should have come to eat husks with the swine, to be misused by their human counterparts, and to die the death of a drunkard, in the refuge which society offers to the most forlorn and hopeless of its castaways.

Isolation.

Decorative feeling.

A tragedy.

VII.

A singular and pathetic career.

SEEKING our illustrations of the poetic life, we find no career of more touching and peculiar interest than that of Poe. It is said that disaster followed him even after death, in the vicious memoir which Griswold prefixed to his collected works; and doubtless the poet should have had for his biographer a man of kind and healthy discernment, like Kennedy, his townsman and generous friend. Yet Poe showed tact in choosing Griswold, and builded better than he knew. He could select no more indefatigable bookwright to bring together his scattered writings, and he counted upon Death's paying all debts. In this Poe was mistaken. For once Griswold wrote as he thought and felt, and his memoir, however spiteful and unchivalrous, was more sincere than many of the sycophantic sketches in the bulky volumes of his "Poets and Poetry." Malice made him eloquent, and an off-hand obituary notice of the poet was the most nervous piece of work that ever came from his pen. It was heartless, and, in some respects, inaccurate. It brought so much wrath upon him that he became vindictive, and followed it up with a memoir, which, as an exhibition of the ignoble nature of its author, scarcely has a parallel. Did this in the end affect Poe's fame injuriously? Far otherwise; it moved a host of writers, beginning with Willis and Graham, to recall his habit of life, and reveal the good side of it. Some have gone as far in eulogy as Griswold went toward the opposite extreme. It seemed a cruel irony of fate that Poe's own biographer should plant thorns upon his grave, but he also planted laurels. He paid an unstinted tribute to the poet's genius, and this was the only concession which Poe himself would care to demand. With sterner irony, Time brings in his revenges! In a familiar edition of the poet's works, for which Griswold laid the groundwork, the memoir by Ingram is devoted largely to

Griswold's memoir.

Effect upon Poe's fame.

correcting the errors of the Doctor's long-since excluded sketch, and to exposing every act of malice against Poe which Griswold committed, either before or after his foeman's death.

Poe's habits and temperament.

After years of censure and defence, and in the light of his own writings, the poet's character is not "beyond all conjecture." Here was a man of letters who fulfilled the traditions of a past century in this western world and modern time; one over-possessed and hampered by the very temperament that made him a poet — and this, too, when he thought himself deliberate and calculating. His head was superbly developed, his brain-power too great for its resources of supply and control. The testimony of some who knew his home-life is that he was tender and lovable. Graham and Willis aver that he was patient and regular in work, and scrupulous to return a just amount of labor for value received. But many who knew and befriended him have spoken, more in sorrow than in anger, of his treachery and thanklessness, of his injustice to himself, and of the degrading excesses which plunged him into depths from which it grew more and more difficult to lift him.

Love of the ideal a restraint upon sensuality.

Nevertheless, Poe was not a man of immoral habits. I assert that scholars, writers, and artists, in spite of a tradition to the contrary, are less given, as a class, to forbidden pleasures than business-men and idle men of the world. Study and a love of the ideal protect them against the sensuality by which too many dull the zest of their appetites. Poe was no exception to the rule. He was not a libertine. Woman was to him the impersonation of celestial beauty, her influence soothed and elevated him, and in her presence he was gentle, winning, and subdued. There is not an unchaste suggestion in the whole course of his writings,

Chastity of Poe's writings.

— a remarkable fact, in view of his acquaintance with the various schools of French literature. His works are almost too spiritual. Not of the earth, earthy, their personages meet with the rapture and co-absorption of disembodied souls. His verse and prose express devotion to Beauty in her most ethereal guise, and he justly might cry out with Shelley: —

> " I vowed that I would dedicate my powers
> To thee and thine; have I not kept the vow?"

Not a scoffer nor an habitual drunkard.

Nor was he undevotional. His sense of the sublime and mystical filled him with thoughts of other worlds and existences than ours; if there is pride, there is reverence, in his bold imaginings. He felt a spark of the divine fire within him, and the pride of his intellectual disdain was, like the Titan's, a not inglorious sin. Finally, Poe was not an habitual drunkard. He had woful fits of drunkenness, varying in frequency, and sometimes of degradation; for a single glass made him the easy prey of any coarse and pitiless hands into which he might fall. He was a man inebriate when sober, his brain surging with emotion, and a stimulant that only served to steady common men bewildered him. As with women, the least contamination was to him debasement. His mature years were a battle with inherited taint, and there were long periods in which he was the victor. This taint had been increased by drugging in infancy, and by the convivial usages of his guardian's household. Bearing in mind, also, the lack of self-control inherent in Celtic and Southern natures, I think he made a plucky fight. The duty of self-support was not one to which he had been trained, and was more than he could bear. Imagine Shelley, who made his paper boats of bank-notes, Byron and Landor, who had their old estates,

His hereditary taint.

forced to write by the column for their weekly board. "Poverty has this disease: through want it teaches a man evil." More, it limits the range of his possibilities. Doudan has said, with truth and feeling, that he who is without security for the morrow can neither meditate upon nor accomplish a lasting work. The delicate fancies of certain writers are not always at quick command, and the public is loath to wait and pay for quality. Poe, more than once, fell into disgrace by not being able to meet his literary engagements on time. His most absurd and outrageous articles, such as the one put forth after his Boston lecture, were the bluster of a man who strove to hide a sense of humiliation and failure. Doubtless, he secretly invoked the gods in his own behalf. He knew, like Chénier going to his death, that it was a pity — he was worth saving. Generous efforts, in truth, were made to save him, by strong and tender friends, but these were quite in vain. He carried a death-warrant within him. Well might he feel that a spell was on him, and in one tale and another try to make the world — which he affected to despise — comprehend its fatality, and bespeak the sympathetic verdict of the future upon his defeat and doom.

Effects of poverty. Cp. "Victorian Poets": p. 81.

It is just that well-balanced persons should rebuke the failings of genius. But let such an one imagine himself with a painfully sensitive organization, — "all touch, all eye, all ear"; with appetites almost resistless; with a frame in which health and success breed a dangerous rapture, disease and sorrow a fatal despair. Surmount all this with a powerful intelligence that does not so much rule the structure as it menaces it, and threatens to shake it asunder. Let him conceive himself as adrift, from the first, among adverse surroundings, now combating his environment, now

His sensitive temperament.

struggling to adjust himself to it. He, too, might find his judgment a broken reed; his passions might get the upper hand; his perplexities bring him to shamelessness and ruin. It was thus the poet's curse came upon him, and the wings of his Psyche were sorrowfully trailed in the dust. I have said to friends as they sneered at the ill-managed life of one whose special genius perhaps could not exist but in union with certain infirmities, that instead of recounting these, and deriding them, they should hedge him round with their protection. We can find more than one man of sense among a thousand, but how rarely a poet with such a gift! When he has gone his music will linger, and be precious to those who never have heard, like ourselves, the sweet bells jangled.

The priceless rarity of genius.

Making every allowance, Poe was terribly blamable. We all are misunderstood, and all condemned to toil. The sprites have their task-work, and cannot always be dancing in the moonlight. At times, we are told, they have to consort with what is ugly, and even take on its guise. Unhappily, Poe was the reverse of one who "fortune's buffets and rewards has ta'en with equal thanks." He stood good fortune more poorly than bad; any emotion would upset him, and his worst falls were after successes, or with success just in sight. His devotion to beauty was eagerly selfish. He had a heart, and in youth was loyal to those he loved. In this respect he differed from the hero of "A Strange Story," born without affection or soul. But his dream was that of "The Palace of Art"—a lordly pleasure-house, where taste and love should have their fill, regardless of the outer world. It has been well said, that if not immoral, he was unmoral. With him an end justified the means, and he had no conception of the law and limitations

Lack of self-poise.

Not immoral, but unmoral.

of liberty, no practical sense of right or wrong. At the most, he ignored such matters as things irrelevant. Now it is not essential that one should have a creed; he may relegate theologies to the regions of the unknowable; but he must be just in order to fear not, and humane that he may be loved; he must be faithful to some moral standard of his own, otherwise his house, however beautiful and lordly, is founded in the sand.

Is genius the product of neurotic disorder?

The question always will recur, whether, if Poe had been able to govern his life aright, he would not also have been conventional and tame, and so much the less a poet. Were it not for his excesses and neurotic crises, should we have had the peculiar quality of his art and the works it has left us? I cannot here discuss the theory that his genius was a frenzy, and that poetry is the product of abnormal nerve-vibrations. The claim, after all, is a scientific statement of the belief that great wits are sure to madness near allied. An examination of it involves the whole ground of fate, free will, and moral responsibility. I think that Poe was bounden for his acts. He never failed to resent infringements upon his own manor; and, however poor his self-control, it was not often with him that the chord of self passed trembling out of sight. Possibly his most exquisite, as they were his most poetic, moments, were at those times when he seemed very wretched, and avowed himself oppressed by a sense of doom. He loved his share of pain, and was an instance of the fact that man is the one being that takes keen delight in the tragedy of its own existence, and for whom

"Joy is deepest when it springs from woe."

Wandering among the graves of those he had cherished, invoking the spectral midnight skies, believing himself the Orestes of his race — in all this he was fulfilling his nature, deriving the supremest sensations, feeding on the plants of night from which such as he obtain their sustenance or go famished. They who do not perceive this never will comprehend the mysteries of art and song, of the heart from whose recesses these must be evoked. They err who commiserate Poe for such experiences. My own pity for him is of another kind; it is that which we ever must feel for one in whom the rarest possibilities were blighted by an inherent *lack of will.* In his sensitiveness to impressions like the foregoing, he had at once the mood and material for far greater results than he achieved. A violin cracks none the sooner for being played in a minor key. His instrument broke for want of a firm and even hand to use it — a virile, devoted master to prolong the strain.

Secret of Poe's disasters.

Poe's demand for his present wish was always strong, yet it was the caprice of a child, and not the determination that stays and conquers. He was no more of an egoist than was Goethe; but self-absorption is the edged tool that maims a wavering hand. His will, in the primary sense, was weak from the beginning. It became more and more reduced by those habits which, of all the defences of a noble mind, attack this stronghold first. It was not able to preserve for him the sanity of true genius, and his product, therefore, was so much the less complete.

No real strength of will.

> "O well for him whose will is strong!
> He suffers, but he will not suffer long."

Poe suffered, in bitter truth, and the end came not through triumph, but in death. His fame is not what it might have been, we say; yet it is greater than he

Fame waits on worth and work.

— dying with a sense of incompleteness — probably expected it to be, and more than he could have asked. In spite, then, of the most reckless career, the work a man really accomplishes — both for what it is in itself and for what it reveals of the author's gift — in the end will be valued exactly at its worth. Does the poet, the artist, demand some promise that it also may be made to tell during our working life, and even that life be lengthened till the world shall learn to honor it? Let him recall the grave, exalted words which Poe took at hazard for his "Ligeia," and stayed not to dwell upon their spiritual meaning: "Man doth not yield himself to the angels, nor unto death utterly, save only through the weakness of his own feeble will."

CHAPTER VIII.

OLIVER WENDELL HOLMES.

I.

A DISCUSSION of any art or artist readily enough might begin with a chapter on Fashion. Of this I ask no livelier illustration than the experience of a poet whose time-honored method is just now fresh in favor, as if he were at matins instead of even-song. It is somewhat strange that the Greeks — at least those late Athenians who spent their time in nothing else but either to tell or to hear some new thing — should have left vacant the seat in their hemicycle to which their gay inheritors have directed that puissant goddess, La Mode. The dullest know that to her are sacred, as the school-books say, not only dress and manners, but styles of furniture, decoration, and all that caters to the lust of the eye and the pride of life. But the adept perceive that fashion often decides our taste in literature, our bent of study, and even of religious thought; how much it has to do with the spirit, no less than the outcome, of human effort. Progress comes by experiment, and this from ennui — ennui that leads to voyages, wars, revolutions, and plainly to change in the arts of expression; that cries out to the imagination, and is the nurse of the invention whereof we term necessity the mother. The best of modes is not above challenge. No stroke can always hold the trophy. Pretty much the same instinct that makes a

Fashion, or Vogue, in Art. *Cp. "Victorian Poets": p. 150.*

woman accept the later, perhaps the uglier, style of dress, secures a trial, even a vogue, to some new method in art or letters. Few demur longer than Taglioni's sister, who stared at a bonnet, the last new thing from Paris, then laughed outright and said, "How very ridiculous you look, my dear. . . . Can you get me one like it?" In fact, we must have discovery, and that by licensing the fashions of successive times, most of them defective, many retrogressive, a few on the path to higher use and beauty. These few may return again and again; they go out of sight, but on an elliptic orbit. Contemporary judgment is least of all judicial. The young forestall novelty itself. The old mistrust or look backward with a sense of loss. It is hard for either to apply tests that are above each fashion, yet derived from all. I suppose that in vicious, and in barren, periods of our English song, men's faculties were much the same as ever; that a sense of beauty was on the alert. There is an exhortation to critical humility when some despised style of a past century suddenly appears fit and attractive; when, from caprice or wholesome instinct, we pick up the round-bowed spectacles of our forbears and see things as they saw them. Their art, dress, accent, quaintly rebuke us; their dainty spirit lives again, and we adopt, as lightly as we formerly contemned, a fashion which we avow that at last we rightly interpret.

Revival of old time modes.

It is wholly natural, then, that a poet like Dr. Holmes should have been in vogue and out of vogue; one who easily can afford to regard either position with tranquillity, but at times, it may be, and solely as to his metrical theories, thought somewhat too antiquated by wits of the new dispensation. At this moment, — the favorite both of Time, to whom thanks for touching him so gently, and of a tide that again bears him forward, — he is warmly appreciated by verse-makers of the latest mode. As a scientific homilist, his popular gauge has been less subject to fluctuations. Science has but one fashion — to lose nothing once gained; and Holmes's pluck and foresight kept him ahead till his neighbors caught up and justified him. His verse, however, puts us on terms with a man of certain tastes and breeding; it is the result of qualities which may or may not be fashionable at a given date. Just now they connect him with the army of occupation, — a veteran, it is true, but, despite his ribbons and crosses, assuredly not "retired."

Holmes's method a survival, and not a renaissance.

The distinction between his poetry and that of the new makers of society-verse is that his is a survival, theirs the attempted revival, of something that has gone before. He wears the seal of "that past Georgian day" by direct inheritance, not from the old time in England, but from that time in England's lettered colonies, whose inner sections still preserve the hereditary language and customs as they are scarcely to be found elsewhere. His work is as emblematic of the past as are the stairways and hand-carvings in various houses of Cambridge, Portsmouth, and Norwich. Some of our modern verse is a symptom of the present renaissance, — which itself delights in going beyond its models. More spindles, more artifice, more furbelows and elaborate graces. Its originals were an imitation, as we find them in the villas of Pope and Walpole, in Hogarth's toilet-party, in architecture, gardening, costume, furniture, manners. Here were negro pages, gewgaws, silks and porcelain from China (as now from Japan) — a mixture of British, Gallic, and Oriental fashions and decorations.

The new vogue.

Now we are working in much the same spirit, and

even more resolutely, with novelties added from regions then unfamiliar, but reviving in both life and literature the manner of that day. A new liking for the Georgian heroics and octosyllabics is queerly blended with our practice in the latest French forms, — themselves a revival of a far more ancient minstrelsy. Such things when first produced, the genuine expression of their time, may yield a less conscious pleasure, but are of more worth; they have the savor of honest purpose, which their imitation lacks. Among living old-style poets, Dr. Holmes, the least complex and various, seems most nearly to the manner born; his work, as I say, being a survival, and not an experiment. It is freshened, however, by the animation which, haplessly for compilers of provincial literature, was wanting in the good Old Colony days. The maker wears the ancestral garb, and is a poet in spite of it. His verses have the courtesy and wit, without the pedagogy, of the knee-buckle time, and a flavor that is really their own. There are other eighteenth-century survivors, whose sponsors are formality and dulness; but Holmes has the modern vivacity, and adjusts without effort even the most hackneyed measures to a new occasion. Throughout the changes of fifty years he has practised the method familiar to his youth, thinking it fit and natural, and one to which he would do well to cling. The conservative persistency of his muse is as notable in matter as in manner. On the whole, so far as we can classify him, he is at the head of his class, and in other respects a class by himself.

Holmes, the leader of his class.

Always a University poet.

Though the most direct and obvious of the Cambridge group, the least given to subtilties, he is our typical university poet; the minstrel of the college that bred him, and within whose liberties he has taught, jested, sung, and toasted, from boyhood to what in common folk would be old age. Alma Mater has been more to him than to Lowell or Longfellow, — has occupied a surprising portion of his range; if we go back to Frere and Canning, even to Gray, for his like, there is no real prototype, and yet, as a university poet, he curiously illustrates his own theories of natural descent. Behind him figure many Harvard rhymesters, — scholars and divines, who, like the Wartons at Oxford, wrote verse whether poets or not, English and Latin *nullo discrimine*, and few indeed were our early verse-makers that were not college men. Holmes would be Holmes, if Norton and Urian Oakes, — to say nothing of their Tenth Muse, Mistress Bradstreet, whose Augustan features, if some Smybert only had preserved them for us, assuredly should distinguish the entrance to the Harvard Annex, — if these worthies, even if Byles and Green, had not flourished before him; but he is the lawful heir to their fervor, wit, and authority, and not until he came into his estate could Harvard boast a natural songster as her laureate. Two centuries of acclimation, and some experience of liberty, probably were needed to germinate the fancy that riots in his measures. Before his day, moreover, the sons of the Puritans hardly were ripe for the doctrine that there is a time to laugh, that humor is quite as helpful a constituent of life as gravity or gloom. Provincial-wise, they at first had to receive this in its cruder form, and relished heartily the broad fun of Holmes's youthful verse. Their mirth-maker soon perceived that both fun and feeling are heightened when combined. As a wit, no writer of English, unless it be Lowell, at this day vies with him. As a humorist, the poet of "The Last Leaf" was among the first to teach his countrymen that pathos is an equal part of

Disperser of the ancestral gloom.

true humor; that sorrow is lightened by jest, and jest redeemed from coarseness by emotion, under most conditions of this our evanescent human life.

II.

Oliver Wendell Holmes: born in Cambridge, Mass., Aug. 29, 1809.

WHAT one does easily is apt to be his forte, though years may pass before he finds this out. Holmes's early pieces, mostly college-verse, were better of their kind than those of a better kind written in youth by some of his contemporaries. The humbler the type, the sooner the development. The young poet had the aid of a suitable habitat; life at Harvard was the precise thing to bring out his talent. There was nothing of the hermit-thrush in him; his temper was not of the withdrawing and reflective kind, nor moodily introspective, — it throve on fellowship, and he looked to his mates for an audience as readily as they to him for a toast-master. He seems to have escaped the poetic measles altogether; if not, he hid his disorder with rare good sense, for his verse nowhere shows that he felt himself "among men, but not of them"; on the contrary, he fairly might plume himself on reversing the Childe's boast, and declare "I have loved the world, and the world me." The thing we first note is his elastic, buoyant nature, displayed from youth to age with cheery frankness, — so that we instinctively search through his Dutch and Puritan ancestries to see where came in the strain that made this Yankee Frenchman of so likable a type. Health begets relish, and Holmes has never lacked for zest, — zest that gives one the sensations best worth living for, if happiness be the true aim of life. He relished from the first, as keenly as an actor or orator or a clever woman, appreciation within sight and sound. There is

At Harvard, 1825–29.

Light of heart, and full of health and zest.

an unwritten Plaudite at the end of every poem, almost of every stanza. He has taken his reward as he went along, even before printing his songs; and if he should fail of the birds in the bush, certainly has held to every one in hand. It is given to few to capture both the present and the future, — to Holmes, perhaps, more nearly than to most of his craft, yet he would be the last to doubt that he stands on lower ground than those to whom poetry, for its own sake, has been a passion and belief. In his early work the mirth so often outweighed the sentiment as to lessen the promise and the self-prediction of his being a poet indeed. Some of one's heart-blood must spill for this, and, while many of his youthful stanzas are serious and eloquent, those which approach the feeling of true poetry are in celebration of companionship and good cheer, so that he seems like a down-East Omar or Hafiz, exemplifying what our gracious Emerson was wont to preach, that there is honest wisdom in song and joy.

"The Collegian," 1830.

If the Rev. Abiel Holmes had serious thoughts of finding his boy so animated by the father's "Life of Dr. Stiles" as to be set upon entering the ministry, they must have faded out as he read the graceless rhymes, the comic and satiric verse, which the vivacious youth furnished to "The Collegian." His metrical escapades also boded ill, as in Lowell's case, for a long allegiance to the law, — which, it seems, he read after graduation. No one can long remain a good lawyer and a fertile man of letters. The medical profession, however, has teemed with poets and scholars; for its practice makes literary effort a delightful change, an avocation, rather than a fatiguing addition to scriptural labor for daily bread. Dr. Samuel Latham Mitchill, for instance, fifty years ago in New York, was almost the prototype,

Medical men of letters.

mutatis mutandis, of our Autocrat, by virtue of his wit, learning, literary work, and civic and social importance. Holmes is a shining instance of one who has done solid work as a teacher and practitioner, in spite of his success in literature. As a versifier, he started with the advantage of hitting the public by buffo-pieces, and with the disadvantage of being expected to make his after-hits in the same manner, — to write for popular amusement in the major rather than the minor key. His verses, with the measured drum-beat of their natural rhythm, were easily understood; he bothered his audience with no accidental effects, no philandering after the finer lyrical distinctions. It is not hard to surmise what "standard" poets had been found on his father's book-shelves. Eloquence was a feature of his lyrics, — such as broke out in the line, "Ay, tear her tattered ensign down!" and the simple force of "Old Ironsides" is indeed worth noting as it culminates in the last stanza. The making of verse that is seized upon by school-day spokesmen barely outlived the influence of Croly, of Drake and Halleck, of Pierpont with his "Stand! the ground's your own, my braves!" and Holmes himself would scarcely write in this way now. Yet one who sees, looming up by the Portsmouth docks, a fine old hulk to which these lines secured half a century of preservation will find them coming again to mind. "The Meeting of the Dryads," another early poem, is marked by so much grace that it seems as if the youth who wrote its quatrains might in time have added a companion-piece to "The Talking Oak." The things which he turned off with purely comic aim were neatly finished, and the merriment of a new writer, who dared not be "as funny" as he could, did quite as much for him as his poems of a higher class. The fashion of the latter,

Qualities of Holmes's early verse.

Rhetoric.

however, we see returning again. There is the pathetic silhouette of the old man, who so

Knee-buckle verse.

> "shakes his feeble head,
> That it seems as if he said,
> 'They are gone.'"

This equals the best recent knee-buckle verse, and excels most of it in simplicity. It taught a lesson to Locker and Saxe, and more than one among younger favorites look up to Holmes affectionately, conscious that the author of "The Last Leaf," "My Aunt," "The Dilemma," and of later trifles still more refined, like "Dorothy Q.," is the Nestor of their light-armed holiday encampment.

Personal characteristics.

A poet so full of zest is wont to live his life, rather than to scorn delights in service of the thankless muse. Dr. Holmes's easy-going method, and a sensible estimate of his own powers, have defined the limits of his zeal. His poetry was and is, like his humor, the overflow of a nervous, original, decidedly intellectual nature; of sparkling life, no less, in which he gathered the full worth of heyday experiences. See that glimpse of Paris, a student's pencilled sketch, with Clemence tripping down the Rue de Seine. It is but a bit, yet through its atmosphere we make out a poet who cared as much for the sweets of the poetic life as for the work that was its product. He had through it all a Puritan sense of duty, and the worldly wisdom that goes with a due perception of values, and he never lost sight of his practical career. His profession, after all, was what he took most seriously. Accepting, then, with hearty thanks, his care-dispelling rhyme and reason, pleased often by the fancies which he tenders in lieu of imagination and power, — we go through the collection of his verse, and see that it has amounted to a great deal in the course of a bustling fifty years.

These numerous pieces divide themselves, as to form, into two classes, — lyrics and poetic essays in solid couplet-verse; as to purpose, into the lighter songs that may be sung, and the nobler numbers, part lyrical, part the poems, both gay and sober, delivered at frequent intervals during his pleasant career. He is a song-writer of the natural kind, through his taste for the open vowel-sounds, and for measures that set themselves to tune. Lyrics of high grade, whose verbal and rhythmical design is of itself sufficient for the spiritual ear, are not those which are best adapted to the musician's needs. Some of Holmes's ballads are still better than his songs. Lines in "The Pilgrim's Vision" have a native flavor: —

A natural songster and balladist.

> "Come hither, God-be-Glorified,
> And sit upon my knee;
> Behold the dream unfolding
> Whereof I spake to thee,
> By the winter's hearth in Leyden,
> And on the stormy sea."

Even his ballads are raciest when brimmed with the element that most attracts their author, that of festive good-fellowship. He gives us a brave picture of Miles Standish, the little captain, stirring a posset with his sword: —

> "He poured the fiery Hollands in, — the man that never feared, —
> He took a long and solemn draught, and wiped his yellow beard;
> And one by one the musketeers — the men that fought and prayed —
> All drank as 't were their mother's milk, and not a man afraid."

Yet if the poet's artistic conscience had been sterner, the last two stanzas of this ballad "On Lending a

Punch-bowl" would not have been spared to weaken its proper close.

His rhymed Addresses.

In his favorite department Holmes always has been an easy winner, gaining in quality as fast as the standard of such work has advanced. In fact, he has advanced the standard by his own growth in brain-power and wisdom. There was a time when half our public men wrote poems for recitation, — when every set oration was paired with a platform-poem. The Phi Beta Kappa Society was answerable for many labored pentameters of Everett, Winthrop, Sprague, and other versifiers, born or made, — equally so the numberless corporations of the federative Saxon race in our aspiring municipalities. Of all these orators in rhyme, Holmes, by natural selection, survives to our day, — and how aptly he flourishes withal! From his start as class-poet, and his step to the front with *Poetry, a Metrical Essay*, the intervals have not been long between his rhymed addresses of the standard platform length: at first named, like the books of Herodotus, after the Muses, — *Urania*, *Terpsichore*, and so on, — a practice shrewdly abandoned, seeing that the Graces, the Fates, and all the daughters of Nereus hardly would suffice to christen the long succession of the Doctor's metrical disquisitions, greater or less, that ceases not even with our day. In the years that followed his graduation, while practising in Boston and afterward a lecturer at Dartmouth, he was summoned, nothing loath, whenever a dinner-song or witty ballad was needed at home, and calls from transpontine and barbaric regions came fast upon him as his popularity grew. Here are some forty printed poems, which cheered that lucky class of '29, and how many others went before and after them we know not. Among college-poets the para-

"Poetry: a Metrical Essay," 1836.

"Poems of the Class of '29," 1851–81.

gon, — and surely this the ideal civic bard, who at the outset boasted of his town,

> "Her threefold hill shall be
> The home of art, the nurse of liberty,"

Boston, and its poet.

and who has celebrated her every effort, in peace or war, to make good the boast. He is an essential part of Boston, like the crier who becomes so identified with a court that it seems as if Justice must change her quarters when he is gone. The Boston of Holmes, distinct as his own personality, certainly must go with him. Much will become new, when old things pass away with the generation of a wit who made a jest that his State House was the hub of the solar system, and in his heart believed it. The time is ended when we can be so local; this civic faith was born before the age of steam, and cannot outlast, save as a tradition, the advent of electric motors and octuple-sheets. Towns must lose their individuality, even as men, — who yearly differ less from one another. Yet the provincialism of Boston has been its charm, and its citizens, striving to be cosmopolitan, in time may repent the effacement of their birth-mark.

Society Verse. *See Chap. XII., and cp. "Victorian Poets": pp. 272, 273.*

I have referred to the standing of Dr. Holmes as a life-long expert in the art of writing those natty lyrics, satires, and *jeux d'esprit*, which it has become the usage to designate as society-verse. Ten years ago, when discussing this "patrician" industry, I scarcely foresaw how actively it soon would be pursued. Its minor devotees certainly have a place in the Parnassian court; but, if content with this petted service, must rank among the squires and pages, and not as lords of high degree. To indulge in a conceit, — and no change of metaphor is too fanciful with respect to the poetry of conceits and graces, — much of our modish verse is only the soufflée and syllabub of a banquet from which strength-giving meats and blooded wine are absent. Taken as the verse which a drawling society affects to patronize, it figures even with the olives and radishes scattered along the meal, wherefrom arrogance and beauty languidly pick trifles while their thoughts are on something else, — or with the comfits at the end, lipped and fingered by sated guests, or taken home as a souvenir and for the nursery. And yet society-verse, meaning that which catches the secret of that day or this, may be — as poets old and new have shown us — picturesque, even dramatic, and rise to a high degree of humor and of sage or tender thought. The consecutive poems of one whose fancy plays about life as he sees it may be a feast complete and epicurean, having solid dishes and fantastic, all justly savored, cooked with discretion, flanked with honest wine, and whose cates and dainties, even, are not designed to cloy. Taken as a whole, Holmes's poetry has regaled us somewhat after this fashion. His pieces light and wise — "Contentment," the "Epilogue to the Breakfast-table Series," "At the Pantomime," "A Familiar Letter," etc. — are always enjoyable. One or two are exquisite in treatment of the past. "Dorothy Q.," that sprightly capture of a portrait's maiden soul, has given, like "The Last Leaf," lessons to admiring pupils of our time. For sheer humor, "The One-hoss Shay" and "Parson Turell's Legacy" are memorable, — extravagances, but full of character, almost as purely Yankee as "Tam O'Shanter" is purely Scotch. In various whimsicalities, Holmes sets the key for Harte and others to follow. "The First Fan," read at a bric-à-brac festival in 1877, proves him an adept in the latest mode. There is also a conceit of showing

Holmes the true Amphitryon.

the youngsters a trick or two, in the story "How the Old Horse Won the Bet," told to the class of '71 by the minstrel of the class of '29, and pointed with the moral that "A horse *can* trot, for all he 's old."

His most ideal poems.

Good and bright as these things are, some of his graver work excels them. Where most in earnest he is most imaginative; this, of course, is where he is most interested, and this again, in moods the results of his scientific bent and experience. Here he shows himself akin to those who have both lightness and strength. Thackeray's reverential mood, that was so beautiful, is matched by the feeling which Holmes, having the familiarity with nature that breeds contempt in grosser men, exhibits in his thoughts upon "The Living Temple." The stanzas thus named, in measure and reverent effect, are not unworthy to be read with Addison's lofty paraphrase of the Nineteenth Psalm. Humility in presence of recognized law is the spirit of the flings at cant and half-truth in his rhymed essays. There are charity and tenderness in "The Voiceless," "Avis," "Iris," and "The Silent Melody." Another little poem, "Under the Violets," reveals the lover of Collins. But "The Living Temple" and "The Chambered Nautilus" doubtless show us their writer's finest qualities, and are not soon to be forgotten. There is a group of his "Vignettes," in recollection of Wordsworth, Moore, Keats, and Shelley, whose cadence is due to that gift of sympathetic vibration which poets seem to possess. These pieces are as good as any to furnish examples of the sudden fancies peculiar to Holmes's genius, whose glint, if not imagination, is like that of the sparks struck off from it. One from the stanzas on Wordsworth: —

Cp. "Elegy on a Shell — The Nautilus": Duyck. "Cyc. Am. Lit." I., 537.

"This is my bark, — a pigmy's ship;
Beneath a child it rolls;

Fear not, — one body makes it dip,
But not a thousand souls."

And this from the Shelley poem, which has an eloquent movement throughout: —

"But Love still prayed, with agonizing wail,
'One, one last look, ye heaving waters, yield!'
Till Ocean, clashing in his jointed mail,
Raised the pale burden on his level shield."

Faults and merits of the "occasional" verse.

The things which, after all, sharply distinguish Holmes from other poets, and constitute the bulk of his work, are the lyrics and metrical essays composed for special audiences or occasions. Starting without much creative ambition, and as a bard of mirth and sentiment, it is plain that he was subject to faults which an easy standard entails. His aptitude for writing, with entire correctness, in familiar measures, has been such that nothing but an equal mental aptness could make up for the frequent padding, the inevitably thin passages, of his longer efforts, and for the conceits to which, like Moore and Hood, he has been tempted to sacrifice the spirit of many a graceful poem. To this day there is no telling whither a fancy, once caught and mounted, will bear this lively rider. Poetry at times has seemed his diversion, rather than a high endeavor; yet perhaps this very seeming is essential to the frolic and careless temper of society-verse. The charm that is instant, the triumph of the passing hour, — these are captured by song that often is transitory as the night which listens to it. In Holmes we have an attractive voice devoted to a secondary order of expression. Yet many of his notes survive, and are worthy of a rehearing. A true faculty is requisite to insure this result, and it is but just to say that with his own growth his brilliant occasional pieces strengthened in thought, wit, and feeling.

Eighteenth Century style and thought.

With respect to his style, there is no one more free from structural whims and vagaries. He has an ear for the "classical" forms of English verse, the academic measures which still bid fair to hold their own — those confirmed by Pope and Goldsmith, and here in vogue long after German dreams, Italian languors, and the French rataplan had their effect upon the poets of our motherland across the sea. His way of thought, like his style, is straightforward and sententious; both are the reverse of what is called transcendental. When he has sustained work to do, and braces himself for a great occasion, nothing will suit but the rhymed pentameter; his heaviest roadster, sixteen hands high, for a long journey. It has served him well, is his by use and possession, and he sturdily will trust it to the end: —

> "Friends of the Muse, to you of right belong
> The first staid footsteps of my square-toed song;
> Full well I know the strong heroic line
> Has lost its fashion since I made it mine;
> But there are tricks old singers will not learn,
> And this grave measure still must serve my turn.
>
> . . . . .
>
> Nor let the rhymester of the hour deride
> The straight-backed measure with its stately stride;
> It gave the mighty voice of Dryden scope;
> It sheathed the steel-bright epigrams of Pope;
> In Goldsmith's verse it learned a sweeter strain;
> Byron and Campbell wore its clanking chain;
> I smile to listen while the critic's scorn
> Flouts the proud purple kings have nobly worn;
> Bid each new rhymer try his dainty skill
> And mould his frozen phrases as he will;
> We thank the artist for his neat device, —
> The shape is pleasing, though the stuff is ice."

He compares it, as contrasted with later modes, to

"the slashed doublet of the cavalier," — the costume that would be chosen by Velasquez or Van Dyke. Now, the heroic measure is stately, but if picturesqueness is to be the test, few will back his opinion that in this measure, as written by Pope's adherents, "Unfading still the better type endures." In the course of English song, the rhymed pentameter has included more distinct styles than even blank-verse, and quite as plainly takes on the stamp of its moulder. For the man, after all, makes or mars it; it lends itself with fatal readiness to merely didactic uses, and hence has been the patient slave of dullards. As written by Chaucer, it *was* picturesque, full of music and color, — the interfluent, luxurious pentameter couplet, revived by Hunt and Keats, and variously utilized for metrical narrative by successive nineteenth-century poets. Still, the "straight-backed," heroic measure of Queen Anne's time, say what we will, must be a natural and generic English form, that could so maintain itself to our own day. Recall Pope's measure in "The Dunciad," and again, in "The Rape of the Lock," — that elegant mock-epic which yet stands at the head of all poetry à-la-mode. How it delights a class that still read Byron and Campbell and Scott, the learned body of jurists and other professional men, sensible and humane, who care little for the poetry of beauty alone. I observe that lawyers, veteran judges, merry and discreet, enjoy the verse of Holmes. It was asked concerning Landor, "Shall not the wise have their poets as well as the witless?" and shall we begrudge the wigged and gowned their rations of wit and epigram and lettered jest? Not the form, but the informing spirit, is the essential thing, and this many, who are on the watch for American originality, fail to comprehend. An apt taster

The rhymed pentameter.

See p. 89.

Sententiousness.

knows which wine has the novel flavor, though the vintages look alike to the eyes.

Master of his own field.

The mechanism of Holmes's briefer occasional poems is fully as trite and simple. Whether this may be from choice or limitation, he has accumulated a unique series of pieces, vivacious as those of Tom Moore, but with the brain of New England in them, and notions and instances without end. How sure their author's sense of the fitness of things, his gift of adaptability to the occasion, — to how many occasions, and what different things! He outrivals Kossuth, the adroit orator who landed in a new world, master of its language, and had forensic arguments for the bar, grace and poetry for women, statistics for merchants, and an assortment of local allusions for the respective towns and villages in which he pleaded his cause. A phantasmagory of the songs, odes, and rhymed addresses, of so many years; collegiate and civic glories; tributes to princes, embassies, generals, heroes; welcomes to novelists and poets; eulogies of the dead; verse inaugural and dedicatory; stanzas read at literary breakfasts, New England dinners, municipal and bucolic feasts; odes natal, nuptial, and mortuary; metrical delectations offered to his brothers of the medical craft — to which he is so loyal — bristling with scorn of quackery and challenge to opposing systems, — not only equal to all occasions, but growing better with their increase. The half of his early collections is made up from efforts of this sort, and they constitute four fifths of his verse during the last thirty years. Now, what has carried Holmes so bravely through all this, if not a kind of special masterhood, an individuality, humor, touch, that we shall not see again? Thus we come, in fine, to be sensible of the distinctive gift of this poet. The

A distinctive gift.

achievement for which he must be noted is, that in a field the most arduous and least attractive he should bear himself with such zest and fitness as to be numbered among poets, and should do honor to an office which they chiefly dread or mistrust, and which is little calculated to excite their inspiration.

III.

His works in prose.

Having in mind the case of our Autocrat, one is moved to traverse the ancient maxim, and exclaim, "Count no man unhappy till his dying day." There are few instances where a writer, suddenly, and after the age when fame is won "or never," compels the public to readjust its estimate of his powers. Holmes was not idle as a rhymester from 1836 to 1857; but his chief labor was given to medical practice and instruction, and it was fair to suppose that his literary capacity had been gauged. Possibly his near friends had no just idea of his versatile talent until he put forth the most taking serial in prose that ever established the prestige of a new magazine. At forty-eight he began a new career, as if it were granted him to live life over, with the wisdom of middle-age in his favor at the start. Coming, in a sense, like an author's first book, *The Autocrat of the Breakfast-Table* naturally was twice as clever as any "first book" of the period. It appears that this work was planned in his youth; but we owe to his maturity the experience, drollery, proverbial humor, and suggestion that flow at ease through its pages. Little is too high or too low for the comment of this down-East philosopher. A kind of attenuated Franklin, he views things and folks with the less robustness, but with keener distinction and insight. His pertinent maxims are so

"The Autocrat of the Breakfast-Table," 1858.

frequent that it seems, as was said of Emerson, as if he had jotted them down from time to time and here first brought them to application; they are apothegms of common life and action, often of mental experience, strung together by a device so original as to make the work quite a novelty in literature. The Autocrat holds an intellectual tourney at a boarding-house table; there jousts against humbug and stupidity, gives light touches of knowledge, sentiment, illustration, coins here and there a phrase destined to be long current, nor forgets the poetic duty of providing a little idyl of human love and interest. Here, also, we find his best lyrical pieces, — on the side of beauty, "The Chambered Nautilus" and "The Living Temple"; on that of mirth, "The One-Hoss Shay" and its companion-piece. How alert his fancy! A tree blows down in his woods; he counts the rings — there are hundreds of them. "This is Shakespeare's. The tree was seven inches in diameter when he was born, ten inches when he died. A little less than ten inches when Milton was born; seventeen when he died. . . . Here is the span of Napoleon's career. . . . I have seen many wooden preachers, never one like this." Again, of letters from callow aspirants: "I have two letters on file; one is a pattern of adulation, the other of impertinence. My reply to the first, containing the best advice I could give, conveyed in courteous language, had brought out the second. There was some sport in this, but Dullness is not commonly a game fish, and only sulks after he is struck." In fine, the Autocrat, if not profound, is always acute, — the liveliest of monologists, and altogether too game to be taken at a disadvantage within his own territory.

The "Autocrat" Series.

Two later books, completing the Autocrat series, follow in a similar vein, their scene the same boarding-house, their slight plots varied by new personages and by-play, the conductor of the Yankee symposia the same Autocrat, through the aid of a Professor and a Poet successively. The best comment on these works is made by their sagacious author, who likens them to the wine of grapes that are squeezed in the press after the first juice that runs of itself from the heart of the fruit has been drawn off. In this lies a recognition of the effect of a market that comes to an author somewhat late in his life. It is too much to expect that one who makes a wonderfully fresh start at fifty should run better and better, as if in the progressive and not the decadent course of life, which latter our author himself reckons from a much earlier stage. And a paying American market for purely literary work began with the foundation of the "Atlantic." Poe's will had been too weak to wait for it; Hawthorne had striven for years; others had struggled and gone down. A lucrative demand for Holmes's prose was too grateful not to be utilized; besides, the income of the magazine required his efforts. I have laid stress upon the need of a market to promote literary activity, but it is worth while to note how far, at certain times and in special cases, too ready a sale tends to lower the grade of ideal work. This may even now be observed. On the one hand, new writers certainly are brought out by the competition between our thriving publishers of books and periodicals; on the other, those who prove themselves capable, and are found available by the caterers, are drawn into a system of over-methodical production at stated intervals. The stint is furnished regularly; each year or half-year the new novel is thrown off, cleverly adapted to the popular taste. Ideal effort is deadened; the natural bent of a poetic mind is subordinated to labor

Dangers of a sure market.

that is best paid. The hope, patience, aspiration that should produce a masterpiece are cast aside. If there be a general advance it is monotonous, and at the expense of individual genius. My deduction is that matter supplied regularly for a persistent market, though of a high order of journey-work, is not improperly designated by that name.

"*The Professor at the Breakfast-Table*," 1859.

The Professor is written somewhat in the manner of Sterne, yet without much artifice. The story of Iris is an interwoven thread of gold. The poems in this book are inferior to those of the Autocrat, but its author here and there shows a gift of drawing real characters; the episode of the Little Gentleman is itself a poem, — its close very touching, though imitated from the death-scene in Tristram Shandy. *The Poet at the Breakfast-Table*, written some years after, is of a more serious cast than its predecessors, chiefly devoted to Holmes's peculiar mental speculations and his fluent gossip on books and learning. He makes his rare old pundit a liberal thinker, clearly of the notion that a high scholarship leads to broader views. I do not think he would banish Greek from a college curriculum; but if he should, the Old Master would cry out upon him. Between the second and third works of this series, his two novels had appeared, — curious examples of what a clever observer can do by way of fiction in the afternoon of life. As conceptions, these were definite and original, as much so as Hawthorne's; but that great romancer would have presented in a far more dramatic and imaginative fashion an Elsie Venner, tainted with the ophidian madness that so vexed her human soul, — a Myrtle Hazard, inheriting the trace of Indian savagery at war with her higher organization. The somewhat crude handling of these tales betrays the fact that

"*The Poet at the Breakfast-Table*," 1873.

"*Elsie Venner*," 1861.

"*The Guardian Angel*," 1867.

the author was not trained by practice in the novelist's art. But they have the merit of coming down to fact with an exhibition of common, often vulgar, every-day life in the country towns of Massachusetts. This, and realistic drawings of sundry provincial types, Holmes produces in a manner directly on the way to the subsequent evolution of more finished works, like Howells's "A Modern Instance" and "The Undiscovered Country." Meanwhile he verifies his birthright by adapting these narratives to the debate on inherited tendency, limited responsibility, and freedom of the will. On the whole, the novels and the Autocrat volumes were indigenous works, in plot and style behind the deft creations of our day, but with their writer's acumen everywhere conspicuous. If their science and suggestion now seem trite, it must be owned that the case was opposite when they were written, and that ideas now familiar were set afloat in this way. Little of our recent literature is so fresh, relatively to our period, as these books were in consideration of their own. As Holmes's humor had relaxed the grimness of a Puritan constituency, so his prose satire did much to liberalize their clerical system. This was not without some wrath and objurgation on the part of the more rigid clergy and laity alike, and at times worked to the disadvantage of the satirist and his publishers. The situation now seems far away and amusing: equally so, the queer audacity of his off-hand pronunciamentos upon the gravest themes. He was responsible, I fear, for a very airy settlement of distracting social problems, to his own satisfaction and that of a generation of half-informed readers; for getting ready sanction to his postulate of a Brahmin caste, and leading many a Gifted Hopkins to set up for its representative. Yet his dialogues

Realistic prototypes.

A shaking of the dry bones.

and stories are in every way the expression of a stimulating personage, their author, — a frank display of the Autocrat himself. If one would learn how to be his own Boswell, these five books are naïve examples of a successful American method.

Holmes's later work.

Holmes's mental fibre, sturdier with use, shows to advantage in a few poems, speeches, and prose essays of his later years. These illustrate the benefits to an author of having, in Quaker diction, a concern upon him; each, like the speech "On the Inevitable Crisis," is the outflow of personal conviction, or, like "Homeopathy *vs.* Allopathy," "The Physiology of Versification," etc., the discussion of a topic in which he takes a special interest. Jonathan Edwards he had epitomized in verse: —

> "the salamander of divines.
> A deep, strong nature, pure and undefiled;
> Faith, strong as his who stabbed his sleeping child."

The notable prose essay on Edwards excites a wish that he oftener had found occasion to indulge his talent for analytic characterization. He has few superiors in discernment of a man's individuality, however distinct that individuality may be from his own.

Address on Emerson (Mass. Hist. Soc.), 1882.

Emerson, for example, was a thinker and poet whose chartered disciples scarcely would have selected Holmes as likely to proffer a sympathetic or even objective transcript of him. Yet, when the time came, Holmes was equal to the effort. He presented with singular clearness, and with an epigrammatic genius at white heat, if not the esoteric view of the Concord Plotinus, at least what could enable an audience to get at the mould of that serene teacher and make some fortunate surmise of the spirit that ennobled it. I do not recall a more faithful and graphic *outside* portrait. True, it was done by an artist who applies the actual eye, used for corporal vision, to the elusive side of things, and who thinks little too immaterial for the test of reason and science, — who looks, we might say, at unexplored tracts by sunlight rather than starlight. But it sets Emerson before us in both his noonday and sundown moods; in his character as a town-dweller, and also as when "he looked upon this earth very much as a visitor from another planet would look on it." With no waste words, the poet's walk, talk, bearing, and intellect are illustrated by a series of images, and in a style so vehicular as to deserve unusual praise. Before the appearance of Dr. Holmes's full treatise on the theme, I read this Boston address and suspected that in understanding of the Emersonian cult he was not behind its votaries. His acceptance of it may be another thing, depending, like his religion, upon the cast of his own nature.

Holmes, as an epigrammatist and proverb-maker.

Many were surprised to find Mr. Arnold rating Emerson, as a writer, below Montaigne. The latter, however rare and various, depended largely in his essays on citations from the ancients, — in fact, from writers of every grade and period; while of Emerson's infrequent borrowing it may be said that his paraphrase often is worth more than the original, and that otherwise each of his fruitful sentences contains some epigram, or striking thought, illuminated by a flash of insight and power. Holmes, among our poets, is another original writer, but his prose is a setting for brilliants of a different kind; his shrewd sayings are bright with native metaphor; he is a proverb-maker, some of whose words are not without wings. When he ranges along the line of his tastes and studies, we find him honestly bred. Plato and the Stagirite, the Elzevir classics, the English essayists, the fathers of the healing art, must be in sight on his shelves, even though

> "the damp offspring of the modern press
> Flaunts on his table with its pictured dress."

A believer in the Reign of Law.

But his proper study is man, the regard of people and movements close at hand. Somewhat distrustful of the "inner light," he stands squarely upon observation, experience, induction; yet at times is so volatile a theorist that one asks how much of his saying is conviction, and how much mirth or whim. His profession has put him on the alert for natural tendency, in the belief that fortune goes by inheritance. Crime and virtue are physically foreordained. He takes unkindly to sentimental attempts at reform. His temper and training so largely affect his writings that the latter scarcely can be criticised from the merely literary point of view. Holmes's conservatism, then, goes well enough with a poet of the old régime, and with the maker of light satires and well-bred verse. In these the utterance of a radical would be as out of keeping as Brown of Osawatomie in a court-suit. There is no call for diatribes on his lack of sympathy with the Abolitionists, with the transcendentalists, with new schools of medicine and art. What has this to do with the service of our gallant and amiable *chanteur?* He sticks to his own like the wearer of "The Entailed Hat." Innovation savors ill to his nostril; yet we feel that if brought face to face with a case of wrong or suffering, his action would be prompted by a warm heart and as swift as any enthusiast could desire. When the Civil War broke out, this conservative poet, who had taken little part in the agitation that preceded it, shared in every way the spirit and duties of the time. None of our

Conservatism.

Loyalty.

poets wrote more stirring war lyrics during the conflict, none has been more national so far as loyalty, in the Websterian sense, to our country and her emblems is concerned. He always has displayed the simple instinctive patriotism of the American minute-man. He may or may not side with his neighbors, but he is for the nation; purely republican, if scarcely democratic. His pride is not of English, but of long American descent. The roundheads of the old country were the cavaliers of the new, — a band of untitled worthies moving off to found clans of their own. "Other things being equal," the doctor does prefer "a man of family." He goes "for the man with a gallery of family portraits against the one with a twenty-five cent daguerreotype," unless he finds "that the latter is the better of the two." Better, he thinks, accept asphyxia than a *mésalliance*, that lasts fifty years to begin with, and then passes down the line of descent. Even our "chryso-aristocracy" he thinks is bettered by the process which secures to those "who can afford the extreme luxury of beauty" the finest specimens of "the young females of each successive season." Thus far our sacerdotal celebrant of genealogies and family-trees. It is likely that he takes more interest than his compeers in the *Proc. Mass. Hist. Soc.* But he represents his section within these limits as strictly as the poet of the library, the poet of the new and radical upper class, the fervent poet of liberty and exaltation, — or even as Emerson, that provincial citizen of the world at large. Our Eastern group of poets is unique; we shall have no other of one caste and section so distinct in its separate personages. The Puritan strain in Holmes's blood was kept pure in the secluded province of Connecticut, where the stern Calvinism of the migra-

A true New-Englander.

Dr. Coles.

tion yet holds sway. Another beloved physician, Dr. Abraham Coles, — our best translator of the Latin Hymns, and the author of "The Microcosm," "The Evangel," and other poems and paraphrases in the same last-century verse that we have been considering, — also is but a strayed inheritor, as his theology and pentameters unite in showing, of the colonial type. Dr. Holmes stands for the ancestral feeling as squarely as he refutes the old belief; and it is well enough that such a poet should be the minstrel of established feasts, and loyal to his class, rather than the avatar of new classes and conditions. He is of Cambridge and Beacon Hill, and in point of style, usage, social life, will maintain his ground with rhyme and banter, — small swords allowed the Ruperts of to-day. Otherwise he gives his judgment free scope, and no superstition trammels the logic of his inquisitive mind. It has required some independence for a man of letters, the friend of Lowell and Emerson, to be a Tory, and for a trimontane poet to be a progressive and speculative thinker.

Holmes's personal charm and magnetism

There is an unconscious sense of the artistic in the self-differentiation of social life. It organizes a stage performance; each one makes himself auxiliary to the whole by some dramatic instinct that loyally accepts the part allotted. Holmes has filled that of hereditary chamberlain, the staff never leaving his hand, and has performed its functions with uncommon ardor and distinction. It would not be strange if those who often have seen at their ceremonies this "fellow of infinite jest, of most excellent fancy," appreciate less than others the strength of his ripest years. The younger men who gathered to pay him their tributes on his seventieth birthday felt that if he did not sing at his own fête his thought might well be: —

—"You are kind; may your tribe be increased,
But at this I can give you such odds if I will!"

He did sing, and the mingled gayety and tenderness of the song made it, as was fitting, one of his sweetest. The occasion itself mellowed his voice, and a mere fancy has not often played more lightly around the edge of feeling than when he said:—

"As on the gauzy wings of fancy flying
From some far orb I track our watery sphere,
Home of the struggling, suffering, doubting, dying,
The silvered globule seems a glistening tear."

His gift of delivery.

Six more years have been added to the youth of his old age, and in them, if not so prolific as once, he has given us some of his neatest work in verse and prose. These efforts have not died with the occasions that called them out. Their beauty, it is true, took on increase by the manner in which the author suited his action to his word. The youth, who has heard this last of the recitationists deliver one of his poems, will recall in future years the fire and spirit of a veteran whose heart was in his work, who reads a stanza with the poetic inflection that no elocutionist can equal, who with it gives you so much of himself—the sparkling eye, the twinkling by-play of the mouth, the nervous frame on tip-toe in chase of imagery unleashed and coursing. Such a poet lifts the glow and fancy of the moment into the region of art, but of the art which must be enacted to bring out its full effect, and in which no actor save the artist himself can satisfactorily essay the single rôle.

IV.

Final impressions of his verse and prose.

If the question is asked, Would the verse of Doctor Holmes be held in so much favor if he had not confirmed his reputation by prose replete with poetic humor and analogy? the fairest answer may be in the negative. Together, his writings surely owe their main success to an approximate exhibition of the author himself. Where the man is even more lively than his work, the public takes kindly to the one and the other. The jester is privileged though in the court of art and letters; yet if one could apply to Holmes — the jester, homilist, and man of feeling — his own process, we should have analysis indeed. Were the theme assigned to himself, we should have an inimitably honest setting forth of his merits and foibles, from this keen anatomist of mind and body, this smile-begetter, this purveyor to so many feasts. As a New Englander he long ago was awarded the highest sectional praise, — that of being, among all his tribe, the cutest. His cleverness and versatility bewilder outside judges. Is he a genius? By all means. And in what degree? His prose, for the most part, is peculiarly original. His serious poetry scarcely has been the serious work of his life; but in his specialty, verse suited to the frolic or pathos of occasions, he has given us much of the best delivered in his own time, and has excelled all others in delivery. Both his strength and weakness lie in his genial temper and his brisk, speculative habit of mind. For, though almost the only modern poet who has infused enough spirit into table and rostrum verse to make it worth recording, his poetry has appealed to the present rather than the future; and, again, he has too curious and analytic a brain for purely artistic work. Of Holmes as a satirist, which it is not unusual to call him, I have said but little. His metrical satires are of the amiable sort that debars him from kinsmanship with the Juvenals of old, or the Popes and Churchills of more recent times. There is more real satire in one of Hosea Biglow's lyrics than in all our laughing philosopher's irony, rhymed and unrhymed. Yet he is a keen observer of the follies and chances which satire makes its food. Give him personages, reminiscences, manners, to touch upon, and he is quite at home. He may not reproduce these imaginatively, in their stronger combinations; but the Autocrat makes no unseemly boast when he says: "It was in talking of Life that we came together. I thought I knew something about that, that I could speak or write about it to some purpose." Let us consider, then, that if Holmes had died young, we should have missed a choice example of the New England fibre which strengthens while it lasts; that he has lived to round a personality that will be traditional for at least the time granted to one or two less characteristic worthies of revolutionary days; that a few of his lyrics already belong to our select anthology, and one or two of his books must be counted as striking factors in what twentieth-century chroniclers will term (and here is matter for reflection) the development of early American literature.

His harp "the harp of Life."

CHAPTER IX.

JAMES RUSSELL LOWELL.

I.

A typical man of letters.

IN a liberal sense, and somewhat as Emerson stands for American thought, the poet Lowell has become our representative man of letters. Not as our most laborious scholar, though of a rich scholarship, and soundly versed in branches which he has chosen to follow. Not as an indomitable writer, yet, when he writes, from whom else are we as sure to receive what is brilliant and original? Nor yet chiefly as a poet, in spite of the ideality, the feeling, the purpose, and the wit that belong to his verse and that first brought him into reputation. But, whatsoever the conjunction that has enabled Mr. Lowell to reach and maintain his typical position, we feel that he holds it, and, on the whole, ought to hold it. His acquirements and versatile writings, the conditions of his life, his international honors, the mould of the man, his speech, bearing, and the spirit of his whole work, have given him a peculiar distinction, and this largely without his thought or seeking. Such a nimbus does not form around one who summons it: it glows and gathers almost without his knowledge, — and not at once, but, like the expression of a noble face, after long experience and service.

Representing, also, American

I have spoken of one poet as excelling others in the adroitness of a man of the world. Lowell's qualities secure him honor and allies without the need of adroitness. He is regarded not only as a man of letters, but as a fine exemplar of culture, and of a culture so generous as to be thought supra-American by those observers who, while pronouncing him a citizen of the world, are careful to exclude this country from his range. Professor Dowden, for instance, says: "Taken as a whole, the works of Lowell do not mirror the life, the thoughts, and passions of the nation. They are works, as it were, of an English poet who has become a naturalized citizen of the United States; who admires the institutions and has faith in the ideas of America, but who cannot throw off his allegiance to the old country and its authorities." But here is a manifest assumption. Doubtless, Lowell's mirror does not reflect Dr. Dowden's conception of the life, the thoughts, and passions of this nation, but that conception, formed at such a distance, might be revised upon a close approach. In the poet's writings we find the life and passion of New England, to a verity, and the best thought of our people at large. For, when I say that he is a type of American culture, I mean of republican culture, and nothing more or less. Those who hold to the republican idea believe that its value is to be found in its levelling tendency; by which I do not mean a general reduction to the lowest caste, but the gradual elevation of a multitude to the standard which individuals have reached, — among them so many of the writing craft, from Franklin's generation to our own. In this respect I do not, of course, mention Lowell's position as distinctive, — the names of other scholars and writers instantly come to mind, — nor have our men of culture been confined to any guild or profession. Marshall and Story, Pinkney, Wirt, Winthrop, Sumner and Bayard, jurists,

culture at its best.

Dowden's "Studies in Literature," p. 472.

The Republican idea, viz.

To advance the general grade of Culture, equally with that of material welfare.

20

orators, and statesmen, — soldiers, merchants, artisans, Americans of every class, — have shown that culture is a plant that thrives in a republic no less than under royal care. Their number is increasing; the average grade is advanced. If this were not so, republicanism would be a failure: in this matter it is on trial no less than in its ability to promote the establishment of first-class museums, libraries, academies, even without governmental aid.

Lowell's special quality and standing.

We count Lowell, among others, as a specimen not of foreign, but of home, culture, and especially of our Eastern type. His life shows what the New England training, not always so fortunate, can do for a man of genius. And thus, even aside from his writings, he is a person of note. The tributes frequently paid him would of themselves keep his name before us. Many of his sayings, like those of Emerson, are a portion of our usual discourse and reference, and the people have taken some of his lyrics faithfully to heart. He has written one work that has become a classic. Whether as a poet and critic, or as a man of affairs, of rare breeding and the healthiest moral tone, Lowell is one of whom it may be affirmed, in the words applied to another, that a thing derives more weight from the fact that he has said it. Are we conscious, then, of having in view a man better than his best writings? But this may be said of many authors, and there must be, at all events, a live personality behind good work.

Catholicity.

Lowell's sense of this, and of the strength and fulness of existence, keep him void of conceit. He often has seemed impatient of his art, half-ready to cry out upon it, lest it lead him from green fields and forests, from the delight of life itself. He is not swift to magnify his office above the heroic action of other men.

This catholicity is rare among poets and artists, whose dearest failing is a lack of concern for people or things not associated with their own pursuits. On the other hand, poetry is the choicest expression of human life, and the poet who does not revere his art and believe in its sovereignty is not born to wear the purple. Lowell, in fortunate seasons, goes back from life to song with new vigor and wisdom, and with a loyalty strengthened by experiences. After all, the man dies, while his imaginative works may survive even the record of his name. Therefore the work is the essential thing; and Lowell's work, above all, is so imbued with his individuality, that none can overlook the relations of the one to the other, or fail, in comprehending his poetry, to enter into the make and spirit of the poet himself.

Musa Regina.

II.

Mr. Underwood has given some account of Lowell's ancestry, and of the conditions which led to the birth and breeding of a poet. We have a picture of the Cambridge manor, Elmwood, — a home not wanting in the relics of an old-time family, — portraits, books, and things of art. Lowell's father, and his father's father, were clergymen, well-read, bearing honored names; his mother, a gifted woman, the mistress of various languages, and loving the old English songs and ballads, — no wonder that three of her children came to be authors, and this one, the youngest, a famous citizen and poet. It is not hard to fill in these outlines with something of the circumstance that, as I pointed out in the case of Mrs. Browning, fore-ordains the training of a genius; that supplies, I repeat, the means of its self-training, since the imagination de-

James Russell Lowell: born in Cambridge, Mass., Feb. 22, 1819.

Cp. "Victorian Poets": p. 118.

rives its sustenance like a plant, selecting and assimilating for itself. All it needs is food, atmosphere, a place to grow. In these Lowell was exceptionally favored, under the influence of local and family traditions, the home-culture, the method of his father, and the taste of the mother from whom he inherited his bent toward letters and song.

Entered Harvard in 1834.

His college course made little change in this way of growth. He might fail of advantages to be gained from drill and drudgery; but was sure to extend his reading in the direction of his natural tastes, until acquainted with many literatures. His subsequent study of the law probably added the logical discipline that enables one to formulate ideas. But any voice that would restrict him to his profession must have fallen "vainlier than the hen's to her false chickens in the pool." Instinct, judgment, everything, pointed to letters as his calling. The period of his start, and his father's literary tastes, are indicated by his avowal that he was brought up "in the old superstition" that Pope "was the greatest poet that ever lived." This would account for his escape to the school of beauty and romance; just as the repression of a clerical surrounding may have had much to do with his early liberalism in politics and theology.

Bent.

Surroundings.

It seems that the light-hearted Cambridge student was eager for all books except those of the curriculum, and troubled himself little as to mathematics and other prosaic branches. This was quite in accordance with precedent, *teste* Landor or Shelley, yet I doubt not that he was more than once sorry for it in after years. One may assume, however, that he passed for what he was, or promised to be, with the Faculty, and became something of an oracle among his mates. There was more eagerness then, at Harvard, than now;

Old Style vs. New.

the young fellows were not ashamed to wear their hearts upon their sleeves. The gospel of indifferentism had not been preached. The words "clever" and "well-equipped" now seem to express our highest good; we avoid sentimentalism, but nourish less that genius which thrives in youth upon hopefully garnished food.

"A Poem recited at Cambridge," 1839.

Lowell wrote the Class Poem, and took leave to print it, being under discipline at the time appointed for its delivery. Mr. Sanborn neatly points out that it abounded in conventional satire of the new-fangled reformers whom the poet was soon to join. As a law graduate, he shortly clouded his professional chances by writing for the Boston "Miscellany," and issuing a little book of verse. A writer's first venture is apt to be a novel or poem. Should he grow in station, it becomes rare, or valued for its indications. The thin, pretty volume, *A Year's Life*, does show traits of its author's after-work, but not so distinctly as many books of the kind. Three years later he termed its contents, —

"A Year's Life," 1841.

> "the firstlings of my muse,
> Poor windfalls of unripe experience."

But three years are a long time in the twenties. There are a few ideal passages in this book, and some that suggest his forming tendencies. It was inscribed to "Una," whom he aptly might have called Egeria, for she was already both the inspirer and the sharer of his best imaginings. A few well-chosen pieces are retained in the opening division of Mr. Lowell's standard collection. Of these, "Threnodia" is a good specimen of his early manner. The simple and natural lines "With a Pressed Flower" are in contrast with vaguer portions of the first book, and have a characteristic thought in the closing stanza, where he says of flowers, that

Maria White.

"Nature, ever kind to love,
Hath granted them the same sweet tongue,
Whether with German skies above,
Or here our granite rocks among."

The cullings from "A Year's Life," with various and riper odes, lyrics, and sonnets, make up the "Early Poems" of his latest edition, showing his range at the date of their production.

Early range and tendencies.

Some of the longer pieces lack compactness, and betray an imagination still somewhat nebulous. "The Sirens," "Irené," "My Love," "Rosaline," are like the first poems of Tennyson, then a risen star. There is a trace of Shelley in the lines "To Perdita, Singing," and "The Moon." "Allegra" is sweet, direct, original. The sonnets upon reading Wordsworth, a sonnet to Spenser (in "A Year's Life"), and one to Keats, afford hints of the poet's healthy tastes. Those to Phillips and Giddings prove that he was no laggard in the unpopular antislavery movement. As to other reforms, it is plain that he began to have convictions, — or, at least, to have a conviction that he had convictions. "The Heritage" and "A Rich Man's Son" were taken up by the press, and are still found in our school-readers. Lowell's voice was for independence, human rights, the dignity of labor. Some of the love-poetry is exquisite. Its serenity declares that no other word than happiness is needed for the history of the time between the dates of his first and second books.

"The Pioneer": ed. by Lowell and Robert Carter.

To be sure, he set himself to edit *The Pioneer*, the conditions being so adverse that poets and essayists who now should make the fortune of a magazine could not prolong its short existence. But we think of Lowell as enjoying to the full those three zestful years, — a briefless barrister, perhaps, yet guarded by the Muse, and having the refined companionship of the girl whose love he sought and won. In the year of his marriage to Maria White, he published a second volume, whose contents, with other verse composed before "Sir Launfal," exhibit his poetic genius in its fresh maturity.

"Poems," 1844.

The "Legend of Brittany," an artistic and legendary poem, was, for that time, quite a significant production, so much so that Poe said it was "the noblest poem yet written by an American." It commended itself to him because, unlike some of Lowell's verse, it was designed for poetry and nothing else — it is not in the least didactic. And that Poe said this, and meant it, shows how few were the longer poems of merit we then had produced. The Legend is a sweet, flowing tale, in the *ottava rima*, after the mode of Keats and up to the standard of Leigh Hunt. It needs dramatic force in the climax, but is simple and delicately finished.

"A Legend of Brittany."

A still better piece of art-work is "Rhœcus," that Greek legend of the wood-nymph and the bee. The poet by chance subjected himself, and not discreditably, to the test of a comparison with the most bewitching of Landor's Hellenics, "The Hamadryad." Much might be said, in view of these two idyls, upon the antique and modern handlings of a theme. Landor worked as a Grecian might, giving the tale in chiselled verse, with no curious regard for its teachings. Its beauty is enough for him, and there it stands — a Periclean vase. His instinct became a conscious method. In a letter to Forster he begs him to amend the poem by striking out a bit of "reflection" which a true hamadryad should "cut across": —

"Rhœcus," compared with Landor's "The Hamadryad."

> "Why should the beautiful
> (And thou art beautiful) disturb the source
> Whence springs all beauty?"

The antique and modern purposes contrasted.

Mr. Lowell's "Rhœcus" is an example of the modern feeling. Passages such as that beginning: —

"A youth named Rhœcus, wandering in the wood,"

are simple and lovely; the scene where Rhœcus, playing dice, rudely treats the winged messenger, is a picture equalling the best of Landor's. But the story itself is preceded by a moralizing commentary, and other glosses of the same kind are here and there. The whole is treated as an allegory conveying a lesson. The wood-nymph herself draws one, tenderly and sadly, at the close: —

> "'Alas!' the voice returned, ''tis thou art blind,
> Not I unmerciful. I can forgive,
> But have no skill to heal thy spirit's eyes;
> Only the soul hath power o'er itself.'"

This method confuses the beauty of the poem, though distinct enough in purpose, and characteristic of the New England school.

The poet obeys a "call."

The poet, in truth, felt himself called upon for secular work. With all his love of beauty, he had a greater dread of dilettanteism. The air was full of "progress," and he made a general assay of the new thoughts and enthusiasms. Reform-verse came naturally from the young idealist portrayed by his friend Page. The broad collar and high-parted, flowing hair set off a handsome, eager face, with the look of Keats and the resolve of a Brook-Farmer. But he was wholly himself, incapable of the affectation which — in a time when poetry is not the first choice of readers — markets its wares by posing for the jest and zest of fashion, and brings into contempt the grand old name of poet among those who know poetry only as a name. Affectation and self-seeking in art, as elsewhere, are detestable. All the genius of Byron, in a romantic period, could not atone for his trace of the former.

His earnestness sincere.

It makes no difference whether the affectation be one of virility or of refinement; the self-seeking is apt to be that of the author or artist who devotes one day in the month to work, and all the rest to advertising it. You may see his outward type in the water-fly Osric, of whom Hamlet says that "'t is a vice to know him." Such creatures and their habits are the breed of special times — men with some bit of talent, gaining their paltry ends, and sure to be duly classified at last. And so Osric, as Hamlet disdainfully perceives, with "many more of the same breed that the drossy age dotes on," has "only got the tune of the time . . . a kind of yesty collection, which carries them through and through the most fond and winnowed opinions." But Lowell, I say, was himself alone, wearing his Arcadian garb, yet hasting to throw aside his crook at the sound of the trumpet. His "progressive" verse often was fuller of opinion than beauty, of eloquence than passion. Some of it is in a measure which reformers have seemed to hit upon by an exasperating instinct — the much-abused verse shown at its best in "Locksley Hall." With the typical radical, it is enough to make a thing wrong that it is accepted by a majority. Lowell found himself with the minority, but the minority then chanced to be the party of a future, and, in essentials, wholly right. If Whittier and himself, like the Lake Poets before them, became didactic through moral earnestness, it none the less aided to inspire them. Their verse advanced a great cause, and, as years went by, grew in quality — perhaps as surely as that of poets who, in youth, reject all but artistic considerations.

Affectation the bane of art.

Lowell's reform-verse.

Before Lowell's thought and imagination had gained their richness, he had to contend with a disproportionate flow of language, if using forms that did not of

"*Poems*," 1848; *and* "*Poetical Works*," 2 v., 1850.

Diffuseness.

themselves restrict it. "Prometheus," "Columbus," "A Glance Behind the Curtain," are studies upon massive themes, weakened because their matter is not compactly moulded. Yet the poet had a terse art of saying things, as when he made Cromwell assert that

Frequent strength of thought and manner.

> "New times demand new measures and new men";

and himself said: —

> "They are slaves who dare not be
> In the right with two or three,"

or, similarly, declared for

> "One faith against a whole earth's unbelief,
> One soul against the flesh of all mankind."

His manner often was fine: —

> "All other glories are as falling stars,
> But universal Nature watches theirs,
> Such strength is won by love of human kind."
>
> "The moon will come and go
> With her monotonous vicissitude."
>
> "The melancholy wash of endless waves."

His analytic turn early cropped out in the "Studies for Two Heads," which is all Lowell — as one now would say. The poem "To the Past" is written with more circumstance than Bryant's, but the latter is the more imaginative. To indicate, finally, the chief reservation of Mr. Lowell's admirers, I must own that these poems often are marked with technical blemishes, from which even his later verse is not exempt. In trying both to express his conviction and to find a method of his own, he betrayed an irregular ear, and a voice rare in quality, but not wholly to be relied upon. He had a way, moreover, of "dropping" like his own bobolink, of letting down his fine passages with odd conceits, mixed metaphors, and licenses

Eccentricities of style.

which as a critic he would not overlook in another. To all this add a knack of coining uncouth words for special tints of meaning, when there are good enough counters in the language for any poet's need. Space can be more agreeably used than by citing examples of these failings, which a reader soon discovers for himself. They have perplexed the poet's friends and teased his reviewers. Although such defects sometimes bring a man's work nearer to us, the question is as to their influence upon its permanent value. Verse may be faultily faultless, or may go to the other extreme. We are indebted, as usual, to Lowell himself for our critical test. Writing of Wordsworth, he says that "the work must surpass the material," and refers to "that shaping imagination which is the highest criterion of a poet."

Lyrical beauty.

It is a labor that physics pain to recall the verse by which he gained that hold upon his countrymen which strengthens through lengthening years. The public was right in its liking for "The Changeling," "She Came and Went," "The First Snow-Fall," than which there are few more touching lyrics of the affections. "The Shepherd of Admetus" and "An Incident in a Railway Car" are on themes which moved the poet to harmonize his taste and thought. When called upon, as he supposed, to make a choice between Taste and his conception of Duty, Taste sometimes went to the wall. Doubtless, he grew to see that the line of Beauty does not always follow Duty's follower, and that the surrender of the former itself may be in the nature of a crime. His sense never was more subtle, his taste never more delightful, than in the recent and flawless stanzas on the "Phœbe." The public keeps in store for him the adage of the wilful songster. That he "can" sing was discovered at the outset. One such piece as "Hebe" decided that point:—

> "I saw the twinkle of white feet,
> I saw the flash of robes descending;
> Before her ran an influence fleet
> That bowed my heart like barley bending."

Lowell's theory of song.

It also included his theory of song, and a sound one:—

> "Coy Hebe flies from those that woo,
> And shuns the hands would seize upon her;
> Follow thy life, and she will sue
> To pour for thee the cup of honor."

To this lesson of his own experience he recurs again and again:—

> "Whither? Albeit I follow fast,
> In all life's circuit I but find,
> Not where thou art, but where thou wast,
> Sweet beckoner, more fleet than wind!
>
> . . . . . .
>
> All of thee but thyself I grasp;
> I seem to fold thy luring shape,
> And vague air to my bosom clasp,
> Thou lithe, perpetual Escape!"

Like other poets of quality, Lowell has found the Muse, between her inspirations, a coquette and evader. He forms his rule accordingly:—

> "Now, I've a notion, if a poet
> Beat up for themes, his verse will show it;
> I wait for subjects that hunt me,
> By day or night won't let me be,
> And hang about me like a curse,
> Till they have made me into verse."

From a poet who does this, we shall get flavor, and, in any event, the best of himself. Lowell's career, telling equally of use and song, has proved the wisdom of his admonitions:—

"Harass her not; thy heat and stir
But greater coyness breed in her;
. . . . . .
The Muse is womanish, nor deigns
Her love to him that pules and plains;
. . . . . .
The epic of a man rehearse,
Be something better than thy verse;
Make thyself rich, and then the Muse
Shall court thy precious interviews,
Shall take thy head upon her knee,
And such enchantment lilt to thee,
That thou shalt hear the life-blood flow
From farthest stars to grass-blades low."

To which one may add, without malice, that Mr. Lowell can give the Muse lessons in the art of flirting; knowing from long practice that, when she once has yielded her heart, she forgives even the infidelities of a favored lover.

A born poet of nature.

There is a beautiful feeling in his poems of nature. Wordsworth has dwelt upon the contrast between the youthful regard for nature, — the feeling of a healthy and impassioned child, — and that of the philosopher who finds in her a sense "of something far more deeply interfused." The latter is a gift that makes us grave. It led Bryant to worship and invocation; and now, in the new light of science, we seek for, rather than feel, the soul of things. The charm of Lowell's outdoor verse lies in its spontaneity; he loves nature with a child-like joy, her boon companion, finding even in her illusions welcome and relief, — just as one gives himself up to a story or a play, and will not be a doubter. Here he never ages, and he beguiles you and me to share his joy. It does me good to see a poet who knows a bird or flower as one friend knows another, yet loves it for itself alone. He sings among the woods, as Boone hunted, refusing to be edified, and with no wish for improvements. This one section he reserves for life itself: —

> "Away, my poets, whose sweet spell
> Can make a garden of a cell!
> I need ye not, for I to-day
> Will make one long sweet verse of play."

His manhood shall not make him lose his boyhood; the whiff of the woods, the brook's voice, the spangle of spring-flowers, — these never fail to stir the old-time thrill; our hearts leap with his, and for once forget to ask the reason why.

His pastoral tastes.

Outside the "Pictures from Appledore" there is little of the ocean in his verse: the sea-breeze brings fewer messages to him than to Longfellow and Whittier. His sense of inland nature is all the more alert, — for him the sweet security of meadow-paths and orchard-closes. He has the pioneer heart, to which a homestead farm is dear and familiar, and native woods and waters are an intoxication. The American, impressed at first by the oaks and reaches of an Old-World park, soon wearies of them, and takes like a partridge to the bush. What Lowell loves most in nature are the trees and their winged habitants, and the flowers that grow untended. "The Indian Summer Reverie" is an early and delightful avowal of his pastoral tastes. His favorite birds and trees, the meadows, river, and marshes, all are there, put in with strokes no modern descriptive poet has excelled. Browning's capture of the thrush's song is rivalled by such a touch as this: —

> "Meanwhile that devil-may-care, the bobolink,
> Remembering duty, in mid-quaver stops
> Just ere he sweeps o'er rapture's tremulous brink,
> And 'twixt the winrows most demurely drops."

The poems "To a Pine-Tree" and "The Birch-

Tree," with their suggestive measures, are companion-pieces that will last. The poet shares the stormy reign of the monarch of Katahdin; yet loves the whisper of the birch in the vale: —

> "Thou art the go-between of rustic lovers;
> Thy white bark has their secrets in its keeping;
> Reuben writes here the happy name of Patience,
> And thy lithe boughs hang murmuring and weeping
> Above her, as she steals the mystery from thy keeping."

Poem "To the Dandelion."

Of Lowell's earlier pieces, the one which shows the finest sense of the poetry of Nature is that addressed "To the Dandelion." The opening phrase ranks with the selectest of Wordsworth and Keats, to whom imaginative diction came intuitively, —

> "Dear common flower, that grow'st beside the way,
> Fringing the dusty road with harmless gold,"

and both thought and language are felicitous throughout: —

> "Thou art my tropics and mine Italy;
> To look at thee unlocks a warmer clime;
> The eyes thou givest me
> Are in the heart, and heed not space or time:
> Not in mid June the golden-cuirassed bee
> Feels a more summer-like warm ravishment
> In the white lily's breezy tent,
> His fragrant Sybaris, than I, when first
> From the dark green thy yellow circles burst."

This poem contains many of its author's peculiar beauties and none of his faults; it was the outcome of the mood that can summon a rare spirit of art to express the gladdest thought and most elusive feeling.

"The Vision of Sir Launfal," 1848.

I think, also, that *The Vision of Sir Launfal* owed its success quite as much to a presentation of nature as to its misty legend. It really is a landscape-poem, of which the lovely passage, "And what is so rare as a day in June?" and the wintry prelude to Part Second, are the specific features. Like the Legend of Brittany, it was a return to poetry as poetry, and a sign that the author was groping for a theme equal to his reserved strength. The Vinland fragment hints at a wider range of experiment. Thus far, in fact, no positively *new* notes. Lowell had shown his art and insight, a brave purpose, absolute sympathy with nature. The ferment of his youth had worked itself clear. "Occasional" pieces, the stanzas to Kossuth, the poem on the English graves at Concord, came from definite convictions and a strong hand. He was a man, well girded, who had not found his best occasion; who needed the pressure of imminent events to bring out his resources and make his work enduring. The question, "How can I make a real addition to literature?" often must have come to one so penetrative. Possibly he was hampered, also, by his own culture. The Dervish's ointment may be too freely applied to the eyes; too close a knowledge of the verities may check ideal effort, — too just a balance of faculties produces indecision. Practical success in art must come from every-day ambition and experiment.

Estimate of his work thus far.

But creative results are apt to follow upon the gift to look at things from without. If Lowell had not utilized his surroundings, he was none the less aware of them. The solution of his problem came when least expected, and as a confirmation of his theory of the Unsought. The clew was not in ancestral or Arthurian legends, but in his own time and at his doorstone. It was woven of the homeliest, the most ungainly, material. It led to something so fresh and unique that its value, like that of other positively new work, at first hardly could have been manifest, even to the poet himself.

A new field.

III.

THE *Biglow Papers* ended all question of Lowell's originality. They are a master-work, in which his ripe genius fastened the spirit of its region and period. Their strength lies in qualities which, as here combined, were no man's save his own. They declare the faith of a sincere and intelligent party with respect to war, — a sentiment called out by the invasion of Mexico, unjust in itself, but now seen to be a historical factor in the world's progress. This was a minority faith, held in vulgar contempt, and there was boldness in declaring it. Again, the "Biglow Papers" were the first, and are the best, metrical presentation of Yankee character in its thought, dialect, manners, and singular mixture of coarseness and shrewdness with the fundamental sense of beauty and right. Never sprang the flower of art from a more unpromising soil; yet these are eclogues as true as those of Theocritus or Burns. Finally, they are not merely objective studies, but charged with the poet's own passion, and bearing the marks of a scholar's hand.

"The Biglow Papers," 1846–48.

The work plainly shows its manner of growth. The first lyric struck the vein, the poet's mind took fire by its own friction, and one effort inspired another. The "Papers" made an immediate "hit"; the public instinctively passed a judgment upon them, in which critics were able to concur after the poet had made an *opus* of the collected series. Here was now seen that maturity of genius, of which Humor is a flower revealing the sound kind man within the poet. Such a work is, also, an illustration and defence of the tenure of Wit in the field of art. Verse made only as satire belongs to a lower order. Of such there are various didac-

Wit and Humor. Their tenure in art. *See pp. 259, 277, and cp. "Victorian Poets": pp. 73, 77, 352.*

tic specimens. But Wit has an imaginative side, and Humor springs like Iris — all smiles and tears. The wit of poets often has been the faculty that ripened last, the overflow of their strength and experience. In the "Biglow Papers," wit and humor are united as in a composition of high grade. The jesting is far removed from that clownish gabble which, if it still increases, will shortly add another to the list of offences that make killing no murder.

A broadly original work.

Lowell was under thirty at this time, and fairly may be reckoned among poets who have done great work in youth. His leap from provincialism is seen in the accessory divisions of his completed satire. The "Notices of an Independent Press" are a polygonal mirror in which journalism saw all its sins reflected, and wherewith he scanned not others' follies only, but his own, mocking our spread-eagleism, anglophobia, and the weaker phases of movements in which he himself had joined. He burlesqued in mock Latin the venerable pomp of college-catalogues and down-East genealogies. Then followed a clever analysis of the Yankee dialect, extended and made authoritative in a prefix to his second series. In the very first contribution of Mr. Biglow, the native Yankee is immortally portrayed.

Realism.

The ludicrous realism of the transcript is without parallel: —

> "Jest go home an' ask our Nancy
> Wether I'd be sech a goose
> Ez to jine ye, — guess you'd fancy
> The etarnal bung wuz loose!
> She wants me fer home consumption,
> Let alone the hay's to mow, —
> Ef you're arter folks o' gumption,
> You've a darned long row to hoe."

How the poet must have enjoyed that stanza! What rollicking delight! But he quickly recalls the inborn pride and patriotism, the sacred wrath, of the true New England, and cries out from a wounded spirit: —

> "Massachusetts, God forgive her,
> She 's a-kneelin' with the rest,
> She thet ough' to ha' clung ferever
> In her grand old eagle-nest!"

His rejection of the popular ideal of Webster, his branding ridicule of Robinson, Cushing, and their like, and his scorn of trimmers, vitalized the "Biglow Papers" and make their hits proverbial. The first series was a protest not only against the slave-holders' invasion of Mexico, but against war itself. Fifteen years later a greater war arose, a mortal struggle to repress the wrong that caused the first. To such a conflict even Lowell could not say nay; his kinsmen freely gave their blood, and bereavement after bereavement came fast upon him. In the second series of the "Biglow Papers" the humor is more grim, the general feeling more intense. Still they are not Tyrtæan strains, but chiefly called out by political episodes, — like the Mason and Slidell affair, — and constantly the poet seeks a relief from the tension of the hour. One feels this in reading the dialogue between the Bridge and the Monument at Concord suggested by Burns's "Twa Briggs," the return to "Sunthin' in the Pastoral Line," or, most of all, "The Courtin'." This bucolic idyl is without a counterpart; no richer juice can be pressed from the wild-grape of the Yankee soil. It is a most artistic idealization of the theme and method essayed years before by a New Hampshire poet and wit, Fessenden, in "The Country Lovers." Of the Biglow epistles, the tenth has the most pathetic undertone. It was composed, seemingly at a heat, in answer to a request for —

"The Biglow Papers," Second Series, 1862-66.

"The Courtin'."

> "sunthin' light an' cute,
> Rattlin' an' shrewd an' kin' o' jingleish."

Mr. Biglow justifies the tone of his new series by avowing the immeasurable anguish and perplexity of the time: —

> "Where 's Peace? I start, some clear-blown night,
> When gaunt stone walls grow numb an' number,
> An', creakin' 'cross the snow-crus' white,
> Walk the col' starlight into summer."

"Out of the abundance of the heart."

His heart is full with its own sorrows; he half-despises himself "for rhymin'," when his young kinsmen have fallen in the fray: —

> "Why, hain't I held 'em on my knee?
> Did n't I love to see 'em growin',
> Three likely lads ez wal could be,
> Hahnsome an' brave an' not tu knowin'?
> . . . . .
> 'T ain't right to hev the young go fust,
> All throbbin' full o' gifts an' graces,
> Leavin' life's paupers dry ez dust
> To try an' make b'lieve fill their places!"

He longs for Peace, but invokes her to come, —

> "not like a mourner, bowed
> For honor lost and dear ones wasted,
> But proud, to meet a people proud,
> With eyes thet tell o' triumph tasted!
> Come, with han' grippin' on the hilt,
> An' step that proves ye Victory's daughter!
> Longin' fer you, our sperits wilt
> Like shipwrecked men's on raf's for water."

These final lyrics, less varied and sparkling than their predecessors, are, in not infrequent passages, more poetical. The author's statement of the causes and method of his work is more suggestive than Poe's whimsical analysis of "The Raven," and not open to the suspicion of being written for effect.

A unique addition to literature.

The "Biglow Papers," as we now have them, form a strongly proportioned work, and are a positive addition to the serio-comic literature of the world. They are almost apart from criticism; there is no prototype by which to test them. Lowell has been compared to Butler, but "Hudibras," whether as poetry or historical satire, is vastly below the master-work of the New England idyllist. The titles of a few great books, each of which has no fellow, come to mind as we think of its possible rank and duration, and I observe that Mr. Sanborn does not fear to mention the highest. It is a point in favor of transatlantic judgment that the "Biglow Papers" first gave Lowell the standing, with those who make opinion in England, which his choicest poems of art and nature had failed to procure for him. From that time their interest in himself and his work has been apparent. Their university degrees, their estimates of his genius and his character, declare him to be one whom the motherland delights to honor, and have made more distinct the position which, as I have said, he holds among our men of letters.

"*A Fable for Critics*," 1848.

His literary satire, *A Fable for Critics*, was a good-natured tilt at the bards of Griswold's Parnassus, — a piece of uneven merit, but far from being open to the charge — that of malevolence — which Poe brought against it. The estimate of Poe is not unfair, and other sketches — such as those of Bryant, Hawthorne, Whittier, and Dwight — are deftly made. Nor could one put a surer finger upon Lowell's short-comings than his own in the lines upon himself. The allegory of the fable is trite. Its sections are loosely united, the language and rhythm are at hap-hazard, and, on the whole, it is a rather careless production, however true to the time and tribe it celebrates.

IV.

Lowell's prose writings.

A POET of intellectual scope will not content himself with verse, as the sole outlet of his thought and feeling. Lowell's essays display his genius in free activity, and have added greatly, and justly, to his authority and standing. One could not select better illustrations of the union of the critical and artistic faculties, or of the distinctions and analogies between the verse and prose of a poet.

"Conversations on Some of the Old Poets," 1844.

It is to be noted that Lowell's political and moral convictions appear chiefly in his verse. His prose appertains to literature, and, with the exception of some graceful sketch-work, bits of travel and reminiscence, has been restricted to criticism. His earliest prose volume was of this kind, in the form of *Conversations* on the old poets and dramatists. These are the ardent generalizations of a young poet, appreciative rather than searching. They are superseded by his maturer survey of their field, but had a stimulating influence in their time. Many who were students then remember the glow which they felt when Lowell's early lectures and essays directed them to a sense of what is best in English song. Young enthusiasts, at Cambridge, found him an ideal teacher and professor of belles-lettres. As years went on, his critical pen was rarely idle. A good fate determined that he should be subjected to the demands of journalistic routine — that he should carry the "Atlantic Monthly" to a sure foot-hold, advancing the standard of our magazine literature; and that he should afterward hold for nine years an editorship of the "North American Review." Such responsibilities overcome a writer's *vis inertiæ*. He naturally becomes his own best con-

Ed. the "Atlantic Monthly," 1857-62.

Ed., with C. E. Norton, of the "No. Am. Review," 1863-72.

tributor, and it was, in a measure, to the spur of his engagements that we owe a notable series of literary essays, many of which first appeared in the review I have named. Publishers have not found his study a reservoir into which they might insert their taps at pleasure. But one must spend time in gathering knowledge to give it out richly, and few comprehend what goes to a page of Lowell's manuscript. The page itself, were it a letter or press-report, could be written in a quarter-hour; but suppose it represents, as in one of his greater essays, the result of prolonged studies — the reading, indexing, formulating works in various languages, upon his shelves or in the Harvard library? Of all this he gives the ultimate quintessence, a distillation fragrant with his own genius. Who can estimate the toil of such work? What can adequately pay for it? There are two guerdons that raise the spirit to scorn delights and live laborious days: Milton sings of one — but the surer is the "exceeding great reward" of the work itself.

"Fireside Travels," 1864.

"Among My Books," 1870.

"My Study Windows," 1871.

"Among My Books," Second Series, 1876.

Lowell's important reviews and studies, selected with excellent discretion, are contained in *My Study Windows*, and in the first and second series of *Among My Books*. These, with the *Fireside Travels*, make up the collection, in four volumes, of his prose works. His style is marked by individuality. Underwood suggests that "the distinctive prose of a poet is necessarily quite removed from general apprehension." The word "distinctive" seems the one qualification that justifies the remark. And how is a poet's prose distinctive? Not in rhythmic undulations, if he be a true poet and artist. Such a writer does not lend the semblance of verse to his prose. To do this, he must produce something inferior to either. Few metrical cadences in the prose of Milton, Goldsmith, Coleridge, Byron, Landor, or

The prose of poets. *Cp. "Victorian Poets:" p. 37.*

Bryant. Its strength and beauty are of another kind. Many of Dickens's passages, we know, can be assorted into lengths of semi-metrical verse; but Dickens, when he tried to make poems, had no great success. Thackeray, whose prose is prose, was, within his range, a charming poet. Longfellow's "Hyperion" is exceptional — written as a "prose-poem" by a young artist fresh from the sentiment of German mystics and romances. As for Carlyle, he was a poet, as Lowell says, "without the gift of song." He invented a special kind of prose as his form of poetic expression. I infer that a poet's prose is not removed from general apprehension by its technique; all things considered, I expect to find it as clear and unadulterate as that of any layman — not more illogical, not more dependent on the reader's intuition to fill out its lapses. A poet's instinct is constructive, little given to omissions in prose syntax. If his prose is hard to understand, it may be that he is a learned thinker, whose thoughts and references do not come at once within popular apprehension.

Individuality of Lowell's prose.

It is because a poet is more original, not more erratic, than many laymen, that his prose often is so individual. Lowell's is clear enough to those familiar with the choicest literature. In critical exploits that bring out his resources, he is not a writer for dullards, and to read him enjoyably is a point in evidence of a liberal education. His manner, in fact, is Protean, adjusted to his topic, and has a flexibility that well expresses his racy wit and freshness: combined with this, peculiarities that irritate the most catholic minds.

The strictures upon it.

Outspoken reviewers have subjected it to minute analysis, and declared their sense of its shortcomings. Their statement that it is not creative, but critical, is true in the ordinary meaning; yet I doubt if "creative" criticism and that which is truly critical differ like the experimental and analytic chemistries. Certainly Lowell is a most suggestive essayist. He sets us a-thinking, and, after a stretch of comment, halts in by-paths, or enlivens us with his sudden wit. He has the intellect, held to be a mark of greatness, that "puts in motion the intellect of others." But he is charged with querulousness, inconsistency of judgment, contempt for unity, and with the habit of becoming entangled in expression. Attention is directed to the conceits, the whimsical diction and recondite instances, to be found in these essays. Verse, not prose, is declared by a few to be his proper vehicle. The indictment has some foundation, but to what extent does it affect his general merits? Things bad in themselves are often part of an author's essential quality. It seems to me that there is a close analogy between the styles of Lowell's verse and prose, distinct as the two forms are, — an analogy to be observed, if I had space to point it out, in the verse and prose of other poets, and inevitable from an author's habits of mind. I cannot better state the matter than by saying that the beauties and faults of the one are those of the other; both are open to the criticisms already made, and to which I may refer again; but each is sustained by a spirit which makes the reader forgive and forget. Under the drift and stubble that float on the surface is the strong, deep current which bears them along, or throws them to the side and keeps a central channel clear.

How far justifiable.

Lowell's lighter touches have the grace that is always modern. The "Fireside Travels" make his censors withhold their arrows of the chase, pleased with the landscape and the guide. However exquisite the art of our latest sketch-writers, who is better company

Sketch-work.

than Lowell in Old-World loiterings or more deft in wood-craft and garden-craft at home? His other prose volumes have sturdier characteristics. Here are the companion-pieces on Lessing and Rousseau; the series — a labor of years — upon the great English masters, from Chaucer to Keats and Carlyle; the elaborate study of Dante; the off-hand portraits of Josiah Quincy, Lincoln, Thoreau; no common subjects these, — who grapples them must do his best, or suffer a fall. Other essays, too, that are not soon forgotten: "Witchcraft in New England," the famous treatise "On a Certain Condescension in Foreigners," and two papers — "My Garden Acquaintance," and "A Good Word for Winter," — outdoor studies that would have delighted the man of Selborne. The style of the critical prose certainly is not modelled upon Addison and his school; it is scarcely what Lowell himself describes as "that exquisite something called Style, which makes itself felt by the skill with which it effaces itself, and masters us at last with a sense of indefinable completeness." To some it may seem a stumbling-block; but to most, I fancy, it is the self-expression of a versatile, learned, original man. When over-freighted with words from other languages, new and old, the polyglotism implies so close a familiarity with many literatures that he cannot avoid drawing on them for his purpose. A pedant quotes for the sake of a display of learning; Lowell, because he has mastered everything connected with his theme. His style, as I have hinted, sometimes is quaintly influenced by his topic and its associations. "Witchcraft" revives here and there the manner of more than one seventeenth-century homilist. The English proper of this curious and learned essay, with all its auroral qualities, is less simple and strong than that

Greater Essays.

His style.

of the critic's noble discourse of Dryden, whose very Latinism seems to befit the spirit of its hero. It should be noted that Lowell's polysyllables — and few writers have more — do not weigh down the page; they are accelerative, galloping, even charging, in leap on leap, from section to section. His word-coining is less venial, for he does not lack taste, and at times exercises it rigidly. But his humor, learning, and caprice audaciously put it by, with a "Go thy way till I need thee!" His comments on Spenser's innovations should be self-applied, and especially the words culled from Bellay, who bids his poet "Fear not to innovate somewhat . . . with modesty, however, with analogy, and judgment of ear." His linguistic arsenal serves him well: nor does he fail of fine exordiums and perorations, and sentences whose "beauty and majesty," as he says of Spenser's, he refuses to endanger by "experiments of this kind." But we should miss something if we held him to his own formula of the best writing, that in which the "component parts" of English "are most exquisitely proportioned one to the other."

Caprice.

Authors who do lay-work for a living, and pursue their art in hours which are the breathing-time of other men, are permitted few of the common pleasures for which they needs must crave. Their manuscripts are written in their blood, and the ink grows pale apace. Even the delight of reading, that at once stimulates and draws upon the brain, is forbidden to one who is harnessed in the van of a professional career. But Lowell, I suspect, has been shy of any harness from which he could not bolt at will. His book-feeding has been unstinted, omnivorous: he was born among books, reared upon them, and has taken from them that which enriches him yet leaves

Thorough equipment.

them none the poorer. Of all writing-men, he who can read without stint is to be envied. Take the essay on Chaucer; it is the result of perfect equipment for a literary task. It is a spring-time brew of philological comment and poetic induction: it reeks with fact, flavored by originality. Here is a rare elucidation of both the letter and the spirit of Chaucer's song; no mere scholar could so illumine the process, and no poet who was not a scholar would venture upon it. Lowell is the contratype of Poe, who made a flourish of scholarship, and was sure of little for which he did not cram. Poe's humor, moreover, was a heavy lance, awkwardly and maliciously couched; Lowell holds his weapon with grace and courtesy, and has a sword of wit in reserve, should affairs grow serious. His faculty of scholarly assimilation and reproduction resembles Montaigne's. What he thoroughly enjoys is work like his review of the "Library of Old Authors." This paper opens with a talk upon books, pleasant as Lamb's gossip and with latter-day thought and criticism beneath the winning style; then follow swift but searching etymological tests of early authors and modern editors, from which the latter come out with some loss of lustre. Lowell's idea of translation is free reproduction by a man of genius. He values Chapman, and declares that Keats, of all men, was the one to have translated Homer. One would like to see a translation from his own hand, say of Aristophanes: should the text halt, the commentary alone would repay us, and the freest versions by Lowell might be something "more original than his originals." His wit inclines him to condense professional truths in expressions that stick in the memory. The monograph on Spenser sparkles with clever, pointed sayings: "Chaucer had been in his grave one hundred

Lowell and Poe.

Theory of translation. *See p. 209.*

Point and wisdom.

and fifty years ere England had secreted choice material enough for the making of another great poet." Of ancient poetasters, it cannot be said "that their works have perished because they were written in an obsolete dialect; for it is the poem that keeps the language alive, and not the language that buoys up the poem." . . . "The complaints one sometimes hears of the neglect of our older literature are the regrets of archæologists rather than of critics. One does not need to advertise the squirrels" (this sentence is like Landor) "where the nut-trees are, nor could any amount of lecturing persuade them to spend their teeth on a hollow nut." . . . "Any verse that makes you and me foreigners is not only not great poetry, but no poetry at all." Speaking of Dunbar's works, "Whoso is national enough to like thistles may browse there to his heart's content. I am inclined for other pasture, having long ago satisfied myself by a good deal of dogged reading that every generation is sure of its own share of bores without borrowing from the past." And in "Witchcraft" he says that Sidney "seems to have divined the fact that there is but one kind of English that is always appropriate and never obsolete, namely, the very best." With all this point and wisdom, he often cannot refrain from unleashing conceits that fly without "stamping" their imagery. In a single page he compares Chaucer's style to a river and a precious vintage, and contrasts it with the froth of champagne and the folly of Milo. In relation to Shakespeare's birth, we have astrology, vinous processes, and alembic projection, following upon one another as illustrations of the coming nativity. Afterward, while censuring language that is "literary, so that there is a gap between the speech of books and that of life," Lowell

Abundant conceits.

tells us that "a mind in itself essentially original becomes in the use of such a medium of utterance unconsciously reminiscential and reflective, lunar and not solar, in expression and even in thought!" Passages of this sort not unnaturally move other critics, in their turn, to fling a *de te fabula* at the writer. An author, in truth, "should consider how largely the art of writing consists in knowing what to leave in the inkstand." But Mr. Lowell is not unconscious of these things: he toys with licenses, as if to prove that, next to Chapman, "he has the longest wind . . . without being long-winded," of all authors. Nor have we any writer whose imagery is oftener strong and exquisite: as in the description of a snowy winter landscape, or at the close of his "Milton," or where, in "Spenser," he glorifies the handiwork of "the witch, Imagination."

Imagery.

A sure and independent critic.

Lowell's scrutiny is sure, and his tests are apt and instant. He is a detective to be dreaded by pretenders. He wastes no reverence upon traditional errors, but no man is more impatient of sham-reform, less afraid of *odia*, whether theological, scientific, or æsthetic. As a comparative critic, there are few so well served by memory and reading. In the essay on Milton he treats with novel discrimination the respective modes of Shakespeare, Milton, and Tasso. Writing of Wordsworth, Swinburne, and others, he uses the comparative method to good purpose. No one is a better judge of what is original. Most things have been said more than once, and he knows by whom. His standard is the manner of saying. "In the parliament of the present," he declares, "every man represents a constituency of the past"; and again, "Writers who have no past are pretty sure of having no future"; and "It is the man behind the words that gives them value." He names Chaucer, Shakespeare, Dryden, in evidence of the truth that "It is not the finding of a thing, but the making something of it after it is found, that is of consequence." In his paper on Wordsworth, he draws a distinction between originality and eccentricity which, I fear, will not soon become obsolete for want of cases in illustration. Striking points are frequent in his critical prose. It is Lowell who says, of Shakespeare, that the manner of a first-class poet is incommunicable, and therefore he never can found a school. His essay on Carlyle, undertaken at a time when few ventured to dispute the old Norseman's autocracy, is, on the whole, as just as it is independent; that on Lincoln could only have been written by one whose convictions rendered him prophetic. Lowell's analogical gift is seen in his comparison of Lincoln to Henry IV. — made before the President's assassination had completed the parallel. His declaration, in "Spenser," of the qualities of voice that "define a man as a poet," is not to be gainsaid, and he also gives us a clever test of the worth of allegory, — it must be that which the reader "helps to make out of his own experience." It is true that his verdicts are not always such as we agree with, nor do they always agree among themselves. Being a poet, he is prone to express his immediate feeling without submitting it to the principles that, in fact, govern his final judgment. This imparts life to a writer, but subjects him to the charge of inconsistency, especially if it is not his habit to revise past work. Lowell scarcely does justice to Wordsworth's imagination, though keenly alive to the bard's puerilities and want of humor. His essay on Dryden, as a presentation of the man and poet, is the best of its length, and contains some of the writer's finest apo-

Impulse.

thegms; that on Pope is inferior, — the critic being so out of personal liking for the figure-head of his youth as to treat him not without fairness and discrimination, but, I think, inadequately. He possibly overrates Clough, as a signal representative of modern feeling, yet may be forgiven for this, as he knew and loved him, and was joined with him in the freemasonry of comrades and poets. He has touched very lightly, once and again, on Emerson, but with precision and truth. His analysis of Thoreau is sharply criticised as being narrow, but it did expose the defective side of a unique character, and, all things considered, is the subtlest of his minor reviews.

Structural imagination.

Lowell rightly holds the highest imagination to be, not so much that which "gathers into the intense focus of passionate phrase," as "the faculty that shapes and gives unity of design and balanced gravitation of parts." His work, as we have seen, at times displays the former kind, rather than the latter. It is in dwelling on special traits, with praise or censure, that he seems discursive. Thus, while his "Shakespeare Once More" includes a masterly exposition of the dramatist's style, it is fragmentary — even more than need be — in the special touches that follow. Other papers fall short in construction; they are not sustained upon the scales indicated at commencement. This lack of balance, I am sure, is due quite as much to circumstances as to the critic's temperament, and largely to the limits of the periodicals for which he has written. His mind seizes upon a great theme, in mass and in detail, and he begins as if to cover it thoroughly. "Lessing" opens with a broad view of the German intellect and literature; "Chaucer" with a survey of the Troubadour period; and the analogous introductions to Spenser, Dryden,

Pope, are of the utmost value. But to complete an essay upon this plan a book must be written. We are none the less grateful for Lowell's noble vestibules, even though we find them too large for the structures. Surplusage is a royal fault. We see that he can be an artist at will, though constantly setting the law of his nature above all laws. Some of the greater essays are both various and complete. That upon Dante is a superb example; one need not be a Dantean scholar to comprehend the scope and strength of this prolonged, cumulative, coherent analysis of the Florentine's career — fortified by citations, and enriched with a knowledge of Italian history, literature, atmosphere, at the close of the thirteenth century, such as few living men possess.

Copiousness.

Have I not indicated that the unfailing value of Lowell's prose work consists in freedom and variety that are the true reflex of the man himself? His resources make him prodigal, and he has the brave impatience of a skilled performer who trusts his ear and is none too careful of the written score. We seem to have his first notes, and find them better than the revised drafts of other men. It is a fellow-feeling which leads him to say of Dryden, that "one of the charms of his best writing is that everything seems struck off at a heat, as by a superior man in the best mood of his talk." This transfer of his own nature is delightful. He *will* be free, and his censors should rate his freedom at its worth, and not hold him too rigidly to conventionalities which he understands, yet chooses to forego. Even the arrangement of his essays seems to be a chance one, but there is an art in the chance. He has given us a series of literary monographs in which Americans may take just pride, for his genius has imparted new

Essential value of his prose work.

light and freshness to the greatest themes. To these he might add equally notable studies of Cervantes, Molière, and Goethe. No living man could venture with less presumption to summon up once more the spirits of those masters. But already the wealth of his critical product is surprising. I think that a selection of apothegms and maxims could be made from it, which, for original thoughts and wise teaching of the author's art, would be worth more to the literary neophyte, and afford more satisfaction to veteran readers, than a digest of the English prose of any other writer since Landor in his prime.

V.

"Under the Willows, and other Poems," 1868.

LOWELL'S prose diversions, so wide in range, could not have been made without some lapse of fealty to the muse of song. When, in 1868, the volume *Under the Willows* appeared, a note stated that the poems mostly had been written at intervals during many years. There is, none the less, an air of afternoon about them. They are the songs of a man who in truth has *gelebt und geliebet* — to revive the motto of his juvenile book — and who has lived to love again. Their thought is subtler, their subjectivity that of one who reads the hearts of others in his own. The title-piece is a most refreshing stretch of pastoral verse. Here and elsewhere his sympathy with birds and trees continues, and much resembles Landor's: —

"But I in June am midway to believe
A tree among my far progenitors,
. . . . .
And I have many a life-long leafy friend,
Never estranged nor careful of my soul.
That knows I hate the axe."

The close recalls the feeling of the "Thalysia" of Theocritus, yet escapes the parallel displayed in certain idyls of Tennyson. The opening gives us a finer rhapsody of June, though less apt to catch the popular ear, than the one in "Sir Launfal." No common musician can touch so variously a well-worn theme.

I do not read these later poems without remembering the moods to which Arthur Clough was subject, and which also affect the verse of another with whom his too brief life was associated. "Auf Wiedersehen" and its "Palinode"—delicate, brooding, dithyrambic—might seem the work of either Clough or Matthew Arnold, and "A Mood" and "The Fountain of Youth" are quite in sympathy with that of the last-named poet. Arnold, like Lowell, delights in "accidentals" and in haunting measures, often admirably rendered. But I think few of his lines are both so suggestive and so vibratory as these from Lowell's exquisite fantasy, "In the Twilight":—

Lowell, Clough, and Matthew Arnold. Cp. "*Victorian Poets*": pp. 243, 244 and pp. 95–99.

"Sometimes a breath floats by me,
An odor from Dreamland sent,
That makes the ghost seem nigh me
Of a splendor that came and went,
Of a life lived somewhere, I know not
In what diviner sphere,
Of memories that stay not and go not,
Like music once heard by an ear
That cannot forget or reclaim it,—
A something so shy, it would shame it
To make it a show,
A something too vague, could I name it,
For others to know,
As if I had lived it or dreamed it,
As if I had acted or schemed it,
Long ago!

"And yet, could I live it over,
This life that stirs in my brain,
Could I be both maiden and lover,
Moon and tide, bee and clover,
As I seem to have been, once again,
Could I but speak and show it,
This pleasure, more sharp than pain,
That baffles and lures me so,
The world should not lack a poet,
Such as it had
In the ages glad
Long ago!"

Between verse like this, and that of Mr. Hosea Biglow, each definite in flavor, the range is phenomenal. To extend a comparison made for the sole purpose of illustrating Lowell's bent, I will say that in a former review I extolled the beauty of Arnold's objective verse — a kind to which his early preface would restrict the modern poet. But with reference to his occasional hardness of touch, and to the mental conflicts revealed by Clough and himself, I scarcely did full justice to a suggestive class of his poems, in a form peculiarly his own, — poems which grow upon the reader and stand the test of years, — and of these I will name, as good examples, "The Buried Life" and "A Summer Night." Lowell and Arnold, poets nearly equal in years, both scholars, both original thinkers, occupy representative positions, — the one in the Old England and the other in the New, — which are singularly correspondent. Two things, however, are to be noted. The American has the freer hand and wider range as a poet. Humor, dialect-verse, and familiar epistles come from him as naturally as his stateliest odes. Again, while both poets feel the perplexities of the time, Arnold's difficulties are the more restrictive of his poetic glow; with him

Lowell and Arnold.

the impediments are spiritual, with Lowell they are material and to be overcome. Mr. Lowell at times has found himself restricted by our local conditions set forth in my early chapters. Like Mr. Arnold, he also feels the questioning spirit of our age of unrest; but his nature is too various and healthy to be depressed by it. The cloud rests more durably on Arnold. Lowell always has one refuge, — to which, also, the poet of the Highland "Bothie" did not resort in vain. Give him a touch of Mother Earth, a breath of free air, one flash of sunshine, and he is no longer a book-man and a brooder; his blood runs riot with the Spring; this inborn, poetic elasticity is the best gift of the gods. Faith and joy are the ascensive forces of song. Lowell trusts in Nature and she gladdens him. How free and unjaded the spirit of "Al Fresco," and of the sprayey "Pictures from Appledore!" At times he places you

In sympathy with Nature,

> "So nigh to the . . . heart of God,
> You almost seem to feel it beat
> Down from the sunshine and up from the sod."

Men are no less near to him. Like Thoreau, — who knew the world, having "travelled" many years in Concord, — he believes that

and with men.

> "Whatever moulds of various brain
> E'er shaped the world to weal or woe,
> Whatever empires wax and wane,
> To him that hath not eyes in vain
> Our village-microcosm can show."

His rustics act and speak for themselves. Some of his lyrics are as dramatic, in their way, as those of Browning, — a poet whose erratic temper, also, is not unlike his own.

It is worth the consideration of those who deplore the effect of "over-culture" upon our poets, that the

The question of culture. Cp. "Victorian Poets": p. 120.

verse of Lowell and Emerson seems the product of their instant moods. The highest culture has learned to unlearn, and Lowell, when he wrote "A Winter Hymn to my Fire," had surely reached its freehold. A masterly, unstinted improvisation — the freshness of youth, with the off-hand ease of an accomplished workman — the mellow thought and rich imagination of a poet in his prime. Lowell's culture has not bred in him an undue respect for polish, and for established ways and forms. Precisely the opposite. Much learning and a fertile mind incline him to express minute shades of his fancy by a most iconoclastic use of words and prefixes. This trait lessened the dignity of his blank-verse poem, *The Cathedral*, admired for its noble passages and justly censured for things that jar and seem out of place. It is not so much a stately pile, conforming to itself, that has risen "like an exhalation," as a structure builded part by part, and at different periods of grandeur or grotesqueness. Contrast the imposing finale — the dome of the edifice — with the whimsical by-play of the tourists airing their French. A sensitive reader, himself a poet and critic, not long ago said to me that he never could wholly forgive Mr. Lowell for using the word "undisprivacied" in this elevated poem. But I do not know in what other production the changeful thoughts of a mind swiftly considering the most complex modern problems, are caught so naturally, and as if on the instant by some psychographic process. "A Familiar Epistle," without the extreme finish of Dobson's work, adds no less to the raciness of Swift or Gay a poet's blood and fire. It has been said that Lowell's verse and prose are marked by a manner, rather than by style, in the modern sense, — which latter I take to be an airy, elusive perfection of language

"The Cathedral," 1870.

Style

and syntax, that of itself wins the reader, and upon which writers of a new school have built up reputations. The thought, the purpose, — these are the main ends with Lowell, though prose or metre suffer for it, and there is no doubt that his manner exactly repeats his habit of mind; and so in this case, as ever, the style is again the man. My own explanation of things which annoy us in his loftier pieces is that his every-day genius is that of wit and humor. His familiar and satiric writings are consistent works of art. It is upon his serious and exalted moods that these things seem to intrude, like the whisperings of the Black Man in the ears of a Puritan at prayers.

Rationale of Lowell's manner.

Where he has bravely exorcised his annoyer is in the lyric efforts that hold a poet responsible, not only to himself, but also to the needs of great occasions. In these there is nothing erratic or perverse. The handiwork is unequal, but not seldom the vigorous intellect and throbbing heart of the man lift him to the airiest heights of a nation's song. I refer, of course, to his odes, delivered since the close of our civil war.

Of these the first, and strongest, is the *Ode Recited at the Harvard Commemoration*. The poet was fresh from the woes and exaltations of the war. He had an occasion that comes but once in a lifetime. The day, the place, the memories of inexorable events, his heart wrung with its own losses and sharing the proud grief of his Alma Mater, — these all united to call forth Mr. Lowell's highest powers. Another poet would have composed a less unequal ode; no American could have glorified it with braver passages, with whiter heat, with language and imagery so befitting impassioned thought. Tried by the rule

The "Commemoration Ode," 1865.

that a true poet is at his best with the greatest theme, Lowell's strength is indisputable. The ode is no smooth-cut block from Pentelicus, but a mass of rugged quartz, beautified with prismatic crystals, and deep-veined here and there with virgin gold. The early strophes, though opening with a fine abrupt line, "Weak-winged is song," are scarcely firm and incisive. Lowell had to work up to his theme. In the third division, "Many loved Truth, and lavished life's best oil," he struck upon a new and musical intonation of the tenderest thoughts. The quaver of this melodious interlude carries the ode along, until the great strophe is reached, —

> "Such was he, our Martyr-Chief,"

in which the man, Abraham Lincoln, whose death had but just closed the national tragedy, is delineated in a manner that gives this poet a preëminence, among those who capture likeness in enduring verse, that we award to Velasquez among those who fasten it upon the canvas. "One of Plutarch's men" is before us, face to face: an historic character whom Lowell fully comprehended, and to whose height he reached in this great strophe. Scarcely less fine is his tearful, yet transfiguring, Avete to the sacred dead of the Commemoration. The weaker divisions of the production furnish a background to these passages, and at the close the poet rises with the invocation, —

> "Bow down, dear Land, for thou hast found release!"

— a strain which shows that when Lowell determinedly sets his mouth to the trumpet, the blast is that of Roncesvalles. Three other heroic odes were composed, it is just to repeat, "after he had precluded himself," by the Harvard poem, "from many of the

"Three Memorial Poems," 1875, 1876.

natural outlets of thought and feeling." That upon Washington, delivered "Under the Old Elm," is the longest and most imposing. Despite its form, it is too long for an ode, and Mr. Lowell has more fitly entitled it a poem. The characterization of Washington is less bold and sympathetic than that of Lincoln. Better the superb tribute to the Mother of Presidents, —

> "Virginia gave us this imperial man,"

which ends the poem with forty unbroken lines that again bring us to the height of Lowell's power. The closing strophes of the Centennial Ode — "Flawless his hand," and "They steered by stars the elder shipmen knew" — are quite as notable. Underwood has called the three odes an Alpine group, — yet each in its length and unevenness brings to mind a Rocky Mountain chain, in which snow-clad, sunlit peaks arise, connected by vaguely outlined ridges of the Sierra.

In a passage of the last-named ode there is food for thought between the lines: —

> "Poets, as their heads grow gray,
> Look from too far behind the eyes,
> Too long-experienced to be wise
> In guileless youth's diviner way;
> Life sings not now, but prophesies."

"The Unfinished Window."

But the second-sight of age has been always, I have said, a portion of Lowell's strength and disability. One thing, perhaps, is needed to make his career ideal: some adequate theme, and mode of treatment, for a work of pure poetry, that shall be, through its imaginative beauty, the rival and complement of his serio-comic masterpiece. "Fitz-Adam's Story," a portion of the long-projected "Nooning," indicates one direction in which he has felt his way; but he has not followed up the clew with the unhasting, unresting purpose that distinguished Longfellow. Even now, and after his more heroic flights, it might be a diversion to his later years, and certainly would revive an interest in American verse, if he would go back and complete "The Nooning," making it, as he can, the most charming of New England's idyllic poems.

VI.

Recapitulation.

LOWELL, then, is a poet who seems to represent New England more variously than either of his comrades. We find in his work, as in theirs, her loyalty and moral purpose. She has been at cost for his training, and he, in turn, has read her heart, honoring her as a mother before the world, and seeing beauty in her common garb and speech. To him, the Eastern States are what the fathers, as he has said, desired to found, — no New Jerusalem, but a new England, and, if it might be, a better one. His poetry has the strength, the tenderness, and the defects of the down-East temper. His doctrines and reflections, in the midst of an ethereal distillation, at times act like the single drop of prose which, as he reports a saying of Landor to Wordsworth, precipitates the whole. But again he is all poet, and the blithest, most unstudied songster on the old Bay Shore. He is, just as truly, an American of the Americans, alive to the idea and movement of the whole country, singularly independent in his tests of its men and products — from whatever section, or in however unpromising form, they chance to appear. Many have found him the surest to detect and welcome, at the time when welcome was needed and lesser men held back, what there might be in them of worth. He is an artist who recognizes things outside of art, and would not rate the knack of writing lines to a lady's girdle above all other wonders of the age. In default of the motive for a sustained and purely ideal work, he has awaited the visits of the Muse, and acted on the moment at her bidding; none of our poets, indeed, has so thrown the responsibility on a monitor whom no industry can placate, who is deaf to entreaty, but gives without stint at her own will. He will sing when she bids him, or not at all. But this is in the nature of genius, and thus brings me to a conclusion. The world readily perceives the genius that is set off by an eccentric or turbid life. Taking advantage of this, false Amphitryons often vaunt themselves for a while. But let a true poet be born to culture and position, and have a share of things which constitute good fortune, and his rarer gift has no romantic aid to bring it into notice: its recognition comes solely through its product, and not fully until "after some time be past." And if Lowell be not, first of all, an original genius, I know not where to look for one. Judged by his personal bearing, who is brighter, more persuasive, more equal to the occasion and himself, — less open to Doudan's stricture upon writers who hoard and store up their thoughts for the betterment of their printed works? Lowell's treasury can stand the drafts of both speech and composition. Judged by his works, as a poet in the end must be, he is one who might gain by revision and compression. But think, as is his due, upon the high-water marks of his abundant tide, and see how enviable the record of a poet who is our most brilliant and learned critic, and who has given us our best native idyl, our best and

A poet of original genius.

most complete work in dialectic verse, and the noblest heroic ode that America has produced, — each and all ranking with the first of their kinds in English literature of the modern time.

CHAPTER X.

WALT WHITMAN.

I.

OF things counted dear to a minstrel's heart, and which can make him patiently endure the common ills of life, this poet has secured a bounteous share. No one more conspicuously shines by difference. Others are more widely read, but who else has been so widely talked of, and who has held even a few readers with so absolute a sway? Whatever we may think of his chantings, the time has gone by when it was possible to ignore him; whatever his ground may be, he has set his feet squarely and audaciously upon it, and is no light weight. Endeavor, then, to judge him on his merits, for he will and must be judged. He stands in the roadway, with his *Salut au Monde*: —

Walter Whitman born in West Hills, Long Island, May 31, 1819.

A challenger.

> "Toward all
> I raise high the perpendicular hand, — I make the signal,
> To remain after me in sight forever,
> For all the haunts and homes of men."

There are not wanting those who return his salutation. He is in very good society, and has been so for a long while. At the outset he was favored with the hand of Emerson, and, once acknowledged at court, allies quickly flocked around him. No writer holds, in some respects, a more enviable place than burly Walt Whitman. As for public opinion of the profes-

Publicity at home and abroad.

sional kind, no American poet, save Longfellow, has attracted so much notice as he in England, France, Germany, and I know not what other lands. Personal items of his doings, sayings, and appearance constantly have found their way to the public. In a collection of sketches, articles, debates, which have appeared during the last fifteen years, relating to American poets, the Whitman and Poe packages, before the deaths of Emerson and Longfellow, were each much larger than all the rest combined. Curiously enough, three fourths of the articles upon Whitman are written by friends who assert that he is neglected by the press. Not only in that publicity which is akin to fame, and stimulating to the poet, has he been thus fortunate; but also in the faculty of exciting and sustaining a discussion in which he has been forced to take little part himself; in an aptitude for making disciples of men able to gain the general ear, and vying with one another to stay up his hands; in his unencumbered, easy way of life; finally, in a bodily and mental equipment, and a tact or artistic instinct to make the most of it, that have established a vigorous ideal of himself as a bard and seer. These incidental successes, which of course do not confirm nor conflict with an estimate of his genius, are brought to mind as the features of a singular career.

Incidental successes.

Such a poet must find a place in any review of the course of American song. Otherwise, however observant of his work from the beginning, I well might hesitate to express my own judgment of thoughts and modes which, like questions in philology or medicine, seem to provoke contention in which men act very much like children and little to the advantage of all concerned. The disputants who arise when an innovator comes along never were divided more

A difficult poet to estimate.

The debate concerning him.

sharply, — not even in that classico-romantic conflict which would have made the fortune of a lesser poet than the author of "Hernani." Perhaps it would be found, upon examination, that the class which declines to regard Whitman as a hero and poet has been content with saying very little about him. If his disciples are in a minority, it is they who chiefly have written the contents of the package mentioned, who never lose a point, who have filled the air with his name. Our acceptance of their estimate almost has seemed the condition of their intellectual respect. At times we are constrained to infer that this poet is to be canonized, not criticised, — that he, they and others may say to Emerson, Lowell, Tennyson, "Thou ailest here, and here"; but woe unto them that lay hands on the Ark of the Covenant. Two points belong to my own mode of inquiry: How far does the effort of a workman relate to what is fine and enduring? and, how far does he succeed in his effort? Nor can I pay Mr. Whitman any worthier tribute than to examine fairly his credentials, and to test his work by the canons, so far as we discover them, that underlie the best results of every progressive art. I recall his own comment on Emerson: "As I understand him, the truest honor you can pay him is to try his own rules." If his poetry is founded in the simplicity and universality which are claimed for it, and which distinguish great works, the average man, who reads Shakespeare and the English Bible, ought to catch glimpses of its scope and meaning, and therefore I am guilty of no strange temerity in forming some opinion of these matters.

Points and method of inquiry.

On the other hand, if there be any so impatient of his assumptions, or so tired of the manifestoes of his friends, as to refuse him the consideration they

Fair play.

would extend to any man alive, against such also I would protest, and deem them neither just nor wise. Their course would give weight to the charge that in America Whitman has been subjected to a kind of outlawry. And those most doubtful of his methods, beliefs, inspiration, should understand that here is an uncommon and striking figure, which they will do well to observe; one whose words have taken hold in various quarters, and whose works should be studied as a whole before they are condemned. Not only a poet, but a personage, of a bearing conformed to his ideal. Whether this bearing comes by nature only, or through skilful intent, its possessor certainly carries it bravely, and, as the phrase is, fills the bill, — a task in which some who have tried to emulate him have disastrously failed. Not only a poet and personage, but one whose views and declarations are also worth attention. True, our main business is not so much to test the soundness of his theories as to ask how poetically he has announced them. We are examining the poets, not the sages and heroes, except in so far as wisdom and heroism must belong to poetry. But Whitman is the most subjective poet on record. The many who look upon art solely as a means of expression justly will not be content unless the man is included in the problem. I, who believe that he who uses song as his means of expression is on one side an artist, wish to consider him both as an artist and a man.

A romantic and significant bearing.

The personal equation.

Questions involving the nature of verse, of expression, of the poetic life, cannot be adequately discussed in a single chapter; but a paragraph, at least, may be devoted to each point, and should be given its full weight of meaning. It is the fashion for many who reject Whitman's canticles to say: "His poetry is good for nothing; but we like him as a man," etc. To me, it seems that his song is more noteworthy than his life, in spite of his services in the hospitals during our civil war. His life, at its best periods, was an emblem of the nobleness of a multitude of his country-men and country-women; at other times, doubtless, and as his poem of "Brooklyn Ferry" permits us to surmise, it has been no more self-forgetting than the lives of countless obscure toilers who do their best from day to day. If, then, I do not think his heroism so important as his art, nor admire him chiefly as an annunciator, but as a poet, it is because I know more than one village where each workman is a philosopher in his way, and something of a priest, and because poets are rarer among us than preachers and heroes, — and I wish to take him at his rarest. That there may be no doubt, from page to page (amid the seeming inconsistencies that must characterize a study of Whitman), as to my conclusion on this point, I may as well say now that both instinct and judgment, with our Greek choruses in mind, and Pindar, and the Hebrew bards, long since led me to number him among the foremost lyric and idyllic poets. If any fail to perceive what I mean by this, let him take a single poem, composed in Whitman's finer mood, — "Out of the Cradle Endlessly Rocking," — and read it with some care. Had he not chanted like this, the exorbitant world would hear little of his philosophy and consecration, and care for them still less. Yet it is no less plain to me, reading long and often his early volume, — "starting from Paumanok" with this full-throated poet, — that many years ago he formed an inspired and inspiring conception of the spirit and destiny of his own land, his own people, and of the future of a

Whitman's life not so exceptional as his works.

Without doubt a poet of lyric and idyllic genius.

world guided by the example of our continental Democracy; and that, — whatever his personal ambition, motive, strength, or weakness, — he bravely and with true genius set forth this conception by methods as bold and free as that which they expressed. What that conception was is to be discovered most readily in the poems which embody it, and not in one but in the mass of them from that day to this. He singularly fails to convey it with justice to himself in the rhetorical preface to the second volume of his Centennial edition.

II.

"Leaves of Grass": Brooklyn, N. Y., 1855.

The first edition of *Leaves of Grass*, now so valued by collectors, is a long, thin volume, curious to behold, with wide pages that give the author's peculiar lines their full effect. Here was a man with measureless "bounce" and ambition, but with a coequal range of demands for his country, and professedly for all mankind. At that time the sale of most books of poetry or abstract thought was small enough; critical authorities were few, and of little weight. "Putnam's Monthly" certainly had influence, and was the periodical to which our favorite writers contributed some of their choicest work. Its reviewer gave the strange book the best reception possible, by filling three columns with extracts from its pages. He could not have selected any passages more original than those beginning with the lines, "I play not a march for victors only," and "A child said, What is the grass?" — than the death-scene of the mashed fireman, for whose sake is the pervading hush among the kneeling crowd, — the ringing story of the old-fashioned frigate and the little captain who won by

Reviewed in "Putnam's Monthly Magazine."

the light of the moon and stars, — the proud humility, the righteous irony and wrath of "A Slave at Auction" and "A Woman at Auction," — the Hebraic picture of the Quakeress with face clearer and more beautiful than the sky, "the justified mother of men." These, and a few masterly bits of description and apostrophe, were given in a manner just to the poet, while rude and coarser parts, that might displease even a progressive reader, were kindly overlooked. The study of Emerson and Carlyle had bred a tolerance of whatever was true to nature and opposed to sham. "Leaves of Grass" was a legitimate offspring of the new movement. Howsoever differing from the latter, or going beyond it, the book would not have found life had not the Concord school already made for it an atmosphere. Whitman — a man of the people — applied the down-East philosophy to the daily walks of life, and sang the blare and brawn that he found in the streets about him. In his opening lines: —

The transcendental movement.

> "I celebrate myself;
> And what I assume you shall assume;
> For every atom belonging to me as good belongs to you.
>
> "I loafe and invite my soul;
> I lean and loafe at my ease . . . observing a spear of summer grass,"

he simply took Alcott and Emerson at their word. His radical demonstration, extended in later years even to rebuke of their own failure to go farther, brought them, perchance, like Frankenstein, to regard with little complacençe the strides of their prodigy. The difference between Emerson and Whitman illustrated that between certain modes of advanced thought in Massachusetts and New York. If the

Massachusetts vs. New York.

philosophy of the former professed to include the people, in its genesis and application it often was somewhat provincial and aristocratic; the other also was theoretically broad, professing to include the scholarly and refined, but in spirit was no less provincial, —suspicious of all save the masses. A true universalism yet may come from them both. It was in no unfriendly humor, but with perfect justice, that the "Putnam" critic declared the new poems to be a "mixture of Yankee transcendentalism and New York rowdyism," which here were "seen to combine in harmony." For their author prophesied in New York with a selfhood that observed but kept aloof from the West side; insensibly the East-sider was set above the man of training or affairs whose teams he drove, whose fires he subdued, whose boats he piloted, and whose manhood perchance was as sturdy and virile as his own. Hence, there was a just reason in the pleasantry of the reviewer, who, after acknowledging that the poet was "one of the roughs," said: "That he is a kosmos is a piece of news we were hardly prepared for. Precisely what a kosmos is, we trust Mr. Whitman will take an early occasion to inform the impatient world." Nothing worse than this sally befell our poet in the leading magazine, and it was added that there were to be found "an original perception of nature, a manly brawn, and an epic directness in the new poet, which belong to no other adept of the transcendental school." Here, at all events, the book was not treated after any Philistine mode.

Class feeling.

Doubtless many young readers of those quotations felt as if they came with a fresh breeze from old Paumanok and the outer bay. I remember my own impression that here, whether his forms were old or

First impressions of this poetry.

new, was a real poet, one who stirred my pulses; and of whom — in spite of his conceit, familiarity, assumption that few could understand him and that all needed his ministrations — I wished to know more. I would not surrender that first impression of his genius for any later critical feeling. Nor since that time, having closely read him, have I found reason to disavow it. And I could sympathize with him, now that his old age really is at hand, in the serene approval of his own work, read twenty years afterward, under some ominous conjunction of Saturn and Mars: —

> "After an interval, reading, here in the midnight,
> With the great stars looking on — all the stars of Orion looking,
> And the silent Pleiades — and the duo looking of Saturn and ruddy Mars;
> Pondering, reading my own songs, after a long interval (sorrow and death familiar now),
> Ere closing the book, what pride! what joy! to find them
> Standing so well the test of death and night,
> And the duo of Saturn and Mars!"

The poet's likeness and attitude.

The picture of Whitman in trousers and open shirt, with slouched hat, hand in pocket, and a defiant cast of manner, resolute as it was, had an air not wholly of one who protests against authority, but rather of him who opposes the gonfalon of a "rough" conventionalism to the conventionalism of culture. Not that of the man "too proud to care from whence" he came, but of one very proud of whence he came and what he wore. Seeing him now, with his gracious and silvery beard, it seems hardly possible that the early portrait was at any time his own. But it has become historical, and properly is retained in later editions.

The "Leaves of Grass" contained the gist of his

Analysis of the "Leaves of Grass."

opinions, and some of its episodes equal in beauty anything he has ever written. He was in his thirty-sixth year, — close upon the age at which more than one famous poet has ended his mission. His book was eminently one with a purpose, or purposes, to which he has been consistent. First, and chiefly, to assert the "Religion of Humanity," — the mystery and development of man, of woman; the sufficiency of the general plan; the inherent and equal nobility of our organs, instincts, desires; the absolute equality of men, irrespective of birth and training. Secondly, to predict a superb illustration of this development, in "These States," the great republic of the present, the pure democracy of the future. Thirdly, to portray an archetypal microcosm, a man embracing in his passionate and ideal sympathy all the joys, sorrows, appetites, virtues, sins, of all men, women, and children, — himself being, doing, and suffering with them, — and that man Walt Whitman. Finally, and to lay the groundwork for a new era in literature (in his view the most essential stimulant of progress), the "Leaves" were written in contempt of established measures, formal rhymes, stock imagery and diction, — and in a most irregular kind of dithyramb, which left the hack reviewer sorely in doubt whether it was verse broken off at hap-hazard, or prose run mad. Whatever motives led to these results, we must admire the courage of a poet who thus burned his ships behind him, and plunged into a wilderness thenceforth all his own. Various passages of the book were resolutely coarse in their naturalism, and were thought by some, who perhaps knew little of the author, to reveal his tendencies. It seemed as if certain passions appeared to him more natural, certain sins more venial, than others, and that these were those which

Bewilderment of the critics.

he felt to be most obstreperous in his own system, — that his creed was adjusted to his personal aptitudes. But many also found in him strength, color, love, and knowledge of nature, and a capacity for lyrical outbursts, — the utterance of a genuine poet. Such was the "Leaves of Grass," although the book is hard to formulate in few and scientific terms; such, at least, it was, so far as I understand its higher meaning.

Whitman's habits, haunts, and conspicuous daily walk.

If the successive editions of "Leaves of Grass" had the quiet sale accorded to books of verse, the work did not lack admirers among radicals on the lookout for something new. Emerson, with one of his cheery impulses, wrote a glowing welcome, which soon was given to the public, and directed all eyes to the rising bard. No poet, as a person, ever came more speedily within range of view. His age, origin, and habits were made known; he himself, in fastidiously studied and picturesque costume, was to be observed strolling up Broadway, crossing the ferries, mounting the omnibuses, wherever he could see and be seen, make studies and be studied. It was learned that he had been by turns printer, school-master, builder, editor; had written articles and poems of a harmless, customary nature, — until, finding that he could not express himself to any purpose in that wise, he underwent conviction, experienced a change of thought and style, and professed a new departure in verse, dress, and way of life. Henceforward he occupied himself with loafing, thinking, writing, and making disciples and "camerados." Among the young wits and writers who enjoyed his fellowship, his slow, large mould and rathe-grizzled hair procured for him the hearty title of "Old Walt." In the second year of the war his blood grew warm, and he went to

Experiences during the War.

Washington, whither all roads then led. His heart yearned toward the soldiery, and in the hospitals and camps he became the tenderest of nurses and the almoner of funds supplied to him by generous hands. After three years of this service, and after a sickness brought on by its exertions, he was given a place in the Interior Department. Then came that senseless act of a benighted official, who dismissed him for the immorality of the "Leaves of Grass." To Whitman it was a piece of good luck. It brought to a climax the discussion of his merits and demerits. It called out from the fervent and learned pen of William D. O'Connor a surging, characteristic vindication, "The Good Gray Poet," in which the offending Secretary was consigned to ignominy, and by which the poet's talents, services, and appearance were so fastened upon public attention that he took his place as a hoar and reverend minstrel. He then, with Lowell, Parsons, Holland, Brownell, and Mrs. Howe, had reached the patriarchal age of forty-six. Another Cabinet officer, a man of taste and feeling, gave him a new position — which he held for nine years, and until somewhat disabled by a paralytic affliction. Meanwhile, influential writers, on both sides of the ocean, skilful in polemic criticism, had avowed allegiance to himself and his works. In England, W. M. Rossetti edited a selection of his poems, and Swinburne, Dowden, Clifford, Symonds, Buchanan, Clive, have joined in recognizing them. In America, — besides O'Connor, — Linton, Conway, Sanborn, Charles Whiting, the Swintons, Benton, Marvin, the sure-eyed and poetic Burroughs, and others, in turn have guarded his rights or ministered to him, some of them with a loyalty unprecedented in our literary annals. Like Fourier, he may be said to have his propagandists in

A fortunate persecution.

"The Good Gray Poet. A Vindication." New York, 1866.

Disciples and friends in Europe and America.

many lands. Making allowance for the tendency to invest with our own attributes some object of hero-worship, a man must be of unusual stuff to breed this enthusiasm; and under any privations the life is a success which has created and sustained such an ideal.

Charges of neglect and unfair treatment.

The appearance of Whitman's "Centennial edition," and his needs at the time, gave occasion for an outcry concerning American neglect and persecution of the poet, and for a debate in which both London and New York took part. But little evidence was found of unfriendliness to him among the magazine-editors, to whom our writers offer their wares. Several of them averred that they would rather accept than decline his contributions; they had declined them only when unsuited to their necessities. What magazine-writer has a smoother experience? In a democracy the right most freely allotted is that of every man to secure his own income. Nor am I aware that, with two exceptions, any American has been able to derive a substantial revenue from poetry alone. A man ahead of his time, or different from his time, usually gathers little of this world's goods. Whitman's fellow-countrymen regard him kindly and with pride. An English poet declared that it was not America, but the literary class in America, that "persecuted" him. Who constituted such a class I know not, since at present it would be hard to find an American author or editor who does not keep a warm place in his heart for the sage of Camden and hold his genius in honor. What opposition the poet really incurred has done him no harm. The outcry led to plain-speaking, and the press gave the fullest hearing to Whitman's friends. It was of benefit, in showing that our writers were misunderstood, in stimulating his

"Leaves of Grass." "Two Rivulets." 2 vols. Author's Centennial Edition. Camden, N. J., 1876.

Portraits and characteristics.

friends to new offices in his behalf, and especially in promoting the sale of the unique *Centennial Edition* (or "Author's") of his collected poems. Never was a collection more aptly named. The two volumes bear the material as well as the spiritual impress of their author. Of the many portraits for which he has sat, they give, besides the earliest, a bold and recent photograph, and the striking wood-cut by his friend Linton — that master of the engraver's craft. Here and there are interpolated later poems, printed on slips, and pasted in by the poet's own hand. It is Whitman, His Book. The edition has an indescribable air; one who owns it feels that he has a portion of the author's self.

Order of contents.

The collection embraces the revised series of "Leaves of Grass," preceded by "Inscriptions," and divided by a group of poems, "Children of Adam," on the sexual conditions of life; by another group, "Calamus," on the love of comrades, and by certain pieces, of which "Crossing Brooklyn Ferry" is a good specimen, in which the aspect and occupations of the people at large, the glory of the American race, and of the dwellers in Mannahatta, are specifically chanted by this bard of New York. Then follow the "Drum-Taps," so full of lyrical fervor that Whitman may be called a chief singer of that great conflict to which the burning songs of other poets had been an overture. There also are "Marches Now the War is Over," with a few pieces that celebrate the republican uprisings in Europe, and the first volume closes with "Songs of Parting." The second, after a general preface, opens with "Two Rivulets," parallel streams of prose and verse, followed by a prose essay of a Carlylese type, possibly suggested by Carlyle's strictures on America. Much of all this portion, prose

"Drum-Taps."

"Two Rivulets."

and verse, is the least satisfactory of Whitman's writings, although greatly in earnest and of most import to the author. "The Centennial Songs" (1876) and the poems of 1872 (including that fine burst, "The Mystic Trumpeter") come next. Reverting to his prose "Rivulet" and the "Democratic Vistas," I do not find, — in these contradictory views of the present, notices of weak joints in our armor, and dreams of the future, — much that has not been considered by many who have helped to guide our republic thus far, much that has not occurred to the poet's fellow-thinkers, or is not, at least, within their power to understand and amend. Neither are they expressed in that terse and sufficient language common to rare minds, — nor in a way at all comparable to the writer's surer way of expressing himself in his chosen verse. Well-written articles like his recantation of Emerson lead one to suspect that his every-day prose is distorted intentionally, otherwise I should say that, if he is a poet of high rank, he is an exception to the conceit that the truest poets write also the most genuine and noble prose; for certainly his usual style is no nearer that of healthy, self-sustained English than his verse is to ordinary rhythm. A poet's genius may reconcile us to that which Cosmo Monkhouse terms poetry in solution, but prose in dissolution is undesirable. A continuous passage of good prose, not broken up with dashes and parentheses, and other elements of weakness, nor marred by incoherent and spasmodic expressions, is hard to find in his "Rivulets" and "Vistas." Both his prose and verse have one fault in common, that he underrates the intelligence of readers. This is visible in constant repetition of his thoughts, often in forms that grow weaker, and in his intimation that we are even unwilling to

"Democratic Vistas," etc.

Defects of Whitman's prose.

comprehend ideas which are familiar to all radical thinkers in modern times.

"Memoranda during the War."

More impressive in their vivid realism, and as evidence not to be gainsaid of Whitman's personal qualities, are the "Memoranda during the War," homely and fragmentary records of his labors among the soldiers. Three years and more were covered by these acts of devotion, and it is well they should be commemorated. Their records constitute a picture of his life at its highest moment, and are interludes between his poems of life and those upon death. The latter, under the title, "Passage to India," express the maturest yearning of his soul. Chastened by illness and wise through experience, the singer whose pulses have beaten with life's full tide now muses upon Death, — the universal blessing. With lofty faith and imagining he confronts the unknown. To one so watchful of his own individuality, any creed that involves a merger of it is monstrous and impossible. He bids his soul voyage through death's portals, sure to find

Poems on Death.

"The untold want, by life and land ne'er granted."

He is at the farthest remove from our modish Buddhism, nor can any Nirvâna satisfy his demands. In this section his song is on a high key, and less reduced than elsewhere by untimely commonplace. Here are the pieces inspired by the tragic death of Lincoln. The burial hymn, "When Lilacs last," etc., is entitled to the repute in which it is affectionately held. The theme is handled in an indirect, melodious, pathetic manner, and I think this poem and Lowell's "Commemoration Ode," each in its own way, the most notable elegies resulting from the war and its episodes. Whitman's is exquisitely idyllic, Lowell's the more heroic and intellectual. Even the "Genius of These States" might stoop for an instant

Lincoln's "Burial Hymn."

to hear the Cambridge scholar, and I can yield the "Burial Hymn" no truer homage than to associate it with his Ode.

A "Poem of Joys" makes an artistic contrast with these death-carols, and a group of "Sea-shore Memories," with their types and music of the infinite, add to the climacteric effect of this division. Unable here to cite passages from Whitman, I can at least direct the reader how to get at his real capabilities. For his original mood, and something of his color, imagination, hold upon nature, lyric power, turn then to the broad harmonies of the "Sea-shore Memories"; to "Lincoln's Burial Hymn," and the shorter poems beyond it; to "The Mystic Trumpeter," and "The Wound-Dresser"; and then, after reading the sixth section of the poem, "Walt Whitman,"

Suggestions to the reader.

"A child said, 'What is the grass?'"

find the two hundred and sixth paragraph,

"I understand the large hearts of heroes,"

and read to the end of the frigate-fight. These passages are a fair introduction to the poet, and you will go with him farther, until checked by some repulsive exhibition, or wearied by pages cheap in wisdom and invective or — intolerably dull. Often where he utters truths, it is with an effort to give offence, or with expressions of contempt for their recipient that well might make even the truth offensive. A man does not care to be driven with blows and hard names, even to a feast, nor to have the host brag too much of the entertainment.

III.

Whitman's physical and sexual themes and illustrations.

HERE we may as well consider a trait of Whitman's early work that most of all has brought it under censure. I refer to the blunt and open manner in which the consummate processes of nature, the acts of procreation and reproduction, with all that appertain to them, are made the theme or illustration of various poems, notably of those with the title "Children of Adam." Landor says of a poet that, "on the remark of a learned man that irregularity is no indication of genius, he began to lose ground rapidly, when on a sudden he cried out in the Haymarket, 'There is no God.' It was then rumored more generally and more gravely that he had something in him. . . . 'Say what you will,' once whispered a friend of mine, 'there are things in him strong as poison, and original as sin.'" But those who looked upon Whitman's sexuality as a shrewd advertisement justly might be advised to let him reap the full benefit of it, since, if he had no more sincere basis, it would receive the earlier judgment — and ere long be "outlawed of art." This has not been its fate, and therefore it must have had something of conviction to sustain it. Nevertheless, it made the public distrustful of this poet, and did much to confine his volumes to the libraries of the select few. Prurient modesty often is a sign that people are conscious of personal defects; but Whitman's physical excursions are of a kind which even Thoreau, refreshed as he was by the new poet, found it hard to keep pace with. The fault was not that he discussed matters which others timidly evade, but that he did not do it in a clean way, — that he was too anatomical and malodorous withal; furthermore, that in this department he showed a morbid interest, and applied its imagery to other departments, as if with a special purpose to lug it in. His pictures sometimes were so realistic, his speech so free, as to excite the hue and cry of indecent exposure; the display of things natural, indeed, but which we think it unnatural to exhibit on the highway, or in the reading-room and parlor.

Alleged indecency.

On the poet's side it is urged that the ground of this exposure was, that thus only could his reform be consistent; that it was necessary to celebrate the body with special unction, since, with respect to the physical basis of life, our social weakness and hypocrisy are most extreme. Not only should the generative functions be proclaimed, but, also, — to show that "there is in nature nothing mean or base," — the side of our life which is hidden, because it is of the earth, earthy, should be plainly recognized in these poems; and thus, out of rankness and coarseness, a new virility be bred, an impotent and squeamish race at last be made whole.

The Poet's defence: "a sane sensuality."

Entering upon this field of dispute, what I have to say — in declaring that Whitman mistakes the aim of the radical artist or poet — is perhaps different from the criticism to which he has been subjected. Let us test him solely by his own rules. Doing this, we presuppose his honesty of purpose, otherwise his objectionable phrases and imagery would be outlawed, not only of art but of criticism. Assume, then, first, that they were composed as a fearless avowal of the instincts and conditions which pertain to him in common with the race which he typifies; secondly, that he deems such a presentation essential to his revolt against the artifice of current life and sentiment, and makes it in loyal *reliance upon the excellence, the truth, of nature.* To judge him in conformity with these

How to test this matter.

ideas lessens our estimate of his genius. Genius is greatly consistent when most audacious. Its instinct will not violate nature's logic, even by chance, and it is something like obtuseness that does so upon a theory.

Genius is consistent.

Wherein this poet misconceives the instinct and method of Nature.

In Mr. Whitman's sight, that alone is to be condemned which is against nature, yet, in his mode of allegiance, he violates her canons. For, if there is nothing in her which is mean or base, there is much that is ugly and disagreeable. If not so in itself (and on the question of absolute beauty I accept his own ruling, "that whatever tastes sweet to the most perfect person, that is finally right"), if not ugly in itself, it seems so to the conscious spirit of our intelligence. Even Mother Earth takes note of this, and resolves, or disguises and beautifies, what is repulsive upon her surface. It is well said that an artist shows inferiority by placing either the true, the beautiful, or the good, above its associates. Nature is strong and rank, but not externally so. She, too, has her sweet and sacred sophistries, and the delight of Art is to heighten her beguilement, and, far from making her ranker than she is, to portray what she might be in ideal combinations. Nature, I say, covers her slime, her muck, her ruins, with garments that to us are beautiful. She conceals the skeleton, the frame-work, the intestinal thick of life, and makes fair the outside of things. Her servitors swiftly hide or transform the fermenting, the excrementitious, and the higher animals possess her instinct. Whitman fails to perceive that she respects certain decencies, that what we call decency is grounded in her law. An artist should not elect to paint the part of her to which Churchill rashly avowed that Hogarth's pencil was devoted. There is a book — the *Affaire Clémenceau* — in which a Frenchman's regard for the lamp of beauty, and his indif-

"Affaire Clémenceau." Paris.

ference to that of goodness, are curiously illustrated. But Dumas points out, in the rebuke given by a sculptor to a pupil who mistakenly elevates the arm of his first model, a beautiful girl, that the Underside of things should be avoided in art, — since Nature, not meaning it to be shown, often deprives it of beauty. Finally, Whitman sins against his mistress in questioning the instinct we derive from her, one which of all is most elevating to poetry, and which is the basis of sensations that lead childhood on, that fill youth with rapture, impress with longing all human kind, and make up, impalpable as they are, half the preciousness of life. He draws away the final veil. It is not squeamishness that leaves something to the imagination, that hints at guerdons still unknown. The law of suggestion, of half-concealment, determines the choicest effects, and is the surest road to truth. Grecian as Whitman may be, the Greeks better understood this matter, as scores of illustrations, like that of the attitude of the Hermaphroditus in the Louvre, show. A poet violates Nature's charm of feeling in robbing love, and even intrigue, of their esoteric quality. No human appetites need be pruriently ignored, but coarsely analyzed they fall below humanity. He even takes away the sweetness and pleasantness of stolen waters and secret bread. *Furto cuncta magis bella.* The mock-modesty and effeminacy of our falser tendencies in art should be chastised, but he misses the true corrective. Delicacy is not impotence, nor rankness the sure mark of virility. The model workman is both fine and strong. Where Whitman sees nothing but the law of procreation, poetry dwells upon the union of souls, devotion unto death, joys greater for their privacy, things of more worth because whispered between the twilights. It

The law of Reserve, in Nature and Art.

The antique feeling.

Delicacy not inconsistent with strength.

is absolutely true that the design of sexuality is the propagation of species. But the delight of lovers who now inherit the earth is no less a natural right, and those children often are the finest that were begot without thought of offspring. There are other lights in which a dear one may be regarded than as the future mother of men, and these — with their present hour of joy — are unjustly subordinated in the "Leaves of Grass." Marked as the failure of this pseudo-naturalism has been hitherto, even thus will it continue, — so long as savages have instincts of modesty, — so long as we dream of and draw the forms and faces, not the internal substance and mechanism, of those we hold most dear, — so long as the ivy trails over the ruin, the southern jessamine covers the blasted pine, the moss hides the festering swamp, — so long as our spirits seek the spirit of all things; and thus long shall art and poesy, while calling every truth of science to their aid, rely on something else than the processes of science for the attainment of their exquisite results.

Spirituality essential.

From the tenor of Mr. Whitman's later works, I sometimes have thought him half-inclined to see in what respect his effort toward a perfect naturalism was misdirected. In any case, there would be no inconsistency in a further modification of his early pieces, — in the rejection of certain passages and words, which, by the law of strangeness, are more conspicuous than ten times their amount of common phraseology, and grow upon the reader until they seem to pervade the whole volume. The examples of Lucretius, Rabelais, and other masters, who wrote in other ages and conditions, and for their own purposes, have little analogy. It well may be that our poet at first had more claim to a wide reading in England than here, since his English editor, without asking consent, omitted

An inference and a suggestion.

"Walt Whitman's Poems." Selected

entirely every poem "which could with tolerable fairness be deemed offensive." Without going so far, and with no falseness to himself, Whitman might re-edit his editions in such wise that they would not be counted wholly among those books which are meat for strong men, but would have a chance among those greater books that are the treasures of the simple and the learned, the young and the old.

and edited by W. M. Rossetti, London.

IV.

THE entire body of his work has a sign-metrical by which it is recognized — a peculiar and uncompromising style, conveyed in a still more peculiar unrhymed verse, irregular, yet capable of impressive rhythmical and lyrical effects.

This poet's lyrical and rhythmical method.

The faults of his method, glaring enough in ruder passages, are quite his own; its merits often are no less so, but in his chosen form there is little original and new. It is an old fashion, always selected for dithyrambic oracular outpourings, — that of the Hebrew lyrists and prophets, and their inspired English translators, — of the Gaelic minstrels, — of various Oriental and Shemitic peoples, — of many barbarous dark-skinned tribes, — and in recent times put to use by Blake, in the "Prophetic Visions," and by other and weaker men. There are symptoms in Whitman's earlier poems, and definite proof in the later, that his studies have included Blake, — between whose traits and his own there is a superficial, not a genuine, likeness. Not as an invention, then, but as a striking and persistent renaissance, the form that has become his trade-mark, and his extreme claims for it, should have fair consideration. An honest effort to enlarge the poet's equipment, too long unaided, by something rich

Not a new invention.

William Blake.

It demands a fair examination.

and strange, deserves praise, even though a failure; for there are failures worthier than triumphs. Our chanter can bear with dignity the provincial laughter of those to whom all is distasteful that is uncommon, and regard it as no unfavorable omen. From us the very strangeness of his chant shall gain for it a welcome, and the chance to benefit us as it may. Thereby we may escape the error pointed out by Mr. Benjamin, who says that people, in approaching a work, instead of learning from it, try to estimate it from their preconceived notions. Hence, original artists at first endure neglect, because they express their own discoveries in nature of what others have not yet seen, — a truth well to bear in mind whenever a singer arrives with a new method.

"What is Art?" S. G. W. Benjamin. Boston: 1877.

Probably the method under review has had a candid hearing in more quarters than the author himself is aware of. If some men of independent thought and feeling have failed to accept his claims and his estimate of the claims of others, it possibly has not been through exclusiveness or malice, but upon their own impression of what has value in song.

Outcry against wonted forms.

Whitman never has swerved from his primal indictment of the wonted forms, rhymed and unrhymed, dependent upon accentual, balanced, and stanzaic effects of sound and shape, — and until recently has expressed his disdain not only of our poets who care for them, but of form itself. So far as this cry was raised against the technique of poetry, I think not merely that it is absurd, but that when he first made it he had not clearly thought out his own problem. Technique, *of some kind*, is an essential, though it is equally true that it cannot atone for poverty of thought and imagination. I hope to show that he never was more mistaken than when he supposed he was throw

The question of Technique.

ing off form and technique. But first it may be said that no "form" ever has sprung to life, and been handed from poet to poet, that was not engendered by instinct and natural law, and that will not be accepted in a sound generalization. Whitman avers that the time has come to break down the barriers between prose and verse, and that only thus can the American bard utter anything commensurate with the liberty and splendor of his themes. Now, the mark of a poet is that he is at ease everywhere, — that nothing can hamper his gifts, his exultant freedom. He is a master of expression. There are certain points — note this — where expression takes on rhythm, and certain other points where it ceases to be rhythmical, — places where prose becomes poetical, and where verse grows prosaic; and throughout Whitman's productions these points are more frequent and unmistakable than in the work of any other writer of our time. However bald or formal a poet's own method, it is useless for him to decry forms that recognize the pulses of time and accent, and the linked sweetness of harmonic sound. Some may be tinkling, others majestic, but each is suited to its purpose, and has a spell to charm alike the philosopher and the child that knows not why. The human sense acknowledges them; they are the earliest utterance of divers peoples, and in their later excellence still hold their sway. Goethe discussed all this with Eckermann, and rightly said there were "great and mysterious agencies" in the various poetic forms. He even added that if a sort of poetic prose should be introduced, it would only show that the distinction between prose and poetry had been lost sight of completely. Rhyme, the most conventional feature of ballad verse, has its due place, and will keep it; it

Unbounded liberty of the Poet.

Time, Accent, Rhythm.

Goethe's view.

Rhyme.

is an artifice, but a natural artifice, and pleases accordingly. Milton gave reasons for discarding it when he perfected an unrhymed measure for the stateliest English poem; but what an instrument rhyme was in his hands that made the sonnets and minor poems! How it has sustained the whole carnival of our heroic and lyric song, from the sweet pipings of Lodge and Chapman and Shakespeare, to the undertones of Swinburne and Poe! There are endless combinations yet in the gamut. The report is that Whitman's prejudice is specially strong against our noblest unrhymed form, "blank-verse." Its variety and freedom, within a range of accents, breaks, cæsural effects, — its rolling organ-harmonies, — he appreciates not at all. Rhythmical as his own verse often can be, our future poets scarcely will discard blank-verse in its behalf — not if they shall recall "The Tempest," "Hail, Holy Light," "Tintern Abbey," "Hyperion," the "Hellenics," "Ulysses," and "Thanatopsis." Mr. Parke Godwin, in a private letter, terms it "the grandest and most flexible of English measures," and adds, with quick enthusiasm: "Oh, what a glory there is in it, when we think of what Shakespeare, Milton, Wordsworth, and Landor made of it, to say nothing of Tennyson and Bryant!" I doubt not that new handlings of this measure will produce new results, unsurpassed in any tongue. It is quite as fit as Mr. Whitman's own, if he knows the use of it, for "the expression of American democracy and manhood." Seeing how dull and prolix he often becomes, it may be that even for him his measure has been too facile, and that the curb of a more regular unrhymed form would have spared us many tedious curvetings and grewsome downfalls.

Whitman upon English blank verse.

Glory of this supreme measure. Cp. "Victorian Poets": pp. 160–162.

Strenuous as he may be in his belief that the old

methods will be useless to poets of the future, I am sure that he has learned the value of technique through his long practice. He well knows that whatever claims to be the poetry of the future speedily will be forgotten in the past, unless consonant with the laws of expression in the language to which it belongs; that verse composed upon a theory, if too artificial in its contempt of art, may be taken up for a while, but, as a false fashion, anon will pass away. Not that his verse is of this class; but it justly has been declared that, in writing with a purpose to introduce a new mode or revolutionize thought, and not because an irresistible impulse seizes him, a poet is so much the less a poet. Our question, then, involves the spontaneity of his work, and the results attained by him.

Whitman's reasonable statement of his own endeavor.

His present theory, like most theories which have reason, seems to be derived from experience: he has learned to discern the good and bad in his work, and has arrived at a rationale of it. He sees that he has been feeling after the irregular, various harmonies of nature, the anthem of the winds, the roll of the surges, the countless laughter of the ocean waves. He tries to catch this "under-melody and rhythm." Here is an artistic motive, distinguishing his chainless dithyrambs from ordinary verse, somewhat as the new German music is distinguished from folk-melody, and from the products of a preceding, especially the Italian, school. Here is not only reason, but a theoretical advance to a grade of art demanding extreme resources, because it affords the widest range of combination and effect.

Its true origin.

But this comprehension of his own aim is an afterthought, the result of long groping. The genesis of the early "Leaves" was in motives less artistic and penetrating. Finding that he could not think and work to advantage in the current mode, he concluded that the mode itself was at fault; especially, that the poet of a young, gigantic nation, the prophet of a new era, should have a new vehicle of song. Without looking farther, he spewed out the old forms, and avowed his distaste for poets who still employ them. His off-hand course does not bring us to the conclusion of the whole matter. So far as the crudeness of the *juventus mundi* is revived by him, it must be temporal and passing, like the work of some painters, who, for the sake of startling effects, use ephemeral pigments. A poet does not, perforce, restore the lost foundations of his art by copying the manner natural to an aboriginal time and people. He is merely exchanging masters, and certainly is not founding a new school. Only as he discovers the inherent tendencies of song does he belong to the future. Still, it is plain that Whitman found a style suited to his purposes, and was fortunate both as a poet and a diplomatist. He was sure to attract notice, and to seem original, by so pronounced a method. Quoth the monk to Gargantua, "A mass, a matin, or vesper, well rung, is half said." It was suited to him as a poet, because he has that somewhat wandering sense of form, and of melody, which often makes one's conceptions seem the more glorious to himself, as if invested with a halo or blended with concurrent sound, and prevents him from lessening or enlarging them by the decisive master-hand, or at once perfecting them by sure control.

Quality of his eye and ear.

A man who finds that his gloves cripple him does right in drawing them off. At first, Whitman certainly meant to escape all technique. But genius, in spite of itself, makes works that stand the test of scientific laws. And thus he now sees that he was grop-

The results attained.

ing toward a broader technique. Unrhymed verse, the easiest to write, is the hardest to excel in, and no measure for a bardling. And Whitman never more nearly displayed the feeling of a true artist than when he expressed a doubt as to his present handling of his own verse, but hoped that, in breaking loose from transmarine forms, he had sounded, at least, the key for a new pæan. I have referred to his gradual advances in the finish of his song. Whether he has revived a form which others will carry to a still higher excellence is doubtful. Blank-verse, limitless in its capacities, forces a poet to stand without disguise, and reveals all his defects. Whitman's verse, it is true, does not subject him to so severe a test. He can so twist and turn himself, and run and jump, that we are puzzled to inspect him at all, or make out his contour. Yet the few who have ventured to follow him have produced little that has not seemed like parody, or unpleasantly grotesque. It may be that his mode is suited to himself alone, and not to the future poets of These States, — that the next original genius will have to sing "as Martin Luther sang," and the glorious army of poetic worthies. I suspect that the old forms, in endless combinations, will return as long as new poets arise with the old abiding sense of time and sound.

Adaptability of true genius.

The greatest poet is many-sided, and will hold himself slavishly to no one thing for the sake of difference. He is a poet, too, in spite of measure and material, while, as to manner, the style is the man. Genius does not need a special language; it newly uses whatever tongue it finds. Thought, fire, passion, will overtop everything, — will show, like the limbs of Teverino, through the clothes of a prince or a beggar. A cheap and common instrument, odious in foolish hands, becomes the slave of music under the touch of a master. I attach less importance, therefore, to Whitman's experiment in verse than he and his critics have, and inquire of his mannerism simply how far it represents the man. To show how little there is in itself, we only have to think of Tupper; to see how rich it may be, when the utterance of genius, listen to Whitman's teacher, William Blake. It does not prove much, but still is interesting, to note that the pieces whose quality never fails with any class of hearers, — of which "My Captain" is an example, — are those in which our poet has approached most nearly, and in a lyrical, melodious manner, to the ordinary forms.

The style is the man.

A significant fact.

Copious and original diction.

He is far more original in his style proper than in his metrical inventions. His diction, on its good behavior, is copious and strong, full of surprises, utilizing the brave, homely words of the people, and assigning new duties to common verbs and nouns. He has a use of his own for Spanish and French catchwords, picked up, it may be, on his trip to Louisiana or in Mexican war times. Among all this is much slang that now has lived its life, and is not understood by a new generation with a slang of its own. This does not offend so much as the mouthing verbiage, the "ostent evanescent" phrases, wherein he seems profoundest to himself, and really is at his worst. The titles of his books and poems are varied and sonorous. Those of the latter often are taken from the opening lines, and are key-notes. What can be fresher than "Leaves of Grass" and "Calamus"? What richer than "The Mystic Trumpeter," "O Star of France!" "Proud Music of the Storm"; or simpler than "Drum-Taps," "The Wound-Dresser," "The Ox-Tamer"; or more characteristic than "Give me the Splendid

Effective titles and epithets.

Silent Sun," "Mannahatta," "As a Strong Bird on Pinions Free," "Joy, Shipmate, Joy"? Some are obscure and grandiose — "Eidòlons," "Chanting the Square Deific," but usually his titles arrest the eye and haunt the ear; it is an artist that invents them, and the best pieces have the finest names. His epithets, also, are racier than those of other poets; there *is* something of the Greek in Whitman, and his lovers call him Homeric, but to me he shall be our old American Hesiod, teaching us works and days.

V.

General estimate of his merits and defects.

His surest hold, then, is as an American poet, gifted with language, feeling, imagination, and inspired by a determined purpose. Some estimate, as I have said, may be made of his excellence and short-comings, without waiting for that national absorption which he himself declares to be the test.

A veritable poet of nature

As an assimilating poet of nature he has positive genius, and seems to me to present his strongest claims. Who else, in fact, has so true a hand or eye for the details, the sweep and color, of American landscape? Like others, he confronts those superb physical aspects of the New World which have controlled our poetry and painting, and deferred the growth of a figure-school, but in this struggle with Nature he is not overcome; if not the master, he is the joyous brother-in-arms. He has heard the message of the pushing, wind-swept sea, along Paumanok's shore; he knows the yellow, waning moon and the rising stars, — the sunset, with its cloud-bar of gold above the horizon, — the birds that sing by night or day, bush and brier, and every shining or swooning flower, the peaks, the prairie, the mighty, conscious river, the dear common grass that children fetch with full hands. Little escapes him, not even "the mossy scabs of the worm fence, and heap'd stones, mullein and poke-weed"; but his details are massed, blended, — the wind saturates and the light of the American skies transfigures them. Not that to me, recalling the penetrative glance of Emerson, the wood and way-side craft that Lowell carried lightly as a sprig of fir, and recalling other things of others, does Whitman seem our "only" poet of nature; but that here he is on his own ground, and with no man his leader.

The human element often present.

Furthermore, his intimacy with Nature is always subjective, — she furnishes the background for his self-portraiture and his images of men. None so apt as he to observe the panorama of life, to see the human figure, — the hay-maker, wagoner, boatman, soldier, woman and babe and maiden, and brown, lusty boy, — to hear not only "the bravuras of birds, bustle of growing wheat, gossip of flames, clack of sticks cooking my meals," but also "the sound I love, the sound of the human voice." His town and country scenes, in peace or in war, are idyllic. From utter want of sympathy, he can only name and designate anything above the *genre* — he does not depict it. A single sketch, done in some original way, often makes a poem; such is that reminiscence (in rhyme) of the old Southern negress, "Ethiopia Saluting the Colors," and such the touching conceit of Old Ireland — no fair and green-robed Hibernia of the harp, but an ancient, sorrowful mother, white-haired, lean and tattered, seated on the ground, mourning for her children. He tells her that they are not dead, but risen again, with rosy and new blood, in another country. This is admirable, I say, and the true way to escape tradition; this is imaginative, — and there is imagina-

His imagination.

tion, too, in his apostrophe to "The Man-of-War-Bird" (carried beyond discretion by this highest mood, he finds it hard to avoid blank-verse) : —

"Thou who hast slept all night upon the storm,
Waking renewed on thy prodigious pinions!
. . . . . .
Thou, born to match the gale (thou art all wings)!
To cope with heaven and earth and sea and hurricane;
Thou ship of air that never furl'st thy sails,
Days, even weeks, untired and onward, through spaces — realms gyrating.
At dark that look'st on Senegal, at morn, America;
That sport'st amid the lightning-flash and thunder-cloud!
In these — in thy experiences — hadst thou my soul,
What joys! What joys were thine!"

Imagination is the essential thing; without it poetry is as sounding brass or a tinkling cymbal. Whitman shows it in his sudden and novel imagery, and in the subjective rapture of verse like this, but quite as often his vision is crowded and inconsistent. An editor writes to me: "In so far as imagination is thinking through types (*eidullia*), Whitman has no equal," adding that he does not use the term as if applied to Coleridge, but as limited to the use of types, and that "in this sense it is really more applicable to a master of science than to a poet. In the poet the type is lodged in his own heart, and when the occasion comes . . . he is mastered by it, and he must sing. In Whitman the type is not so much in his heart as in his thought. . . . While he is moved by thought, often grand and elementary, he does not give the intellectual satisfaction warranted by the thought, but a moving panorama of objects. He not only puts aside his 'singing-robes,' but his 'thinking-cap,' and resorts to the stereopticon." How acute, how true! There is, however, a peculiar quality in these long catalogues

H. M. Alden's analysis of this quality.

"Catalogues" in

Whitman's verse.

Their meaning.

of types, — such as those in the "Song of the Broad-Axe" and "Salut au Monde," or, more poetically treated, in "Longings for Home." The poet appeals to our synthetic vision. Look through a window; you see not only the framed landscape, but each tree and stone and living thing. His page must be seized with the eye, as a journalist reads a column at a glance, until successive "types" and pages blend in the mind like the diverse colors of a swift-turning wheel. Whitman's most inartistic fault is that he overdoes this method, as if usually unable to compose in any other way.

Pathos and tenderness.

The tenderness of a strong and robust nature is a winning feature of his song. There is no love-making, no yearning for some idol of the heart. In the lack of so refining a contrast to his realism, we have gentle thoughts of children, images of grand old men, and of women clothed with sanctity and years. This tenderness, a kind of natural piety, marks also his poems relating to the oppressed, the suffering, the wounded and dying soldiers. It is the soul of the pathetic, melodious threne for Lincoln, and of the epilogue — "My Captain!" These pieces remind us that he has gained command of his own music, and in the matter of tone has displayed strength from the first. In revising his early poems he has improved their effect as a whole. It must be owned that his wheat often is more welcome for the chaff in which it is scattered; there is none of the persistent luxury which compels much of Swinburne's unstinted wealth to go unreckoned. Finally, let us note that Whitman, long ago, was not unread in the few great books of the world, nor inapt to digest their wisdom. He was among the first to perceive the grandeur of the scientific truths which are to give impulse to a new and

Relations of Poetry and Science. Cp.

loftier poetic imagination. Those are significant passages in the poem "Walt Whitman," written by one who had read the thirty-eighth chapter of Job, and beginning, "Long I was hugg'd close — long and long."

"Victorian Poets": pp. 7–21, 170, 193, 343.

The "Leaves of Grass," in thought and method, avowedly are a protest against a hackney breed of singers, singing the same old song. More poets than one are born in each generation, yet Whitman has derided his compeers and scouted the sincerity of their passion. In two things he fairly did take the initiative, and might, like a wise advocate, rest his case upon them. He essayed, without reserve or sophistry, the full presentment of the natural man. He devoted his song to the future of his own country, accepting and outvying the loudest peak-and-prairie brag, and pledging These States to work out a perfect democracy and the salvation of the world. Striking words and venturesome deeds, for which he must have full credit. But in our studies of the ideal and its votaries, the failings of the latter cannot be lightly passed over. There is an inconsistency, despite the gloss, between his fearful arraignment, going beyond Carlyle's, of the outgrowth of our democracy, thus far, and his promise for the future. In his prose, he sees neither physical nor moral health among us: all is disease, impotency, fraud, decline. In his verse, the average American is lauded as no type ever was before. These matters renew questions which, to say the least, are still open. Are the lines of caste less sharply divided every year, or are the high growing higher, and the low lower, under our democracy? Is not the social law of more import than the form of government, and has not the quality of race much to do with both? Does Americanism in speech and literature depend upon the form and letter, or upon the

Protest against conventionalism.

Realism, and Democracy: the cardinal principles of Whitman's song.

His incomplete judgment of Democracy in America.

See pp. 4–11.

spirit? Can the spirit of literature do much more than express the national spirit as far as it has gone, and has it not, in fact, varied with the atmosphere? Is a nation changed by literature, or the latter by the former, in times when journalism so swiftly represents the thought and fashion of each day? As to distinctions in form and spirit between the Old-World literature and our own, I have always looked for these to enlarge with time. But with the recent increase of travel and communication, each side of the Atlantic now more than ever seems to affect the other. Our "native flavor" still is distinct in proportion to the youth of a section, and inversely to the development. It is an intellectual narrowness that fails to meditate upon these things.

Narrowness his main defect.

Thus we come to a defect in Whitman's theories, reasoning, and general attitude. He professes universality, absolute sympathy, breadth in morals, thought, workmanship, — exemption from prejudice and formalism. Under all the high poetic excellences which I carefully have pointed out, I half suspect that his faults lie in the region where, to use his own word, he is most complacent: in brief, that a certain *narrowness* holds him within well-defined bounds. In many ways he does not conform to his creed. Others have faith in the future of America, with her arts and letters, yet hesitate to lay down rules for her adoption. These must come of themselves, or not at all. Again, in this poet's specification of the objects of his sympathy, the members of every class, the lofty and the lowly, are duly named; yet there always is an implication that the employer is inferior to the employed, — that the man of training, the "civilizee," is less manly than the rough, the pioneer. He suspects those who, by chance or ability, rise above the crowd.

Class feeling.

What attention he does pay them is felt to be in the nature of patronage, and insufferable. Other things being equal, a scholar is as good as an ignoramus, a rich man as a poor man, a civilizee as a boor. Great champions of democracy — poets like Byron, Shelley, Landor, Swinburne, Hugo — often have come from the ranks of long descent. It would be easy to cite verses from Whitman that apparently refute this statement of his feeling, but the spirit of his whole work confirms it. Meanwhile, though various editions of his poems have found a sale, he is little read by our common people, who know him so well, and of whose democracy he is the self-avowed herald. In numberless homes of working-men — and all Americans are workers — the books of other poets are treasured. Some mental grip and culture are required, of course, to get hold of the poetry of the future. But Whittier, in this land, is a truer type of the people's poet, — the word "people" here meaning a vast body of freemen, having a common-school education, homes, an honest living, and a general comprehension far above that of the masses in Europe. These folk have an instinct that Whittier, for example, has seized his day with as much alertness and self-devotion as this other bard of Quaker lineage, and has sung songs "fit for the New World" as he found it. Whitman is more truly the voice and product of the culture of which he bids us beware. At least, he utters the cry of culture for escape from over-culture, from the weariness, the finical precision, of its own satiety. His warmest admirers are of several classes: those who have carried the art of verse to super-refined limits, and seeing nothing farther in that direction, break up the mould for a change; those radical enthusiasts who, like myself, are interested in whatever hopes to

Not the people's poet.

Whittier.

Whitman a product of the times, and a favorite with special classes.

bring us more speedily to the golden year; lastly, those who, radically inclined, do not think closely, and make no distinction between his strength and weakness. Thus he is, in a sense, the poet of the over-refined and the doctrinaires. Such men, too, as Thoreau and Burroughs have a welcome that scarcely would have been given them in an earlier time. From the discord and artifice of our social life we go with them to the woods, learn to name the birds, note the beauty of form and flower, and love these healthy comrades who know each spring that bubbles beneath the lichened crag and trailing hemlock. Theocritus learns his notes upon the mountain, but sings in courts of Alexandria and Syracuse. Whitman, through propagandists who care for his teachings from metaphysical and personal causes, and compose their own ideals of the man, may yet reach the people, in spite of the fact that lasting works usually have pleased all classes in their own time.

The charm of Thoreau and Burroughs.

Reflecting upon his metrical theory, we also find narrowness instead of breadth. I have shown that the bent of a liberal artist may lead him to adopt a special form, but not to reject all others; he will see the uses of each, demanding only that it shall be good in its kind. Swinburne, with his cordial liking for Whitman, is too acute to overlook his formalism. Some of his eulogists, those whom I greatly respect, fail in their special analysis. One of them rightly says that Shakespeare's sonnets are artificial, and that three lines which he selects from "Measure for Measure" are of a higher grade of verse. But these are the reverse of "unmeasured" lines, — they are in Shakespeare's free and artistic, yet most measured, vein. Here comes in the distinction between art and artifice; the blank-verse is conceived in the broad

Whitman's excessive formalism.

Art vs. Artifice.

spirit of the former, the finish and pedantry of the sonnet make it an artificial form. A master enjoys the task of making its artifice artistic, but does not employ it exclusively. Whitman's irregular, manneristic chant is *at the other extreme of artificiality*, and equally monotonous. A poet can use it with feeling and majesty; but to use it invariably, to laud it as the one mode of future expression, to decry all others, is formalism of a pronounced kind. I have intimated that Whitman has carefully studied and improved it. Burroughs does him injustice in admitting that he is not a poet and artist in the current acceptation of those terms, and another writer simply is just in declaring that when he undertakes to give us poetry he can do it. True, the long prose sentences thrown within his ruder pieces resemble nothing so much as the comic recitativos in the buffo-songs of the concert-cellars. This is not art, nor wisdom, but sensationalism. There is narrowness in his failure to recast and modify these and other depressing portions of various poems, and it is sheer Philistinism for one to coddle all the weaknesses of his experimental period, because they have been a product of himself.

One effect of reading his verse.

One effect of the constant reading of his poetry is that, like the use of certain refections, it mars our taste for the proper enjoyment of other kinds. Not, of course, because it is wholly superior, since the most subtile landscape by Corot or Rousseau might be utterly put to nought by a melodramatic neighbor, full of positive color and extravagance. Nor is it always, either, to our bard's advantage that he should be read with other poets. Consider Wordsworth's exquisite lyric upon the education which Nature gives the child whom to herself she takes, and of whom she declares: —

Comparative criticism.

"The stars of midnight shall be dear
To her; and she shall lean her ear
In many a secret place,
Where rivulets dance their wayward round,
And beauty born of murmuring sound
Shall pass into her face."

It happens that Whitman has a poem on the same theme, describing the process of growth by sympathy and absorption, which thus begins and ends:—

"There was a child went forth every day;
And the first object he look'd upon, that object he became;
And that object became part of him for the day, or a certain part of the day, or for many years, or stretching cycles of years.
. . . .
The horizon's edge, the flying sea-crow, the fragrance of salt-marsh and shore-mud;
These became part of that child who went forth every day, and who now goes, and will always go forth every day."

Plainly there are some comparative advantages in Wordsworth's treatment of this idea. It would be just as easy to reverse this showing by quoting other passages from each poet: the purpose of my digression is to declare that by means of comparative criticism any poet may be judged unfairly, and without regard to his general claims.

The charge of affectation.

So far as Whitman's formalism is natural to him, no matter how eccentric, we must bear with it; whenever it partakes of affectation, it is not to be desired. The charge of attitudinizing, so often brought against his writings and personal career, may be the result of a popular impression that the border-line is indistinct between his self-assertion as a type of Man and the ordinary self-esteem and self-advancement displayed by men of common mould.

Pretensions.

Pretensions have this advantage, that they challenge analysis, and make a vast noise even as we are forced to examine them. In the early preface to the "Leaves" there is a passage modelled, in my opinion, upon the style of Emerson, concerning simplicity, — with which I heartily agree, having constantly insisted upon the test of simplicity in my discussion of the poets. Yet this quality is the last to be discerned in many portions of the "Leaves of Grass." In its stead we often find boldness, and the "pride that apes humility," — until the reader is tempted to quote from the "Poet of Feudalism" those words of Cornwall upon the roughness which brought good Kent to the stocks. Our bard's self-assertion, when the expression of his real manhood, is bracing, is an element of poetic strength. When it even seems to be "posing," it is a weakness, or a shrewdness, and 't is a weakness in a poet to be unduly shrewd. Of course a distinction must be carefully made between the fine extravagance of genius, the joy in its own conceptions, and self-conscious vanity or affectation, — between, also, occasional weaknesses of the great, of men like Browning, and like the greatest of recent masters, Hugo, and the afflatus of small men, who only thus far succeed in copying them. And it would be unjust to reckon Whitman among the latter class.

Frequent want of true simplicity.

It may be that his strictures upon the poets of his own land at one time made them hesitate to venture upon the first advances in brotherhood, or to intrude on him with their recognition of his birthright. As late as his Centennial edition, his opinion of their uselessness was expressed in withering terms. He declared that he could not except "a single writer" from his indictment of the "genteel" producers of "pistareen, paste-pot work," and inveighed against the "copious dribble, either of our little or well-known

Whitman's criticism of other poets. E. g. "Democratic Vistas," (Centl. Ed.), pp. 32, 54, 58.

rhymesters." It is just to add that recently, if the reports of interlocutors are trustworthy, he has excepted "Bryant, Emerson, Whittier, and Longfellow — these only and proportionately in the order given" — from his former criticism, and has stated that his general attitude is eminently respectful. If it were not, there would be no inconsistency, in view of his purpose and convictions, nor any reason for complaint. There was no consistency, however, in complaints that arose in various quarters, to some of which I have before referred, concerning a lack of recognition and encouragement from his fellow-craftsmen. There is ample ground for his scorn of the time-serving, unsubstantial quality of much of our literature. But I should not be writing this volume, did I not well know that there are other poets than himself who hear the roll of the ages, who look before and after, above and below. The culture which he deprecates may have done them an ill turn in lessening their worldly tact. I am aware that Whitman's poems are the drama of his own life and passions. His subjectivity is so great that he not only absorbs all others into himself, but insists upon being absorbed by whomsoever he addresses. In his conception of the world's equality, the singer himself appears as the one Messianic personage, the answerer and sustainer, the universal solvent, — in all these respects holding even "Him that was crucified" to be not one whit his superior. It is his kiss, his consolation, that all must receive, — whoever you are, these are given especially to you. But men are egotists, and not all tolerant of one man's selfhood; they do not always deem the affinities elective. Whitman's personality is too strong and individual to be universal, and even to him it is not given to be all things to all men.

An egoist by nature, and on principle.

VI.

BUT there is that in venerableness which compels veneration, and it is an instinct of human nature to seek the blessing and revere the wisdom of the poet or peasant transfigured by hoary hairs: —

A benign and lovable old age.

"Old age superbly rising! O welcome, ineffable grace of dying days!"

I was one of a small but sympathetic audience gathered in New York to hear Mr. Whitman, at the cordial request of authors, journalists, and artists, deliver a lecture upon Abraham Lincoln. As he entered, haltingly, and took the seat placed for him, his appearance satisfied the eye. His manly figure, clothed in a drab suit that loosely and well became him, his head crowned with flowing silvery hair, his bearded, ruddy and wholesome face, upon which sat a look of friendliness, the wise benignity that comes with ripened years, all these gave him the aspect of a poet and sage. His reminiscences of the martyr President were slight, but he had read the hero's heart, had sung his dirge, and no theme could have been dearer to him or more fitly chosen. The lecture was written in panoramic, somewhat disjointed, prose, but its brokenness was the counterpart of his vocal manner, with its frequent pauses, interphrases, illustrations. His delivery was persuasive, natural, by turns tender and strong, and he held us with him from the outset. Something of Lincoln himself seemed to pass into this man who had loved and studied him. A patriot of the honest school spoke to us, yet with a new voice — a man who took the future into his patriotism, and the world no less than his own land.

Lecture upon Lincoln: New York, 1878.

I wished that the youths of America could hear him, and that he might go through the land, reading as he did that night, from town to town. I saw that he was by nature a rhapsodist, like them of old, and should be, more than other poets, a reciter of the verse that so aptly reflects himself. He had the round forehead and head which often mark the orator, rather than the logician. He surely feels with Ben Jonson, as to a language, that "the writing of it is but an accident," and this is a good thing to feel and know. His view of the dramatic value of Lincoln's death to the future artist and poet was significant. It was the culminating act of the civil war, he said: "Ring down the curtain, with its muses of History and Tragedy on either side." Elsewhere his claim to be an American of the Americans was strengthened by a peculiarly national mistake, that of confounding quantity with quality, of setting mere size and vastness above dramatic essence. When the brief discourse was ended, he was induced to read the shorter dirge, "O Captain! My Captain!" It is, of his poems, among those nearest to a wonted lyrical form, as if the genuine sorrow of his theme had given him new pinions. He read it simply and well, and as I listened to its strange, pathetic melodies, my eyes filled with tears, and I felt that here, indeed, was a minstrel of whom it would be said, if he could reach the ears of the multitude and stand in their presence, that not only the cultured, but "the common people heard him gladly."

A rhapsodist.

Summary.

Although no order of talent or temperament, in this age, can wholly defy classification, there nevertheless is a limbo of poets, artists, thinkers, men of genius, some of whose creations are so expressive, and others so feeble and ill-conceived, that any discussion of their quality must consist alternately of praise and adverse criticism. Reviewing what has been written, I see that the career and output of the poet under notice are provocative of each in some extreme, and unite to render him a striking figure in that disputed estate.

Walt Whitman, then, has seemed to me a man who should think well of Nature, since he has received much at her hands; and well of Fortune, since his birth, training, localities, have individualized the character of his natural gifts; and well of Humanity, for his good works to men have come back to him in the devotion of the most loyal and efficient band of adherents that ever buoyed the purpose and advanced the interests of a reformer or poet. He has lived his life, and warmed both hands before its fire, and in middle-age honored it with widely praised and not ignoble deeds. Experience and years have brought his virile, too lusty nature to a wiser harmony and repose. He has combined a sincere enthusiasm with the tact of a man of the world, and, with undoubted love for his kind, never has lost sight of his own aim and reputation. No follower, no critic, could measure him with a higher estimate than that which from the first he has set upon himself. As a poet, a word-builder, he is equipped with touch, voice, vision, zest, — all trained and freshened, in boyhood and manhood, by genuine intercourse with Nature in her broadest and minutest forms. From her, indeed, he is true-born, — no bastard child nor impostor. He is at home with certain classes of men; but here his limitations begin, for he is not great enough, unconscious enough, to do more than assume to include *all* classes in his sympathy and brotherhood. The merits of his verse are lyrical

Whitman's equipment.

His genius and limitations.

passion and frequent originality, — a copious, native, surprising range of diction, — strong feeling, softened by consummate tenderness and pity, — a method lowered by hoarseness, coarseness, and much that is very pointless and dull, yet at its best charged with melody and meaning, or so near perfection that we are irked to have him miss the one touch needful, — a skill that often is art, but very seldom mastery. As a man of convictions, he has reflected upon the idea of a true democracy, and sought to represent it by a true Americanism; yet, in searching for it and for the archetypal manhood chiefly in his own personality, it is not strange that he has frequently gratified his self-consciousness, while failing to present to others a satisfactory and well-proportioned type of either. His disposition and manner of growth always have led him to overrate the significance of his views, and inclined him to narrow theories of art, life and song. He utters a sensible protest against the imitativeness and complacency that are the bane of literature, yet is more formal than others in his non-conformity, and haughtier in his plainness than many in their pride. Finally, and in no invidious sense, it is true that he is the poet of a refined period, impossible in any other, and appeals most to those who long for a reaction, a new beginning; not a poet of the people, but eminently one who might be, could he in these days avail himself of their hearing as of their sight. Is he, therefore, not to be read in the future? Of our living poets, I should think him most sure of an intermittent remembrance hereafter, if not of a general reading. Of all, he is the one most sure — waiving the question of his popular fame — to be now and then examined; for, in any event, his verse will be revived from time to time by dilettants on the hunt for curious treasures

His future reputation.

in the literature of the past, by men who will reprint and elucidate him, to join their names with his, or to do for this singer what their prototypes in our day have done for François Villon, for the author of "Joseph and his Brethren," and for William Blake.

CHAPTER XI.

BAYARD TAYLOR.

Taylor's career to be noted in illustration of recent conditions.

THIS poet, the last and youngest of those here made the subjects of distinct review, is no longer a living comrade. The consecrating hand that removed him enables us to free our judgment from bias of rivalry or affection.

> "Far off is he, above desire and fear;
> No more submitted to the change and chance
> Of the unsteady planets."

He was taken in his prime, with work spread out before him, yet not until after years of unceasing production. We find ourselves observing one whose ideal was higher than anything which his writings, abundant as they are, express for us, and one who none the less has claims to be estimated in some degree by that ideal. His life was noteworthy; it was a display of heroic industry, zest, ambition, the bravest self-reliance, — and from slight beginnings he achieved much. But he was one whose success must be gauged from within. What was his dream? Did he realize it? If not, what hindered him? These questions must be asked; and, in trying to answer them, we see the peculiar advantages which the career of Taylor proffers for an understanding of the literary movement, the social and working life, in which he was involved. Not that he was our most famous singer, nor one whose score was completed, —

The question of success.

but what American poet ever touched life and letters more variously? He let nothing go by him, he essayed everything, and he furnishes examples of what to do — and what to avoid. Moreover, his story enables us to study American authorship under somewhat different conditions from those which have affected the Cambridge group, and with it a period whose bisecting line is indicated by the date of the beginning of our civil war.

New York. *See p. 53.*

The task laid upon the pioneers of letters in New York has been sufficiently hard, — always the need of devotion, toil, patient laying of foundations on which others shall build. Inherited names and resources, and the advantage of university life, have favored the growth of the New England school. Poets who have strayed into New York — and here they are more seldom born than imported — have carried the harp with one hand and some instrument of labor with the other, and have sung their songs in such noonings as they could obtain. Almost without exception they have been thrown upon journalism for a support, and have experienced whatever good and evil that profession brings to the æsthetic sense of its practitioner. Bayard Taylor was not only a sturdy and courageous example of a poet born out of New England, but must be studied with the period already named. Younger than our chief poets still living, he stood with a few companions who found their music broken in upon by the tumult of a national war. Thus, we are to consider the writings of one who dates half-way between the elder and the rising generations; who was not of Cambridge, nor of Concord, but from the Middle States; and in whose works, although the product of a life of action, we always find the influences of the study and the hearth.

Obiter cantata.

The Civil War.

I.

A versatile author.

TAYLOR was the most versatile of authors. This was the result of constitutional tendency, increased by the exigencies of American life and his own life in particular. He was one, I think, whose natural gift could as well be understood through his personal qualities as from his works. His presence and story were so unreservedly before us as to afford paradigms of the birth and breeding of a poet. A critic takes kindly to verse which has a man behind it. He strives to put himself in harmony with the singer's youth, manhood, and intellectual prime, — to measure his ideals no less than his performances, — to feel his aids and restrictions, — to breathe, as it were, the very breath of his inspiration. It is worth while to bear in mind the region from which this poet came, and the kinship that exists between the fields, the trees, the air, and all living and sentient things belonging to a given spot of earth. The happy pastoral county of a central State produced Bayard Taylor from its oldest and purest Quaker stock. Here lie the broad undulating meadows and woodlands of a section wholly characteristic of the temperate zone. Here nature has no extremes of grandeur or picturesqueness, nor any gloomy aspects, but is simple, attractive, strong; here it blends, as in English rural landscape, all attributes in just proportion. The sons of such a soil are rounded and even in their make, sound of brawn and brain, open to many phases of life, — not likely, once having touched the outer world, to content themselves with one experience or one purpose.

Born in Kennett Square, Penn., Jan. 11, 1825.

Early life and longings.

Young Bayard throve upon the nourishment which Nature offered him. His sensibilities were those of her poets and artists. The trees, the flowers, the grasses, he knew them all; he was no sportsman, but "named all the birds without a gun." His farming duties often were forgotten in rovings and reveries, and moods uncomprehended either by himself or by those about him. Then the eager devouring of books, old-fashioned novels, history, travels; above all, of the poetry within his reach. His youth was that of the traditional American boy, and here, as always, the story of Rasselas repeats itself. The fairest native valley palls upon the lad who as yet has nothing by which to measure its worth. Tranquillity for the old; for the young, a longing for a new and larger range. But time rights all things: as no town-bred person ever really knows the country, so no country-lad in older years forgets the secrets Nature taught his childhood. Taylor had through life the frank and somewhat homely simplicity of the yeoman, cosmopolite as he was. In time he learned how glad his youth had been, and again and again returned to the fields of Kennett. But the boy's impatience of his confines was early shown. After the schooling at a country academy, where he studied well, came the revolt from farm-life and the alternative selection of a trade. Of course he chose to be a printer, and at the age of seventeen became an apprentice in West Chester. Already he had found his gift of making verses, and now took fire with the thought of being a poet. The publication of his juvenile pieces grew out of his desire to see the world.

"Ximena; . . . and Other Poems," 1844.

A thin little book, now so hard to find, entitled *Ximena*, was dedicated to Griswold, in gratitude for "kind encouragement" shown the author. It shows the course of his early readings. Byron, Scott, Moore, Mrs. Hemans, Bryant, are echoed here and there. A blank-verse poem is inscribed to Whittier, whose name was a household word in the Quaker home. Though this book contained no new note, it did show the ambition and facile gift of the writer. One quality is apparent which afterward marked his verse, — a peculiar sonorousness, especially in the use of resonant proper nouns, the names of historic persons and places. "Ximena" was printed at a venture, for the purpose of increasing the savings with which to undertake a tramp over Europe, at that time an almost fanciful design. From the proceeds he was enabled to see those patrons in Philadelphia who advanced him, on the pledge of his future labors, the little sum which encouraged him to set out upon his travels. After reaching New York he hastened to the *Tribune* office, at that time the Mecca of rustic enthusiasts, few of whom placed too modest a valuation upon their own powers. However, it was no common youth, this stripling of nineteen, who won the interest of Horace Greeley, and already had found practical friends in Willis, Griswold, Godwin, and the kindly editor of "Graham's Magazine."

Sonorous quality.

Here I may as well consider the sentiment of the journeys which employed so large a portion of his life, and the quality of their record. The latter began in 1846 with the famous *Views Afoot*, and ended with *Egypt and Iceland in the Year 1874*, a date only five years previous to the sudden close of his career.

His "Travels": from "Views Afoot," 1846, to "Egypt and Iceland," 1874. (Eleven vols.)

The gist of the matter is that Taylor was a poet upon his travels. A national instinct was expressed in the going out of this wiry, erect, impetuous young man, "to see the world." The same desire that brings a Western youth to the Atlantic shore has sent our coast-born lads on strange voyages to many lands. Grant White averred that while the air of England was

"Roaming with a hungry heart."

yet new to him, he felt that it was something he was "born to breathe." For us the old strangeness and distance no more yield the charm which belonged to the pages of Irving and Willis and Mitchell.

But in Taylor's case no home-ambition could restrain his desire for travel. He went abroad that he might see and learn and grow. His journals were undertaken chiefly to give him the means of adventure. He made no scientific pretensions. He was something of a botanist, a natural geographer, could see the form beneath the color, and had enough of general knowledge to make his narrative rich and intelligible. Before all, he sought the delight of the eye, and that series of sensations which Pater declares to be the sum of life. He had a poet's sense of the best everywhere, and a poet's sympathy with any land to which he came. Hence we journey with him, and enjoy his own emotions; we experience his passion to reach the summits, the ultimate deserts, the extreme capes. Such is the spirit of his *Travels*. We read much in them of scenery and external things; he reserved for his private letters what he had to say of the men and women whose friendship he gained. His perceptions enabled him, though going rapidly over many regions, to get the special quality of each. In all these books there is the essential truth of the poet; if they are a reporter's letters, they are those of a poet acting as reporter. He wrote of what he saw, and saw with faithful eyes.

His aim and equipment.

Viewing them in this light, I have little to add in respect to their literary merits. The style is that of true prose; no sing-song and sentimentalism; a clear and wholesome medium of expression. Its two extremes, of compact polish and unstudied freshness, are to be found, the one in that collection of sketches

Prose style.

which was almost his last, the "By-Ways of Europe," and the other in the romantic "Views Afoot"—the story of his first tour, whose publication made him widely known, and invested him with a friendly interest. His connections were influential. Greeley and Dana, editors of the journal to whose staff he was attached, which had an immense inland circulation, and with whose radical tenets he was in sympathy, took pleasure in advancing his reputation.

The Tribune."

Early success, and the attention of the public,—great things for any author,—are still not without peril to the faculty divine of the poet. Taylor had kept up the habit of putting his impressions into verse. Two years after his return, he printed the *Rhymes of Travel.* The preface stated that this was the first venture to which he had "intrusted a hope of success, for the sake of Poetry alone." Among the best-remembered lyrics is "A Bacchic Ode." A few Western ballads gave freshness to the book. It was approved by Poe, who found imaginative eloquence in Taylor's style, but on the whole these Rhymes do not seem to me remarkable even as a poet's first offering. Bayard was now twenty-four years old, and surely, recalling the work of Bryant, and Keats, and Shelley, at or before the same age, could not be thought a precocious singer. There was little then in American life to stimulate precocity in song. Besides, his nature was so ardent that slight and common sensations intoxicated him, and he estimated their effect, and his power to transmit it to others, beyond the true value.

"*Rhymes of Travel, Ballads, etc.,*" 1848.

See "The Literati."

Nothing so quaintly indicates the place he now held, and the conception formed of him by his provincial readers, as the sentimental portrait by Buchanan Read which served as a frontispiece to the "Rhymes of Travel." The steel engraving gives us Taylor as he

A portrait by Read.

pauses in the act of climbing the Alps. A slender youth, in face and form resembling Shelley, and equipped like one of Bunyan's Pilgrims, with a palmer's hat, blouse and belt, and a shepherd's crook in his hand for an alpenstock; lofty peaks in the background; all deliciously operatic and impossible. Such was the popular notion of Taylor, and it often brought out a merry laugh from him and his friends in later years. But those were simple, fortunate times for the young minstrel, who took his success modestly and gladly, nor forgot his work withal; and he now enjoyed a season as poetic as ever afterward came to him. Indeed, he now was in circumstances more favorable than in later years for the cultivation of his art. He had secured the means of support, and formed associations which gave him the fellowship and rivalry of comrades in taste and ambition. He got hold of what he needed, art-life, and embraced it with a zest. Through his established success he could aid and encourage his friends, and they in turn did good to his hand and training. Sooth to say, he prized his Arcadian life far more than his sudden honors; it always was first in his affections. He loved his brother bards with the full strength of his large mould, gave them freely of his praise, and frankly welcomed their appreciation in return.

"Excelsior!"

The "consonancy of our youth."

A newspaper mission to the new Eldorado gave him some picturesque themes. In that pioneer time the scenes and groups upon the Pacific coast had not the aspect which Bret Harte has caught and used so well. But there was a fresh atmosphere in the pictures of Taylor's "Californian Ballads," and a ring in their tone. Stoddard and himself had met shortly before this journey. They were within a year of each other in age, and their friendship, when Taylor settled down

Californian ballads, of 1849.

Taylor and Stoddard.

again to city journalism, became close and stimulative. The aspirations of the two poets were the same. They held counsel together in their sky-chambers, and wrote and studied in concert. Their books were dedicated to each other. Soon Boker, of Philadelphia, a year or two their senior,—born to what Griswold termed "a life of opulent leisure," but always the ally of his brother-poets,—became the third in a chivalrous trio. His "Calaynos" had given him reputation as a dramatic poet. A life-long friendship was established among the three. All this seems the memory of salad-days, but it is from such enthusiasms that new poetic fashions grow. Ten years more, and younger poets were added to the group,—O'Brien, Aldrich, and others,—among whom Taylor was a central figure, holding the friendship of all.

Boker.

Meanwhile these Arcadian influences had told upon his genius. He brought out in Boston, under the classic auspices of the Ticknor house, a volume which gave the first measure of his lyrical powers. *A Book of Romances* contained pieces that rank among the best he wrote. Here was the style, quite matured, which seems most genuinely his own. The chief value of the collection was in miscellaneous pieces that have the quality which makes good art always fresh to us. These rank with the best American verse written up to that time. Nor do I know one of our elder or younger poets who might not be glad to have composed such an idyl as "Hylas," with its strong blank-verse made soft and liquid by feminine endings, the Dorian grace infused with just enough sentiment to make it effective in modern times. It is worthy of a place in Landor's "Hellenics," and in my own mind always is associated with "The Hamadryad." None of Taylor's later classical pieces is quite so good as this.

"A Book of Romances, Lyrics, and Songs," 1851.

"Hylas."

See p. 311.

There also are two charming oriental stories, in blank-verse, — a measure which he managed well, — "Kubleh," and "The Soldier and the Pard." "Ariel," "Sorrowful Music," and the "Ode to Shelley," remind us too much of that poet, from whose influence Taylor never quite freed himself, nor desired to free himself, until his dying day. These are fine poems, and so are others notably his own — "Sicilian Wine," "Taurus," "Serapion," and "The Metempsychosis of the Pine." The last-named lyric may be taken as a specimen of his characteristic mode.

Influence of Shelley.

I have said that this volume contained the first fruits of an interval when the poet felt most keenly the compensations of art-life. And so it did; for it was by work like this that he was able to pass beneath and out from the shadow of a sombre cloud. The painful romance of his youth; the lingering illness of the girl to whom he was betrothed, the marriage only a month before she died, — all this broke in upon precious days, and effected more than a temporary change. It was Taylor's nature not to take lightly such a loss, nor to hold loosely so tender a memory. His grief was foretokened in the December lyric, "Moan, ye wild winds, around the pane!" It was the motive of a succession of memorial pieces, expressing moods of sorrow, that ended only years afterward, with the "vision" of "The Poet's Journal." But now it wore him down, sent him again on his wanderings, and determined that his life should become one of restless, varying action.

Mary Agnew: died, Dec., 1850.

See "Life and Letters of Bayard Taylor. Edited by Marie Hansen-Taylor and Horace E. Scudder," 1884.

His most extended journey began in 1851, shortly after the appearance of the "Romances." He travelled in Spain, Egypt, the Orient, etc., until 1854, and during this time not only wrote the letters which made three volumes of prose, but also continued to

"Poems of the Orient," 1854.

exercise his poetic skill. The main result was the *Poems of the Orient.*

This volume contains the best work of his purely lyrical period, and may justly be characterized as vivid, spontaneous, harmonious in tone and artistic in execution. Of all the regions which Taylor now had traversed, the Orient seemed most nearly to touch his own nature. His adaptability to the life and sentiment of any land was surprising; he was our typical example of the only being that can accommodate itself to all extremes of climate and custom. But he seemed to have been born for the Orient, and if his Songs do not set forth the East as orientals know it, they do set forth Taylor in the East: —

His best lyrical work.

> "The Poet knew the Land of the East, —
> His soul was native there."

It needed not Hicks's picture of the bronzed traveller, in his turban and Asiatic costume, smoking, cross-legged, upon a roof-top of Damascus, to show how much of a Syrian he then was. Others saw it in those down-drooping eyelids which made his profile like Tennyson's; in his aquiline nose, with the expressive tremor of the nostrils as he spoke; in his thinly tufted chin, his close-curling hair; his love of spices, music, coffee, colors, and perfumes; his sensitiveness to out-door influences, to the freshness of the morning, the bath, the elemental touch of air and water and the life-giving sun. It is to be found in the "Poems of the Orient," where we have these traits reflected in diverse lyrics that make a fascinating whole. In them he seemed to give full vent to his flood of song. Whether from regard to the criticism that charged him with rhetoric and exuberance,

A western Asiatic.

or from the languor of work and travel, in after life his poetry often was more restrained, less fervid and exhilarating.

The tone of the Eastern poems is by turns glowing and languorous, and usually rich in color and sound. The poet's intellect keeps him above the race he celebrates. A western Epicurean, he gets the best out of the East, — its finest passion and wisdom and its changeless soul. A sonnet interprets Nubia, the land of dreams and sleep: —

> "Hush! for she does but sleep; she is not dead:
> Action and Toil have made the world their own,
> But she hath built an altar to Repose."

The varying skies of Egypt, the Desert, the Syrian Coast, of Damascus, of Persia, free these poems from the honeyed monotony of Moore's orientalism, and the bookishness of Southey's. In manner, however, they sometimes remind us of Byron and of Hunt, and even of Tennyson, whose melodies have haunted so many singers, and whose "Maud" appeared in the same year with the lyrics before us. Here are some oriental tales in rhymed pentameter, and one in octosyllabic verse. "The Temptation of Hassan Ben Khaled" is the longest and best, the model of a narrative poem. William Morris has done nothing better of the kind. One wishes that Taylor had paid more attention to narrative poetry, availing himself, like Morris, of legends ready to his hand. He told a story in verse so easily and delightfully that he always underrated both the art and the poets who have excelled in it. "Amran's Wooing" is another good story — a tale of the Desert. Here also are songs, that will last as long as anything the poet wrote: —

Narrative verse.

Two notable songs.

> "Daughter of Egypt, veil thine eyes!"

and the favorite "Bedouin Song": —

> "From the Desert I come to thee
> On a stallion shod with fire;
> And the winds are left behind
> In the speed of my desire.
> Under thy window I stand,
> And the midnight hears my cry:
> I love thee, I love but thee,
> With a love that shall not die —
> *Till the sun grows cold,*
> *And the stars are old,*
> *And the leaves of the Judgment Book*
> *unfold!*"

There is a reminiscence of Shelley in one stanza; but this song has its own character. There is a faultless idyl in quatrains, celebrating the Hindoo legend of the coming of Camadeva, that affords a fine instance of a quality which marks the "Poems of the Orient," that of restraint — the reserved strength which will not give one stroke too much. At last the poet folds his tent and unwinds the turban from his brow: —

> "The sun has ceased to shine; the palms that bent,
> Inebriate with light, have disappeared;
> And naught is left me of the Orient
> But the tanned bosom and the unshorn beard."

These lyrics are free from moralizing and show little of the influence of Longfellow, which at that time was so visible in American verse; they are poetry uttered for poetry's sake, and with the voice that sings independently.

"Poems of Home and Travel," 1855.

A revised edition was issued of Taylor's earlier poems, including also maturer pieces written for the magazines. Stoddard, Taylor, and others, were now engaged with the elder poets in supplying the verse which made attractive the first series of "Putnam's Monthly Magazine." This periodical was fortunate,

"Putnam's Monthly," etc.

like a successor, "The Atlantic Monthly," in its choir of songsters. Nor was it wanting in prose-poems, such as the delicate and haunting stories by the author of "Lotus-Eating" and "Nile Notes of a Howadji." These books and Taylor's oriental poems were the complements of one another, and equally refreshing to the stay-at-home public that welcomed them.

Curtis's ideal writings.

The poet-traveller was now in his thirtieth year. Assuming that his work now showed the quality of his developed gift, we may examine its value. If he never had done anything more, if his summons had come at this time, — there would have been, even as now, few whose taking-off would be so deplored, around whose memory would gather a more regretful interest. We should speak of the promise of a career, and say, "Had he but lived!" He did live, and for years was a working man of letters, and must be judged by his product to the end. His life was consecrated to poetry, yet not devoted to it. How much this means! Possibly he gained all the laurels he had a right to expect, under the conditions in which he acquiesced. To look further involved the surrender of immediate honors, of rare experience, of growth in various directions. It would have been strange indeed if, at his age, he had not accepted "the goods the gods provide," — trusting, through strength and future occasion, to make even his half service of the muse as effective as the entire fealty of others who have won the crown.

Characteristics.

A divided ambition.

Taylor had the elements of prolonged growth. Being what he was at thirty, the undisturbed practice of his art, a devotion like that of Tennyson's or Longfellow's, should have given him indisputable poetic fame. He would have refined that subtler sense which, as no one knows more surely than the present writer, is so elusive, so often dulled or stunted by the force, the outcry, the perturbing conflicts of the social, the trading, the professional, or even the patriotic and political, world of action and toil. Still, this poet's capabilities, aside from his gift of song, were unique, and pressed for employment. His memory was prodigious. Nothing that he learned was forgotten, and he learned without effort. After a single reading he knew a poem by heart, and could repeat whole pages of his favorite authors; and there was little that he did not read or see. His perception of externals was alert and true; but he did not so readily catch by intuition the thoughts and feelings of those about him. He had a fine sense of form and color, drew and painted creditably, and seemed a natural artist. His linguistic powers were well known. He taught himself something of the classical texts, and was more infused with the antique sentiment than many a learned Theban. He quickly caught the pass-words and phrases of any language, Shemitic or Aryan, wherever he journeyed. German he mastered, wrote in, thought in; it became so much like a native tongue with him as to refute the theory that one gains of a new language only so much as he loses of his own. His personal traits were no less admirable. To think of him is to recall a person larger in make and magnanimity than the common sort; a man of buoyancy, hopefulness, sweetness of temper, — loyal, shrinking from contention, yet ready to do battle for a principle or in the just cause of a friend; stainless in morals, and of an honesty so natural that he could not be surprised into an untruth or the commission of a mean act. His open delight over any work of his own that pleased him was the reverse of egotism, yet often misunderstood by those who slightly knew him. He was without jealousy,

Capabilities.

Personal traits.

though sometimes ruffled by the prosperity of quacks and pretenders. Yet his personal ambition and aspiration were very great, only equalled by his industry and scrupulous fulfilment of any task he undertook. In social life he was generous and unrestrained, full of the knightly, mirth-loving, romantic spirit; a poet who kept his heart green to the last, even when disease was upon him, and the plethoric habit of his middle life. These dulled his eye, but never broke his spirit nor turned his thoughts to gall.

Style as a poet.

As a poet, I say, the qualities of his mature style were now fairly displayed. From the beginning, rhythm, the *surreusis* of liquid measures, had much to do with his sense of the beautiful in verse, and reacted upon his imagination. He revelled in the effect of the broad English vowels, the "hollow ae's and oe's," and in the consonantal vigor of our language. He enjoyed reading aloud the poetry of Darley, of Byron and Shelley, and read his own with such melody and resonance that one who listened to its chanting sound was no more able than himself to tell whether it was of his poorest or his best. Its dominant quality, therefore, was often that of eloquence, as in the verse of Croly and Campbell. Poe quoted from one of his early pieces, to show that eloquence and imagination may go together. I have said that Bryant was "elemental" in his communion with sea and forest and the misty mountain winds.

An ethnical range.

Taylor, as to the general range of his poetry, was ethnical and secular. Nations, races, eras, the past and future of mankind, were the objects of his regard; he got his material, his imaginative pictures, from their aspect, and his most elevated verse relates to their historic and prophetic phases. His art-method was simple and direct, obvious rather than suggestive, and he generally composed in a major key. Some of his measures are fresh with the breeze and spray. In other moods he would write a ballad, or a tender lyric like "The Song of the Camp." He had the spontaneity of a born singer; but with it a facility that was dangerous indeed. His first draft was apt to be his best if not his only one. He had few affectations; his instinct being against obscurity and oddness of expression. He made his verse, as far as might be, the clear vehicle of his feeling. Of late years, in the desire to convey his deeper, more intellectual thought and conviction, he frequently became involved, and a metaphysical vagueness was apparent even in his lyrics. At such times critics thought his efforts strained, and his friends declared that he was not working in his best vein.

Over-facility.

Involved expression.

II.

MUCH of Taylor's poetry does not bear its maker's hand-mark so distinctly as that of Longfellow or Whittier is wont to do. His subjects and modes of treatment are varied, and the former may be assorted in groups, — the classical pieces, the dithyrambic lyrics, the poems of travel, and those of hearth and home. In any mood he was apt to reach a certain standard of merit; he rarely failed. But there was one field — though he scarcely seemed to realize its value — so much his own as to breed for him a number of rough imitators. From it he made such studies, of the rural scenes and characters he best knew, as "John Reid," "The Old Pennsylvania Farmer," and that lovely ballad, unexcelled in truth and tenderness of feeling — "The Quaker Widow." The poet more rarely gave voice to the extremes of pas-

His Pennsylvanian idyls.

"The Quaker Widow," etc.

sion. Even his noon-day health and manliness sometimes blunted his delicacy of touch. And yet, when he felt with his whole heart, he could be not only refined but highly imaginative, as in "Euphorion," — a poem addressed to friends who had lost a dreamy and beautiful child: —

"Euphorion."

"For, through the crystal of your tears,
His love and beauty fairer shine;
The shadows of advancing years
Draw back, and leave him all divine.

"And Death, that took him, cannot claim
The smallest vesture of his birth, —
The little life, a dancing flame
That hovered o'er the hills of earth, —

"The finer soul, that unto ours
A subtle perfume seemed to be,
Like incense blown from April flowers
Beside the scarred and stormy tree, —

"The wondering eyes, that ever saw
Some fleeting mystery in the air,
And felt the stars of evening draw
His heart to silence, childhood's prayer!"

These stanzas are at the highest reach, I think, of Taylor's lyrical genius. The man who could write them, and who composed the Bedouin Song and the Pennsylvanian idyls, was a poet whose fame should be dear to his countrymen. But he did much more. Of what kind, and under what conditions? Here comes in the lesson of his life as a poet, and it is chiefly as a poet that we are considering him.

Remarks on the life of this poet

Authors are pretty sure to give us something of value when they render the feeling of localities to which they belong. A sympathetic poet is in danger of lessening his birthright through much knowledge of the world at large. Taylor was patriotic, always

Burns and Whittier.

American; yet I think his lyrical mark would have been still higher had his relations been confined, if not to the section that gave him birth, at most to his own land and people. His native qualities were not unlike those of Burns and Whittier; these three poets were more similar, as they came from the mould, than any others whom I call to mind. Burns was a healthy country lad, full of the prodigal force of nature, blown on by her breezes, nurtured by her soil, thrilled by emotions as he felt the rich sap of youth coursing through his veins. His influences were those of his own people. His first efforts imitated the plodding of the "Caledonian Bards." When somewhat matured, he awoke to the beauty of the true Scottish minstrelsy, and adapted his own song to it. Suppose that opportunities for travel, wider culture, varied reading, the mastery of languages, had been given him. One nail drives out another. He might have been hampered with his acquisitions; his muse would have subdued her strength in diverse strains; he no longer would have been the fine, untrammelled specialist, — and might have wholly lost his native wood-notes wild. Whittier owes his fame to his seclusion — voluntary or involuntary — and to his presentation of the themes and feeling nearest the heart of New England. His work is thus a specific addition to American song. His early pieces, like those of Burns, were artificial. It was not until after growth and fervid conviction that his lips were really touched with fire.

Taylor's more varied experiences.

It was Taylor's good fortune, as a man who would live his life, — his ill fortune, it may be, as a poet, — to obtain the multiform experience for which his youth had longed. We admire his pluck and adventure, but lament what was lost to poetry. At times when his fine spirit, bound within a home range, would have made the most of its surroundings, he was able to gratify without stint his love of travel and observation. His poetic gift was always by him; but surely he lost much in exchange for what he gained. One can readily conceive the lyrical genius of Whittier as subject to be diffused or perplexed under similar conditions. The question lies between personal attainment and the extreme utilization of an artist's special gift. Taylor chose the former. He said, "If I have any ambition, it is to enjoy as large a store of experience as this earth can furnish." In a letter which I received from him he wrote: "If I were to write about myself for six hours, it would all come to this: that life is, for me, the establishing of my own *Entelecheia*, — the making of all that is possible out of such powers as I may have, without violently forcing or distorting them." Circumstances aided him in his choice. As a youth, he thought little of the effect upon his poetic career, or possibly thought he was promoting it. Later on, however "rich and ample" his life, he felt a sense of uneasiness. He cared most of all, in his heart of hearts, to be a poet, and saw that, while going afar to invoke the Muse, he had given her the less chance to seek him. Choose between the ideal and the actual — such is the alternative of art. Few can eat their cake and have it, too. Delight of life and action has turned aside many a swift runner, as I have shown in reference to Domett and Horne. Again, whatever may be said of the benefits and disadvantages of culture, it often has been a practical injury to the poet — since no one is sure of life's full limit — to set before him too high and broad an ideal. It may not always be best to aim at the sun. We ask of a man

His own theory of life and art.

An alternative.

the one thing he can do better than other men, and often, as in the legend of Gaspar Becerra, "that is best which lieth nearest." Then there are hindrances born of success itself, and to these Taylor was peculiarly subjected.

His environment.

He became involved with the literary life of New York, and at a trying time. It was just early enough for him to receive a good word from Poe, and late enough for him to witness the rout of the "literati." Even a sham literary feeling may be better than no feeling at all. Has New York gained since then as a literary centre? Yes, and no. It is now the base from which our authors draw their supplies. The great journals, the profitable magazines, the largest publishing houses, with few exceptions, are located there. It is the chief centre of distribution, and will so remain until some future period shall number as many great centres of distribution as there may be characteristic sections. But the atmosphere, — the public feeling which alone can foster rising art and make its workmen glad and creative, — this gathers more slowly. Authors are tolerated, respected, valued as accessories; but not always understood, nor often intrusted with the care of important movements. New York has a sufficiency of writers and of literary elements for the needs of many smaller cities; but the former do not feel themselves sustained by that sympathetic interest which, for example, encourages the music of Naples, the art of Paris or Rome. New York is great in material progress, generous in charities; but still too practical to do much more than to affect an æsthetic sentiment. Her wealthy classes are groping toward the comprehension of what is beautiful. They have schools of design, and are surpassing not only the troglodytes, but our more immediate an-

Art and letters in the New World metropolis.

cestors, in mural decoration. What is intellectually fine we have yet to pursue with any general ardor. The city took a pride in Bryant as a man and as a picturesque figure on state occasions; but how many of his townsmen had read the most of his poems, or cared to read them? Herein is no reason for complaint; all is as it should be. If individuals are not coddled in New York, they at least have an equal chance, and there are not lacking assurances of future development.

Journalism vs. ideality.

Thus Taylor's lot was cast in a somewhat uncongenial city, and he often found himself praised and courted where he needed the stimulus of intelligent sympathy. He took to journalism, and it was his mainstay through life. During the last thirty years, journalism has absorbed much of our best talent, and well it might, for it demands the best. No severer test can be applied to a writer than that of his ability to furnish leading articles regularly. More than one, who has succeeded easily as a bookwright or essayist, has found his equipment and his power of composition inadequate to the off-hand production of compact, polished, well-informed leaders, such as are needed for the editorial pages of great newspapers. Journalism is an art; but under our system it brings little beyond his weekly stipend to the sub-journalist. The stipend is sure, and that means a great deal to one who lives by his pen. Newspapers thus far have supplied the readiest market to a writer, and the magazines next to them. The task of daily writing for the press, while a good staff, is a poor crutch; it diffuses the heat of authorship, checks idealism, retards the construction of masterpieces. Besides, it brings an author into attrition with members of the craft who possibly know him so familiarly as to underrate him.

See pp. 75–108, and cp. "Victorian Poets": pp. 81, 82.

He is subjected to local jealousies, to the over-praise of the newspaper which befriends him, and sometimes to the unjust or ungenerous treatment of rival sheets. All this may be thought an evil peculiar to New York, and one which we shall outgrow. But the same phenomena are visible in the matured capitals of England and France, and must be accepted as part of a journalist's warfare and surroundings.

Lecturing.

Newspaper-work, then, to which Taylor owed so much of his current reputation, also restricted his advance as a creative author. He felt constrained to hold, by this and by lecturing, the popularity he had gained, and likewise to obtain the means of carrying out his scheme of life. As a man of note, his home-pride grew upon him. He chose to realize a dream of possessing a sightly house and broad acres in Kennett, — a manor-home where he could place his parents, and find a retreat in times of rest. All this he did, in his early prime; such a man can have anything for which he will pay the price. Its cost to him, no doubt, was a lessening of his quality as a poet. A pressure of social and professional duties — meetings, speeches, correspondence — bore upon him severely. Under it he made a good fight; hopeful, generous, considerate, trying to do something in a field where the laborers were too few. But men do not escape from tasks they once assume, and he had undertaken to earn a large income and survey the world, on the one hand, and to hold the Muse by her pinions on the other. His poetry had to be composed "between spells" and on the wing; more than all, the versatile habit of his life became a second nature to him.

"Cedarcroft."

"Little foxes."

Question of American overwork.

There is much unfairness, however, in the blame to which public men in this country are subjected for their overwork. This is rather a matter of necessity than of choice. People in the old world largely inherit their means and methods from their forbears; new men, even there, often have the habit of overwork fixed upon them by the time their footholds are secured. But the statesmen and thinkers of Europe start with assured incomes more commonly than do our own, and are not forced to earn their bread as they go along. Our Eastern Brahmins, however, have had for the most part resources which they have enlarged by the help of such gentle, scholarly pursuits as the service of a university affords. They have shown themselves quite willing to indulge a spirit of restfulness and calm. So long as Americans who do not inherit estates have the Anglo-Saxon pride and domestic tenderness, they will be tempted to do work elsewhere than in a garret, and rarely be able to drive from their minds the thought of its effect upon an income-paying constituency.

III.

Married to Marie Hansen, of Gotha: 1857.

TAYLOR married in Germany, and his choice was fortunate. She whose hand he gained was by her talents and acquirements in every sense his companion, — in full sympathy with his purposes, for happy years the wise and tender guardian of his household, as she is now the faithful treasurer of his memory and fame. Her translations made his works known to her countrymen; she confirmed his taste for the thought and letters of her Fatherland, and was his constant aid in the study of them.

"The Poet's Journal," 1862.

The Poet's Journal was an expression of the happiness for which its author had now exchanged the trials of the past. Its chief interest is found in a revelation of the author's heart. The prelude, to the mistress of Cedarcroft, is not excelled by anything which follows. Years afterward, he made a still more earnest avowal of his wedded content: —

> "With thee was the ceasing of sorrow.
> Hope from thy lips I have drawn, and subtler strength from thy spirit,
> Sharer of dream and of deed, inflexible conscience of Beauty!
> Though as a Grace thou art dear, as a guardian Muse thou art earnest,
> Walking with purer feet the paths of song that I venture,
> Side by side, unwearied, in cheerful encouraging silence.
> Not thy constant woman's heart alone I have wedded;
> One are we made in patience and faith and high aspiration."

Middle life.

The poet's life of travel, writing, lecturing, means-providing, now went forward busily. Duties and honors grew upon him. His interest in the civil war gave birth to some vigorous popular ballads. We need not follow his public career, nor his periodical returns to the shade of his own chestnuts and tulip-trees. His friend Aldrich compares Taylor's life to a drama, of which the intervals were filled with the music of his poetic work at home. Four fifths of this he was to enact, and we thought to see his mind's "noblest offspring" with the last; but the curtain fell abruptly, and the putting out of the lights ended a performance that steadily had grown in worth. What there was of it was marked by rare experiences. Among his friends, he counted the wise and gifted of many lands. He had their respect and confidence; and his correspondence with them was most extensive. His private letters were delightful, and a sheet covered with his beautiful handwriting and flowing thoughts was a thing to prize and store away.

Taylor's Novels.

Partly with the thought to try his hand — like Goethe, whom he seemed to have taken as a master — at every kind of work, and partly as a form of literature suited to the times, he essayed novel-writing. His novels sold well, and appeared to hit the popular taste. They mostly were realistic transcripts of what he had seen, and contained his own views of what was, and what was lacking, in American life at that time. The plot of *Hannah Thurston* is nothing; the tale was written to illustrate types of character and phases of society, — especially to show up the mock-reforms of the day. The heroine is a Quakeress, as good and original a creation as is to be found in the whole course of these novels. The hero, like most of their heroes, is something of a muff. Taylor's second novel, *John Godfrey's Fortune*, has commonplace and unattractive New York scenes, but these are truthful records of the side of life with which the author first became acquainted in the growing city. *The Story of Kennett* is the cleverest and most artistic of the series; a romance of the old-fashioned kind, and a true idyl of Pennsylvanian country-life in the early prime. Meantime, the author's short stories, contributed to magazines, were always fresh and good, as indeed were all his miscellaneous essays. The amount he threw off was remarkable. He wrote prefaces, edited books of travel and biography, did everything a man of letters could do, with cheerfulness and facility. His prose was simple, clear, good English, if not great. Upon the whole, his literary criticisms seemed to me the ripest and most valuable portion of his prose labor. In them he was compact, learned, writing to the point, and his opinions were just and good with regard to both the spirit and technique of a work. In later years, his reviews were so catholic, sound of canon and exact in detail, as to be models; and it became evident that he could have been a notable critic, had

"*Hannah Thurston*," 1863.

"*John Godfrey's Fortune*," 1864.

"*The Story of Kennett*," 1866.

"*Joseph and His Friend*," 1870.

Shorter Tales, Essays, etc.

See "*Critical Essays*," 1880.

he devoted himself to criticism alone. He had abundant humor, and this, with his judicial faculty, and his talent for parody and burlesque, found play in the serio-comic papers which were collected a few years before his death, in a volume called *The Echo Club.*

See "Studies in German Literature," 1879.

Few men, not excepting Lewes and Carlyle, have been so well informed as Taylor with respect to German literature. His lectures upon that subject were prepared originally as a university course. For years he was a student of Goethe and Schiller and their times, and it was the dream of his life to write their biography. To this end he made extended researches in Germany, and collected material under auspicious conditions. Had he lived to complete such a work, it would have been a masterpiece. In the midst of his labors, he was enabled to make a complete English translation of "Faust," in the original metres, and to supervise its publication.

IV.

"Faust: Translated, in the Original Metres." Parts I. and II., 1870–71.

THE surprising rapidity with which the two parts of *Faust* were brought out, the original commentary and notes, the avowal that the editor had read all the translations and commentaries made in any language, were phenomena of that kind which sometimes led people to distrust the thoroughness of Taylor's work. The scholarly character of this performance is now well established. That to which more than one of his predecessors had given a lifetime, he apparently completed in three years. He had borne it in mind, however, for two decades, and it was his habit to think upon a task until able to execute it at a dash and with great perfection.

The most poetic and scholarly version.

The result was an advance upon any previous rendering of the entire work. The preface demonstrates that poetry sometimes absolutely requires a retention of the original metres for its translation. Illustrations of this are found in Freiligrath's perfect transcript of Scott's "Come as the wind comes," and in Strodtmann's fine "Es fällt der Strahl auf Burg und Thal,"—the "Bugle-Song" of Tennyson. To me these seem extreme cases: in others the result might be otherwise. A translator must choose the best method for the work in hand. It is doubtful whether the test would apply equally well to each of several poets who differ among themselves as widely as Homer, Theocritus, and Pindar.

Its method.

The characteristics of Taylor's "Faust" are sympathetic quality, rapid poetic handling, absolute fidelity to the text. Now and then his realistic version of the first part has an unusual or quaint effect, detracting from its imaginative design. Hence some of the best portions are those not in rhyme, such as the Cathedral scene, where Margaret is harassed by the Evil Spirit:—

> "How otherwise was it, Margaret,
> When thou, still innocent—"

which is reproduced with thrilling power. The regular verse also is well rendered, Goethe's "Dedication" never having been so well given by any other translator. Its firm, sonorous stanzas are in harmony with Taylor's own manner and poetic feeling:—

The "Dedication."

> "Again ye come, ye hovering Forms! I find ye,
> As early to my clouded sight ye shone!
> Shall I attempt, this once, to seize and bind ye?
> Still o'er my heart is that illusion thrown?
> Ye crowd more near! Then, be the reign assigned ye,
> And sway me from your misty, shadowy zone!

My bosom thrills, with youthful passion shaken,
From magic airs that round your march awaken.

. . . .

"And grasps me now a long-unwonted yearning
For that serene and solemn Spirit-Land:
My song, to faint Æolian murmurs turning,
Sways like a harp-string by the breezes fanned.
I thrill and tremble; tear on tear is burning,
And the stern heart is tenderly unmanned.
What I possess, I see far distant lying,
And what I lost grows real and undying."

Handling of the Second Part.

To the mystical and much disputed Second Part the lineal method of translation is specially adapted, and serves to preserve the fantastic nature of the original. Taylor had the gift and knowledge which enabled him to succeed where others had failed. He felt his ability, and perhaps too readily estimated the greatness of this part by the difficulties he mastered. The best poet, other things being equal, is the best translator. Opinions may differ as to the merits of his handling of the First Part of "Faust," but with respect to that of the Second there is little question. It is unlikely that any great English poet soon will undertake to excel it. Carlyle could have made the venture, for he was essentially a poet, despite his outcry against verse. Shelley, had he essayed a complete version and made his studies accordingly, might have left us the ideal translation—for he was the ideal translator. His paraphrase of the "Hymn to Mercury" is, as Emerson would say, more original than the original. His overture of "Faust" is in some way more grand and rapturous than Taylor's. His "Walpurgis Night" is full of enchantment—too soon the waving ended of that magic wand.

Shelley.

Taylor's notes and commentary are the best we

have, learned and intelligible, equally marked by poetic feeling and good sense. His critical views of the Second Part should be more authoritative than those of others less conversant with the subject and less truly poets. He approves of Lewes's statement: "I have little sympathy with that philosophy of art which consists in translating Art into Philosophy, and I trouble myself very little with 'considerations on the Idea.'" In disputed passages, he seeks for light from his master's other writings, rather than from German and English commentators. The result of this course is excellent, and I do not believe that any other translator has so nearly reproduced both the text and spirit of Goethe's life-long work.

Taylor's Notes on Faust.

V.

An art-poem, *The Picture of St. John*, was published by Taylor some years after the appearance of "The Poet's Journal." His talent for drawing has been mentioned; he was exceedingly fond of art, and not a few of its votaries were his attached friends. The new poem was dedicated to this gentle brotherhood. Its theme may be termed the development of an artist's powers through experience of the joy and suffering of life. The tale is Italian, as regards both feeling and incident; and the scene is laid in Italy and the Alps. There are four books, of stanzas which seem a variation upon the *ottava rima*. The poet spent much time upon this work, and it has many graceful passages. But as a fresh and original conception and a charming piece of workmanship, I prefer *Lars*, the only sustained poem in narrative form which he subsequently composed. It is finely conceived, and executed in a style worthy of the conception — which

"The Picture of St. John," 1866.

"Lars: a Pastoral of Norway," 1873.

could not always be said of Taylor's works. In "Lars" he took a subject quite within his powers, and realized his ideal. The scenes change from the Norwegian coast to the Quaker borders of the Delaware, and the author thoroughly understood the landscape, manners, and sentiment of the two regions. The atmosphere is, by turns, fragrant with the balsam of Norseland firs, and thymy with the smell of new-mown fields across the western sea. A contrast is drawn between the half-savage habit of the Norse-folk and the placid religious quality of our pastoral midland settlements. The combat with knives between the rival Norsemen, Lars and Per, is a virile piece of work. Less Tennysonian and even more poetic are the idyls of Norwegian cottage life, which precede this scene. This blank-verse poem is a delightful production; we have no idyl of similar length, except "Evangeline," that equals it in finish and interest.

"Home Pastorals, Ballads, and Lyrics," 1875.

A subsequent collection of miscellaneous pieces — the *Home Pastorals*, to some of which I have referred — was made by the poet. Four contemplative poems of the seasons, as observed from the porches of Cedarcroft, are excellent of their kind, and have been undervalued; they are in English hexameter verse, for which Taylor had a good ear, and only narrative pieces in that measure obtain a popular reading. To me they seem wise, beautiful, true to nature; resembling in ease and freshness Clough's "Bothie," and very faithful to the scenery and sentiments of the Pennsylvanian border. This book also contains some of the poet's best ballads; but has other lyrics quite uneven in merit. It is notable for three of the odes (exhibiting his taste for sweeping Pindaric measures) which he recited upon various public occasions in his later years.

The Goethe ode and the one delivered at Gettysburg are manly and heroic poems. The Shakespeare ode is less successful. In a crowning lyrical effort, he had as wide an audience as poet could desire. He was addressing not only the assemblage in Independence Square, on the 4th of July, 1876, but millions of his countrymen, — in truth, the reading world. It was a fine occasion, and all his ambition was aroused. What poet ever had a more historic opportunity? Should the verse of all his contemporaries be forgotten, the first Centennial Ode will be revived and re-examined.

"The National Ode," 1876.

The National Ode was not unworthy of the occasion, from a conventional point of view. It was sonorous, patriotic, mindful of our traditions, full of dignity and rhetorical power. As such it was received. But it was not the one new, bold, original production, which appeals alike to the wise and the unlearned, rouses the imagination, imprints itself upon the memory of all who read it, and becomes a lasting portion of national literature. Marvell's ode "On the Return of the Lord Protector" and Lowell's "Commemoration Ode" are poems of this kind; in sooth, Taylor's effort, coming after the latter, demanded all his courage. I remember urging him to adopt some regular stanzaic form, however complicated, or else to write his poem in blank-verse or rhymed-heroic, — either of these measures being more likely than the irregular Pindaric to touch and hold the popular heart. It seemed to me that the simplest vehicle would best convey, on such an occasion, the noblest thought. His adverse decision was guided partly by precedent, more by his instinctive sense of an ability to compose and recite musically his Pindaric verse. He did deliver his ode with superb effect, and felt the occasion in every fibre of his mould. Americans refer without distrust to this poem, but few recall its phrases; and it must be acknowledged that even of Lowell's elaborate odes only one has really succeeded in fastening itself upon the public mind.

VI.

Dramatic Writings.

ONE more division of Taylor's manifold productions remains for consideration, — to wit, his dramatic works. Of these, two are philosophical studies cast in dramatic form; the intervening one, however, is a five-act play, the interest being human rather than speculative.

"The Prophet: a Tragedy," 1874.

The Prophet has certain claims to attention. This work, a closet-drama perhaps as easily adapted for the stage as one or two of Browning's, was an attempt to treat dramatically a modern and peculiar American theme, and to make what could be made of it. Hints are taken from the early history of Mormonism, but the central figure, instead of being a vulgar impostor like Joseph Smith, is a simple and pious young farmer, such a man as the author's own county might have produced; intelligent withal, but the victim of the religious ecstasy that comes to one without knowledge of books and the world. The devices of shrewder comrades and the jealousy of women unite to deceive him, and to persuade him, by signs and miracles, of his prophetic mission. The incidents follow naturally; the scenes being laid first in New England, then in the far West, whither the Prophet and his followers have gone to found a sacred city. Internal plots and external foes bring about a catastrophe, ending with the death of the hero of the play.

The drama, poetry's

The highest form of poetry is the drama, for it includes *all other forms*, and should combine them in their greatest excellence. At its best it is the supreme flower of the literature of any nation, and demands a poet's rarest and most comprehensive genius. It scarcely proffers a method which he can fully master, late in life, after years of lyrical or idyllic minstrelsy. The dramatic instinct must be born in him : again, his formative period must find him in a region where a dramatic tendency already fills the air. Otherwise his work as a playwright, like that of Tennyson or Longfellow, must be accomplished by an artificial effort, and will lack the touch that makes the whole world kin. Even Browning, with his immense dramatic resources, early found a greater hindrance than his own subjectivity in the non-sympathetic spirit of his people and time. "The Prophet" failed, in view of its author's theme and purpose, not solely from his lack of early dramatic practice, but from causes which hardly could be overcome. Such a plot might be treated idealistically, by giving the widest range to imagination, fearing no extravagance, creating one's own facts and atmosphere, and the result might be a great dramatic poem if not an acting drama; or it might be treated realistically, — the course which Taylor naturally pursued. To insure success by the latter mode, the time and events of a drama must be poetic in themselves. In this story of our own time, there is, perforce, a lack of the illusive and entrancing atmosphere of the far-away past. That which is too modern and familiar seems commonplace. The time may come when as much shall be made of the Mormon episode as of the traditions of the Druses or of John of Leyden; at present it furnishes a store of clap-trap to melodramatic playwrights who derive from it substantial gains. Taylor drew his personages with skill, but their unheroic character was against the passion of

highest form.

Modes of treatment.

the play. The work illustrates the importance of certain canons. First, nobility of theme has much to do with the value of art; secondly, realism is not the chief end in matters of design. There is truth — and truth; the truth of what is or has been, and the truth of what may be.

Cp. "Victorian Poets": p. 53.

The lack of interest felt in "The Prophet" deterred its author from further experiments of the kind. His other dramas are purely ideal. *The Masque of the Gods* presents that side of his nature which was most exalted and aspiring. His religious temper, it has been seen, was bred under other influences than those which restrict the faith of many poets. He was a believer in direct inspiration, but a questioner of revelation. The creed of the Progressive Quakers was liberal and humane, and the boy grew up to regard men of all races as his brethren, and every form of worship as acceptable to an Unknown God whom he himself addressed in the spirit of Pope's "Universal Prayer." This sense was strengthened by his travels and studies, and his religion became broader than any man's theology. "The Masque of the Gods" — a title with a tinge of quaintness below the dignity of the subject — is a drama of three dialogues, managed in a severe and classical fashion. It approaches as near to the highest grade as intellect, eloquence, and fervent glow, — it was written in four days, "almost at white heat," — can lift such a poem. What it lacks is the unconscious flight into that empyrean where the wings move without sound and touches of flame hover at the tips of the pinions. The conception is vast, daring, — far more imaginative than its working out.

"The Masque of the Gods," 1872.

This drama, which Taylor rated high among his productions, and which is in every sense an expression of his devotion to the nobler forms of song, renders

A poet of noble ideals.

it possible for one to assert that a writer may be judged somewhat by his ideals, and that, so far as this mode of judgment is concerned, its author held a significant place in the group of American poets. It was the precursor — the overture, we may say — to the work that was his swan-song, the larger drama which he lived to complete, and of which a fair broad copy reached him but a day before the lyre dropped from his hand forever. "Of his last work," wrote his bereaved wife, — "*sein Schwanen Gesang*, as I call it, — as I would call it in my mind involuntarily, long before I knew he was deadly ill, he only saw one copy, and that of the English edition."

His swan-song.

A strange interest belongs to the drama of *Prince Deukalion*. The poet deferred his serious work upon the life of Goethe, that he might be sure of completing this one poem which he strove to make his best. Attention may be directed to the artistic skill with which it is composed, to the sounding qualities of the main body of its verse, and to the varying interludes marked by the author's lyrical felicities in their maturest range. Even here his expression retains a mannerism which grew out of the limited vocabulary prevailing when he learned his art in youth. Certain words and effects are of too frequent recurrence; but, allowing for all this, "Prince Deukalion" will bear examination for its excess of rhythmical beauty. America has produced few poems so admirable for richness and variety of measures.

"Prince Deukalion: a Lyrical Drama,' 1878.

Rhythmical beauty.

The subject is one that lay near Taylor's heart, and to him was the most elevating of poetic themes — to wit, the progress of mankind, from the ignominy and suffering belonging to the youth of the world, to the golden age of the future. The thought and treatment of the drama are entirely characteristic of the

A characteristic theme.

author. The early portion is unquestionably fine. Passages in the middle and latter sections show a falling off, due, it may be, to the languor of illness and to the pressure of the instinct which made the poet hasten to the completion of his task, but at the close he again rose to a noble height. It is easy to select an example of the vigorous handling of the structural verse. His Poet declares:—

> "I am a voice, and cannot more be still
> Than some high tree that takes the whirlwind's stress
> Upon the summit of a lonely hill.
> Be thou a wooing breeze, my song is fair;
> Be thou a storm, it pierces far and shrill,
> And grows the spirit of the starless air:
> Such voices were, and such must ever be,
> Omnipotent as love, unforced as prayer,
> And poured round Life as round its isles the sea!"

Agathon's avowal.

In the fourth act, the words of Agathon are an expression of the sentiment and hopeful philosophy which animated Taylor's whole career:—

> "But I *accept*—even all this conscious life
> Gives in its fullest measure—gladness, health,
> Clean appetite, and wholeness of my claim
> To knowledge, beauty, aspiration, power!
> Joy follows action, here; and action bliss,
> Hereafter!"

But at last, and even here, it seemed as if—to change the line of John Webster—the years of this loyal and eager poet had felicities too many. His rest was not to be that upon which he counted. Had he drawn his own horoscope it could not have appeared more perfect. He went again to the land of his earliest pilgrimage, encouraged with honors and affection, and with the best opportunities for the production of a work to which his own choice and the desire of the entire republic of letters strongly impelled him. Hereafter, he was to have calm and leisure. But within the year his soul was required of him, and one more broken shaft was added to the endless colonnade by which we testify to the incompleteness of this our earthly life, and express the pity of it.

Died in Berlin, Germany, Dec. 19, 1878.

Final considerations

Shortly after Taylor's death, a fellow-writer, who knew him well, spoke to me of his literary career. "A man so aspiring and sagacious," this critic said, "could be satisfied with nothing less than the highest achievement, the soundest professional judgment in his favor." Recognizing the point thus made, I would not accept it as a test of his genius. It seemed to me that it was his fortune, however wide his popular reputation, to be underestimated by his professional compeers. His gift was genuine and inherent, but it became too much diffused; he strove to survey too large a precinct, and it was surprising how far, in more than one direction, he made his lines extend. With all his facility and purpose, he found himself in a too arduous struggle between the duty of the hour and the still higher work fashioned after "the pattern which was shewed him in the Mount." He set himself to carry out an almost impossible plan of life. His manliness in this and other respects we all concede. During his experience of a time and region which made Poe a weakling, — almost an Ishmaelite, — with what pluck and heartiness Taylor faced the situation, until it seemed as if the very god of strength took pleasure in befriending him! After all, he had some right to count upon length of years, and to shape his plan accordingly. He grew in taste and judgment as he grew older, and even his devotion of so much time to hack-work was not without its requitals. He led a singularly happy life throughout, and the cloud foretokening its close was but of brief duration. He was fond of festivals, of joy; he had honor, love, and loyal "troops of friends." More was given to him than was taken away, and his memory is something to dwell upon with pleasure, not with pain. The volumes of his song are left to us, the bequest of that which he thought the choicest product of his years. No one who would acquaint himself with American poetry can overlook Bayard Taylor's share of it. Those who would understand its growth, or predict its future, must bear in mind the generation for which he wrote and the story of his efforts and environment.

CHAPTER XII.

THE OUTLOOK

Retrospective.

IN writing upon the leaders of American song, I have sought to make our various studies as comprehensive as possible within due bounds. That they might be both critical and sympathetic, and afford new illustrations of the poetic principle and the temperament of poets, it has been my effort to approach the subject of each from his own ground, — to comprehend his motive and judge him at his best; at the same time, to see where he has failed of that standard and of the true spirit of ideal expression. Such an effort requires to be taken as a whole. Isolated phrases, and even sections, may be misconstrued as unfair stricture or, on the other hand, as if biased by personal considerations. Yet, in the course of each study, I have tried to draw a just portrait, and so to analyze the work of its original as to obtain at least an approximately correct resultant.

Design of this chapter.

For this final chapter, — relating to various persons and questions of the time, and necessarily less cohesive and animate than those which it supplements, — I would ask that its parts be weighed together, if at all. It has a distinct purpose, — to glance at the existing condition of our poetry, and to speculate concerning the near future. Not to prophesy — we scarcely can forecast next month's weather from the numberless shifting currents of to-day. Yet one may hopefully surmise, for example, that a dull spell will not last beyond all reason and experience. The past teaches us what signs indicate the change, — where blue sky will first appear, — and that, if the wind "backs," or proves fickle, a brightening will be temporary and delusive. In the mood of a cautious weather-sage, then, let us examine the late reports from the signal-stations that together show the probabilities. In reviewing the poetry of England, the general drift was indicated more plainly by the choir at large than by the solos of a few striking and independent voices.

Cp. "Victorian Poets": p. 234.

I.

Recent forebodings.

When some of our elder poets, their careers felicitously rounded, were taken from us, there soon arose a cry of foreboding. Who, it was asked, are to occupy the places of Bryant, Longfellow, Emerson? What younger men can equal the work executed by those pioneers when the latter were of corresponding age? A period of decline has been predicted. It may be noted, as we seek to determine whether the prediction is well based, that a similar cry is heard from across the sea. The work of Tennyson and the Brownings, in their prime, is contrasted with that of their juniors, and critics are not boastful as to the promise of another saengerfest. I venture to recall that ten years ago I saw the beginning of a poetic dusk, and expressed a belief in its temporary continuance. It is now generally perceived and lamented; nevertheless it seems to me that it is near an end, and that we may begin to look for a new day. If this is to differ from the last, — if we who enjoyed the old fashion shall find it hard to accustom ourselves to the new, — the young will speedily interpret it for us. Their estimate of relative values will have its own gauge.

Duration and close of our first poetic term.

The rise of Poetry in America, its first noteworthy and somewhat original endeavor, was clearly marked, and in the main coincident with that of the Victorian School abroad. Before long, our poetry took its place with standard literature; its authors won the interest, even the affection, of an attentive public. The close of the term involved may not have been so clear to us. Literary periods shift with mingled sounds, like those of bands following one another at intervals in a procession. But, as in the case of the parallel term abroad, it was defined sufficiently for us now to look back and recognize it. The influences to which was due a diversion of interest, and which brought poetic aims and methods into doubt, may be briefly recapitulated. They include all that we have seen prevailing throughout Christendom and resulting from its accelerated evolution of knowledge and energy: the radical change in the course of imagination, enforced by the advance of science,—the disturbance of tradition and convictions,—the leap from romance to realism. We must allow, too, for the diversion of genius to material conquests, adventure, the creation of fortunes; and for the growth of journalism, and of prose fiction answering to the demands of the time. All the resulting influences are fully as dynamic here as in the Old World, and some of them far more so. But other factors, peculiar to this country, must not be overlooked. The civil war was a general absorbent at the crisis when a second group of poets began to form. Their generation pledged itself to the most heroic struggle of the century. The conflict not only checked the rise of a new school, but was followed by a time of languor in which the songs of Apollo

Recapitulation of distracting influences. *Cp. "Victorian Poets": pp. 7–29.*

See pp. 17, 26, 27.

The War.

seemed trivial to those who had listened to the shout of Mars. A manly reaction from the taste for rhetoric and sentiment which existed before the war degenerated into the indifferentism lately affected by our clever youths. Those whose lyrical instinct survived through all conditions, and still impelled them to sing, found themselves subject to a novel disadvantage. The favorite senior bards were still in voice; their very longevity, fitting and beautiful as it was, restrained the zeal and postponed the opportunities of pupils who held them in honor. Our common and becoming reverence prevented both the younger writers and the people from suspecting that these veterans were running in grooves and supplying little new; finally, when this was realized, and there was a more open field, it became evident that the public was satiated with verse and craved a change, not merely of poets, but to some new form of imaginative literature. Original genius will find an outlet through all hindrances; be the air as it may, its flight will be the eagle's; but it will be apt, at such a time, to take some other direction than that of its predecessors. All in all, the subsequent incitement to lyrical effort was not so effective, nor was the opening so clear, as in the period that favored the rise of Longfellow and his compeers.

Preëmption.

A new public taste.

In the course of these studies I have referred at some length to a few poets next succeeding those veterans, — some who now, but for the regard shown them by younger contestants, would scarcely realize how surely they are becoming veterans themselves. Thus age succeeds to age, and still Poesy, —

See pp. 54–58.

> "blazoned as on heaven's immortal noon,
> . . . leads generations on."

It only remains for us to take an outlook, and make

A brief survey

note of what poetic activity is discoverable at the present time. With respect to my near associates, and to the increasing circle of fresh recruits, whose chances are all before them, I repeat my statement that it would be out of taste and purpose for me to assume the functions of a critical censor or appraiser. The situation can be studied, and some conjecture made of the future, upon a rapid (and in the main uncritical) summary of what a representative number of these have done and are doing, and I do not think our conclusions can be so well reached in any other way.

now requisite.

Its character.

II.

WHITTIER and Holmes, the two oldest survivors of their group, find their audience still extending with the rapid spread of culture in this land. Their eyes are scarcely dimmed, and their natural strength serves them for periodic flights of song. Lowell's apparent retirement in favor of younger writers, though doubtless only temporary, is the one courtesy they desire him to forego. From Whitman, more picturesque than ever, we have now and then some passing, half-broken, yet harmonic strain, striving to capture the substance of things seen and unseen. I have written already of Taylor, Stoddard, Boker, Trowbridge, and their comrades, with whom our poetry began to show less of the ethical and polemic fervor that brought their predecessors into repute. No new cause required the lifting up of hands, and they meditated the muse from simple love of beauty and song. Stoddard, although a hard-worked man of letters, has been true to his early vows, and adds to our songs of summer in the autumn of his life. Occasionally also he writes, with his old finish and tranquil power, one of those

Emeriti.

Next in age. See Chap. II., etc.

Stoddard.

sustained and characteristic blank-verse poems in which his faculty is at its highest. Of poets a decade younger, Hayne, Aldrich, Winter, Piatt, Howells, and a few others, still remain. It was their lot to begin at just the time when the country had forsworn peace and its pipings; but they none the less took heart, and did good service in keeping our minstrel line unbroken through good and evil days alike.

A younger group.

William Winter: 1836–

Winter's extreme poetic temperament, and his loyalty to an ideal, have made his frequent sketches of travel very charming, and have imparted to his dramatic criticisms the grace and proportion for which they are distinguished. The melody, ease, and sincere feeling of his personal tributes and occasional pieces for delivery render them quite unique. The poem read at the dedication of the monument to Poe is an elevated production. His best lyrics have caught the spirit of the early English muse.

Thomas Bailey Aldrich: 1836–

To Aldrich, now in his sunny prime,—the most pointed and exquisite of our lyrical craftsmen,—justly is awarded a place at the head of the younger art-school. He is a poet of inborn taste, a votary of the beautiful, and many of his delicately conceived pieces, that are unexcelled by modern work, were composed in a ruder time, and thus a forecast of the present technical advance. They illustrate the American instinct which unites a Saxon honesty of feeling to that artistic subtilty in which the French surpass the world. Though successful in a few poems of a more heroic cast, his essential skill and genius are found in briefer lyrics comparable to faultless specimens of the antique graver's art. Such picces as the "Palabras Cariñosas" and the lines "On an Intaglio Head of Minerva" have a high-bred quality that still keeps them at the head of our *vers de société;* nor is their

Beauty of his verse and prose.

author dependent for his effect on novel and elaborate forms. Apparently spontaneous, they are perfected with the touch of a Gautier. His quatrains and trifles expressive of fleeting moods rank with the best of our time. Aldrich's restraint in verse is a notable contrast to the sudden wit and fancy of his speech; as a writer, he never has stood in need of the injunction,—

> "O Poet, then forbear
> The loosely sandalled verse,
> Choose rather thou to wear
> The buskin straight and terse."

His shorter tales and sketches are finished like so many poems in prose, sparklingly original, and delightful for the airy by-play, the refined *nuances*, of a captivating literary style.

Edgar Fawcett: 1847–

Fawcett's verse displays tendencies which class him with the art-school, and an inclination to profit by the Gallic taste and motive. The poems in his two volumes are selected, I presume, from a copious store, as he has been from youth a prolific writer. In *Fantasy and Passion* were many cabinet pictures in rhyme, drawn with fastidious care, and an occasional lyric, like "The Meeting," upon a weird theme and suggestively wrought. The leading pieces in *Song and Story* have fewer mannerisms,—a less fanciful, a freer and more imaginative, treatment. Mr. Fawcett's versatility leads him to essay almost every form of inventive, satirical, and critical literature, and as a playwright he has made not the least successful of his ventures. Two of our prominent New York authors seem, aside from their professional work as journalists, to have devoted themselves without reserve to poetry. Their characteristics are very dis-

Gilder and de Kay.

Richard Watson Gilder: 1844–

similar. Gilder, whose vein is so unlike that of Mr. Aldrich, vies with him in artistic conscientiousness. There is no slovenly work in *The New Day* and *The Poet and his Master;* each is a cluster of flawless poems, — the earlier verse marked by the mystical beauty, intense emotion, and psychological distinctions, of the select illuminati. He appears to have studied closely, besides the most ideal English verse, the Italian sonnets and canzoni which ever deeply impress a poet of exquisite feeling. An individual tone dominates his maturer lyrical efforts; his aim is choice and high, as should be that of one who decides upon the claims of others, and at his age there are fine things left for him to do. Charles de Kay is also conspicuous for height of aim, and certainly for a most resolute purpose. In these days it is bracing to see a man of his ability in earnest as a poet. It would be premature to judge of the strange, affluent, and broadly handled Visions, *Nimrod* and *Esther*, at this near view, or until completed by the final section of their trilogy. *Hesperus* and the *Poems of Barnaval* show his impassioned and more subjective moods, and his resources for a prodigal display of varied, uneven, but often strongly effective lyrical work.

Charles de Kay: 1849–

George Arnold: 1834–65.

John Aylmere Dorgan: 1836–67.

George Parsons Lathrop: 1851–

Hjalmar Hjorth Boyesen: 1848–

The deaths of Arnold and Dorgan, at ages when practice-work ended and individual traits began to appear, stilled two voices of no little promise. Among our Northern poets there are some whose verse is the expression of their choicest impulses rather than the most substantial portion of their literary outcome. Lathrop's too infrequent lyrics give token of sensitive feeling and a beautiful poetic vein. Professor Boyesen's verse, like his prose, belongs so thoroughly to his adopted language, and is so fresh and classic, that we scarcely think of him as a Norwegian. The Oriental songs of Edward King are healthy and virile, and add variety to our recent product. Sill, Benton, Dr. Powers, Weir Mitchell, Professor Beers, Riordan, S. H. Thayer, W. S. Shurtleff, McKay, Conant, Abbey, Duffield, Blood, Proudfit, Butterworth, Saltus, Tilton, the late Robert Weeks, among our writers of lyrical verse, represent widely different grades of motive and execution. Of the late Henry Work, that instinctive composer of songs (and their music) for the people, I have spoken elsewhere. Robert Grant has a frolic talent for satire, and something like that masterhood of current styles for which we still read Frere and Aytoun. Houghton's *St. Olaf's Kirk* is a good romantic poem, in the Tennysonian manner, finished with much care. Maurice Thompson's *Songs of Fair Weather* are well named; in breezy, out-of-door feeling he is a kinsman of Walter Mitchell, who wrote "Tacking Ship off Shore." It is chiefly through a close observation of nature that the influence of the elder poets, especially of Emerson, is prolonged by the new choir. *Monte Rosa*, Nichols's long descriptive poem, is a not unworthy counterpart to *The Brook* — for which the late Dr. Wright is held in recollection. The transcendental instinct, that follows upon Nature's elusive and spiritual trails, survives in the thoughtful lines of her born communicant, John Albee, whose individuality is none the less apparent. Cheney's lyrics of nature and emotion have kindred yet distinct traits. "The Modern Job," by Peterson, is an eccentric, but original and suggestive work, and there are striking passages in his minor poems. McKnight's volume of sonnets on "Life and Faith" is fraught with poetic meditation. Montgomery and "Paul Hermes," the former

Edward King 1848–

(See Index.)

Robert Grant: 1852–

George Washington Wright Houghton: 1850–

James Maurice Thompson: 1844–

Walter Mitchell: 1826–

Starr Hoyt Nichols: 1834–

Wright: *see p. 52.*

John Albee: 1833–

John Vance Cheney: 1848–

Henry Peterson. 1818–

George McKnight: 1840–

George Edgar Montgomery: 1856–

William Roscoe Thayer. ("Paul Hermes"): 1859–

avowedly, are inspired by the marvels of the new learning, and find no surer tonic for the imagination than modern scientific discovery. Emerson's song was a verification of Wordsworth's faith in the identity of philosopher and poet. Our future imagery will shape itself unconsciously, without much need of a poet's wilful effort, and will be his adjunct and vehicle rather than the object of his aim. Montgomery's command of rhythm is finely evident, and the young author of *Hermes* seems to have good service within his power.

John Boyle O'Reilly: 1844–

Robert Dwyer Joyce: 1813–83.

Maurice Francis Egan: 1852–

(See Index.)

Boyle O'Reilly attests his Irish blood by the *verve* and readiness of his ballads. He may be more justly claimed as an American than the late Dr. Joyce, whose *Deirdrè* fulfilled the promise of a bard who in youth wrote the "Ballads of Irish Chivalry." Among other and recent Celtic minstrels of this greater Ireland, besides Maurice Egan, a sweet and true poet, have been the gallant O'Brien and Halpine, John Savage, McDermott, — and Father Ryan, whose emotional strains reach a larger audience than that which more studied verse is wont to gain.

Female poets: see p. 50.

A Scotch critic, whose resources as our literary historian are confined mostly to periods before the civil war, repeats an old fling at "the plague of American poetesses." This *vieux garçon* of letters, if acquainted with their work, might beseech us, like Benedick, not to flout at him for what he had said against them. Our daughters of song outnumber those in England, and some of them, like some of their brethren, have thin voices; but it is just as true that much genuine poetry is composed by others, and that, while we have none whose notes equal those of at least one Englishwoman, in average merit they are not behind their fair rivals. Their lyrics, sonnets,

Their relative excellence.

ballads, are feminine and spontaneous, and often highly artistic. To be sure, our aspirants of either sex are attempting few works of invention; where all are sonneteering, it is not strange that women should hold their own. Yet their advance in discipline and range is apparent also in novels and other prose-work; they know more than of old, their thought is deeper, their feeling more healthy. The morale of their verse is always elevating; in other respects it fluently adapts itself to the conventions of the day.

An advance noted.

Among these sweet-voiced singers, to some of whom I have alluded heretofore, Miss Larcom, with her orchard notes, well retains her popularity. Mrs. Cooke and Mrs. Stoddard are too seldom heard, — each so original, so true in verse and prose to characteristic types. The former's poetry always has been admired for motive and execution; Mrs. Stoddard's, though less in amount, has the condensed power and vivid coloring that render it difficult to mistake the source of anything from her hand. The verse of the brilliant and devoted "H. H." (the sense of whose loss is fresh upon us) is more carefully finished, though perhaps it sings the less for its union of intellectuality with a subtile feeling whose intenseness is realized only by degrees. Her pieces, mostly in a single key, and that grave and earnest, have won the just encomiums of select critics, but certainly lack the variety of mood which betokens an inborn and always dominant poetic faculty. Mrs. Spofford's various lyrics are rich in cadence; she has a fine choice of measures, and always interests us both with her theme and its treatment. Her passion is genuine, and unusual resources of diction, color, effect, are brought to play in her poems. Mrs. Fields, the most objective of these writers, veils her personality, except as it be-

Lucy Larcom.

Rose Terry Cooke.

Elizabeth Drew Barstow Stoddard.

Helen Maria Fiske Jackson. ("H. H.")

Harriet Elizabeth Prescott Spofford.

Annie Adams Fields.

comes revealed by a free rhythmical method, and an obvious inclination toward the classical and antique. The zest, the enchanting glamour, of Northern coast-life are known to Celia Thaxter, our daughter of the isles. Her sprayey stanzas give us the dip of the sea-bird's wing, the foam and tangle of ocean, varied interpretations of clambering sunrise mists and evening's fiery cloud above the main. Mrs. Allen, Mrs. Mapes Dodge, Mrs. Moulton, Nora Perry, Miss Coolbrith and Miss Shinn of California, are natural singers, in their several degrees. The stanzas of Mrs. Moulton and Mrs. Dodge are marked by charming fancy, and always tender and sweet. Miss Perry is an instinctive melodist, with a sure ear for the telling, original refrains that heighten the effect of such lyrics as "Cressid" and "Riding Down."

Celia Leighton Thaxter.

Mrs. Moulton, Mrs. Dodge, Miss Perry, and others. (See Index.)

Our best-known Western poetess, Mrs. Piatt, though often obscure, has traits resembling those of Miss Rossetti, — a vivid consciousness of the mystery of life and death, a conjuring indirectness of style, and a gift, which she shares with Mrs. Dodge, of seeing into the hearts of children. She will not, however, be rightly measured by one who reads the wrong volume of her poems, or the wrong poem. Miss Phelps's deeply religious nature, warring with its own doubts, leads her on adventurous paths. That she is essentially a poet was evident from her prose, long before she made a collection of verse. She is the modern vine from a Puritan stock, subject to inherited tendencies, but yielding blossoms of feminine grace and aspiration. The names of the late Mrs. Hudson, of Mrs. Bradley, "Marian Douglas," Mrs. Sangster, Miss Bushnell, Miss Woolsey, Mrs. Searing, Miss Bates, Mrs. Smith, Miss Bloede, Miss de Vere, Ella Dietz, Miss Proctor, Mrs. Rollins, Miss Osgood, and Miss

Sarah Morgan Bryan Piatt.

Elizabeth Stuart Phelps.

(See Index.)

Cone, may be cited in a list of those whose songs are pleasantly familiar. Miss Lazarus, to whose translations of Heine I have referred elsewhere, is on her own ground in rendering the Hebrew poets of old Spain; her minor pieces are written with a firm hand, and her tragedy, *The Dance of Death*, is a work of much power. "Owen Innsley" has gained the favor of those who care for poetry of an artistic type, and Miss Thomas, that delightful confidante, yet betrayer, of the secrets of the nymphs and muses, has given us a volume of great beauty. The *Songs and Lyrics* of Miss Hutchinson, and even more her later pieces, striking for their melody, imagination, and unique sense of design, assure us that if she allots to poetry the devotion that has enriched her work in other fields, its very greenest wreath is at her command. There are still younger voices that give us fresh music — like Miss Guiney's, or, like those of the Goodale sisters, artless ditties of the woods and fields, and from which maturer notes are not unlikely to be heard.

Emma Lazarus.

Lucy White Jennison.

Edith Matilda Thomas.

Ellen Mackay Hutchinson.

In the South, we have Mrs. Preston's works, of an ambitious cast and strengthened by dramatic purpose and expression. Like Mrs. Webster in England, she may be called a pupil of Browning. Local color, and much suggestion of the far Southern atmosphere and sentiment, are found in the volumes of Mrs. Townsend, of Louisiana.

Margaret Junkin Preston.

Mary Ashley Townsend. ("Xarifa.")

These poets mostly sing for expression's sake, and therefore without affectation. They often excel the sterner sex in perception of the finer details of life and nature. The critic would be a renegade who, after paying his tribute to feminine genius in England, should not recognize with satisfaction what has been achieved by his own countrywomen. They have their shortcomings, not the least of which in some of them is that even perfection which is in itself a fault; but a general advance is just as evident in their poetry as in the prose fiction for which they now are held in honor throughout the English-speaking world.

Arcadian diversions.

A phase of our verse, illustrating its present station, reflects the new London vogue, and has been mentioned in comparison with Dr. Holmes's lighter vein. I refer to the plenitude of metrical trifles, society-verse, *belles choses* in the French forms that are so taking. Various new-comers make their entrance accordingly; scarcely one but turns you off his rondeau or ballade, and very cleverly withal. Blithe measures written gracefully, like those of Sherman, Minturn Peck, etc., are more agreeable than the prentice-work of sentimentalists. A sprightly Mercutio is better company than your juvenile Harold or Werter. They serve very well, moreover, for the travesties and "satire harming not" of the boulevard press. Our young collegians, of whom Loring, who died in his adventurous youth, was the precursor, are apt at such devices. It is curious to receive rhymes of the same kind from Cambridge, Massachusetts, and Cambridge, England. Mr. Scollard's are just as well turned as Mr. Ropes's, and are not without signs of good omen. The line of advance has been exemplified by a poet who began in this way, the author of *Airs from Arcady*. Bunner's verse, whether of the gayer kind, or rising to the merit of his more ideal lyrics and sonnets, is a hopeful inscription at the parting of the ways. It already commends itself to those who look for feeling under grace, and shows that he now can make his standing with the muse depend upon the constancy of his devotion.

"With pipe and flute."

(See Index.)

H. C. Bunner.

Before discussing further the latest tendencies, let

us see what is doing in those precincts to which we naturally turn for literature of a specific flavor. The South, once so ambitious, has been very barren of poetry during the last thirty years, either mindful of Poe's conviction that there was no equal chance for her native writers, or feeling that they were too remote from the world to keep up with its progressive changes. I think that standard literature, including poetry, is read with more interest in the South than here, and oratory there is still more than a tradition. But the South has been unfortunate in the loss of promising writers. One such was Timrod, whose handiwork was skilful and often imaginative and strong. Timrod's "Cotton Boll" was a forerunner of the method of a still finer poet than he, whose career was equally pathetic. The name of Sidney Lanier brings him clearly to recollection — as I saw him more than once in the study of our lamented Deukalion; the host so buoyant and sympathetic; the Southerner nervous and eager, with dark hair and silken beard, features delicately moulded, pallid complexion, hands of the slender, white, artistic type. The final collection of his writings, with an adequate and feeling memoir by Dr. Ward, confirms me in an already expressed belief that Lanier's difficulties were explained by the very traits which made his genius unique. His musical faculty was compulsive; it inclined him to override Lessing's law of the distinctions of art, and to essay in language feats that only the gamut can render possible. For all this, one now sees clearly that he was a poet, and bent upon no middle flight. He magnified his office, and took a prophetic view of its restored supremacy. The juvenile pieces here first brought together, although his biographer apologizes for them, have little in common with ordinary verse of the time. "Nir-

The South.

Henry Timrod: 1829–67.

Sidney Lanier: 1842–81.

His collected "Poems," 1884.

Lessing's "Laocoön."

Lanier's early and spontaneous vein.

vâna," "Resurrection," and the songs for "The Jacquerie," are such as herald a new voice; and later efforts of the kind also show his gift unadulterated by meditations on rhythmical structure. Among these are the "Song of the Chattahoochee," almost as haunting as "Ulalume," "The Revenge of Hamish,"—than which there are few stronger ballads,—"The Mocking Bird," "Tampa Robins," "The Stirrup-Cup," "The Bee," and "The Ship of Earth." But turn to the productions which he deemed far more significant, in view of their composition upon a new and symphonic method. In time he doubtless might have wrought out something to which these would seem but preliminary experiments. The Centennial cantata was written to be sung, and when rendered accordingly no longer appeared grotesque. We may surmise that the adaptation not of melody alone, but also of harmony and counterpoint, to the uses of the poet, was Lanier's ultimate design. Nor is it safe to gainsay the belief that he would have accomplished this more nearly, but for his early death and the hindrances of sickness and embarrassment that long preceded it. Compositions suggestive and reverberant as "Sunrise" and "The Marshes of Glynn" go far toward vindicating his method. Yet even in these there is a surplusage, and an occasional failure to make not only outlines but impressions decidedly clear. "The Symphony," "Corn," and other over-praised ventures on the same plan, seem to me nebulous, and often mere recitative. The danger of too curious speculation is suggested by the strained effect of several ambitious failures, contrasted with the beauty of his unstudied work. An old foe, didacticism, creeps in by stealth when work upon a theoretical system is attempted. Let critics deduce what laws they may;

His maturer work: its theory.

Symphonic compositions.

Their merit and their failing.

it is not for the poet deliberately to set about illustrating them. The formulas devised by Poe and others often are found to suit, designedly or not, their inventor's personal capabilities. Lanier's movement to enlarge the scope of verse was directly in the line of his own endowment; he has left hints for successors who may avoid his chief mistake — that of wandering along in improvisation like some facile, dreamy master of the key-board. That remarkable piece of analysis, *The Science of English Verse*, serves little purpose except, like Coleridge's metaphysics, to give us further respect for its author's intellectual powers.

"The Science of English Verse," 1880.

Hayne's vitality, courage, and native lyrical impulse have kept him in voice, and his people regard him with a tenderness which, if a commensurate largesse were added, should make him feel less solitary among his pines. Various Southern poets, — Cooke, Randall, Burns Wilson of Kentucky, Boner, and others, open vistas of the life and spirit of their region. Townsend's ballads, in their sturdy, careless way, speak for the poetic side of a peculiarly American writer, true to memories of a boyhood on the "Eastern Shore." His tales, and the strongly dramatic fiction of Cable, Miss Murfree, Page, Johnston, etc., more clearly betoken the revived imagination of a glowing clime. The great heart of the generous and lonely South, too long restrained, — of the South once so prodigal of romance, eloquence, gallant aspiration, — once more has found expression. It enables us to know it, having begun at last to comprehend its true self.

Paul Hamilton Hayne: 1831–

James Ryder Randall: 1839–

George Alfred Townsend: 1841–

Promise of the South.

That the public is always on the alert for what is both good and novel was illustrated by Bret Harte's leap into favor with his portraitures of a new and scenic world. His prose idyls of the camp and coast, even more than his ballads, were the vouchers of a

The Pacific Slope.

Francis Bret Harte: 1837–

poet; familiar as the verse at once became, it is far less creative than the stories. The serious portion of it, excepting a few dialect pieces, — "Jim," "In the Tunnel," etc., — is much like the verse of Longfellow, Whittier, and Taylor; the humorous poems, though never wanting in some touch of nature, are apt to be what we do not recognize as American. But of either class it may be said that it is, like the rhyming of his master, Thackeray, the overflow of a rare genius, whose work must be counted among the treasures of the language. Mr. Harte may be termed the founder, and thus far has been the most brilliant exemplar, of our transcontinental school. Joaquin Miller is, first of all, a poet, if one may judge from the relative merits of his verse and prose, — the latter of which does not show his spirit and invention at their best. The *Songs of the Sierras*, as a first book, was no ordinary production. Its metrical romances, notwithstanding obvious crudities and affectations, gave a pleasurable thrill to the reader. Here was something like the Byronic imagination, set aglow by the freedom and splendor of the Western ranges, or by turns creating with at least a sensuous *vraisemblance* an ideal of the tropics which so many Northern minstrels have dreamed of and sung. Miller still has years before him, and often lyrics from his pen suggest that, if he would add a reasonable modicum of purpose to his sense of the beautiful, the world would profit by the result. Among other poets of the Pacific Slope, Warren Stoddard and Phelps seem more indifferent to local flavor, and refine their work in the usual manner of the Eastern school.

Cincinnatus Hiner (Joaquin) Miller: 1841–

Charles Warren Stoddard: 1840–

Charles Henry Phelps: 1853–

Surveying the broad central region of tilth and traffic between the Mississippi River and the Appalachian Range, — the most fertile land on earth, and tenanted by a people whose average culture exceeds that of any race numerically equal,—we find it sensitive to music and art, but not yet fruitful of that poesy which, as Sidney declared, alone can outvie nature, and "make the too-much-loved earth more lovely." The Ohio valley lost two poets,—one in battle, the other after he had lived to write our most effective ballad of the war,—Lytle and Forceythe Willson, each of whom had unquestionable lyrical talent. John Piatt, the laureate of prairie and homestead life, has won a just reputation for his reflective and idyllic verse. He has a Wordsworthian sympathy with nature, and knowledge of its forms, and a sincere purpose. He transmits with much simplicity the air and bloom of the prairie, the fire-light in the settler's home, and the human endeavor of the great inland States he knows so well. Will Carleton struck a natural vein by instinct, in his farm-ballads, and has been rewarded for the tenacity with which he has pursued it. Others, like Venable and Harney, find their way to the households of a rural constituency; they have the merit of presenting that to which they are wonted—they know whereof they affirm.

The Inland States.

Lytle and Willson. (See Index.)

John James Piatt: 1835–

William Carleton: 1845–

William Henry Venable: 1836–

William Wallace Harney: 1831–

John Hay, whose writings are at once fine and strong, has been so engrossed by a rare experience of "cities, . . . councils, governments," as scarcely to have done full justice to his sterling gifts. With his taste, mental vigor, and mastery of style, he may well be taken to task for neglecting a faculty exceptionally his own. The uncompromising dialect-pieces, which made a hit as easily as they were thrown off, are the mere excess of his pathos and humor. Such poetry as the blank-verse impromptu on Liberty shows the higher worth of a man who should rise above indifference, and the hindrance of his mood, and in

John Hay: 1838–

these spiritless times take up the lyre again, nor fitfully touch the strings.

"Scholar Gypsies."

In places remote from the literary market, we often discover signs of hopeful energy. The best models are read by isolated poets, whose seclusion the capricious standards of the town oracles fail to influence. Snider's *Delphic Days*, for example, a charming idyl in the elegiac distich, was printed in St. Louis, through a singular coincidence, at the same date with Munby's "Dorothy" in England, — the two being the only prolonged specimens of this measure, if I mistake not, which our language affords. *Agamemnon's Daughter*, by the same hand, is another contrast to the bounds of every-day song. Leighton's legendary dramas, *The Sons of Godwin* and *At the Court of King Edwin*, are creditable to our literature. Their romantic themes, by inheritance and the liberties of art, plainly are within the usufruct of an American poet. A drama of like cast, and successfully adapted to the stage, is *Pendragon*, the work of an Illinoisian, William Young.

Denton Jacques Snider: 1841–

William Leighton: 1833–

William Young: 1847–

Recent translators.

The department of translation, which (as well as that of devotional verse) has been noted in a former chapter, is at present somewhat neglected, though there are minor contributions by Lea, F. Peterson, Mrs. Conant, and others. Perhaps the most suggestive of the late efforts in this field are Miss Preston's charming translations from the Provençal and her version of the Georgics. Howland's Æneid is rude and elegant by turns, but of interest to those who believe with me that the English accentuate hexameter is on the whole our best instrument for literal and lineal rendering of the classical measure. The translation of Virgil's complete works, by Wilstach, is more elaborate. It is written in flexible blank-

See p. 55.

(See Index.)

verse, and garnished with copious notes and a review of former English versions. This student, who does not lack temerity, is translating "The Divine Comedy," upon a metrical system hitherto unessayed.

Dialect-verse.

Few dialects of our tongue, except those of Scotland, Lancashire, and Dorset, have been more cleverly handled for metrical effect than those peculiar to the United States. The Atlantic varieties have been used to good purpose, as we have seen, from the time of Fessenden's "Country Lovers" to that wherein are recorded the exploits of Hans Breitmann. Harte's and Hay's successes in a corresponding line increased the popular regard for their better work. Riley's Hoosier lyrics often are more terse and pointed than the numerous ballads of Carleton. Some of the most attractive and piquant of American folk-songs are in the dialect of our African population, North and South. Stephen Foster, the pioneer of "minstrel" song-writers, whose touching or humorous ditties were wedded to genuine melody, deserves remembrance. A group, with the author of "Uncle Remus" included, has diligently cultivated the art of writing plantation-verse. Mrs. Preston, Sidney and Clifford Lanier, the late Mrs. McDowell and Irwin Russell, Miss McLean, Macon, and many others, have contributed to this quaint anthology, which — at its extremes of humor, as in "Reb'rend Quacko Strong," or of melody and devotional pathos, as in "De Sheepfol'" — certainly is an original outgrowth of the cisatlantic muse.

See p. 59, and cp. "Victorian Poets": pp. 278, 279.

James Whitcomb Riley: 1854–

See p. 49

Plantation lyrics.

Joel Chandler Harris: 1848–

Irwin Russell: 1853–79.

(And see Index.)

III.

Such is a fairly representative list of those to whom our recent poetry owes its being. A protest

The foregoing a

representative list.

against so free a range of selection may be entered by some, who fail to consider that for each name here found a score of others could be cited. Doubtless many of the latter have equal claims to notice, this summary having been made with no design of completeness, but as a sufficient basis for remarks on the weakness, quite as much as on the strength, of our present movement, and on the chances of the near future.

Cp. "Victorian Poets": pp. 290, 291.

At the outset it can be honestly asserted, in behalf of the writers named, that as a whole they do not show less favorably than the corresponding modern choir of Great Britain. It would be difficult to assort them in groups such as we have observed abroad; apart from local differences of style they bear an almost monotonous relationship to one another. This common likeness, however, is an illusive something which renders their productions American. If their verse presents few absolutely novel types, it is more charged with national sentiment than that of the late English poets. It pays little regard to pseudo-classicism, middle-age restorations, and to themes borrowed from other lands and languages. It is sincere and impulsive, and has a New World mode of looking at things and considering them. Finally, the work of the most expert among these writers, both sexes included, is often as interesting for technical merit as that of their distant compeers, although it may be that we have fewer in number who reach a faultless standard.

Traits, as compared with those of the general choir abroad.

Question as to the relative importance of our later-day song,

Granting or claiming thus much, a reviewer must put the question directly to his conscience — How does the most of this recent verse impress you? Upon the foregoing summary, what can one honestly declare of its force and significance? Its achievements have been noted; the side on which it is trivial or deficient must be as plainly shown, lest the narrator be forced hereafter to regret that he withheld his convictions. Nor is it easy to gloss over the dynamic insufficiency of our present metrical literature. The belief scarcely can be resisted that there is, if not a decadence, at least a poetic interregnum, as compared with the past and measuring our advance in sundry fields of activity. As I have said, the first influence is ended; there is a pause before the start and triumph of another. This may be frankly acknowledged; in fact, the situation is merely correlative with that observed, ten years ago, in our look across the sea. It is none the less one on which neither our poets nor their countrymen have much reason to plume themselves. If our poetry, since the time of Longfellow, has not kept pace with our general movement, this of itself implies an interregnum. I suspect that it is of less relative importance than if it had held the point already gained. Its new leaders, at all events, are not invested with the authority of those to whom these essays chiefly have been devoted. Their volumes scarcely receive the welcome — nor have they the bearing and import as an indispensable part of literature — that appertained to the poems of "The Seaside and the Fireside," "Evangeline," the "Voices of Freedom," "Snow-Bound," "The Biglow Papers," "Under the Willows," "Poems of the Orient," and the "Poems" of the Concord sage. To the careful eye they seem less suggestive of changes and results than were "The Raven and other Poems," "Songs of Summer," and "Leaves of Grass." They do not, like some of the books here named, supply either lay or professional classes with the most essential portion

Measured by that which we have been considering.

of their reading. We see that this is partly due to conditions which it is just as well should obtain for a season, and which the poets are not able to avert. Before recurring to this difficulty, let us see how far they are their own bafflers and justly to be held responsible.

Our modern poets.

Some of them have given such evidence of the faculty divine as to be sure of enrolment in the Parnassian registry. Others have composed charming bits of verse, — pledges, as yet unfulfilled, of something larger and more creative. We do not ask for masterpieces, but how few the recent poems which approach in breadth and interest those of the veteran school! Do our poets really trust their calling, in defiance of temporal conditions, however discouraging? Do they not share in a measure the sentiment which regards ideality as an amiable weakness, the relic of a Quixotic period, and thus feel half-ashamed of their birthright? Few of them, at the best, cultivate the latter seriously, as their avowed means of expression; and of these few the majority perhaps are women. There are some who will be ungracious enough to say that a time when religion and poesy are sustained by the graceful, devoted, but distinctly minor services of women, is not one of supremacy for either the pulpit or the lyre. Those who demur to this, and who refer to the authors of the "Sonnets from the Portuguese" and "Romola," will be told that Mrs. Browning and George Eliot were forerunners, not exemplars, of a golden era when it shall be no longer true.

One feature.

Spirit of the new school.

Even if our poets are doing the best within their power, their misconception of relative values is much the same as that recently noted of the minor English school. To our predecessors the spirit of a work was all in all; the form was often marred by careless execution. It took years of Keats, Tennyson, and the study of their masters, to rectify this, and then the drift set quite too far in an opposite direction; until at last a Neo-Romantic group wreaked its thoughts upon details of sound and color, placed decoration above construction, the form of verse above its motive, — thus missing the impulsive cadence, the more ethereal structure, to which the evasive spirit of poetry mysteriously inclines. Heine's assertion, that a poet must have natural tones in his lyrics and characters in his narrative or dramatic efforts, was sustained by the impotency of our own verse-makers before the time of Whittier and Longfellow. With them and their comrades American poetry took on at least the merit of being natural, and gained a foothold; but this merit is less apparent in our later verse, whose forms, though neatly mastered, breed a temper as artificial as their own. In brief, our lyrics of the past had the virtue of simplicity, but were less noteworthy for imagination; those which have succeeded them fail equally in poetry's highest attribute, and their interest is due less to simplicity than to art — the art which, being a substitute for imaginative vitality, runs into artifices and mere technique. Over-refinement, through a strict interpretation of that excellent canon, "Art for Art's sake," is a vice of the period. Art is a language, and a seemingly careless workman may be a truer artist than his painstaking fellow. When one has little to say, his technics are a kind of pedantry, while a faulty poem or picture may be great because a great thought or character is in it. The best workman is he who adapts means to the noblest end, and we tire of those who, with no message to deliver, elaborate their style. The oldest races have discovered that no

Cp. "Victorian Poets": pp. 284–6, 289.

Simplicity and artifice.

Art wins by expression. *Cp. "Victorian Poets": p. 288.*

labor is artistic, unless strictly to the purpose; a few sure lines, and the result may be attained. We see, however, that technical experts, though devoid of imagination, often have a sudden following among new men. This is because their skill is addressed to the profession rather than to the public, and also because the young recognize the dexterity which they must acquire, while the creative genius of true masters as yet escapes them. Hence the instant vogue of novel forms, requiring adroitness for their perfection, and so elegant as to conciliate even those they do not capture. When real additions to our English method, they will bear use and reproduction. But, after a few men of exquisite talents have employed them to advantage, the public grows weary of modes so peculiar that we are compelled to dwell upon the form and not the thought.

Passing vogues.

Thus we have in view, if not precisely a mob of gentlemen who write with ease, an increased number of those writing with the profusion of ease and the pain of curious labor, and often at a loss of individual distinction. Lyrics, sonnets, canzonets, are produced on every hand. The average is so good that, despite the beauty of an occasional piece, few can be said to stand out boldly from the rest. Considering the accumulated wealth of English poetry, it is questionable whether more sonnets, etc., are a real addition to it, and if a place worth having can be earned by polishing the countless facets of gems dependent on the fanciful analysis of love and other emotions. Again, some of our poets, like certain painters, avoid continued effort, and satisfy themselves with sketch-work — a facile way of keeping up expectation. Having mastered one's vocation, why not practice it with a determined hand? Too much assurance was the fault

"The accomplishment of verse."

Half-efforts.

of our earlier period, but the ambition that went with it stimulated a few to real achievements. It is hard to account for our easy modern contentment. In older countries the mines have been so well worked that there is an excuse for resorting to the "tailings," but here there should be the broadest encouragement for prospectors. No doubt our reaction from the old-fashioned conceit has its effect on able men, and makes them cleave to ground of which they have no fear. Too much credit is awarded now to the knowledge of one's limitations. A poet, most of all, should not believe in limitations; by ignoring them, a few will reach the heights. But our aspirants seem to feel that nothing better can be done than to amuse readers who consider poetry a diversion, and they either fear to put their fate to the touch "to gain or lose it all," or utterly fail to realize the chance at this moment existing. And so, if poetry has lost its hold, it is in some degree because no brilliant leader compels attention to it, devoting himself to the hazard of arduous and bravely ventured song.

"If thy heart fail thee, climb not at all."

The time, then, is not one of transition, save in the sense that all periods are transitional. It is intercalary, yet as well defined as the middle ring of Saturn, gaining its light and substance from a multitude of little quantities, — notable, in fact, for the profusion and excellence of its minor verse. And here it must be borne in mind that not a few of our idealists are directing their main efforts to prose composition. For example, one of the finest elegiac poems of recent years, *The North Shore Watch*, is privately printed by Mr. Woodberry, who thus far has permitted the ordinary reader to know him only as a biographer and critical essayist. Among the chief Victorian writers, we found but two or three that might be classified as

Profusion of minor verse.

Ideality diverted to prose composition.

"The North Shore Watch."

George Edward Woodberry: 1855.

Novelist-poets, etc. *See p. 75, and cp. "Victorian Poets": pp. 81, 82, 251-3.*

novelist-poets. Hood was almost the only journalist-poet of note, a true vocalist, jaded by hackwork. Nowadays, the conditions are reversed; the rhythmic art is more frequently an avocation. Among our novelists, however, Aldrich always seems the poet, — an author with whom song has the precedence. His tales are the prose of a poetic artist, and owe to this fact their airy charm. Howells furnishes an instance of the apt recognition of existing tendencies. The wisdom he has displayed "in his generation" goes far to justify the diversion we are observing. His early verse, issued conjointly with that of his friend Piatt, bore unusual marks of promise, nor has he quite broken with the muse or ceased to hold her image in his heart. Otherwise his bent, like Mr. James's, was that of a critic, scholar, analyst; and the determined evolution of a masterly novel-writer, from a youth of the qualifications involved, might serve as a text for homilies on the power of the human will. His pen being his fortune, his chosen profession that of a man of letters, he manfully trained himself to the production of literature that he foresaw would be welcome and remunerative; this, in a series of works, — at first descriptive, then inventive, — constantly advancing in perception, in management of incident and character, until he now stands where we find him, in the front rank of those who impress observers with a sense of our literary progress. His poetic gift serves him well in translation, in dramatic adaptation, and with respect to the feeling and artistic effect of his tenderest episodes. Waiving discussion of Mr. Howells's method as a novelist, who can question that he has judged wisely, and has done far better for the public than if he had pursued the art that was his early choice?

William Dean Howells: 1837-

New outlets of imaginative energy.

By such examples more light is cast upon the reduced importance of our song-makers, and ground discovered for a belief that this is transitory and that a fresh departure will anon be made. Fancy and imagination are still rife, but their energy finds vent in new directions. Accomplished craftsmen, some of whom thirty years ago might have been numbered among the poets, now supply the public with its imaginative rations in the guise of prose fiction and romance. Through instinct or judgment, they have occupied the gap in our literature. The time has been opportune; famous innings were made by the elder minstrels; our school of fiction had been represented only by a few rare and exceptional names.

The prevailing impulse.

So keen has been the new impulse, that the young neophyte of to-day, instead of shaping his vague conceptions into rhythm and imitating the poets within his knowledge, longs to emulate the foremost novelists. In the flush of our latest conquest, the rank and file naturally overrate the relative worth of prose fiction, which, at its best, — as will appear on a brief consideration of the world's literary masterpieces, — is not a more vital and enduring creation than the poet's song.

Compensation.

Yet the movement has resulted in a decided gain to the prestige of our national authorship. With a staff of novelists and romancers well equipped in both invention and style, — Howells, Aldrich, Julian Hawthorne, Eggleston, Cable, James, Harte, Crawford, Bishop, Stockton, Lathrop, Kip, Mrs. Stoddard, Miss Jewett, Miss Woolson, Miss Murfree, Miss Howard, Mrs. Foote, and others who also are adequate to cope with the transatlantic experts, — in view of the results already obtained from the field in which these popular authors are so active, none can assume that the diversion of creative energy thus ex-

(See Index.)

emplified has not brought with it a measurable compensation.

IV.

What cheer?

Both exterior and subjective conditions having thus determined the present office of the imagination, the breathing-spell of poetry is not without promise of a stronger utterance than ever when its voice shall be renewed. We shall have more poets yet, and some of those who have been named will contribute, I doubt not, to the hastening of that renewal. They can derive from our fiction itself a shrewd lesson for their guidance. Their predecessors fully met the need for idyllic verse, relating to home, patriotism, religion, and the workaday life of an orderly people. They did not scrutinize, and vividly present, the coils of individual being. Our people have outgrown their juvenescence, tested their manhood, and now demand a lustier regimen. They crave the sensations of mature and cosmopolitan experience, and are bent upon what we are told is the proper study of mankind. The rise of our novelists was the answer to this craving; they depict *Life* as it is, though rarely as yet in its intenser phases. Those who, besides meeting Mr. James's requirement that "the mind of the producer shall be displayed," do reflect life in something more than a commonplace aspect are the chroniclers, chiefly, of provincial episodes, confined to sections so narrow that it is scarcely needful to linger in them throughout the narrative of a sustained work. Their welcome is partly due to the fact that their studies are bolder and more dramatic than those of the restrained Eastern school. The muster-roll of the latter has increased somewhat more rapidly than its market. We have seen poetry out of demand; the same thing be-

A lesson from the novelists.

Need of a Life-School.

An opportune time.

gins to be observed of prose fiction. Renewed attention is given to history, memoirs, travels; but many signs declare that there never was a time when a live and glowing poet would have a better chance than now. In the multitude of ambitious novelists, distinction is less easily gained. Only the poet can excite the subtlest thrills, the most abiding sensations. The promise of his return lies in the truth that our spiritual nature does abhor a vacuum, — the need insures the supply. Though our public has resorted to prose literature for its wants, it now and then still reads a poem with avidity. The sudden popularity of Arnold's "Light of Asia" — the work of a scholar and enthusiast rather than of a strongly original hand — was of real significance. That production gave a sensuous and legendary idealization of the religious feeling of an impressible body of readers; it appealed to an existing sentiment; it focalized the rays in which the faiths of the East and the West are blending throughout the modern world. In short, it was most timely, and it was both attractive and dimensional. If, then, the people care little for current poetry, is it not because that poetry cares little for the people and fails to assume its vantage-ground? Busying itself with intricacies of form and sound and imagery, it scarcely deigns to reach the general heart. Your skill is admirable, say the people, and of interest to your own guild, but we ask that it shall be used to some purpose. Convey to us the intellect and passion wherewith poets are thought to be endowed, the gloom and glory of human life, the national aspiration, the pride of the past and vision of the future.

The poets and the public.

Rhythmical productions will be acceptable that compare with those of the past, as vigorous figure-paint-

The former must respond to

the new dramatic instinct.

ings with the canvases of our elder artists. Even in landscape we have reached the stage where human feeling, and that American, pervades the most favored work. Nor will it be enough to depict life in aggregated and general types. Whitman has achieved this, conveying a national spirit in his symphonic echoes of the murmuring towns and forests and ocean-waves. He gives us life and movement, but the specific character, the personal movement, seldom animate his pages. Individuals, men and women, various and real, must be set before us in being and action,— above all, in that mutual play upon one another's destinies which results from what we term the dramatic purport of life. Thus rising above mere introspection and analysis, poetry must be not so much a criticism as the objective portrayal and illumination of life itself — and that not only along the uneventful, quiescent flow of rural existence, but upon the tides of circumstance where men are striving for intense sensations and continuous development.

Cp. "*Victorian Poets*": *p.* 344.

In other words, the time has come for poetry, in any form, that shall be essentially *dramatic*. This kind has rounded each recurring cycle in other literatures than our own. It is a symptom of maturity, and we, in our turn, approach the age when life attains fire and color and is full of experiences that give tone to art. I think that our future efforts will result in dramatic verse, and even in actual dramas for both the closet and the stage. I am aware that this belief has been entertained before, and prematurely; it was as strong in the time of Tyler and Dunlap and Payne, nor would our own experiments be much more significant than theirs, were it not for the recent and encouraging efforts of our younger authors, several of whom are among the poets already

Promise of a dramatic movement.

named. Playwrights still feel compelled to offer rudimentary work to their audiences. The primary and denominative element of the actor's art, that of action, with every aid of scenic effect, just now is all in all. The text is but an adjunct to the pantomime. Realism, also, is as conspicuous in our theatres as in the latest French and English novels. It was desirable to get beyond stale and absurd conventionality, yet certain conventions are indispensable to art; there is nothing ideal in a slavish, mechanical reproduction of speech and manners. Unduly favored as the text once may have been, we now err as plainly in the opposite way. A poet turns playwright, and there begins the inevitable conflict with the stage itself. He yields to the conviction of actor and manager that the text will never regain the critical interest of audiences. I make bold to think otherwise; to hold that belief is to overlook the recorded equipoise of text and action at every epoch when the theatre has been preëminent. The sentiment of the hour may be against the production of what are termed literary plays; yet nothing, after all, is surer to draw than some familiar tragedy or comedy of the great dramatic poets. In Italy, France, Germany, it is the same. The people want amusement, and in all times they prefer the best offered; when there were none but poetic dramas, they sustained them, and intelligently traversed the rendering of dialogue and phrase. On the other hand, wretched mounting and acting will make the finest text wearisome. The whole dispute turns largely upon circumstance and fashion. Notwithstanding Tennyson's undramatic cast of genius, he has succeeded — but only, as was predicted long ago, after successive trials and by a *tour de force* — in producing an excellent drama. "Becket," with

Text and action.

Cp. "*Victorian Poets*": *p.* 266.

The Stage.

Cp. "*Victorian Poets*": *pp.* 191, 413.

"*Becket.*"

respect to action, plot, and language, is greatly superior to many plays of the Knowles and Talfourd period, which still hold the stage; and yet the public, and various theatrical critics, will have none of it. The time has been simply unpropitious. Boker's "Francesca da Rimini" waited twenty-five years for an actor and a manager fully to utilize its possibilities.

"Francesca da Rimini."

Audience and playwright.

We see that for the development of an ideal drama the public taste and sentiment must rise accordingly. The stage reflects these; but it also can anticipate and help to form them, through works of genius which the people in the end will appreciate. The ambitious playwright, on his part, must realize that his faculty is the greater when adaptable and inventive. Writer, actor, theatre and public, must unite to give effect to any drama. Brander Matthews says that "for a poetic play to have a success, it must be the work of one who is both poet and playwright; who is, in fact, playwright first and poet after," — and cites the examples of Molière and Shakespeare and Hugo, and of lesser men. Playwrights not familiar with the stage from youth have succeeded only after failures.

Effects of town-life.

Our dramatists are likely to spring from those who, if not used to theatrical "business" and people, are thoroughly acquainted with town life. We know the retardant effect of society upon artists of exalted sensibility. Liszt's rival declares that social distractions have prevented the Abbé from being a great composer; that Bach's seclusion and Beethoven's deafness protected them from outside voices and made them hear the voice of God within. Yet the dramatist, whose theme is human action, must have observed that action under the excitements and among the contrasted types of civic life. The increase of our cities itself betokens a change from idyllic to dramatic methods in literary art.

But I have allowed my faith in the need of such a change to lead me into surmises concerning the rise of the stage-drama in America. The latter certainly would give a rapid impulse to the former. As it is, a young playwright like Carleton finds it prudent to adapt his labors to the immediate requirements of the stage, after testing his literary faculty by the composition of a metrical drama, *Memnon*, a work indebted to Elizabethan models in its rhetoric and emblazonry, and not devoid of fine diction and poetic glow. Among the numerous plays offered to the managers, there probably are some of an elevated class that would be available under conditions which I think will not be long delayed. Meanwhile, under existing conditions, our few playwrights who combine tact with refinement, — and Bronson Howard should have the credit due to a pioneer who still works among the foremost, — probably have done the best that could be done, with a sense of what is now practicable, and a hopeful willingness to prepare the way for their successors, poetic or otherwise, in the early future. Time is all that is needed to give us the heroic temper and coadequate themes. Of the two, tradition is less essential to romance and the drama than a favoring atmosphere. The wreath must be held out by a public that delights in the Pythian games, and won by contestants worthy to receive it.

Henry Guy Carleton: 1855-

"Memnon," 1884

Pioneer efforts.

V.

THERE are questions that come home to one who would aid in speeding the return of "the Muse, disgusted at" the "age and clime." Can I, he asks, be

The poet's faculty compulsive and lasting.

reckoned with the promoters of her new reign? Yes, it will be answered, if your effort is in earnest and if you are in truth a poet. To doubt of this is almost the doubt's own confirmation. That writer to whom rhythmic phrases come as the natural utterance of his extremest hope, regret, devotion, is a poet of some degree. At the rarest crises he finds that, without and even beyond his will, life and death and all things dear and sacred are made auxiliary to the compulsive purpose of his art; just as in the passion for science, as if to verify the terrible irony of Balzac and Wordsworth, the alchemist will analyze his wife's tears, the Linnæan will botanize even upon his mother's grave: —

> "Alas, and hast thou then so soon forgot
> The bond that with thy gift of song did go —
> Severe as fate, fixed and unchangeable?
> Dost thou not know this is the poet's lot!"

If, when his brain is in working humor, its chambers filled with imaged pageantry, the same form of utterance becomes his ready servant, then he is a poet indeed. But if he has a dexterous metrical faculty, and hunts for theme and motive, — or if his verse does not say what otherwise cannot be said at all, — then he is a mere artisan in words, and less than those whose thought and feeling are too deep for speech. The true poet is haunted by his gift, even in hours of drudgery and enforced prosaic life. He cannot escape it. After spells of dejection and weariness, when it has seemed to leave for ever, it always, always, returns again — perishable only with himself.

Favoring conditions:

Again he will ask, What are my opportunities? What is the final appraisement of the time and situation? We have noted those latter-day conditions that vex the poet's mind. Yet art is the precious outcome of all conditions; there are none that may not be transmuted in its crucible. Science, whose iconoclasm had to be considered, first of all, in our study of the Victorian period, has forced us to adjust ourselves to its dispensation. A scientific conflict with tradition always has been in progress, though never so determinedly as now. But the poet and artist keep pace with it, even forestall it, so that each new wonder leads to greater things, and the so-called doom of art is a victorious transition: —

Intellectual,

"If my bark sinks, 't is to another sea."

As to material conditions, we find that the practical eagerness of the age, and of our own people before all, has so nearly satisfied its motive as to beget the intellectual and æsthetic needs to which beauty is the purveyor. As heretofore in Venice and other commonwealths, first nationality, then riches, then the rise of poetry and the arts. — After materialism and the scientific stress, the demands of journalism have been the chief counter-sway to poetic activity. But our journals are now the adjuvants of imaginative effort in prose and verse; the best of them are conducted by writers who have the literary spirit, and who make room for ideal literature, even if it does not swell their lists so rapidly as that of another kind. The poet can get a hearing; our Chattertons need not starve in their garrets; there never was a better market for the wares of Apollo, — their tuneful venders need not hope for wealth, but if one cannot make his genius something more than its own exceeding great reward, it is because he mistakes the period or scorns to address himself fitly to his readers. Finally, criticism is at once more catholic and more discriminating than of old. Can it make a poet, or teach him his mission? Hardly; but it can spur him to his best,

Material, and

Literary.

and point out the heresies from which he must free himself or address the oracle in vain.

Requirements.

Such being our opportunities, we have seen that the personal requirements are coequal, and their summing-up may well be the conclusion of the whole matter. Warmth, action, genuine human interest, must vivify the minstrel's art; the world will receive him if he in truth comes into his own. Taste and adroitness can no longer win by novelty. Natural emotion is the soul of poetry, as melody is of music; the same faults are engendered by over-study of either art; there is a lack of sincerity, of irresistible impulse, in both the poet and the composer. The decorative vogue has reached its lowest grade — that of assumption for burlesque and persiflage; just as Pre-Raphaelitism, at first a reform in art, extended to poetry, to architecture, to wall-decoration, to stage-setting, finally to the dress of moonstruck blue-stockings and literary dandies. What has been gained in new design will survive. But henceforth the sense of beauty must have something "far more deeply interfused": the ideal, which, though not made with hands of artificers, is eternal on the earth as in the heavens, because it is inherent in the soul. There is also one prerequisite, upon which stress was laid by Dr. Storrs in his application to modern art of Goethe's reservation as to the worth of certain engravings: "Still, something is wanting in all these pictures — the Manly. . . . The pictures lack a certain urgent power," etc. Culture, I have said, will make a poet draw ahead of his unstudious fellows, but the resolve born of conviction is needed to sustain the advance. The lecturer rightly declared that only "courageous work will suit America, whose race is essentially courageous and stoical." Our key-note

Poetry not merely an art, but an inspiration.

R. S. Storrs: at Union College, 1883.

assuredly should be that of freshness and joy; the sadness of declining races, only, has the beauty of natural pathos. There is no cause for morbidly introspective verse — no need, I hope, for dilettanteism — in this brave country of ours for centuries to come.

The American ideal.

I think, too, we may claim that there is no better ideal of manhood than the American ideal, derived from an aggregation of characteristic types. Our future verse should be more native than that of the past, in having a flavor more plainly distinct from the motherland. Not that our former contingent misrepresented the America of its time. Even Longfellow's work, with so much of imported theme and treatment, conveyed a sentiment that came, say what we will, from no foreign source. The reason that a decidedly autochthonous kind was not then proffered, unless by Whitman, was that a distinction between the conditions of England and America was not more strongly established. Since the war our novitiate has ended. We welcome home-productions; our servility to foreign judgment has lessened, and we apply with considerable self-poise our own standards of criticism to things abroad. We have outlived the greed of a childhood that depends on sustenance furnished by its elders, and are far indeed from the senile atrophy which also must borrow to recruit its wasting powers. Our debt to acute foreign critics is none the less memorable. They, in truth, were the first to counsel us that we should lean upon ourselves; to insist that we ought at least to escape Old World limitations, — the first to recognize so heartily anything purely American, even our sectional humor, as to bring about our discovery that it was not necessarily "a poor thing," although our "own."

A national type. *See pp. 7–9, 96, 97.*

It is agreed that sectional types, which thus have lent their raciness to various productions, are subsidiary to the formation of one that shall be national. A character formed of mingling components must undergo the phases of defective hybridity; our own is just beginning to assume a coherence that is the promise of a similar adjustment in art. As local types disappear there may be special losses, yet a general gain. The lifting of the Japanese embargo was harmful to the purity of the insular art, but added something to the arts of the world at large. Even now our English cousins, seeking for what they term Americanism in our literature, begin to find its flavor stealthily added to their own.

Its promotion.

Nothing will strengthen more rapidly the native bias of our literature than its increase of dramatic tone. Speech, action, and passion will be derived from life as here seen, from factors near at hand and stuff of which the writer himself is moulded. Our playwrights are now encouraged by a copyright royalty. All classes of literary workmen, however, still endure the disadvantage of a market drugged with stolen goods. Shameless as is our legal plundering of foreign authors, our blood is most stirred by the consequent injury to home literature, — by the wrongs, the poverty, the discouragement to which the foes of International Copyright subject our own writers. The nerve and vitality of the latter can have no stronger demonstration than by the progress which they make while loaded with an almost insufferable burden. When this shall at last be lifted, their forward movement may answer to the most sanguine conjecture. Of two things they already are assured: First, the perception, the inborn taste, of their countrymen stands in need of less tutorage than that of

The copyright question. *See pp. 23–25.*

American taste.

transatlantic Saxon races. Our people have blundered from isolation; confront them with the models of older lands, and they quickly learn to choose the fit and beautiful, and the time is now reached when the finest models are widely attainable. Secondly, our inheritance is a language that is relatively the greatest treasure-house of the world's literature: at once the most laconic and the most copious of tongues, — the sturdiest in its foundations of emotion and utility, the most varied by appropriation of synonyms from all languages, new and old; the youngest and most occidental of the great modes of speech, steadily diffusing itself about the globe, with no possible supplanter or successor except itself at further stages of maturity; finally, elastic and copious most of all in the land which adds to it new idioms, of cisatlantic growth, or assimilated from the dialects of many races that here contribute their diction to its own. A language whose glory is that even corruptions serve to speed its growth, and whose fine achievement long has been to make the neologism, even the solecism, of one generation the classicism of the next. This is the potent and sonorous instrument which our poet has at his command, and the genius of his country, like Ariel, bids him

Our English tongue.

"— take
This slave of music, for my sake."

THE twilight of the poets, succeeding to the brightness of their first diurnal course, is a favorable interval at which to review the careers of those whose work therewith is ended. Although at such a time public interest may set in other directions, I

Past, Present, and Future.

have adhered to a task so arduous, yet so fascinating to the critical and poetic student. When the lustre of a still more auspicious day shall yield in its turn to the recurring dusk, a new chronicler will have the range of noble imaginations to consider, heightened in significance by comparison with the field of these prior excursions. But, if I have not wholly erred in respect to the lessons derivable from the past, he will not go far beyond them. The canons are not subject to change; he, in turn, will deduce the same elements appertaining to the chief of arts, and test his poets and their bequests by the same unswerving laws. And concerning the dawn which may soon break upon us unawares, as we make conjecture of the future of American song, it is difficult to keep the level of restraint — to avoid "rising on the wings of prophecy." Who can doubt that it will correspond to the future of the land itself, — of America now wholly free and interblending, with not one but a score of civic capitals, each an emulative centre of taste and invention, a focus of energetic life, ceaseless in action, radiant with the glow of beauty and creative power.

Art's changeless law.

INDEX.

INDEX.

THE CRITICAL AND POETICAL WORKS

OF

EDMUND CLARENCE STEDMAN

HOUGHTON MIFFLIN COMPANY
BOSTON: 4 PARK STREET. NEW YORK: 16 EAST 40TH STREET
The Riverside Press, Cambridge

An American Anthology, 1787-1900.

SELECTIONS illustrating the editor's critical review of American poetry in the nineteenth century. With brief biographies, a valuable introduction, an engraved title-page, and a photogravure frontispiece of a group of American poets: Longfellow, Lowell, Holmes, Whittier, Bryant, Poe, and Lanier. Large crown octavo, 878 pages, gilt top, $3.00; *Holiday Edition*, full gilt, $3.50; half calf, gilt top, $5.00; full levant or tree calf, $7.00.

A notable contribution to the history of literature of the passing century. In its spirit and in its results this anthology will stand out for the future as distinctly as the year in which it has appeared closes one epoch and begins another. — *Sewanee Review.*

It is a monumental work, and even to be included in it will be to escape the oblivion which awaits so many major and minor poets. — RICHARD HENRY STODDARD, in *Mail and Express*, New York.

"An American Anthology" is not only the bequest of the passing century to future generations, but the most interesting and inclusive of all collections of American verse. — WALLACE BRUCE, in *Chicago Evening Post.*

✠✠✠

A Victorian Anthology, 1837-1895.

SELECTIONS illustrating the editor's critical review of British poetry in the reign of Victoria ("Victorian Poets"). With brief biographies of the authors quoted, a fine frontispiece portrait of Queen Victoria, and a vignette of the Poets' Corner in Westminster Abbey. Large crown 8vo, 784 pages, gilt top, $2.50; *Holiday Edition*, full gilt, $3.00; half calf, $4.50; full levant or tree calf, $6.50.

There is no one on either side the Atlantic better fitted than Mr. Stedman to edit an anthology of the period. — *Boston Advertiser.*

His "Victorian Anthology" is a cyclopedia of modern English poetry edited with signal discretion and delicacy. — *The Times*, London.

✠✠✠

Poems Now First Collected.

12mo, gilt top, $1.50.

MR. STEDMAN'S lyre is one of many strings, all carefully tuned, whereon at will he can make sweet music, stately or gay as befits his mood; and always through his singing one is conscious of a joyous and happy heart whence come the songs — a heart forever young. — *The Book Buyer*, New York.

The Nature and Elements of Poetry.

WITH Frontispiece after Dürer, Topical Analysis, and Analytical Index. Crown 8vo, gilt top, $1.50.

CONTENTS: I. Oracles Old and New. II. What is Poetry? III. Creation and Self-Expression. IV. Melancholia. V. Beauty. VI. Truth. VII. Imagination. VIII. The Faculty Divine: Passion, Insight, Genius, Faith. Index.

If the writer has not said the last word on "the faculty divine," it is doubtful whether any better word remains. And it is all said so reverently and modestly that even if for the moment you do not quite agree with him, his spirit seems to hint that he is probably right and you are wrong. — *Public Opinion*, New York.

✠✠✠

Victorian Poets.

REVISED and extended by a supplementary chapter to the fiftieth year of the period under review. Crown 8vo, gilt top, $2.25; half calf, $3.50.

One of the most thorough, workmanlike, and artistic pieces of real critical writing that we have in English. For the period covered by it, it is the most comprehensive, profound, and lucid literary exposition that has appeared in this country or elsewhere. — Prof. MOSES COIT TYLER, *Cornell University*.

✠✠✠

Poets of America.

A COMPANION volume to Victorian Poets. With full Notes in margin, and careful Analytical Index. Crown 8vo, gilt top, $2.25; half calf, $3.50.

CONTENTS: Early and Recent Conditions; Growth of the American School; William Cullen Bryant; John Greenleaf Whittier; Ralph Waldo Emerson; Henry Wadsworth Longfellow; Edgar Allan Poe. Oliver Wendell Holmes; James Russell Lowell; Walt Whitman; Bayard Taylor; The Outlook.

It is doubtful whether any other living American man of letters could have written a volume at once so comprehensive, so appreciative, so discriminating, and so well defined in respect to the impressions which it makes. — *The Congregationalist*, Boston.